Change Management

Manage the Change
or It Will Manage You

The **Management Handbooks for Results** Series

Change Management

Manage the Change or It Will Manage You

Frank Voehl • H. James Harrington

CRC Press
Taylor & Francis Group
Boca Raton   London   New York

CRC Press is an imprint of the
Taylor & Francis Group, an **informa** business

A PRODUCTIVITY PRESS BOOK

CRC Press
Taylor & Francis Group
6000 Broken Sound Parkway NW, Suite 300
Boca Raton, FL 33487-2742

Printed on acid-free paper
Version Date: 20151106

International Standard Book Number-13: 978-1-4822-1418-5 (Paperback)

Library of Congress Cataloging-in-Publication Data

Names: Voehl, Frank, 1946- | Harrington, H. J. (H. James)
Title: Change management : manage the change or it will manage you / Frank Voehl and H. James Harrington.
Description: Boca Raton : CRC Press, 2016. | Series: Management handbooks for results series ; 5 | Includes bibliographical references and index.
Identifiers: LCCN 2015030296 | ISBN 9781482214185 (hardback)
Subjects: LCSH: Organizational change--Management. | Strategic planning.
Classification: LCC HD58.8 .V634 2016 | DDC 658.4/06--dc23
LC record available at http://lccn.loc.gov/2015030296

Visit the Taylor & Francis Web site at
http://www.taylorandfrancis.com

and the CRC Press Web site at
http://www.crcpress.com

To all the change agents, and to my life-long partner Dr. Jim, who never met a conflict that he couldn't resolve, who is a world-master at asking the right questions. And to my wife Micki, who always tries to understand why the other person sees the situation differently.

Thank you for helping me to think about thinking, and to change the way I see change.

Frank Voehl

It seems like you have many, many friends until you need them to do something for you or when you're taking a position that is not a popular one. I feel I am fortunate to have a number of friends who have always been there through my ups and downs and when I need their help. In particular, I'd like to recognize Chuck Mignosa and Frank Voehl for always being there to cheer me up when I'm down, to lift me up when I've fallen, and who have never done anything that would harm me in any way, even when I'm wrong. True, steadfast friends are hard to find and I'm lucky to have found a few of them as I struggled through life.

H. James Harrington

Contents

SECTION II   Understanding

SECTION III   Applying

SECTION V   Creating

Prologue

This Change Management book represents a substantial core guidance effort for Change Management practitioners. It is organized around the revised version of Bloom's *Taxonomy for Learning Organizations* as it is applied to Change Management. Practice and research have shown that to manage change effectively, organizations need to do change-oriented things very well. Because this book is organized around the modern version of Bloom's *Taxonomy* in its various forms, this taxonomy represents the process of organizational learning as well as individual learning.

> Before we can understand a concept we have to remember it.
> Before we can apply the concept we must understand it.
> Before we analyze it we must be able to apply it.
> Before we can evaluate its impact we must have analyzed it.
> Before we can create we must have remembered, understood, applied, analyzed, and evaluated.*

In 1956, Benjamin Bloom headed a group of educational psychologists who developed a classification of levels of intellectual behavior important in learning. During the 1990s a new group of cognitive psychologists, led by Lorin Anderson (a former student of Bloom), updated the taxonomy to reflect relevance to twenty-first century work. Figure P.1 shows the revised Taxonomy, noting the change from nouns to verbs associated with each level.

For the purposes of Change Management, the Knowledge aspect of Bloom's Taxonomy can be organized into four levels of Knowledge Management,[†] as shown in Figure P.2.

---

* Adapted from the *Three Story Intellect* by Oliver Wendell Holmes and Art Costa.

† See Dianna Fisher, Director of Project Development & Training Office: (541) 737–8658, Cell: (541) 230–4029, Extended Campus Oregon State University, The Valley Library at Corvallis, OR 97331. Also, the four levels of Knowledge Management are covered in the book by Harrington & Voehl, *Knowledge Management Excellence*, Chico, CA: Paton Press, 2009. Organizations contend with increasingly higher levels of knowledge-driven competition. Many attempt to meet the challenge by investing in expensive knowledge management systems. However, these are useless for making strategic decisions because they don't distinguish between what's strategically relevant and what isn't. This book focuses on identifying and managing the specific, critical knowledge assets that your organization needs to disrupt your competitors, including tacit experience of key employees, a deep understanding of customers' needs, valuable patents and copyrights, shared industry practices, and customer- and supplier-generated innovations.

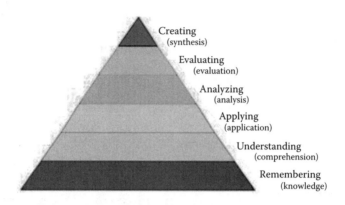

Traditional Bloom	Twenty-First Century Bloom	Change Management Context
Knowledge	*Remembering*: Can the organization recall or remember the information?	Define, duplicate, list, memorize, recall, repeat, reproduce, state
Comprehension	*Understanding*: Can the organization explain ideas or concepts?	Classify, describe, discuss, explain, identify, locate, recognize, report, select, translate, paraphrase
Application	*Applying*: Can the organization use the information in a new way?	Choose, demonstrate, dramatize, employ, illustrate, interpret, operate, schedule, sketch, solve, use, write
Analysis	*Analyzing*: Can the organization distinguish between the different parts?	Appraise, compare, contrast, criticize, differentiate, discriminate, distinguish, examine, experiment, question, test
Evaluation	*Evaluating*: Can the organization justify a stand or decision?	Appraise, argue, defend, judge, select, support, value, evaluate
Synthesis	*Creating*: Can the organization create a new product or point of view?	Assemble, construct, create, design, develop, formulate, write

FIGURE P.1

Bloom's Taxonomy applied to Organizational Change Management.

Factual knowledge	The basic facts required in order to solve problems	• Knowledge of terminology. • Knowledge of specific details and elements
Conceptual knowledge	The interrelationships among the facts that enable them to function together within a larger structure	• Knowledge of classifications and categories • Knowledge of principles and generalizations • Knowledge of theories, models, and structures
Procedural knowledge	How and when to perform particular procedures, such as investigations, treatment, etc.	• Knowledge of subject-specified skills, technique algorithms, criteria for determining when to use appropriate procedures
Meta-cognitive knowledge	Knowledge of cognition in general as well as awareness and knowledge of one's own cognition	• Strategic knowledge • Knowledge of the cognitive demands of different tasks • Self-knowledge: own strengths and weaknesses

Indeed, it is possible to construct a two-dimensional grid in which Bloom's 6 levels are linked to the hierarchy of 4 knowledge levels:

Knowledge dimension	The cognitive process dimension					
	Remember	Understand	Apply	Analyze	Evaluate	Create
Factual knowledge	List	Summarize	Classify	Order	Rank	Combine
Conceptual knowledge	Describe	Interpret	Experiment	Explain	Assess	Plan
Procedural knowledge	Tabulate	Predict	Calculate	Differentiate	Conclude	Compose
Meta-cognitive knowledge	Appropriate use	Execute	Construct	Achieve	Action	Actualize

FIGURE P.2
The four levels of Knowledge Management.

This book's organization around Bloom's Taxonomy consists of 16 chapters:

Section I: Remembering
- Chapter 1: Introduction to Change Management
- Chapter 2: The Philosophy and Evolution of Change Management
- Chapter 3: Making the Case for Change Readiness

Section II: Understanding
- Chapter 4: Dirty Dozen Most Popular Models
- Chapter 5: Sustainable Change Lifecycle
- Chapter 6: Facilitated OCM Workshops
- Chapter 7: Culture Change Management (CCM)

Section III: Applying
- Chapter 8: Applying Methods for Deployment
- Chapter 9: Initiatives' Prioritization
- Chapter 10: The Iterative Development Approach

Section IV: Analyzing and Evaluating
- Chapter 11: Gathering, Analyzing, and Prioritizing Requirements
- Chapter 12: Using Estimates and Time Boxes

Section V: Creating
- Chapter 13: Modeling and Simulation
- Chapter 14: Measurement and Appraisal
- Chapter 15: Risk Management Considerations
- Chapter 16: Deploying and Implementing CCM

It has long been accepted that understanding is best served through dialogue and experimentation. Also, Bloom often stated it should be a new context into which you are applying the understanding but stressed that it should be a unique context with just one solution. Taxonomies, the science or technique of classification, are developed to provide a framework for organizing a continuum along an underlying structure. For example, languages may be classified as Romantic, Germanic, and so forth based on their underlying grammatical structure and origin. The goal of any practitioner using Bloom's Taxonomy is to encourage higher-order thought in their Change Management interventions by building up from lower-level to higher-level organizationally focused cognitive skills, with the goal of creating high-performance organizations. Behavioral and cognitive learning objectives are outlined to highlight how Bloom's Taxonomy can be incorporated into larger-scale Change Management goals or guidelines.

Bloom's Taxonomy primarily provides Change Management practitioners with a focus for developing their Change Management learning objectives. Originally, Bloom's taxonomy was one-dimensional with an exclusive focus on the knowledge domain. The current updated version, which was developed by Anderson and Krathwohl in 2001, reorganizes and highlights the interactions between two dimensions: cognitive processes and knowledge content.

In Harrington's book *Project Change Management—Applying Change Management to Improve Projects*, published in 2000 by McGraw-Hill, he proposed that the Project Management Institute's *A Guide to the Project Management Body of Knowledge* be modified from its present nine project management knowledge areas to include a 10th knowledge area, Managing Organizational Change. Instead of developing a completely separate 10th knowledge area, the Project Management Institute has decided to embed "Managing Organizational Change" into their nine project management knowledge areas. In hindsight, Harrington agrees that this may even be a better approach as it makes managing organizational change a unique part of all the nine project management knowledge areas rather than a separate unique activity and knowledge base. Harrington and Voehl's Organizational Excellence series deals with five components of excellence: People, Process, Project, Knowledge, and Resources, as shown in Figure P.3.

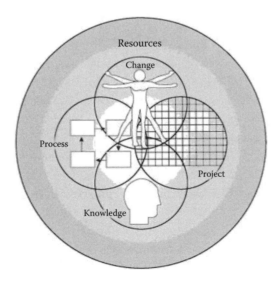

FIGURE P.3
The five dimensions of Organizational Excellence.

As a result, in this book we will be presenting two aspects of Change Management: (1) traditional Change Management as it impacts the project management team's activities and (2) our suggested new approach to Change Management directed at changing the culture and preparing the people impacted by the project change activities to accept and adapt to the new/changed working conditions. The first half of the book deals with traditional Change Management (Chapters 1 through 8) and our new approach to changing the culture (Chapters 9 through 16).

Acknowledgments

We recognize that the content of this book builds upon the work done by many others in developing the change management methodologies and the many innovative and unique ideas that have made the methodology an important part of every organization's operation.

In his work on "standing on the shoulders of giants," Friedrich Nietzsche argues that a dwarf (a.k.a. the academic scholar) brings even the most sublime heights down to his level of understanding. In the section of *Thus Spoke Zarathustra* (1882) entitled "On the Vision and the Riddle," Zarathustra climbs to great heights with a dwarf on his shoulders to show him his greatest thought. Once there, however, the dwarf fails to understand the profundity of the vision and he is reproached for "making things too easy on himself."

If there is to be anything resembling "progress" in the history of philosophy, Nietzsche in *Philosophy in the Tragic Age of the Greeks* (1873) writes that it can only come from those rare giants among men, "each giant calling to his brother through the desolate intervals of time."

Finally, the metaphor of "standing on the shoulder of giants" is often used to promote and validate the free software movement, which is so critical to open innovation and culture change management. In the book *Free as in Freedom*, Bob Young of Red Hat supports the free software movement by saying that it enables people to stand on the shoulders of giants. He also says that standing on the shoulders of giants is the opposite of reinventing the wheel.

About the Authors

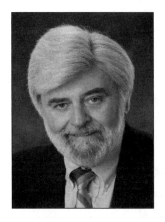

Frank Voehl currently serves as the chairman and president of Strategy Associates, Inc. and as a senior consultant and chancellor for the Harrington Management Systems. He also serves as the chairman of the board for a number of businesses and as a Grand Master Black Belt Instructor and Technology Advisor at the University of Central Florida in Orlando, Florida. He is recognized as one of the world leaders in applying quality measurement and Lean Six Sigma methodologies to business processes.

PREVIOUS EXPERIENCE

Frank Voehl has extensive knowledge of NRC, FDA, GMP & NASA quality system requirements. He is an expert in ISO-9000, QS-9000/14000/18000, and integrated Lean Six Sigma Quality System Standards and processes. He has degrees from St. John's University and advanced studies at NYU, as well as an honorary doctor of divinity degree. Since 1986, he has been responsible for overseeing the implementation of quality management systems with organizations in such diverse industries as telecommunications and utilities, federal, state and local government agencies, public administration and safety, pharmaceuticals, insurance/banking, manufacturing, and institutes of higher learning. In 2002, he joined The Harrington Group as the chief operating officer and executive vice president. He has held executive management positions with Florida Power and Light and FPL Group, where he was the founding general manager and COO of QualTec Quality Services for seven years. He has written and published/co-published over 35 books and hundreds of technical papers on business management, quality improvement, change management, knowledge management, logistics, and teambuilding, and has received numerous awards for community leadership, service to third-world countries, and student mentoring.

CREDENTIALS

The Bahamas National Quality Award was developed in 1991 by Frank Voehl to recognize the many contributions of companies in the Caribbean region, and he is an honorary member of its Board of Judges. In 1980, the City of Yonkers, New York, declared March 7 as "Frank Voehl Day," honoring him for his many contributions on behalf of thousands of youth in the city where he lived, performed volunteer work, and served as athletic director and coach of the Yonkers-Pelton Basketball Association. In 1985, he was named "Father of the Year" in Broward County, Florida. He also serves as president of the Miami Archdiocesan Council of the St. Vincent de Paul Society, whose mission is to serve the poor and needy throughout South Florida and the world.

Frank's contributions to quality improvement around the world have brought him many honors and awards, including ASQ's Distinguished Service Medal, the Caribbean Center for Excellence Founders Award, the Community Quality Distinguished Service Award, the Czech Republic Outstanding Service Award on behalf of its business community leaders, FPL's Pioneer Lead Facilitator Award, the Florida SFMA Partners in Productivity Award, and many others. He was appointed the honorary advisor to the Bahamas Quality Control Association, and he was elected to the Eastern Europe Quality Hall of Fame.

 **Dr. H. James Harrington** now serves as the chief executive officer for Harrington Management Systems. He also serves as the chairman of the board for a number of businesses.

Dr. Harrington is recognized as one of the world leaders in applying performance improvement methodologies to business processes. He has an excellent record of coming into an organization, working as its CEO or COO, resulting in a major improvement in its financial and quality performance.

In the book, *Tech Trending*, Dr. Harrington was referred to as "the quintessential tech trender." The *New York Times* referred to him as having a "… knack for synthesis and an open mind about packaging his knowledge and experience in new ways—characteristics that may matter more as prerequisites for new-economy success than technical wizardry…." The author, Tom Peters, stated, "I fervently hope that Harrington's readers will not only benefit from the thoroughness of his effort but will also 'smell' the fundamental nature of the challenge for change that he mounts." Bill Clinton, former president of the United States, appointed Dr. Harrington to serve as an Ambassador of Good Will. It has been said about him, "He writes the books that other consultants use."

Harrington Management Systems (formerly Harrington Institute) was featured on a half-hour TV program, *Heartbeat of America*, which focuses on outstanding small businesses that make America strong. The host, William Shatner, stated: "You (Dr. Harrington) manage an entrepreneurial company that moves America forward. You are obviously successful."

PREVIOUS EXPERIENCE

In February 2002, Dr. Harrington retired as the COO of Systemcorp A.L.G., the leading supplier of knowledge management and project management software solutions when Systemcorp was purchased by IBM. Prior to this, he served as a principal and one of the leaders in the Process Innovation Group at Ernst & Young; he retired from Ernst & Young when it was purchased by Cap Gemini. Dr. Harrington joined Ernst & Young when Ernst & Young purchased Harrington, Hurd & Rieker, a consulting firm that Dr. Harrington started. Before that, Dr. Harrington was with IBM for over 40 years as a senior engineer and project manager.

Dr. Harrington is past chairman and past president of the prestigious International Academy for Quality and of the American Society for Quality Control. He is also an active member of the Global Knowledge Economics Council.

CREDENTIALS

H. James Harrington was elected to the honorary level of the International Academy for Quality, which is the highest level of recognition in the quality profession.

H. James Harrington is a government-registered Quality Engineer, a Certified Quality and Reliability Engineer by the American Society for Quality Control, and a Permanent Certified Professional Manager by the Institute of Certified Professional Managers. He is a certified Master Six Sigma Black Belt and received the title of Six Sigma Grand Master. H. James Harrington has an MBA and PhD in engineering management and a BS in electrical engineering. Additionally, in 2013, Dr. Harrington received an honorary degree of doctor of philosophy (PhD) from the Sudan Academy of Sciences.

H. James Harrington's contributions to performance improvement around the world have brought him many honors. He was appointed the honorary advisor to the China Quality Control Association and was elected to the Singapore Productivity Hall of Fame in 1990. He has been named lifetime honorary president of the Asia-Pacific Quality Control Organization and honorary director of the Association Chilean de Control de Calidad. In 2006, Dr. Harrington accepted the honorary chairman position of Quality Technology Park of Iran.

H. James Harrington has been elected a Fellow of the British Quality Control Organization and the American Society for Quality Control. In 2008 he was elected to be an Honorary Fellow of the Iran Quality Association and Azerbaijan Quality Association. He was also elected an honorary member of the quality societies in Taiwan, Argentina, Brazil, Colombia, and Singapore. He is also listed in *Who's Who Worldwide* and

Men of Distinction Worldwide. He has presented hundreds of papers on performance improvement and organizational management structure at the local, state, national, and international levels.

RECOGNITION

- The Harrington/Ishikawa Medal, presented yearly by the Asian Pacific Quality Organization, was named after H. James Harrington to recognize his many contributions to the region.
- The Harrington/Neron Medal was named after H. James Harrington in 1997 for his many contributions to the quality movement in Canada.
- The Harrington Best TQM Thesis Award was established in 2004 and named after H. James Harrington by the European Universities Network and e-TQM College.
- The Harrington Chair in Performance Excellence was established in 2005 at the Sudan University.
- The Harrington Excellence Medal was established in 2007 to recognize an individual who uses the quality tools in a superior manner.
- H. James Harrington Scholarship was established in 2011 by the ASQ Inspection Division.

H. James Harrington has received many awards, among them the Benjamin L. Lubelsky Award, the John Delbert Award, the Administrative Applications Division Silver Anniversary Award, and the Inspection Division Gold Medal Award. In 1996, he received the ASQC's Lancaster Award in recognition of his international activities. In 2001, he received the Magnolia Award in recognition for the many contributions he has made in improving quality in China. In 2002, H. James Harrington was selected by the European Literati Club to receive a lifetime achievement award at the Literati Award for Excellence ceremony in London. The award was given to honor his excellent literature contributions to the advancement of quality and organizational performance. Also, in 2002, H. James Harrington was awarded the International Academy of Quality President's Award in recognition for outstanding global leadership in quality and competitiveness, and contributions to IAQ as Nominations Committee Chair, Vice President, and Chairman. In 2003 H. James Harrington received the Edwards Medal from the American Society for Quality (ASQ). The Edwards Medal is presented to the individual who has demonstrated the most outstanding leadership in the application of modern quality control methods, especially through the organization and administration of such work. In 2004, he received the Distinguished Service Award, which is ASQ's highest award for service granted by the Society. In 2008, Dr. Harrington was awarded the Sheikh Khalifa Excellence Award (UAE) in recognition of his superior performance as an original Quality and Excellence Guru who helped shape modern quality thinking. In 2009, Dr. Harrington was selected as the Professional of the Year (2009). Also in 2009, he received the Hamdan Bin Mohammed e-University Medal. In 2010, the Asian Pacific Quality Association (APQO) awarded Harrington the APQO President's Award for his "exemplary leadership." The Australian Organization of Quality NSW's Board recognized Harrington as "the Global Leader in Performance Improvement Initiatives" in 2010. In 2011, he was honored to receive the Shanghai Magnolia Special Contributions Award from the Shanghai Association for Quality in recognition of his 25 years of contributing to the advancement of quality in China. This was the first time that this award was given out. In 2012, Dr. Harrington received the ASQ Ishikawa Medal for his many contributions in promoting the understanding of process improvement and employee involvement on the human aspects of quality at the local, national, and international levels. Also in 2012, he was awarded the Jack Grayson Award. This award recognizes individuals who have demonstrated outstanding leadership in the application of quality philosophy, methods and tools in education, health care, public service, and not-for-profit organizations. Harrington also received the A.C. Rosander Award in 2012. This is ASQ Service Quality Division's highest honor. It is given in recognition of outstanding long-term service and leadership resulting in substantial progress toward the fulfillment of the Division's programs and goals. Additionally, in 2012, Dr. Harrington was honored by the Asia Pacific Quality Organization by being awarded the Armand V. Feigenbaum Lifetime Achievement Medal. This award is given annually to an individual whose relentless pursuit of performance improvement over a minimum of 25 years has distinguished himself or herself for the candidate's work in promoting the use of quality methodologies and principles within and outside of the organization he or she is part of.

CONTACT INFORMATION

Dr. Harrington is a very prolific author, publishing hundreds of technical reports and magazine articles. For the past 8 years he has published a monthly column in *Quality Digest Magazine* and is syndicated in five other publications. He has authored 40 books and 10 software packages.

Dr. Harrington's contact information:
Address: 15559 Union Avenue #187, Los Gatos, CA, 95032
Phone: (408) 358–2476
E-mail: hjh@harrington-institute.com

Section I

Remembering

The knowledge level is defined as information retrieval or recall, with the emphasis on remembering, either by recognition or recall of ideas, information, or facts. The knowledge level represents the lowest level in Bloom's, although, it provides the basis for all higher cognitive activity and is especially important in Change Management activities (see Figure SI.1). The purpose of this level is to assess if an organization has gained specific information from its past historical experiences.

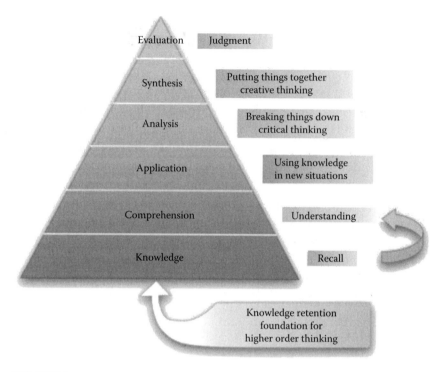

FIGURE SI.1
Bloom's Taxonomy for Thinking.

Remembering: Recall or retrieve previously learned information	**Examples**: Recite a policy. Quote prices from memory to a customer. Recite the safety rules. **Key Words**: defines, describes, identifies, knows, labels, lists, matches, names, outlines, recalls, recognizes, reproduces, selects, states **Technologies**: book marking, flash cards, rote learning based on repetition, reading

This section contains the following chapters:

- Chapter 1: Introduction to Change Management
- Chapter 2: The Philosophy and Evolution of Change Management
- Chapter 3: Making the Case for Change Readiness

1

Introduction to Change Management

In a Nutshell: What Is Change Management? This is the proverbial question that has been asked from the beginning of time (management), one that many practitioners have heard from colleagues or coworkers in passing or in formal presentations, in and around the water cooler each day. While many of us may know intuitively what change management is, we often have a hard time conveying to others what we really mean by it. In thinking about how to define change, it is important to provide context related to two other related concepts—the change itself and related management systems. This book shows how the change management process works with the three management systems—quality, project, and daily work management—as critical disciplines that are applied to a variety of organizational change interventions to improve the likelihood of success and return on investment. Ultimately, the goal of change management is to improve the organization by altering how work is done. Accordingly, there is increasing pressure on organizations to deliver working solutions to business in ever-shorter timescales—without compromising quality. The processes by which solutions are developed must be agile and deliver what the business needs when it needs it. This book presents a framework based on best practice and lessons learned by the authors over their collective 100-year career-span. Its promise is to offer a flexible, yet controlled and sustainable, change process that can be used to deliver solutions, combining effective use of people's knowledge together with techniques such as iterative development and modelling to achieve tight project delivery time frames. Typically, a fast-paced change-oriented change intervention can deliver a workable solution within timescales of three to six months, sometimes even within eight weeks.

INTRODUCTION

Definitions:

1. Change management is a disciplined framework for driving business results by changing behaviors (Nelson and Aaron 2007).* It entails managing the effect of new business processes, changes in organizational structure, or cultural changes within an enterprise. The challenge is to apply effective practices to anticipate and minimize resistance.

2. Organizational change management (OCM) is a systematic approach to planning and integrating change aligned with business strategy that focuses on both the business and its people. From a business standpoint, OCM focuses on planning and implementing transactional change (quick, short-term change activities), along with or in addition to transformational change (deep, long-term fundamental change), in order to facilitate delivery of sustainable organizational outcomes and benefits at minimum cost and risk.

3. Culture change management (CCM) contains many of the elements of the above but focuses on the human side of change as it affects the employees in their day-to-day work activities by creating a culture of assessment.† CCM emphasizes that it is the people that make the change happen (or not, in some cases), and their ability to adapt, absorb, and assimilate new ways of operating ultimately defines success.

---

* *The Change Management Pocket Guide* is a solid resource for people who need to make change happen. This tactical, hands-on guide will lead you through the steps in the entire process from planning for a change through sustaining new ways in your organization. In this book, you will find 31 valuable change management tools that can be easily customized for any organization. These tools are detailed and flexible, and you can adjust the scale to fit your needs. Many can be used throughout the project or with different audiences.

† A culture of assessment is an organizational environment in which decisions are based on facts, research, and analysis, and where services are planned and delivered in ways that maximize positive outcomes and impacts for customers and stakeholders alike. This culture exists in organizations where employees care to know what results they produce and how those results relate to customers' expectations. The organizational mission, vision, values, structures, and systems support behavior that is performance- and learning-oriented.

According to Tim Creasey, Director of R&D for Prosci, change management can be defined as*: "the process, tools and techniques to manage the people-side of change to achieve a required business outcome." When we introduce change to a client organization, we know that we are ultimately going to be impacting two or more of the following four parts of how the organization operates:

1. Processes
2. Systems
3. Organization structure
4. Job roles

While there are numerous approaches and tools that can be used to improve the organization, all of them ultimately prescribe adjustments to one or more of the four parts of the organization listed above. Change typically results as a reaction to specific problems or opportunities the organization is facing based on internal or external stimuli. While the notion of becoming more competitive, becoming closer to the customer, or becoming more efficient can be the motivation to change, at some point these goals must be transformed into the specific impacts on processes, systems, organization structures, or job roles. This is the process of defining the change. However, according to Creasey, it is not enough to merely prescribe the change and expect it to happen—creating change within an organization takes hard work and structure around what must actually take place to make the change happen.

There are three key disciplines required to bring change management to life. These include

- Project management
- Change management
- Daily work management

---

* Source: An interview with Tim Creasey, April, 2014. Prosci's change management methodology is based on research with over 2600 participants over the last 14 years. What is unique about the methodology is that it comes from real project leaders and teams reflecting on what worked, what did not, and what they would do differently on their next projects. At its core, Prosci's methodology is the collective lessons learned by those introducing change across the globe. Based on this research, Prosci's goal has been to develop a methodology that is holistic and at the same time easy to use. The resulting process, tools, and assessments have been developed with one goal in mind: that organizations can put them to use on projects and change initiatives, building upon the organization's own internal change management skill set. See the Prosci website, www.prosci .com, for related details.

To begin, let's look at the formal definitions of each of these. Here are a few commonly accepted definitions that help us begin to think about these distinct but intertwined disciplines.

As described in Table 1.1, both project management and change management support moving an organization from a current state (how things are done today) through a transition state to a desired future state (the new processes, systems, organization structures, or job roles defined by the change). Project management focuses on the tasks to achieve the project requirements while change management focuses on the people impacted by the change. Daily management, on the other hand, is an approach to running an organization where staff members take the time each day to evaluate their progress toward meeting the organization's improvement targets, and then take the time to measure how they compare against the organization's overall progress.

Management decisions are based on facts and data, with equal attention paid to results and processes. In other words, daily management allows the organization to stay on track and creates the groundwork for effective problem solving. Key elements of daily management are the brief 15–20 minute daily huddles, visibility walls, and standard work. Daily huddles, or meetings, bring staff together to get on the same page using visibility walls, which consist of relevant charts and data, making the work of

TABLE 1.1

Definitions of Project Management, Change Management, and Daily Management Activities

Project management	Project management is the application of knowledge, skills, tools, and techniques to project activities to meet project requirements. Project management is accomplished through the application and integration of the project management processes of initiating, planning, executing, monitoring and controlling, and closing. * From PMBOK® Guide, Third Edition
Change management	Change management is the process, tools, and techniques to manage the people side of change to achieve the required business outcome. Change management incorporates the organizational tools that can be utilized to help individuals make successful personal transitions resulting in the adoption and realization of change.
Daily management	Daily management is the process, tools, and techniques used to make the work of the organization or unit visible and create a visual workplace.

the organization or unit visible. Creating a visual workplace makes work abnormalities apparent and able to be addressed through change management improvement work, while the gains can be nurtured and sustained. Standardized work, which requires defining a uniform way a task is done, is an important element because it serves as the baseline for further improvement work.

TECHNICAL AND PEOPLE SIDES OF CHANGE MANAGEMENT

Any change to processes, systems, organizational structures, and/or job roles will have a technical side and a people side that must be managed. Project management and change management have evolved as disciplines to provide both the structure and the tools needed to realize change successfully on the technical and people sides, as shown in Figure 1.1.

The goal of project management is to effectively deploy resources in a structured manner to develop and implement the solution in terms of what needs to be done to processes, systems, organizational structure, and job

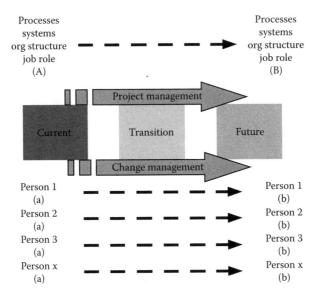

FIGURE 1.1
Transitioning between functions.

roles. The goal of change management is to help each individual impacted by the change to make a successful transition, given what is required by the solution.

BLENDING IN THE RIGHT AMOUNT OF MANAGEMENT

Each initiative or project that we undertake requires some level of involvement of the project management, change management, and daily management systems approach (see Table 1.2). These disciplines are tools used to support the implementation of a variety of changes that you may be undertaking.

Note: Most of the project/intervention types that we have been discussing need both project management and change management, while some need a blend of two or three of the four disciplines. There are very few instances where you will not need at least two of the three disciplines.

ERP: enterprise resource planning.

These management methods and tools must be applied independent of the actual change that you are undertaking. Any time you alter processes, systems, organization structures, or job roles, you need a structured approach to manage both the technical side and the people side of the pending change.

TABLE 1.2

Analysis of Change Management from a Management System's Perspective

Project/Intervention Type	Project Management	Change Management	Daily Management
Deploying an ERP solution across the entire organization	Always	Always	Always
Reengineering the work processes and contact scripts of your call center agents	Always	Always	Always
Integrating two organizations and their information systems following a merger or acquisition	Always	Always	Sometimes
Redesigning the physical layout of an office space	Sometimes	Sometimes	Always
Developing a new sales channel	Sometimes	Sometimes	Sometimes

DIFFERENT VIEWS OF CHANGE MANAGEMENT

While the right amount of project management and change management is often always needed, each of their associated tools are at their best when they are customized for the unique situation that you are facing and are fully integrated. Your organization (with its unique culture and history) and the specific change that you are implementing all influence the right amount of project management, change management, and daily management. So far, in most change-oriented handbooks, project management and change management are discussed as two distinct disciplines, and daily management is rarely brought into the conversation. While separate as fields of study, on a real project intervention, most of these management systems should be (but rarely are) integrated. The steps and activities move in unison as teams work to move from the current state to a desired future state.

As an example, think about what activities occur during the planning phase of a project. On the project management side, teams are identifying the milestones and activities that must be completed. They are outlining the resources needed and how they will work together. They are defining the scope of what will be part of the project and what will not be. From a change and daily management side, teams begin crafting key messages that must be communicated. They work with project sponsors to build strong and active coalitions of senior leaders. They begin making the case of why the change is needed to employees throughout the organization even before the specific details of the solution are complete. The most effective projects integrate these activities into a single project plan.

All major improvements within an organization are driven by the implementation of projects and/or portfolio of projects. For years the project management methodology was based on the major content areas:

1. Project integration management
2. Project scope management
3. Project time management
4. Project cost management
5. Project quality management
6. Project human resource management

7. Project communications management
8. Project risks management
9. Project procurement management

Noticeably lacking from the project management body of knowledge was culture change management and daily management. It is unfortunate for when the body of knowledge for project management was assembled, these methodologies were still in the development stages and the impact that they have on the potential success of the project was not thoroughly understood by most organizations. As a result, there has been an extremely high failure rate in the value created by a high percentage of the project. In the past when the majority of employees were poorly educated, the resistance to change was minimized and it was just accepted that someone "up there" knew what was best. Historically, these employees blindly followed direction, never questioning the legitimacy of the change initiatives. Today with a highly trained and educated workforce, employees are questioning the need for them to change. They are not questioning the need *per se*; in fact, they are all for change as long as the change does not impact them.

SUMMARY

Rapid changes in external environment, consumer behavior, global economics, and disruptive technologies are throwing off the most rigorous business strategies and the best-trained managers. Everyone expects to see big changes ahead but people react differently to change. Over 60 percent of companies out there are operating on a dated business model and 20 percent are operating with a mental model that has been expired for more than five years. There are few reasons for those 20 percent of companies to survive another five years or even three, and the other 60 percent only have a short window of opportunity to design and orchestrate their transformation.

Many people become accustomed to the status quo and don't want to alter the way things are being done regardless of the potential benefits or the disruptive threats from emerging competition. For many, fear of the unknown and the concern about the ramifications on their careers are barriers to acknowledge the need for change. Although people don't like change, winning belongs to those who thrive with change. History shows that any business transformation process is painful. The way many organizations manage change or transformation, using existing change management models, is too slow, and by the time they refreeze, the market has shifted and they find that they will need another transformation.

2

The Philosophy and Evolution
of Change Management

In a Nutshell: It can sometimes be hard to separate out the change, project management, and change management. In practice, these three components are intertwined in order to deliver a positive outcome to the organization. However, there is value in separating out the components. Thinking about the three components and their philosophies separately makes it easier to define and help others understand these distinct elements. Also, separating out these three components is a solid first step when troubleshooting on a particular project that may not be moving ahead as expected. For instance, are our challenges coming from issues around designing the change? Are the issues related to the technical steps, activities, or resources (project management)? Or are concerns coming from how individuals are accepting or resisting the change (change management)?

INTRODUCTION

Some of the earliest writings of mankind were centered on change. Dating back as early as 3000 BC, the *I Ching* (or *Book of Changes*) conceived the notion that change is inevitable and resistance to change is one of humankind's greatest causes of pain. These early agents of change wrote that in order to affect change in a positive way, a balance was required between internal and external forces. But it is one thing to produce a momentary change, and quite another to sustain that change. Traditionally, change management has been used to help project management teams successfully implement projects/programs that involve changing the activities and/or the behavioral patterns of the people within the organization that would be impacted by the change (Campbell 1969). By the early 1980s, some managers were required to have not only an excellent understanding of the technology involved and the processes required to implement the technology, but also awareness that project success was heavily dependent on the degree of acceptance by the people.

Projects in customer relations management, concurrent engineering, Lean, and total quality management (TQM) required that the project be in direct alignment with the organization's culture and mission. In order for the technology to be successful, people were required to change their operating behaviors. Backed by statistics which began to demonstrate that up to 65 percent of the strategic initiatives required significant behavioral change on the part of the employees, project managers came to realize their success relied heavily on the ability of the project team to change the habits and behaviors of the impacted staff and line workers.

This is change management at its essence: *proactive steps taken to enable the passing from one phase or state to the next, with the goal of an improvement over the original condition that is sustained over time.* The purpose of this chapter is to briefly review the development of thought regarding change management over the last 35 years, highlight what we have learned, and propose a path forward that establishes a model for achieving sustainable change.

RISKS IN SYSTEMS IMPLEMENTATION

As stated in a change management plan from the National Institutes of Health (2001),* "The greatest risk to the successful implementation of an enterprise-wide system is the failure to take into consideration major aspects of organizational change management." This report goes on to state that poor communications, inadequate training, or insufficient workforce planning can lead to a lack of acceptance of business changes and poor performance at the end-user level. In many cases, failure to provide for adequate change management planning has resulted in the loss of millions of dollars in failed or delayed implementation.

---

* Source: See http://nbs.nih.gov/pdf/change_management.pdf.

Effective change management can minimize the impact of these factors on the project and ensure that all personnel affected by the change management project intervention receive assistance to help them manage change in their area, as shown in Figure 2.1.

Figure 2.1 depicts the goal of the change management plan which is to minimize the productivity dip that is often caused by new project interventions. It is adapted from an integrated State of Oklahoma CORE project change management plan with the change management model of plan, do, and sustain.

In any large implementation, the change management project team can expect to experience resistance and reluctance to change. The change effort should be described in a business case document that will provide the various stakeholder groups important information about the project's purpose, scope, benefits, timeline, and training opportunities as well as how the individual job environment will change due to the implementation of the applications.* Change management will become the voice of this project and help define the changes required within the customer's business processes, policies, and procedures. The messages provided via this plan should be customized based on the specific needs of each group affected by the project. It is the intent of every change management project team that each change management effort will lessen the production dip that is inevitable in any varied and complex project.

―――――――――

CHANGE MANAGEMENT ACTIVITIES AND GOALS

Change management encompasses all activities aimed at helping an organization successfully accept and adopt new technologies and new ways to serve its customers. Effective change management enables the transformation of strategy, processes, technology, and people to enhance performance and ensure continuous improvement in an ever-changing environment. A

---

* *Making the Case for Change: Using Effective Business Cases to Minimize Project and Innovation Failures* (The Little Big Book Series) by Christopher F. Voehl, H. James Harrington, and Frank Voehl (2015). This book illustrates how to develop a strong business case that links investments to program results, and ultimately, with the strategic outcomes of the organization. In addition, the book provides a template and example case studies for those seeking to fast-track the development of a business case within their organization.

Goal of organizational change management is to minimize the productivity dip

The performance dip

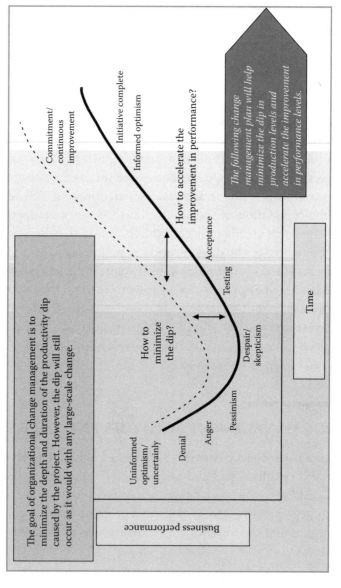

FIGURE 2.1

Goal of the organizational change management plan. (Available at http://www.youroklahoma.com/coreoklahoma/change1.pdf.)

comprehensive and structured approach to change management is critical to the success of any project that will bring about significant change.

Think about what each component is trying to achieve, as shown in Table 2.1. This is a descriptive way to tell someone else what change management is and how it is related to the change and project management.

Change management's activities help identify the inherent people-related risks that can impact the success of any major organization's activity, such as an ERP initiative. This book will help organizations assess overall readiness for change by evaluating various stakeholder groups across the organization. Specifically, it will help the reader to

1. Set and articulate a business case and vision for change, one that creates a long-term view based on solid and credible rationale
2. Develop a change management strategy that includes considerations to manage the magnitude of change and needed stakeholder support in order to mobilize and align leaders to lead, coordinate, and facilitate change
3. Engage and communicate with stakeholders to encourage collaboration and support
4. Align the organization's structure, performance objectives, and incentives with clear metrics to measure the success of change
5. Enable the workforce through learning and facilitating role changes to develop a change-oriented culture that supports the organization's strategy and specific change initiatives

TABLE 2.1

Goal or Objective for Each of the Three Elements of Change Management

Element	Goal or Objective
Quality management	To improve the organization in some fashion; for instance, reduce error rates, reduce costs, improve revenues, solve problems, seize opportunities, align work and strategy, and streamline information flow within the organization
Project management	To develop a set of specific plans and actions to achieve the change given time, cost, and scope constraints and to utilize resources effectively (managing the technical side of the change)
Daily management	To use the process, tools, and techniques to make the work of the organization or unit visible and create a visual workplace

CHANGE MANAGEMENT PROCESSES AND TOOLS

Change management incorporates processes and tools that manage employee needs and requirements during each change at an organizational level. When combined with an understanding of individual change management best practice processes, it can provide a structured approach to effectively transition groups or organizations through change (see Figure 2.2 for details). This book encompasses the main change management activities and is often organized around the plan–do–check–act (PDCA) management model, which loosely form the Prosci change management process of plan, do, and sustain:

1. Plan: identify potential change, analyze change request, plan change
2. Do: evaluate change, implement change
3. Sustain: review and close change

FIGURE 2.2
Key components of traditional change management. Depiction of some of the key components of change management, including techniques for making the change management intervention a successful one.

The following is a description of the six change management components:

1. Creating a change management strategy (readiness assessments)
2. Engaging senior managers as change leaders (sponsorship)
3. Building awareness of the need for change (communications)
4. Developing skills and knowledge to support the change (education and training)
5. Helping employees move through the transition (coaching by managers and supervisors)
6. Developing methods to sustain the change (measurement systems, rewards, and reinforcement)

The change management plan–do–sustain framework* 3 provides an ideal basis for an even-handed development and deployment process, which encompasses people (e.g., organization, staff, skills, and capabilities), the technology that supports them (e.g., Information technology [IT], office automation, and communications), and the processes that bind them all together (in line with the business strategy).

WHY USE CHANGE MANAGEMENT?

The change management approaches described in this book are vendor-independent approaches that recognize that a great many more change management projects fail because of people issues than because of technology issues. This book's focus is on helping people to work effectively together to achieve the business goals. A fundamental assumption of the change management approach is that nothing is built perfectly the first time, but that as a rule of thumb, 80 percent of the solution can be produced in 20 percent of the time that it would take to produce the total solution. Using this approach to change management, it is all right to sacrifice quality for productivity. It is sometimes referred to as letting the customer be the final inspection.

This approach is used by a number of our most advanced innovative companies, such as Microsoft and Apple. A basic problem with less agile approaches is the expectation that potential solution users can predict

---

* See *The Change Management Pocket Guide*, as previously described in footnote on page 15.

what all their requirements will be at some distant point in time. This problem is compounded by the fact that the mere existence of a new solution affects the business requirements because the methods of working have changed. In the classical, sequential (or waterfall), approach, the next step cannot be started until the current step is completed. In practice, a lot of time is spent in getting from the 80-percent solution to the total solution, with the assumption that no step ever needs to be revisited. This means that considerable time is spent going back to completed steps and unravelling the defects from work that has previously been accepted. The result is that projects are delivered late and over budget or they fail to meet the business needs since time is not spent reworking the requirements.

Solutions built using the change management approach address the current and imminent needs of the business rather than the traditional approach of attacking all the perceived possibilities. The resulting solution is, therefore, expected to be a better fit to the true business needs— easier to test and more likely to be accepted into the business working practices. Since the development cost of most IT solutions is only a small part of the total life cycle costs, it makes sense to build simpler solutions that are fit for their specific purpose and are easier to maintain and modify after their initial development. The latter is possible since maintenance can be treated as a further incremental delivery toward the total solution.

PROBLEMS IDENTIFIED BY CHANGE MANAGEMENT STUDY RESEARCH

In addition to addressing many of the problems inherent with a traditional approach, we also address many of the general concerns about change management process development. Specifically, change management is a convergent approach, ensuring that basic foundations for the intervention are agreed upon at an early stage. This allows businesses to understand the scope of the proposed solution before the detail is explored and expanded. Clarifying and agreeing on the foundations ensures no unwelcome surprises on change management projects. In particular, for larger corporate organizations with a complex architecture, agreeing on the solution architecture toward the start of the project is essential, as outlined in our business case handbook.* Managing any business change or developing any solution is never a simple task, and many serious problems occur regularly whenever people from multiple disciplines work together on a project. Change management is specifically designed to address many of these well-known problems.

Some of the details of common problems and change management's approach to addressing these are outlined in the following key problem areas:

1. *Communication problems.* Poor communication is highlighted time after time as a major failing on projects. Setting up clear and concise communication between the different areas and levels of an organization is not an easy task. Change management provides a lot of guidance to strengthen communication and to make it as rich as possible. Change management's emphasis on human interaction (e.g., facilitated workshops), visualization (e.g., modeling, prototyping), and clearly defined roles is at the heart of improved project communication. In particular, visualization has proved to be a far more effective way of communicating than by large, textual documents that are passed from one person to another and sometimes used to apportion blame when an unworkable solution has been delivered.

2. *Late delivery.* Slippage of the completion date causes much frustration and significant knock-on effects for a business. Change management sees this issue as one of the most important problems to address and change management's approach and many of the change management practices are geared toward always being on time. Being on time applies to short-term goals as well as the project as a whole. If there is ever a need for compromise on a project, change management believes that compromising the deadline is not an option. The delivered solution isn't really what the business wanted.

3. *Unwanted/defective features included.* Another frustration is that when the solution is delivered, it doesn't meet the expectations of the business. It may have features that don't do what the business

---

* *Making the Case for Change: Using Effective Business Cases to Minimize Project and Innovation Failures* (The Little Big Book Series) by Christopher F. Voehl, H. James Harrington, and Frank Voehl (2014). The best time to stop projects or programs that will not be successful is before they are ever started. Research has shown that the focused use of realistic business case analysis on proposed initiatives could enable your organization to reduce the amount of project waste and churn (rework) by up to 40 percent, potentially avoiding millions of dollars lost on projects, programs, and initiatives that would fail to produce the desired results.

really wanted it to do, or contain snags and bugs that prevent the deliverable from performing smoothly, or it simply might not be aligned with true business processes. In change management, getting the correct understanding of the needs of the business is of paramount importance. Change management encompasses practices that encourage collaboration and enable rich communications. Most importantly, change management teams are encouraged to embrace change, which allow them to deal with problems that occur, to encompass new ideas that appear, and to build the solution based on a deepening understanding of the solution in detail.

4. *Unused features.* Recent research has highlighted the low percentage of delivered features that are actually used. This often happens because the business tends to overprescribe their needs during a project. Change management helps a business to prioritize its needs and keep the focus on what is important. This also avoids causing delays to a project by developing features that are never used.

5. *Building the right change model.* A frequent cry on a traditional project is that "the users have changed their minds." Although typically treated as a problem, change management embraces change and believes that it isn't a bad thing but a good one! It is often the result of a deepening understanding or sometimes it is due to an external event. Change management capitalizes on the greater depth of understanding and so ensures that the deployed solution fits with the true business requirements. Change management enables change through iterative development, with regular reviews to make sure that what is being developed is what the business really wants. Requirement changes are a natural result of a better understanding, so change management expects it and plans for it.

There are two types of change involved with every change management intervention. They are type I changes—the changes that the individuals impacted by the output from the prototype or solution have to undergo, and type II changes—the changes that the change management team and plan need to undergo in order to accept and support the type I changes.

6. *Delayed or late return on investment (ROI).* Usually, business benefits decrease over time and therefore delivering everything toward the end of a project will reduce the ROI. Change management uses incremental delivery to get the most important and most valuable

features to the business as soon as it can. When appropriate, it can harness the aggressive nature of techniques, such as vertical prototyping, in order to deliver a partial solution to the business very early and therefore to enable early ROI. This is an expanded role and will mean that change management is responsible for playing a very different role than it has been applying in the past.

7. *Overengineering or gold-plating.* There is normally a diminishing return (on value) when trying to make a deliverable perfect. Usually the highest business benefits can be derived by getting something that is good enough into a window of opportunity for the business. Change management is a pragmatic approach that focuses on the business need in order to prevent a team being tempted into adding bells and whistles that the business could live without, and as a result, missing the deadline. Prioritization ensures that the whole team is clear about the relative importance of the work to be done.

CHANGE MANAGEMENT ITERATIVE DEVELOPMENT

The change management sustainable change model (outlined in Chapter 4) involves the solution's end users throughout the change management life cycle, which has many benefits:

- The users are more likely to claim ownership of the solution
- The risk of building the wrong solution is greatly reduced
- The final solution is more likely to meet the users' real business requirements
- The users will be better trained, since their representatives will define and coordinate the training required
- Deployment is more likely to go smoothly because of the cooperation of all parties concerned throughout development

Our model specifically addresses many of the problems that cause projects to struggle or to fail. For many organizations, having the ability to deliver working solutions consistently, on time, and on budget is seen as a major step forward and this provides a perfect match for their change management needs and wants.

BASIC CHANGE MANAGEMENT OBJECTIVES

The basic objectives of change management support the plan–do–sustain cycle. They direct the team in the attitude they must take and the mindset they must adopt in order to deliver consistently. Compromising any principle undermines change management's basic philosophy: If a team doesn't follow all of the principles, then they don't get the full benefit. The collective value of change management's objectives enables organizations to deliver best-value business solutions collaboratively.

Change management's underlying objectives are organized around the plan–do–sustain cycle, as shown below.*

Plan
1. Collaborate
2. Never compromise quality
3. Focus on the business case
4. Ensure practicality of the plan and that risks are considered and built into the plan
5. Ensure impacted personnel change requirements are planned for and funded

Do
6. Ensure scope changes are in line with real business requirements
7. Ensure project output deliverables are not installed prior to the impacted personnel being ready (emotionally and technically) to receive them
8. Deliver on time
9. Build incrementally and iteratively on firm foundations

Sustain
10. Install an effective measurement system
11. Communicate continuously and clearly
12. Demonstrate control

---

* Prosci's research has shown that projects with excellent change management effectiveness are *six times* more likely to meet or exceed project objectives. Change management increases the success of organizational change and project initiatives by applying a structured framework of methods, tools, and processes managing the change from a current state to a future state. Regardless of the scale of change, applying a change management framework increases the probability of staying on schedule and budget, resulting in higher benefit realization and ROI. See: http://www.prosci.com /change-management/why-change-management/.

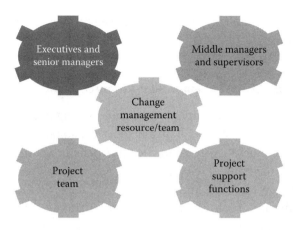

FIGURE 2.3
The roles involved in change management.

Objective 1: Collaborate

Teams that work in a spirit of active cooperation and commitment will always outperform groups of individuals working only in loose association. Collaboration encourages increased understanding, greater speed, and shared ownership that enable teams to perform at a level that exceeds the sum of their parts. In order to fulfil this objective, change management teams should

- Involve the right stakeholders, at the right time, throughout the project
- Ensure that the members of the team are empowered to make decisions on behalf of those they represent
- Actively involve the business representatives
- Build a one-team culture

Change management roles bring the needed subject-matter experts into the project so they can contribute to the solution. The change management resource team* is responsible for facilitating a high level of collaboration between team members, as shown in Figure 2.3. Facilitated workshops

---

* Based on the Prosci change management tutorial. There is a whole system of people in the organization responsible for supporting employees in making this transition. From the highest levels of leadership to front-line supervisors, effectively managing change requires a system of actors all moving in unison and fulfilling their particular roles based on their unique relationships to the change at hand. This tutorial examines the five key change management roles. For more details, see: http://www.change-management.com/tutorial-job-roles-mod2.htm.

enable stakeholders to share their knowledge effectively with other members of the project team.

The Role of the Change Management Resource Team

The resource team role is important because having dedicated resources for change management was high on most consultants' lists of overall greatest contributors to success in the 2007 benchmarking study.* Also, there is a growing body of data that shows a correlation between the success of a change initiative and how well the people side was managed. Without dedicated resources, change management activities will not be completed. Unfortunately, when budgets and schedules are squeezed, change management is pushed to the bottom of the priority list if there are not dedicated resources.

Objective 2: Never Compromise Quality

In change management, the level of quality to be delivered should be agreed to at the start. All work should be aimed at achieving that level of quality—no more and no less. A solution has to be good enough. (Note: Striving for excellence at this point is not necessary with the new change management model.) If the business agrees that the features in the minimum usable subset have been provided adequately, then the solution should be acceptable. In order to fulfil this objective, change management teams will

- Set the level of quality at the outset
- Ensure that quality does not become a variable
- Design, document, and test appropriately
- Build in quality by constant review
- Test early and continuously

The business and technical testing of these products together with regular reviews throughout the project life cycle will help the change management team to build a quality solution. Using change management, everything is tested as early as possible. Test-driven techniques result in a

---

* The Prosci Benchmarking Study, 2007.

test being written before the deliverable is actually produced. Prioritization and timeboxing are used to ensure that testing is appropriate and undertaken without introducing unnecessary risks, as described in Chapters 11 and 12 of this book.

Objective 3: Focus on the Business Case

Every decision taken during a change management project should be viewed in the light of the overriding business case goals and objectives, which is to deliver what the business needs it to deliver, and when it needs to be. A change management project is a means to an end, not an end in itself. In order to fulfill this objective, change management teams will need to

- Understand the true business priorities
- Establish a sound business case
- Update the business case based on information which they collected that was not available when the business case was approved by the executive management team
- Seek continuous business sponsorship and commitment
- Guarantee the minimum usable subset (see Chapter 11)

Specific business roles in change management in conjunction with the business products created in the foundations phase and key techniques such as timeboxing and prioritization enable change management teams to fulfill this objective. Timeboxing allocates a fixed time period, called a time box, to each planned activity.

Objective 4: Deliver on Time

Delivering products on time is a very desirable outcome for a project and is quite often the single most important success factor. Late delivery can undermine the very rationale for a project, especially where market opportunities or legal deadlines are involved. In order to fulfil this principle, change management teams will

- Timebox the work
- Focus on business priorities
- Always hit deadlines

Timeboxing and prioritization enable change management teams to implement this principle and build a reputation for timely and predictable deliveries.

Objective 5: Build Incrementally and Iteratively on Firm Foundations

In order to deliver real business benefits early, change management advocates incremental delivery. This encourages stakeholder confidence and is a source of feedback for use in subsequent increments. Increments that are deployed into operational use may lead to the realization of early business benefit. Change management advocates first understanding the scope of the business problem to be solved and the proposed solution, but not in such detail that the project becomes paralyzed. In order to fulfill this principle, project teams will

- Strive for early delivery of business benefit where possible
- Continually confirm that the correct solution is being built
- Formally reassess priorities and ongoing project viability with each delivered increment

Change management teams implement this principle using a change management life cycle, which delivers a solid base of knowledge initially before developing incrementally. In order to converge on an accurate business solution, change management uses iterative development to deliver the right solution. The concept of iteration is embedded throughout change management's life cycle down to the lowest level of timeboxing.* It is very rare that anything is built perfectly the first time and projects

---

* In the world of change management time management, timeboxing allocates a fixed time period, called a time box, to each planned activity. Several change management project management approaches use timeboxing, which is also used to address personal tasks in a smaller time frame. It often involves having deliverables and deadlines that will improve the productivity of the user. In change management project management, the triple constraints are time or schedule, cost or budget, and scope or performance. Quality is often added, sometimes replacing cost. Changing one constraint will probably impact the rest. Without timeboxing, projects usually work to a fixed scope, such that when it is clear that some deliverables cannot be completed, in which case either the deadline slips to allow for more time, or more people are involved to accomplish more in the same timeframe. Usually when both happen, delivery is late, costs go up, and often quality suffers. This concept is described further in later chapters of this book.

operate within a changing world. Change management time management advocates a pragmatic approach to change that relies on iteration in order to embrace change and produce a better solution.

In order to fulfill this principle, change management teams will

- Do enough design up front to create strong foundations
- Take an iterative approach to building all products
- Build customer feedback into each iteration
- Accept that most detail emerges later rather than sooner
- Embrace change—the right solution will not emerge without it
- Be creative and experiment, learn, and evolve

Change is inevitable, so change management allows for change and harnesses its benefits. Within the constraints of time and cost, change is actively encouraged in order to evolve to the most appropriate solution. Change management uses iteration and constant review to make sure that what is being developed is what the business really needs.

Objective 6: Communicate Continuously and Clearly

Poor communication is often cited as the biggest single cause of project failure. Change management techniques are specifically designed to improve communication effectiveness for both teams and individuals. In order to fulfill this principle, change management teams will

- Run daily team stand-up sessions
- Use facilitated workshops
- Use rich communication techniques such as modeling and prototyping
- Present instances of the evolving solution early and often
- Keep documentation lean and timely
- Manage stakeholder expectations throughout the project
- Encourage informal, face-to-face communication at all levels

Change management emphasizes the value of human interaction through facilitated workshops, clearly defined roles, and user involvement. Modeling and prototyping make early instances of the new culture available for preimplementation scrutiny.

Objective 7: Demonstrate Control (Final Component of Sustain)

It is essential to be in control of an intervention at all times. A change management team needs to be proactive when monitoring and controlling progress in line with the business case. You need to be able to prove you are in control. In order to fulfill this principle, change management teams, especially the project manager and team leader, will

- Use an appropriate level of formality for tracking and reporting
- Make plans and progress visible to all
- Measure progress through focus on delivery of products rather than completed activities
- Manage proactively
- Evaluate continuing project viability based on the business objectives

The use of well-defined time boxes with constant review points and the preparation of the change management plan are designed to assist the project manager and the change management team to follow this principle.

SUMMARY

The concepts and ideas described in this chapter help direct and shape the attitude and mindset of a change management team. Compromising any of the objectives undermines the change management philosophy, as they deliver an endurable approach consisting of three components as follows:

- Component 1: Plan. Identify potential change, analyze change request, plan change
- Component 2: Do. Evaluate change, implement change
- Component 3: Sustain. Review and close change

In this chapter readers were introduced to the following seven change management objectives:

- Objective 1: Collaborate (initial component of plan)
- Objective 2: Never compromise quality (second component of plan)

- Objective 3: Focus on the business case (third component of plan)
- Objective 4: Deliver on time (component of do)
- Objective 5: Build incrementally and iteratively on firm foundations (component of do)
- Objective 6: Communicate continuously and clearly (component of sustain)
- Objective 7: Demonstrate control (final component of sustain)

In Chapter 11 we will show you how these objectives are prioritized and accomplished.

3

Making the Case for Change Readiness

In a Nutshell: A Gartner Group survey of Fortune 500 executives revealed that almost 70 percent of change implementations did not realize their full process and systems benefits due to failure to address the people issues. The survey reveals that enterprises that fail to prepare and support their workforces for major and continuing organizational change will miss business objectives by at least 30 percent and will experience turnover rates of at least 20 percent annually for their key knowledge and leadership workers. A very common theme among these failures is a lack of understanding of the power of the collective human system to obstruct or avoid the progress of initiatives. The result has been to reinforce fear, defensiveness, and cynicism among employees toward change efforts. Over the long haul, a failure of change means that business strategies are not accomplished and that resistance to change increases and the organization's survival is threatened. The success or failure of any change initiatives depends not only on the business demand and strategic decisions of top management, but on attitudes, values, perception, and beliefs of the people and their active participation. In change implementations, human aspects play a crucial role in ensuring that the change really takes root in the DNA of the organization.

INTRODUCTION

As contained in the report *Best Practices in Change Management*,* the authors highlighted a few troublesome statistics: "nearly 60 percent of the companies analyzed lacked the right capabilities to deliver on their

---

* Prosci, Inc. April 2014.

change plans, while about the same percentage of companies didn't have the appropriate individuals, structures and decision-making processes to drive the change initiatives. Furthermore, about 60 percent lacked the right metrics and incentives to make change efforts successful; and more than 63 percent of the companies faced high risks to their change efforts because of significant communications gaps between the leaders of the effort and the employees most affected by it."

Extrapolating from IBM's May 2008 study of CEOs (highlighted in the Project Management Institute [PMI] paper, *Change Agility: Readiness for Strategy Implementation*), we concluded that there are seven common challenges to successful, sustainable strategic change initiatives:

1. Changing mindsets and attitudes
2. Corporate culture
3. Underestimation of complexity
4. Shortage of resources
5. Lack of higher management commitment
6. Lack of change know-how
7. Lack of motivation of involved employees

Although lack of employee motivation still emerges as a key barrier to sustainable change, nonetheless it still ranks at the bottom of this list. A clear challenger emerges with the key need being a global paradigm shift consisting of changing mindsets, attitudes, and organizational culture. Later in this chapter we explore the real impact of changing organizational paradigms and evolving to a culture of alignment and enrollment integral to our Sustainable Change Model. To conclude the assessment of the current state of organizational change (both within the framework of this chapter and within organizations seeking to assess their change readiness), the PMI companion paper, *Building Change Agility: The Strategic Process for Agility Improvement*, posts several key questions that must be addressed to effect change and pave the way for establishing a change sustainability model within organizations:

- Who needs to be ready for a change? This includes both internal and external actors, and requires both alignment at the strategic/structural level as well as enrollment throughout the organization to ensure that impacts from change can be efficiently and empathetically absorbed and reacted upon with an effective response.

- What processes/activities need to be ready for change? This includes both organizational processes, such as strategic alignment, processes integral to OCM mobilization, and execution including change control and governance; and supporting processes for organizational portfolio/program/project monitoring, measuring, managing, and sustaining through lessons learned.
- What changes in operational systems need to support change agility? Change agility defines operational dimensions on which organizations seeking change agility and sustainability need to focus their change readiness assessment efforts:
  - Time: includes responsiveness, prioritization, decision making, and a sense of urgency
  - Leadership: includes cultural trust and transparency, innovation, and openness
  - Work norms: includes decision involvement, collaboration, and participation
  - Learning: includes sharing, mentoring, performance review, and standardization
- What causal drivers need to be addressed in order to improve change agility? Most organizations focus at the outcome level, only addressing problem symptoms as they arise. They rarely get beyond the tip of the iceberg to address the root causes of pervasive, persistent causal factors perennially driving down change adoption rates or get beyond the status quo. Addressing the following causal drivers as part of a comprehensive change readiness assessment is a sure way to break the status quo and move toward a sustainable change management approach:
  - Culture: includes leadership and organizational responsiveness (markets, trends), innovation; holistic/transparent/integrated alignment within boundaries, lean structures/decision making; collaborative, coordinated work efforts; participatory decision making with two-way input and feedback on future direction; and knowledge sharing and individual development
  - Commitment: includes leadership embracing the change paradigm as the norm; rigorous prioritization, qualification, and selection of potential change initiatives; and leaders as active change agents throughout ensuring alignment, enrollment, and strategy execution
  - Capacity: organization embraces lean/agile/adaptability in business practices and processes; standardizes a portfolio management

approach of strategically aligned inventory of initiatives prioritized, organized, and managed through a program management office type infrastructure; processes for strategy development, solution definition, and change management are well defined and utilized; process improvement is a stated and active goal of the organization; planning is inclusive; and resources are allocated and managed proactively

Finally, the change readiness assessment should highlight the degree to which recognition and reward systems support all of these stated objectives and themes, especially those contributing to progress on these key causal drivers of change agility and sustainability.

UNDERSTANDING THE READINESS FOR A CHANGE LIFE CYCLE

There are many situations where an organization needs to incorporate a change life cycle. Many times it is due to an expansion, restructuring, merger & acquisition, regulatory compliance, or an ERP technology. To determine the organization's change management life cycle needs, we need to know at least the following four items on the change checklist:

- How are they managing change today?
- What are their current challenges and opportunities?
- What organizational challenges and changes are they expecting?
- How are they integrating change management and training?

The Team needs to assess the business case and ensure alignment with the organization's vision and goals. Next, they need to look at how they communicate and train their employees today and help them to strategize the best approach for the culture. Risks and business impacts are then identified and communicated to the appropriate level of the organization in order to help the organization become ready for the impact of change through the use of a standardized methodology and some type of external consulting expertise. According to many consultants and CEOs that we interviewed, strategy execution at the level of the individual employee is increasingly proving to be a key to OCM success.* And this is true for all types of organizations be they public, private, or nonprofit organizations, as many senior executives know this and worry about it. When asked what keeps them up at night, CEOs involved in transformation often say they are concerned about how the workforce will react, how they can get their team to work together, and how they will be able to lead their people. They also worry about retaining their company's unique values and sense of identity and about creating a culture of commitment and performance. Leadership teams that fail to plan for the human side of change often find themselves wondering why their best-laid plans have gone awry.†

Most leaders, however, know a lot more about strategy formulation than execution. They know much more about planning than doing, which causes major problems while rolling strategy to work. The worst part is that leaders do not own the execution process; they delegate the task of execution of change versus executing the business to people at lower levels, and very often without proper guidelines and training. The strategy execution problems faced by many organizations are remarkably similar to those viewed by many leaders in the world. The obstacles to effective strategy execution are still real and formidable. While strategy planning is difficult and challenging, as always, it's still obvious that leaders feel more than ever that the successful execution of strategy is more problematic than the formulation of a chosen strategy and even more important for organizational performance. It is still clear that making strategy work is more difficult and challenging than formulating strategy, but the results are worth it, as shown in the typical change life cycle depicted in Figure 3.1.‡

---

* Long-term structural transformation has four characteristics: (1) scale, as the change affects all or most of the organization, (2) magnitude, as it involves significant alterations of the status quo, (3) duration, as it lasts for months, if not years, and (4) strategic importance. However, companies will reap the rewards only when change occurs at the level of the individual employee.

† No single methodology fits every company, but there is a set of practices, tools, and techniques that can be adapted to a variety of situations. What follows in this book is a list of guiding principles for change management. Using these as a systematic, comprehensive framework, executives can understand what to expect, how to manage their own personal change, and how to engage the entire organization in the process.

‡ Figure 3.1 is based on the Suntiva fundamentals of change model, as found on the website http://www.suntiva.com/blog/post/40/the-fundamentals-of-change-management/. Today's business leaders face enormous challenges in combining the right business strategy with the processes, technology, and people who can make it happen. Suntiva has built service and solution offerings around this reality, bringing together deep and specific business domain expertise with their deep doctoral-level knowledge of psychology, human behavior, and organizational performance. Over hundreds of engagements, they have proven the value of this combination, delivering lasting results and measurable business outcomes for their client leadership teams.

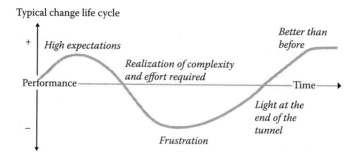

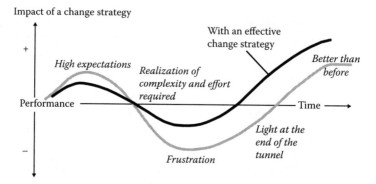

FIGURE 3.1

Typical change life cycle and impact of a change strategy. Given the scope, impact, and frequency of change it stands to reason that organizations invest in using a structured and repeatable process to plan and guide change and build capacity for change and learning along the way. As illustrated, an effective change management strategy can reduce the dip or the disruption and expedite achieving business benefits.

An executive whose relentless focus is on execution and the building of internal capabilities supporting it is the person of the hour. Making strategy work and achieving desired results are the mark of a successful leader. Every organization, of course, has some separation of planning and doing, of formulation and execution. However, when such a separation becomes dysfunctional and planners begin to see themselves as the smart people and treat the doers as grunts, there clearly will be execution problems. When the senior leaders plan and see execution as something below them that detracts from their dignity as top leaders, the successful implementation of strategy obviously is in jeopardy. Ownership of execution and the change processes are vital to execution and are necessary for success.

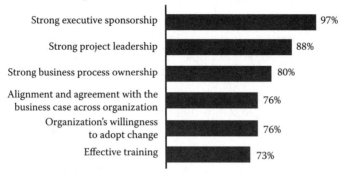

Leadership and change management were cited
most often as the top enablers for achieving value

% of respondent selection of influential value factors

Strong executive sponsorship	97%
Strong project leadership	88%
Strong business process ownership	80%
Alignment and agreement with the business case across organization	76%
Organization's willingness to adopt change	76%
Effective training	73%

FIGURE 3.2
The top enablers for achieving value. As can be seen, strong executive leadership and
project sponsorship are the key success factors.

Change is impossible without commitment to the decisions and actions
that define strategy execution.*

Another major issue facing implementations is that top leaders have discovered the hard way that people impact the success of an implementation. If the organization is not ready for the transformation, the project
will miss timelines (as used earlier) and come in over budget. OCM uses
a solid methodology for assessing all the key areas of the people side of an
implementation and surfacing risks before they become expensive mistakes (Figure 3.2; ASUG Best Practices Survey 2006†).

The results of recent surveys showed major issues with how leaders make
decisions and how information flows through the organization:

- *Decision-to-action time lag.* Only about a third of employees felt that
  important strategic and operational decisions were quickly translated
  into action (versus two-thirds of participants from the high-execution

---

* Three steps should be followed in developing the strategy: First, confront reality and articulate a
convincing need for change. Second, demonstrate faith that the company has a viable future and
the leadership to get there. Finally, provide a road map to guide behavior and decision making.
Leaders must then customize this message for various internal audiences, describing the pending
change in terms that matter to the individuals.

† The benchmarking study includes data from a finance benchmarking study that SAP and
ASUG conducted in late 2005. Data from more than 200 companies comprises the finance
benchmark database averages. For a complete list of all benchmarking studies, see www.asug.com
/Benchmarking/BenchmarkingInitiatives.

benchmark organizations). For example, regional sales teams often had to wait for long periods of time on approvals from headquarters, delaying and at times jeopardizing important transactions.

- *Second-guessing decisions.* Employees were twice as likely as those in benchmark organizations to feel that decisions were frequently second-guessed. For example, in over 90 percent of the cases where management had attempted to empower junior staff by delegating decision-making power, leaders reversed the decision within a year.
- *Information stalled.* Only about half the employees felt that important information about the market environment got to headquarters quickly, compared with nearly three-quarters in the benchmark group. For example, in Asia, new industry entrants often experimented with new product offerings and marketing channels. But because there was not a clear way for information to flow to and from headquarters, this important competitive information reached decision-makers slowly or not at all.

The organization follows a commitment curve on every change implementation. Change management will educate the end users and leadership to make them aware of the changes that are coming their way. There are best practices change practitioners for teaching and encouraging the organization how to understand and accept the changes. Only after all the individuals accept the changes can we say the organization has reached full adoption. Change management works at the individual levels through communication, involvement, training, support, and reinforcement to build consensus throughout the organization.

SUMMARY

A lack of explicit focus on how informal networks could support the change seems to be a major area of concern. Networks of like-minded people that interact to informally exchange information and ideas are essential and are often absent or underutilized. For example, there are informal centers of excellence—loose groupings of people who discuss specific technical topics, such as maintenance strategies or frugal engineering approaches. Since information is always more reliable when it comes from someone you trust, the company could have better understood who interacted with who and used these networks to roll out changes through existing paths. The people in these networks could influence each other to further solidify changes. Changing your company's approach to execution is daunting and there is no perfect way to do it, but following these guidelines and knowing what to watch out for will give you a good place to start.

It is important to understand that an individual's concern and resistance to change is based on how the individual perceives what the change will impact. The following summarizes the degree of impact on an individual that change will have:

- Changes that impact the individual negatively have the highest level of impact
- Changes that impact the individual's immediate family have the next highest level of impact
- Changes that impact the individual team that the employee is part of have a lesser impact
- Changes that impact the organization/company culture and operating habits have an even lower impact
- Changes that impact the organization/company have the least impact

Individuals are inherently rational and will question to what extent change is needed, whether the company is headed in the right direction, and whether they want to commit personally to making change happen. They will look to the leadership for answers. The articulation of a formal case for change and the creation of a written vision statement are invaluable opportunities to create or compel leadership team alignment with the workforce.

All too often, change leaders make the mistake of believing that their employees understand the issues, feel the need to change, and see the new direction as clearly as they do. The best change programs reinforce core messages through regular, timely advice that is both inspirational and practicable. Communications flow in from the bottom and out from the top, and are targeted to provide employees with the right information at the right time and to solicit their input and feedback. Often this will require overcommunication through multiple, redundant channels.

Section II

Understanding

The Understanding Level in Bloom's Taxonomy considers the ability to grasp the meaning of Change Management material. It also involves translating material from one form to another (words to numbers to models), interpreting material (explaining or summarizing or deducting), estimating future trends (predicting consequences or effects or outcomes). This level goes one step beyond the simple remembering of material, and represents the lowest level of understanding. Learning objectives at this level are: understand facts and principles, interpret verbal material, interpret charts and graphs, translate verbal material to mathematical formulae, estimate the future consequences implied in data, justify systems and models, and methods and procedures.

Understanding:
Comprehending the meaning, translation, interpolation, and interpretation of instructions and problems. State a problem in one's own words.

Examples: Rewrite the principles of test writing. Explain in one's own words the steps for performing a complex task. Translate an equation into a computer spreadsheet.

Key Words: comprehends, converts, defends, distinguishes, estimates, explains, extends, generalizes, gives an example, infers, interprets, paraphrases, predicts, rewrites, summarizes, translates

Technologies: create an analogy, participating in cooperative learning, taking notes, storytelling, Internet search

This section contains the following chapters:

- Chapter 4: Dirty Dozen Most Popular Models
- Chapter 5: Sustainable Change Lifecycle
- Chapter 6: Facilitated OCM Workshops
- Chapter 7: Culture Change Management (CCM)

4

Dirty Dozen Most Popular Models

In a Nutshell: The most popular OCM models have evolved from seven main threads or streams over the past 70 years or so. They are outlined in this chapter to provide a background context for your OCM effort. We show how the seven main threads have found their way into the "Dirty Dozen Models for Change Management," as we like to call them. Finally, our Model for Sustainable Change is profiled in this book toward the end of the chapter; it is an amalgam of the best and most workable features of these seven historical threads and the emergent 12 "Dirty Dozen" models for effective change management. We call this model SUSTAIN, which is an acronym for the seven-component Harrington-Voehl Lifecycle Model (see Chapter 5 for a full treatment of the Lifecycle Model). The change management models outlined in this chapter present a convincing argument that traditional management structures and practices that emphasize control and uniformity are in many cases antichange. That is, the culture and structure of traditional organizations are such that adapting to rapid change is inherently difficult and slow. If management's focus is to reduce the variability and instability of human actions to uniform and dependable patterns, the antichange aspects will make creating an organization that adapts quickly to turbulence and complexity a very difficult task indeed.

OVERVIEW

Traditionally, OCM has a long history of being used to help project management teams successfully implement projects/programs that involve changing the activities and/or the behavioral patterns of the people within the organization that would be impacted by the change (Campbell 1969). Our research has led us to some of the earliest writings of humankind that center on change.* But it is one thing to produce a momentary change and quite another to sustain the change, as the findings in this chapter will illustrate.

By the early 1980s, project managers were required to have not only an excellent understanding of the technology involved and the processes required to implement the technology, but also awareness that project success was heavily dependent on the degree of acceptance by the people. Projects in customer relations management, concurrent engineering, Lean, and Total Quality Management (TQM) required that the project be in direct alignment with the organization culture and mission. In order for the technology to be successful, people were required to change their operating behaviors. Backed by statistics which began to demonstrate that up to 65 percent of the strategic initiatives required significant behavioral change on the part of the employees, project managers came to realize their success relied heavily on the ability of the project team to change the habits and behaviors of the impacted employees (Burgelman 1991).

This is change management at its essence: proactive steps taken to enable the passing from one phase or state to the next, with the goal of an improvement and innovation over the original condition that can be effectively sustained over time, which is where the process and quality management aspects come into play. The purpose of this chapter is to briefly review the development of thought regarding OCM over the last 70 years, highlight what we have learned, and propose a path forward that establishes a model for achieving sustainable change.

EVOLUTION OF CHANGE MANAGEMENT

Our studies have shown that very little has been well documented on the evolution of OCM from the sustainability viewpoint at the organizational level. Various articles reflect diverse research into the topic of organizational change. However, many of these studies looked at organizational change from several perspectives. There is no right or wrong theory to OCM, as it is not an exact science. However, by performing some ongoing

---

* Dating back as early as 3000 BCE, the *I Ching* or *Book of Changes* conceived the notion of change as inevitable, and resistance to change as one of humankind's greatest causes of pain. These early agents of change wrote that in order to affect change in a positive way, a balance was required between internal and external forces.

research combined with studies by the industry's leading experts, a clearer picture of what it takes to lead a change effort effectively continues to emerge. It is important that we must continually review and consider how our changing society and culture will require fresh insight on the appropriate change process. Management techniques based on the classical bureaucratic structure described by Max Weber have proven to be inflexible in environments of rapid change and increased turbulence and complexity (Scott 1981; Scott and Davis 2003).

Change management models and theories addressed in our research suggest that the research can be organized into seven main threads or streams as follows:

1. *Thread One: Starting with top management using the Action Research Learning Model/Theory* (began by Collier 1945; Lewin 1946; Trist 1948–1965; French 1969; Agrilis, 1976; Brown and Tandon 1983; Tichy and Ulrich 1984; Robbins and Duncan 1988; Agrylis and Schein 1989)
   - The results: These experts were somewhat viewed as the fathers of modern-era focus on change management. Their models focused on the change itself. Lewin and Trist used a force-field approach to indicate that forces moving toward the future state must be stronger than opposing forces. A potential deficiency was that this approach focused on change as a stand-alone event, and while recognizing with the "freeze" state that change needs to be sustained, did not address *how* to sustain.
2. *Thread Two: Lewin's Three-Step Model Unfreeze-Change-Refreeze* (Lewin 1945, 1951) and Schein's Extension of Lewin's Change Model (Schein 1980)
   - This focused more on the role and responsibility of the change agent using available media than on the evolution of the change itself. Information is continuously exchanged throughout the process.
   - *The results: A concise view of the new state is required to clearly identify the gap between the present state and that being proposed.* This approach used activities that aid in making the change include imitation of role models and looking for personalized solutions through trial-and-error learning; mixed results for success.
3. *Thread Three: Shifting Paradigms Model of Planned Change* by Lippit, Watson, and Westley, which expanded Lewin's Three-Step Model to a Five-Phase Model (Lippit, Watson, and Westley 1958)

- Lippitt, Watson, and Westley point out that changes are more likely to be stable if they allow paradigms to spread to neighboring systems or to subparts of the system immediately affected. Changes are better rooted. Some examples are: the individual meets other problems in a similar way, several businesses adopt the same innovation, or the problem spreads to other departments of the same business. The result: the more widespread imitation becomes, the more the behavior is regarded as normal.

4. *Thread Four: Kotter's Talk and Communicate Eight-Step Model* (Kotter 1996); expanded/contracted by Bridges into the *Transitions Management* model (2000)

   - In 1996 John Kotter wrote *Leading Change*, which looked at what people did to transform their organizations. Kotter introduced an eight-step change model for helping managers deal with communication issues dealing with transformational change. This is summarized in Kotter's eight-step change model. For *The Heart of Change* (2002), John Kotter worked with Dan Cohen to look into the core problems people face when leading change. The result: Kotter and Bridges concluded that the central issue was changing the behavior of people and that successful change occurs when *speaking to people's feelings*. This model focused on the actual movement (i.e., transition) from current state to future state. Similar to Lewin, Bridges did not address sustaining the change, whereas Kotter did. They all assumed that if the transition is done correctly, there would not be a return to the previous state, and this has proven to not always be the case.

5. *Thread Five: Assimilate and Integrate n-Step* Change Models* (Mento, Jones, and Dirmdofers 2002); Jick's abbreviated Ten-Step Model (Jick 2001, 2003); Ten Commandments (Kanter 1983, 1989); Ten Keys (Pendlebury, Grouard, and Meston 1998); 12 Action Steps (Nadler 1989, 1998)

   - This entails following a variety of steps; the exact steps vary depending on the model used; belief that achieving organizational change is assimilated through an integrated and planned approach; claims to be appropriate for all types of change; each of the ten-step models focuses on taking an integrated approach to transformation as a whole.

---

* The n-Step change management concept also includes Transformation Trajectory (Taffinfer 1998), Nine-Phase Change Process Model (Anderson and Anderson 2001), Step-by-Step Change Model (Kirkpatrick 2001), 12 Step Framework (Mento, Jones, and Dirndorfer 2002), RAND's Six Steps (Light 2005), and Integrated Model (Leppitt 2006).

6. *Thread Six: Invest in planning using Shield's Five-Step Model* (Shield 1999) and Prosci's ADKAR Organizational Change model (2000–2014)
   - These models were first introduced in 1999 as an outcome-oriented planning approach to facilitate individual change. The result: the ADKAR model has taken hold as an easy-to-use and proven method, and is now one of the most widely used change management models in the world.
7. *Thread Seven: Negotiated results delivered through project portfolios*
   - The Bain Model and Harrington-Voehl Change Leader Model both focus on negotiating the change management landscape by predicting, measuring, and managing risk associated with the changes being sought. The result: considerable increase in the odds of success and the support of experts and dedicated partners within the client's organization who are focused on achieving the hoped-for OCM results.

These seven historical streams suggest a need for a sustainable change model, which is noticeably missing from the body of knowledge and is presented for review at the end of this chapter. Some recent developments include a growing shift into a more robust focus on strategic initiative management and organizational change to ensure that change management is a competency that is well integrated into the organization's portfolio of programs and projects to achieve intended strategic outcomes.

SOME SPECIFICS FROM THE RESEARCH

According to the Project Management Institute's *Pulse of the Profession*® *In-Depth Report: Enabling Organizational Change through Strategic Initiatives* (PMI 2014), 48 percent of strategic initiatives are unsuccessful, and as a result, nearly 15 percent of every dollar spent is lost due to poor project performance. The good news is that success rates are significantly higher in organizations that report being highly effective at OCM. Bain's 2013 research suggests that in order to realize effective results, the role of the external consultant must be to help clients overcome the odds of failure. Global executives who participated in Bain & Company's Management Tools & Trends survey (Bain & Company 2013) see economic conditions improving in their industries, but their confidence has waned amid a slower recovery than many anticipated. As a result, 55 percent of executives surveyed were concerned about meeting their earnings targets in 2013. Their priority is to grow revenues, and they're taking a more strategic and focused approach.

Too often, projects neglect the human factor (especially in the implementation of enterprise technology). Bain's approach focuses on three key ingredients to improve the odds of success: predicting, measuring, and managing change-associated risk from the very first day of the project.

In the end, even with the best intentions, an application of change management half-measures in most organizational interventions (particularly found in IT initiatives) traditionally tends to run organizations into a state of disorganizational chaos, which leads to (and is fed by) further dysfunctional OCM practices (Burke, Lake, and Paine 2009).

Hornstein (2008) summarized the issue as it relates to IT programs when he stated, "One of the most important and significant outcomes of organizational change efforts that are coupled with IT implementations is the demonstration of the power of community and community action."

There are many different roles and activities that the individuals involved in change management play (see Figure 4.1). Each individual needs to understand his or her role and responsibility for organizational change management to be successful.

The creation of change agent roles, which are populated by organizational members bringing all staff together to engage one another and the leadership in dialogue about the vision going forward, in turn bring out the pride and commitment of employees. Furthermore, it then becomes

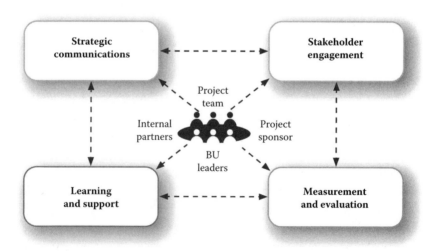

FIGURE 4.1

Various roles involved in change management.

clear that everyone in the organization has great ideas about how the organization can improve itself. Employees often are just waiting for the opportunity to be invited to contribute (see Figure 4.2).

(See the paper "Accelerate End-User Adoption with a Strong Organizational Change Capability" by Emergent Technologies [Jessie Jacoby,

Accelerate End-User Adoption with a Strong Organizational Change Capability

When companies choose to deploy new software to end-users across the enterprise, they are looking to either enhance business performance or minimize IT costs. These goals are often broken down into more discrete objectives such as increasing employee productivity, providing new capabilities, streamlining processes, reducing service desk calls, and so forth. Regardless of whether the software runs "in the cloud" or locally on employees' machines, the economic business case assumes that some percentage of the end-user population will adopt the new software. The projected return on investment (ROI) as defined by the business case depends on achieving a defined target adoption rate.

The Mathematics of End-User Adoption

It is important for IT leaders to understand the role that organizational change plays in driving successful end-user adoption. The most elegant software solution flawlessly deployed will yield a low adoption rate without effective organizational change management. This point is illustrated in the equation below where the *Technical Capability* is your software and hardware selections, IT project governance, risk management, resource prioritization, and deployment approach; and *Organizational Change Capability* represents communications strategy, vision of the future, case for change, stakeholder engagement, and training.

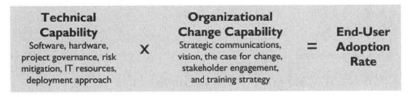

Technical Capability		Organizational Change Capability		End-User Adoption Rate
Software, hardware, project governance, risk mitigation, IT resources, deployment approach	X	Strategic communications, vision, the case for change, stakeholder engagement, and training strategy	=	

Using a 10-point scale where 10 equals 100% confidence, score your project's Technical Capability (TC), then score its Organizational Change Capability (OCC). Typically, IT project teams will score higher on TC than on OCC. When this occurs, the team should focus on increasing the OCC rather than TC score. For example, let's say you scored your project as follows: 8 (TC) x 6 (OCC) = 48. Increasing your TC score by 2 points will yield an overall score of 60. But, increasing your OCC score by 2 points will bump your overall score to 64 – four points higher than if you had focused on the TC score. This simple formula illustrates how Organizational Change Capability serves as a *force multiplier* in driving end-user adoption.

FIGURE 4.2
Accelerate end-user adoption.

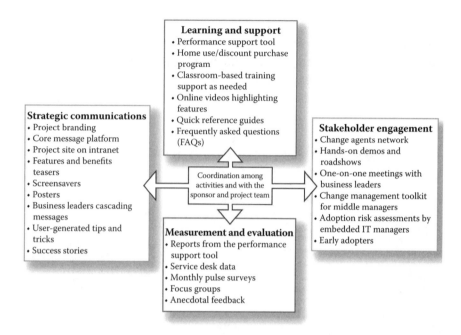

Learning and support
- Performance support tool
- Home use/discount purchase program
- Classroom-based training support as needed
- Online videos highlighting features
- Quick reference guides
- Frequently asked questions (FAQs)

Strategic communications
- Project branding
- Core message platform
- Project site on intranet
- Features and benefits teasers
- Screensavers
- Posters
- Business leaders cascading messages
- User-generated tips and tricks
- Success stories

Coordination among activities and with the sponsor and project team

Stakeholder engagement
- Change agents network
- Hands-on demos and roadshows
- One-on-one meetings with business leaders
- Change management toolkit for middle managers
- Adoption risk assessments by embedded IT managers
- Early adopters

Measurement and evaluation
- Reports from the performance support tool
- Service desk data
- Monthly pulse surveys
- Focus groups
- Anecdotal feedback

FIGURE 4.3
U.S.-based transportation company example.

managing director] for more details, at http://www.mosaichub.com /resources/download/accelerate-end-user-adoption-with-a-strong-organiz.)

Figure 4.3 shows how a transportation company used an OCM software product called LearningGuide as their third-party support tool to help facilitate the adoption of a change management project.

MORE SPECIFICS FROM THE RESEARCH

Since many organizations employ various change management methodologies, approaches, and models, Gavin's emerging OCM Toolkit is designed in a modular fashion to support and boost the effectiveness of the approaches discussed in the seven threads. Specifically, the dozen models below have emerged as being widely adopted and sustainable, hence we affectionately call them The Dirty Dozen. As time-honored models, they activate positive change behaviors during the stages of the most common methodologies, approaches, and models.

The basis of their inclusion was that the model is

1. Effective—it works
2. Economical—it has a ROI
3. Long-lasting—not here today, gone tomorrow
4. Used or has been used by at least 100 organizations
5. Suitable for any type of organization
6. Used or has been used for at least 5 years
7. Suitable for any type of work culture

The Dirty Dozen includes

- The Universal Change Activation Toolkit
- ADKAR Model for Change Management
- Accelerating Implementation Methodology (AIM)
- Beckham and Harris Change Management Process
- Boston Consulting Group (BCG) Change Delta
- Bridges Leading Transition Model for Change
- Harrington-Voehl sustainable change model
- GE's Change Acceleration Process (CAP)
- John Kotter Eight-Step Model for Change
- McKinsey 7S Change Model
- Kurt Lewin's Three-Stage Change Model
- People-centered implementation (PCI) Model

Each model is evaluated in Table 4.1 as they apply to the seven OCM threads that constitute the SUSTAIN Lifecycle.

Each of these 12 (Dirty Dozen) models have been influenced to some extent by the seven threads. For the sake of keeping the discussion and relationships simple, the designations High (H), Medium (M), and Low (L) are used to illustrate the relationships between our SUSTAIN Model for OCM and the seven developmental threads of the past 70 years.

BRIEF DESCRIPTION OF THE 12 MODELS

1. (Universal) OCM Toolkit

The (Universal) Organizational Change Management Toolkit was developed by Gavin Wendell of Better Business Learning,

TABLE 4.1

The Dirty Dozen Models' Relationships to the SUSTAIN OCM Model

The Dirty Dozen Most Popular Change Management Models	The Seven Organizational Change Management Threads							Totals
	S	U	S	T	A	I	N	
Universal Change Activation Toolkit	H	M	H	H	H	H	M	19
ADKAR Model for Change Management	H	M	M	H	H	M	M	17
AIM (Accelerating Implementation Methodology)	M	L	L	H	H	M	L	13
Beckhard and Harris Change Management Process	H	M	M	M	H	M	L	15
Boston Consulting Group (BCG) Change Delta	H	H	M	H	M	L	L	15
Bridges Leading Transitions Model for Change	H	M	M	H	H	M	M	17
The Harrington-Voehl Change Roadmap	H	H	M	H	H	H	M	19
GE's CAP	H	L	M	M	H	M	H	16
Kotter Eight Step Model for Change	H	M	L	H	M	H	M	16
McKinsey 7-S Change Model	M	M	H	M	H	M	L	15
Lewin's Three-Stage Change Model	H	H	M	M	H	M	M	17
PCI Model	L	L	M	H	H	M	M	14
Totals	32	24	24	32	32	26	21	197

Note: SUSTAIN is an acronym broken down as follows: S = Start with Top Management, U = Unfreeze-Change-Refreeze, S = Shifting Paradigms, T = Talk and Communicate, A = Assimilate and Integrate, I = Invest in Planning, N = Negotiate Results. CAP = Change Acceleration Process, H = high, L = low, M = medium, PCI = people-centered implementation.

which specializes in producing unique and effective organizational development resources. The mission of the Toolkit is to improve the way organizations worldwide grow and change. Over 20,000 organizations in 140 countries utilize the Better Business Learning change management guides included in the Change Activation Toolkit. *It is proven to give the change agent an appreciation of where and how this Toolkit can be used to accelerate the development and implementation of the Dirty Dozen Change Management Programs.*

The Change Activation Toolkit is compatible with all change methodologies and models. A detailed compatibility guide maps which of the Toolkit's 18 modules can be used to boost engagement and awareness at the stages and phases of all prominent methodologies, including many of the ones described in this chapter: ADKAR,

AIM, BCG Change Delta, Bridges Leading Transition, Change Leader's Roadmap, GE CAP, Harrington-Voehl Roadmap, Kotter's Eight-Stage model, Kubler Ross Change Curve, Kurt Lewin's Three-Phase model, LaMarsh, PCI, Prosci, and others.

The Universal OCM Toolkit consists of 18 modules. They are:

1. Project and change management
2. Engaging and maintaining sponsor involvement
3. Creating a communication strategy
4. Choosing communication channels
5. Accommodating different communication styles
6. Inspiring action not despair
7. Change stakeholder analysis
8. Change readiness assessment
9. Conducting gap analysis
10. Learning and coaching as change enablers
11. Four common responses to change
12. Managing resistance
13. Telling stories
14. Culture and change
15. Learning and coaching as change enablers
16. Managing change effectiveness
17. Why change fails
18. Thinking about organizational change

In addition, the Toolkit's 18 modules are used to determine the contextual features and implementation options that are required for consideration when an organization undergoes change. The framework of the model helps to design a context-sensitive approach to change. After examining and analyzing different strategic models, we can conclude that strategic change is successful when it has a positive impact on people, systems, and the organization. The clients that we surveyed practiced changes in strategy, leadership, structure, culture, and process. They reengineered the systems, maintained continuous improvement in change, and focused on customer-centered changes. All these changes were aimed at reducing the cost and improving the effectiveness of the operations.

Finally, the change is effective because of the exceptional management style and ability to adapt to that change processes. The companies that are able to provide better services to both the customers and the employees have all used one or more of the OCM models outlined in this book. They excelled in providing better-quality service to the customers by employing a customized OCM model and approach that worked best for their organization, at that time, and in those circumstances; one size does not fit all. They were also able to motivate the employees by providing job opportunities leading them to better performance results, and they were able to achieve their organization's goals and objectives using the OCM models, tools, and techniques outlined in this book. The strategies in an organization emerged over time in an incremental way by learning from partial commitments and previous moves.

The unique animated videos featured in each module contained in this Toolkit's approach to OCM can be shown with or without the accompanying facilitated workshop activities as suits the particular need. For sessions utilizing the workshop facilitation guide and materials, each module features between three and five activities that can be selected depending on group size, experience level, and requirements (see Chapter 7 for details).

The Change Activation Toolkit model empowers change leaders to implement OCM in the context of the following seven generic OCM areas:

1. Leading change
2. Creating a shared need
3. Shaping a vision
4. Mobilizing commitment
5. Making change last
6. Monitoring progress
7. Changing systems and structures

Each of the 18 modules contains six multimedia features or areas of focus.

Figure 4.4 depicts the six multimedia features of the Change Activation Toolkit, and can be arranged according to the particular phase or type of intervention where the components are most likely to be employed.

2. Prosci ADKAR Model

The Prosci ADKAR change management model was first published in the 1998 book *The Perfect Change* by Jeff Hiatt, founder

| Change tools and templates | Informative summary videos | Workshop facilitation guides | Workshop presentation slides | Activity materials and handouts | Further reading guides |

FIGURE 4.4
Multimedia features in universal change activation.

and CEO of Prosci Research. (For more information, see Hiatt, J.M. [2006] *ADKAR: A Model for Change in Business, Government and Our Community.*) The ADKAR model addresses change at the scale of the individual rather than the whole organization. This is a part of the Prosci Change Management Methodology; however, it is often used on its own as a guiding framework for creating change initiatives as shown below. Prosci's ADKAR Model is an individual change management model. It outlines the five building blocks of successful change, whether that change occurs at home, in the community, or at work.

ADKAR is an acronym based on the five building blocks:

- A, *awareness* of the need for change
- D, *desire* to participate and support the change
- K, *knowledge* on how to change
- A, *ability* to implement required skills and behaviors
- R, *reinforcement* to sustain the change

The final three building blocks of Prosci's ADKAR Model—*knowledge, ability, and reinforcement*—are where the individual, who is making the change, ultimately begins doing things the new way. It involves knowing how to make the change, making the change, and ultimately staying with the change. While these building blocks are where the actual change occurs, it is important to remember the building block nature of ADKAR; knowledge, ability, and reinforcement cannot be attained without the prerequisite awareness and desire.

Prosci offers some tips and reflections about knowledge, ability, and reinforcement that can help change management professionals be more effective in implementing change.

- *Change does not begin with knowledge.* Without a holistic model for individual change, such as Prosci's ADKAR Model, teams can easily fall into the trap of simply sending employees to training when a change is being introduced. This rarely drives successful change and can often have negative and lasting impacts on the employees who must bring a change to life in their day-to-day work. Training is critical, but it must occur in the context of sufficient awareness and desire.

- *Do not assume that with knowledge comes ability.* There is often a large gap between knowledge and ability. Ensure that along with training to impart knowledge, employees are given sufficient tools for building their own ability, including hands-on practice, support from coaches, and the availability to network and work with others who have made the change successfully.

- *Keep a focus on reinforcement, even when it is difficult.* There is so much change going on in organizations today that maintaining a focus on reinforcing change is difficult. Acknowledge this fact, and the tendency to simply move on once a change goes live, and build the necessary mechanisms to reinforce a change. You only know if a change was successful if you take a step back afterward to see if employees are actually doing their jobs differently.

The ADKAR change management model was first published in the 1998 book *The Perfect Change* by Jeff Hiatt, founder and CEO of Prosci Research. For more information, see Hiatt, J.M. (2006) *ADKAR: a model for change in business, government and our community.* Learn more at: http://www.change-management.com/tutorial-adkar-overview.htm.

The Change Activation Toolkit can be used with the ADKAR Model to align the five stages and build OCM capability while engaging the staff throughout all five stages, as shown in Figure 4.5.

3. **AIM or accelerated change management for business transformation**

Dealing with multiple, simultaneous types of change are what the model for accelerated change management (ACM) for business transformation is all about. When people are impacted by change in a modern organization, they are usually caught off-guard. Most people are hard-wired to think, view, and deal with change in a natural way. However, for an organization to be lean, successful, and around for the long-term, processes have to transform change into advantage.

ADKAR goal	Change activation toolkit modules that support this goal	CHANGE ACTIVATION TOOLKIT
Awareness	Choosing communication channels / Creating a communication strategy / Thinking about organizational change	
Desire	Inspiring action not despair / Telling stories	
Knowledge	Accommodating different communication styles	
Ability	Learning and coaching as change enablers / Managing resistance / Four common responses to change	
Reinforcement	Culture and change / Measuring change effectiveness	

FIGURE 4.5
Five-Stage ADKAR Model aligned with Change Activation Toolkit.

According to change practitioner Tom McNellis,* the heartbeat of all business is energy (computer hardware, software, databases, phones, applications, etc.). Hundreds of technologies conducted via energy will change every day at an ever more rapid rate, primarily due to continuous innovation. Sometimes one or two types of change(s) can be planned-for through project management, where a project team might plan the change(s), and place a "no-more-change" stake-line into the project base and communicate the words "scope freeze." From that moment on, any change(s) that might impact scope, time, and/or budget has to filter through a change control board. Change control boards are created to determine which changes will move forward and which changes will not, as part of project implementation. However, due to technological innovations, there will be multiple changes impacting organizations.

---

* For more information, contact: tmn@afebresearch.com; or call 1-610-937-2370.

The accelerated change management for business transformation considers six areas of transformation for Agile and Open operational models:

L = Transformation of Operating Models
E = Transformation of Customer Interfaces
A = Transformation of Product Innovation
N = Transformation of Data Mining Hubs
E = Transformation of Optimization Algorithms
R = Transformation of Project Team Approaches

The AIM (or ACM) Model is organized into six phases: (1) Define the Implementation, (2) Generate Sponsorships, (3) Build Change Agent Capability, (4) Develop Target Readiness, (5) Communication, and (6) Define the Reinforcement Strategy.

4. Beckham and Harris Change Management

There are six components to the Beckham & Harris (B&H) change management model:

- Components 1 and 2: Establishing the need for motivating change, and Building the Change team
- Component Three: Creating a shared vision
- Component Four: Communicating and developing political capital and support
- Component Five: Managing the transition by noticing improvements and energizing others
- Component Six: Sustaining momentum by consolidating the gains

Figure 4.6 depicts the 11 organizational change management activities needed for effective interventions, grouped into the five major categories of Motivating Change, Creating a Vision, Developing Political Support, Managing the Transition, and Sustaining Momentum.

5. Boston Consulting Group

The Boston Consulting Group (BCG) Model for change management is also called the Hard Side of change management. They have studied hundreds of major change programs at companies around the world, with a goal of developing a more effective approach—one that would reduce the risks and virtually assure a positive outcome.

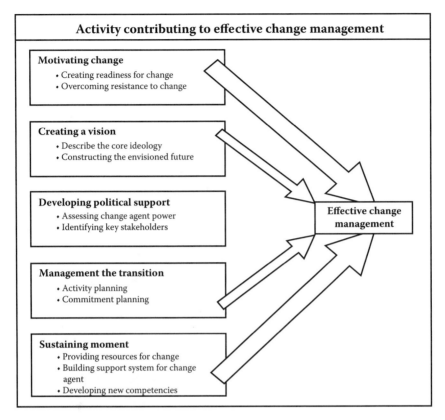

FIGURE 4.6
The Beckham and Harris Change Management Activity Model.

Based on research findings, they created a systematic, Technology-enabled change management approach that addresses operational and organizational changes along with the behaviors that affect program outcomes and are critical to success. Rigorous program development, tracking, and reporting is used to stay on schedule and on budget.

Their model suggests that the outcome of change initiatives is driven by four elements: the *duration* of the project; the performance *integrity* of the team; the organizational *commitment* to change; and the additional *effort* required of staff members; thus the term DICE, as in rolling the dice. Assessing projects against these four elements can greatly help institutions achieve successful change from Ideation to Impact. Also included is a methodology for scoring and statistically analyzing the dynamics of DICE, thereby allowing objective assessment of the likely outcome of transformation, helping to load the dice in your favor. Underlying the DICE concept, the BCG model revolves around four distinct components on a project-level basis: executional certainty, enabled leaders, an engaged organization, and a governance/PMO function, as shown in Figure 4.7.

6. **Bridges Transitions Management Model**

The Bridges Three-Phase Model explores human behaviors relating to change and defines typical emotions that individuals might exhibit during the change process. The Model provides strategies on how to overcome some of the emotional barriers to change without getting stuck. For example, in the new beginning phase, there may be a great

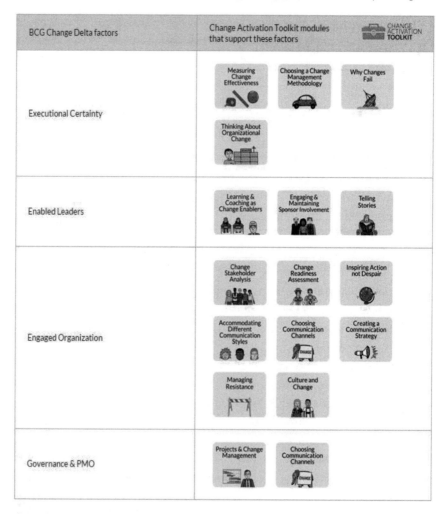

FIGURE 4.7

The Four-Stage BCG Model with Change Activation Toolkit. Depiction of the four BCG Delta Factors model with the related 17 modules of the Change Activation Toolkit.

deal of fear of the unknown. One strategy might be to provide training on specific tools or educational materials. In the neutral zone, allow creative ways to think about work. During the ending and losing phase, people will feel committed and this requires the need to sustain the new way of working, possibly through goal setting. Include individuals through each phase of the transition. For more information, see Bridges, W. (2009) *Managing Transitions: Making the Most of Change.*

The Bridges Model explorers the human behaviors related to change management and defines the typical emotions that employees may exhibit during the change process. The value of the Bridges model is its simplicity in outlining the strategies involved with overcoming the emotional barriers to change.

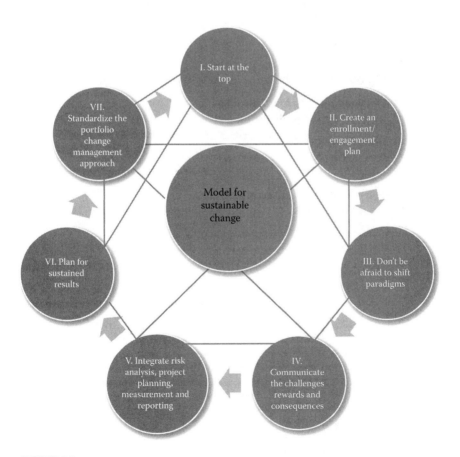

FIGURE 4.8

The Harrington-Voehl sustainable change model. Depiction of the Harrington-Voehl Seven-Stage sustainable change model, which is expanded on in more detail later in this chapter.

7. Harrington-Voehl Change Leader Roadmap

The Harrington-Voehl Change Leader Roadmap was first created in 1995 as a five-step process and was gradually expanded into the present seven-step Model for Sustainable Change (see Figure 4.8). It is based on two major factors for change: a personal context and an organizational context. The personal context for change revolves around positive and negative motivating factors that are evaluated by employees on a personal level. This includes factors such as an employee's personal and family situation, health, financial position, stability, mobility, relationships, and so forth. An employee's professional career history and plans (successes, failures, promotions, aspirations, and years left before retirement) are also considerations. The degree that this change will affect them personally is one of the keys. The organizational context for change involves employees evaluating these positive and negative motivating factors based on an organization's history with change, such as past change success or failure, the likelihood that this change will really happen, and consequences for employees that have resisted change in the past.

8. GE's Change Acceleration Process

About 25 years ago, under the direction of Chairman Jack Welch, GE launched Work-Out, a team based problem-solving and employee empowerment program modeled after the FPL Total Quality Management Systems approach (called the Deming Prize) that was in vogue at the time.* Work-Out was a huge success and Welch was frustrated by the rate of adoption through the business. Welch, the visionary, realized that GE (and everyone else!) was entering an era of constant change, and that those who adapted to change the fastest would be the survivors. He commissioned a team of consultants (including Steve Kerr, who was to become GE's first Chief Learning Officer) to scour industry and academia to study the best practices

---

* FPL pursued the quest for the Deming Prize wholeheartedly. Instead of continuing to implement the company's 1985 quality-improvement initiative QIP gradually, employees were given less than six months to meet Deming Prize requirements. Rigorous weekly training courses were developed for first-line, nonsupervisory employees, and over 1700 teams were formed to come up with problem-solving solutions to reduce costs or improve efficiency. Managers were required to master new managerial theories and complex statistical calculations. Supervisors spent their time tracking and calculating dozens of cross-referenced indicators such as the percentage of street lights installed in 21 days. A functional review team was required to document and analyze 800 different procedures for everything from conducting energy surveys to answering customer complaint letters. An area manager of customer service for the utility's commercial/industrial group summed up the rigid process and the avalanche of paperwork by stating that preparing for the exam was "grueling."

in change management and come back to GE with a toolkit that Welch's managers could easily implement. The result was the Change Acceleration Process, commonly referred to within GE simply as CAP (Becker, Huselid, and Ulrich 2001).

The team studied hundreds of projects and business initiatives. One of their insights was that a high-quality technical strategy solution is insufficient to guarantee success. An astonishingly high percentage of failed projects had excellent technical plans. As an example of such a project, consider a business adopting Siebel Customer Relationship Management (CRM) system enterprise-wide. Typically a great deal of effort is put into the technical strategy to deploy the hardware and software, train the employees, and so forth.

The team found that it is lack of attention to the cultural factors that derail the project when there is a failure—not the technical strategy. Failure, for our purposes, is defined as failing to achieve the anticipated benefits of the project (i.e., the benefits that justified the project in the first place). With the help of Frank Voehl and FPL, the team adopted Maier's Change Effectiveness Equation: $Q \times A = E^*$ as a simple way to describe the phenomena. Translated to English, it reads: the Effectiveness (E) of any initiative is equal to the product of the Quality (Q) of the technical strategy and the Acceptance (A) of that strategy. In other words, paying attention to the people side of the equation is as important to success as the technical side. (Note: It is interesting to note that we decided to use a multiplicative relationship; if there is a zero for the Acceptance factor, the total effectiveness of the initiative will be zero, regardless of the strength of the technical strategy.)

CAP Model

Seven steps were used to implement the CAP Model. They are

Step 1: Leading Change
Step 2: Creating a Shared Need
Step 3: Shaping a Vision
Step 4: Mobilizing commitment

---

* The Change Effectiveness Equation ($E = Q \times A$) was first developed by Norman Maier in his work at the University of Chicago. It was first used in conjunction with the Total Quality program by Frank Voehl in 1983 at the University of Miami, and when he was the COO and General Manager of FPL Qualtec for use by client Design and Development Teams during the late 1980s. In 1988–1989, GE was a client of Qualtec and Voehl worked with their Corporate Design Team to help design the Work-Out program, and in particular the change management components.

Step 5: Making Change Last
Step 6: Monitoring Process
Step 7: Changing Systems and Structures

1. Leading Change: First and foremost, authentic, committed leadership throughout the duration of the initiative is essential for success. From a project management perspective, there is a significant risk of failure if the organization perceives a lack of leadership commitment to the initiative.

2. Creating a Shared Need: The need for change must outweigh the resistance—the inertia in the organization to maintain the status quo. There must be compelling reasons to change that resonate not just for the leadership team, but that will appeal to all stakeholders. To paraphrase Peter Senge in his groundbreaking book, The Fifth Discipline, "Although we are all interested in large scale change, we must change one mind at a time."

3. Shaping a Vision: Leadership must articulate a clear and legitimate vision of the world after the change initiative. Every journey must have a destination; otherwise, you are just wandering. The vision must be widely understood and shared. The end-state must be described in behavioral terms (i.e., observable, measurable terms). Not business results, but individual behavior. Shaping the vision and mobilizing commitment might be the two most critical factors in a successful change initiative, as shown in Figure 4.9.

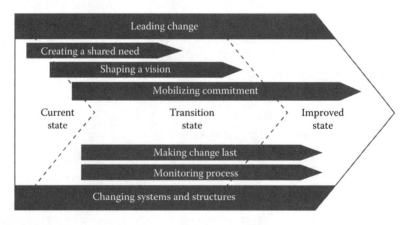

FIGURE 4.9
The GE CAP model.

In order to make change permanent, you must systematically identify how these systems influence the behavior you are trying to change and modify them appropriately. Failure to address these systems and structures is why so many initiatives become the proverbial flavor of the month.

4. Mobilizing commitment: Once you have leadership support, compelling logic for change, and a clear vision of the future, you have the necessary ingredients to roll out your initiative. You now begin to execute an influence strategy to build momentum. You leverage the early adopters to pilot the project where you face low resistance and can learn from mistakes with a forgiving partner.

5. Making Change Last: Steps 2–4 are primarily about accelerating adoption of your changes. Steps 5–7 are about making the changes permanent. You leverage early wins, taking the knowledge gained in your pilots and transfer learning and best practices to your broader rollout. You plan for integrating with other existing, potentially competing initiatives. You assess what is helping and what is hindering the initiative.

6. Monitoring Process: It is important to plan for measuring the progress of your change initiative. Is it real? How will you know? You need to set benchmarks, realize them—and celebrate! Similarly, there must be accountability for lack of progress.

7. Changing Systems and Structures: Every business has underlying systems and structures: hiring and staffing, IT systems, training and development, resource allocation, organizational design, SOPs/workflow, and so forth. These systems were designed to support the current state of the business. If they are not changed to support the desired future state of the business, they will always push you back to the old way, as that is what they are supposed to do.

9. Kotter Eight-Step Model

The Kotter Eight-Step Model, created by Harvard University Professor John Kotter, allows employees to buy into the change after leaders convince them of the sense of urgency for change to occur. There are eight steps involved in this model:

1. Increase the urgency for change
2. Build a team dedicated to change
3. Create the vision for change
4. Communicate the need for change
5. Empower staff with the ability to change
6. Create short term goals
7. Stay persistent
8. Make the change permanent

With over 30 years of research and trial-and-error efforts to his name, Dr. Kotter has proved by surveying over 100 client organizations over a seven-year period that nearly 70 percent of major changes within organizations fail to live up to their expectations. It is Kotter's belief, with a high certainty of success, that organizations who do not adapt to change will not prosper. Since technology and employee bases are ever-changing variables, Kotter recommends that executive management teams implement a holistic approach to improve change.

Without embracing the holistic approach, the team will identify the lack thereof of change, and management could be taking a one-way ride on a rollercoaster that has already been embarked on. Remember, the end goal is to lead change and eventually anchor the changes into the existing framework of corporate culture. Resistance to acknowledge change is only a temporary Band-Aid to the problem, which could ultimately pose negative results.

Kotter's eight-step change model is about showing people a truth that influences their feelings. We've seen how a sense of urgency moves people to action and helps us pull together a guiding team that can go on to prepare a clear and simple vision of the future. Communicating the vision and strategy comes next. The John Kotter Eight-Step Change model is a linear model that focuses on the importance of gaining buy-in. It is relatively simple to understand and works well in organizations that are organized in a relatively narrow organizational structure. The selling point is its simplicity, a memorable eight steps, and a basis in Kotter's thirty-plus years of research into organizational change. For more information, see Kotter, J.P. (1996) *Leading Change* and Kotter, J. (1998) *Leading Change: Why Transformation Efforts Fail*, Harvard Business Review.

10. McKinsey 7S Change Management Model

The McKinsey 7S Framework is a management model developed by well-known business consultants Robert H. Waterman, Jr.

and Tom Peters who also developed the Management by Walking Around (MBWA) motif, and authored *In Search of Excellence* in the 1980s. It was a strategic vision for groups to include businesses, business units, and teams. The 7S components are structure, strategy, systems, skills, style, staff, and shared values.

The model is most often used as an organizational analysis tool to assess and monitor changes in the internal situation of an organization. The model is based on the theory that, for an organization to perform well, these seven elements need to be aligned and mutually reinforcing. Therefore, the model can be used to help identify what needs to be realigned to improve performance or to maintain alignment (and performance) during other types of change.

Whatever the type of change—restructuring, new processes, organizational merger, new systems, change of leadership, and so forth—the model can be used to understand how the organizational elements are interrelated and so ensure that the wider impact of changes made in one area is taken into consideration. The objective is to analyze how well an organization is positioned to achieve its intended objectives. Figure 4.10 depicts the McKinsey 7-S Model, along with the relationship to each of the associated categories.

According to Tom Peters, one of the authors, the shape of the model was also of monumental importance. It suggested that all seven forces needed to somehow be aligned if the organization was

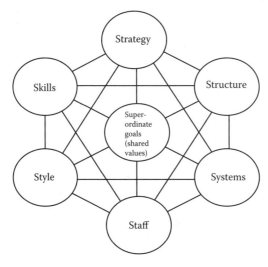

FIGURE 4.10
The McKinsey 7-S process.

going to move forward vigorously—this was the breakthrough (a word I normally despise) that directly addressed Ron Daniel's initial concerns that had motivated the project. As he put it in the 1980 *Business Horizons* article, "At its most powerful and complex, the framework forces us to concentrate on interactions and fit." The real energy required to redirect an institution, Peters claimed, comes when all the variables in the model are aligned.

11. Lewin's Three-Stage Change Model

The three major theories of organizational change that have received considerable attention in the field are Lewin's Change Model, the Action Research Model, and Contemporary Adaptations of Action Research.

Lewin's Change Model: According to the open-systems view, organizations, like living creatures, tend to be continuously working to maintain a steady state. This helps us understand why organizations require external impetus to initiate change and indeed why that change will be resisted even when it is necessary.

Looking at the organization as a system, change can occur at three levels. And since the patterns of resistance to change are different for each, the patterns in each level require different change strategies and techniques (see Figure 4.11). These levels involve

- Changing the individuals who work in the organization—that is, their skills, values, attitudes, and eventually behavior—but making sure that such individual behavioral change is always regarded as instrumental to organizational change
- Changing various organizational structures and systems— reward systems, reporting relationships, work design, and so on
- Directly changing the organizational climate or interpersonal style—how open people are with each other, how conflict is managed, how decisions are made, and so on

According to Kurt Lewin, a pioneer in the field of social psychology of organizations, the first step of any OCM process is to unfreeze the present pattern of behavior as a way of managing and mitigating resistance to change. Depending on the organizational level of change intended, such unfreezing might involve, on the individual level, selectively promoting or terminating employees; on the structural level, developing highly experiential training programs in such

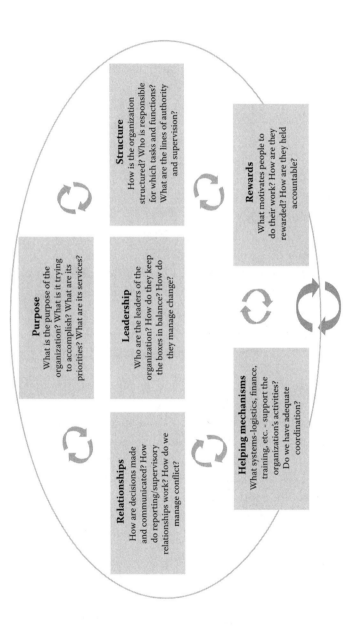

FIGURE 4.11

Lewin's view of the Organization as a System.

new organization designs as matrix management; or, on the climate level, providing data-based feedback on how employees feel about certain management practices.

Whatever the level involved, each of these interventions is intended to make organizational members address that level's need for change, heighten their awareness of their own behavioral patterns, and make them more open to the change process. The second step, movement, involves making the actual changes that will move the organization to another level of response. On the individual level, we would expect to see people behaving differently, perhaps demonstrating new skills or new supervisory practices. And, on the individual level, we would expect to see changes in actual organizational structures, reporting relationships, and reward systems that affect the way people do their work.

Finally, on the climate or interpersonal level, we would expect to see behavior patterns that indicate greater interpersonal trust and openness and fewer dysfunctional interactions. The final stage of the change process, refreezing, involves stabilizing or institutionalizing these changes by establishing systems that make these behavioral patterns "relatively secure against change," as Lewin put it. The refreezing stage may involve, for example, redesigning the organization's recruitment process to increase the likelihood of hiring applicants who share the organization's new management style and value system. During the refreezing stage, the organization may also ensure that the new behaviors have become the operating norms at work, that the reward system actually reinforces those behaviors, or that a new, more participative management style predominates.

Another useful Lewin-based OCM framework to consider is the *Burke-Litwin model*. The model not only provides users with more areas of the system, but also shows where there is higher leverage for transformational shifts. The Burke-Litwin Change Model gives you a map to look at for the alignment of your organization. It contains more dimensions than most other models, which makes it look overly complex at first glance. However, there is some simplicity when you look at the model from a top-down perspective, as it provides a strategic view of the types of shifts you want to initiate. Since his early development days, Lewin has insisted that mission and strategy, leadership, and organization culture are transformational in nature. The other layers of the model are more for transactional and individual changes. For example, some leaders try to create transformation by restructuring or trying to motivate staff. They can be helpful mechanisms to increase organization effectiveness, but they do not normally manifest in transformational shifts.

12. **People-Centered Implementation**

People-centered implementation (PCI) is a proven methodology that has helped over 175 organizations worldwide to deliver change more effectively by engaging people in the change process, following the six critical success factors (CSFs). They are

CSF 1: Effective change leadership
CSF 2: Powerful engagement processes
CSF 3: Committed local sponsors
CSF 4: Strong personal connections
CSF 5: Sustained personal performance
CSF 6: Shared change purpose

The six CSFs are shown in Figure 4.12. PCI creates an environment of sustained change and ultimately increases project success rates.

The PCI Model enables change leaders and project teams to deliver sustainable change through an integrated suite of e-learning

FIGURE 4.12
The PCI change management Model.

modules, online change assessments, collaboration, and a step-by-step change planner.

The Six PCI CSFs

PCI is designed around a set of CSFs that should be addressed at the local and the organizational levels by management in order to drive effective change management program initiatives (see Table 4.2). Table 4.2 shows how each of the categories can be self-evaluated by management on a 100-point score.

Table 4.2 shows the six PCI CSFs that can be used as a self-evaluation tool prior to, during, and after the OCM intervention.

TABLE 4.2

The PCI CSF Index

CSF Category	What the CSFs Enable the Organization to Do	Total Points
Shared change purpose	The focus is on building the sense of urgency, the buy-in, and the commitment that is needed in order to create a shared compelling case for change management that both directs and motivates the people in the organization	10
Effective change leadership	Change leadership starts with changing oneself; then build a network of trained skilled change leaders	15
Powerful engagement processes	Develop and implement the processes needed to communicate with others; need to educate, involve, and reward the workforce	15
Committed local sponsors	Support change management implementation by providing middle and front-line management with the workforce engagement skills, tools, and motivation, allowing them to work closely with their people during the change deployment	20
Strong personal connection	Work up-close and personal with managers and supervisors to deliver a personal commitment, along with skill building and behavior-changing action plans that help the workers to change more effectively	15
Sustained personal performance	Minimize disruption and maximize performance by helping the workers to adapt to the changes and embed the transition in a manner that really sticks in order to ensure that the benefits of the change are continuously realized	25
Total points		100

BEST PRACTICES HIGHLIGHTS

Best Practices in Change Management by Prosci, Inc. April, 2014 highlighted an alarming statistic: nearly 60 percent of the companies analyzed lacked the right capabilities to deliver on their change plans, while about the same percentage of companies didn't have the appropriate individuals, structures, and decision-making processes to drive the change initiatives. Furthermore, about 60 percent lacked the right metrics and incentives to make change efforts successful, and more than 63 percent of the companies faced high risks to their change efforts because of significant communications gaps between the leaders of the effort and the employees most affected by it.[*]

Although lack of employee motivation still emerges as a key barrier to sustainable change, nonetheless it still ranks at the bottom of this list. A clear challenger emerges with the key need being a global paradigm shift consisting of changing mindsets, attitudes, and organizational culture. In Section 3 of this book, we explore the real impact of changing organizational paradigms and evolving to a culture of alignment and enrollment, integral to the Model for Sustainable Change.

The following is from a May 2008 study done by IBM[†]:

1. Changing mindsets and attitudes (58%)
2. Corporate culture (49%)
3. Underestimation of complexity (35%)
4. Shortage of resources (33%)
5. Lack of higher management commitment (32%)
6. Lack of change know-how (20%)
7. Lack of motivation of involved employees (16%)

To conclude the assessment of the current state of organizational change (both within the framework of this book and within organizations seeking to assess their change readiness), the PMI companion paper *Building Change Agility: The Strategic Process for Agility Improvement* posts several key questions that must be addressed to effect change and pave the way for establishing a change sustainability model within organizations:

---

[*] Ibid. http://www.bain.com/publications/articles/results-delivery-busting-3-common-change-management-myths.aspx.

[†] IBM Global Study: Majority of Organizational Change Projects Fail. *Changing Mindsets and Culture Continue to Be Major Obstacles*, October 2008. See: https://www-03.ibm.com/press/us/en/pressrelease/25492.wss.

1. *Who needs to be ready for a change?* This includes both internal and external actors, and requires both alignments at the strategic/structural level as well as enrollment throughout the organization to ensure that impacts from change can be efficiently and empathetically absorbed and reacted upon with an effective response.

2. *What processes/activities need to be ready for change?* This includes both organizational processes, such as strategic alignment, processes integral to OCM mobilization, and execution including change control and governance, and supporting processes for organizational portfolio/program/project monitoring, measuring, managing, and sustaining through lessons learned.

3. *What changes in operational systems need to support change agility?* Change Agility defines for operational dimensions on which organizations seeking change agility and sustainability need to focus their change readiness assessment efforts:

    • Time: includes responsiveness, prioritization, decision making, sense of urgency

    • Leadership: includes cultural trust and transparency, innovation, and openness

    • Work norms: includes decision involvement, collaboration, and participation

    • Learning: includes sharing, mentoring, performance review, and standardization

4. *What causal drivers need to be addressed in order to improve change agility?* Most organizations focus at the outcome level, only addressing problem symptoms as they arise. They rarely get beyond the tip of the iceberg to address the root causes of pervasive, persistent causal factors perennially driving down change adoption rates or get beyond the status quo. Addressing the following causal drivers as part of a comprehensive change readiness assessment (Champy 1997) is a sure way to break the status quo and move toward a Model for Sustainable Change:

    • Culture: includes leadership and organizational responsiveness (markets, trends), innovation; holistic/transparent/integrated alignment within boundaries, lean structures/decision making; collaborative, coordinated work efforts; participatory decision making with two-way input and feedback on future direction; knowledge sharing and individual development

    • Commitment: includes leadership embracing the change paradigm as the norm; rigorous prioritization, qualification, and selection of

potential change initiatives; leaders as active change agents throughout ensuring alignment, enrollment, and strategy execution

- Capacity: organization embraces lean/agile/adaptability in business
practices and processes; standardizes a portfolio management
approach of strategically aligned inventory of initiatives prioritized, organized, and managed through a Program Management
Office type infrastructure; processes for strategy development,
solution definition, and change management are well defined and
utilized; process improvement is a stated and active goal of the
organization; planning is inclusive; resources are allocated and
managed proactively

Finally, our research-oriented* change readiness assessment should
highlight the degree to which recognition and reward systems support
all of these stated objectives and themes, especially those contributing to
progress on these key causal drivers of change agility and sustainability.

CHANGES IN APPROACH LEAD TO SUSTAIN

There is a need to make a shift in most organizations' change culture.
Project managers face continual challenges to keep up with the pace of
change, especially when new technology initiatives are introduced. Most
often in traditional change management, the change effort starts at communication, ends with training, and hopes for the best. To break with this
pattern and embrace the Model for Sustainable Change, project managers
in addition to managing the scope of their projects must also engage those
being impacted by the change and go beyond traditional approaches to
communication and embrace that of alignment and enrollment.

In the Harvard Business Review article *Leading Change: Why Transformation Efforts Fail* (by John P. Kotter, January 2007), we learn that while
some of these traditional efforts have been very successful, many others

---

* 2011, Five Guiding Principles of Change Management, Bain & Company, Inc. See: http://www
.bain.com/Images/2011-01-04%20BAIN%20BRIEF%20Results%20delivery.pdf.
Valutis, W., The Secrets to Creating Sustainable Change, simplicityHR. http://www.simplicityhr
.com/sustainable-change, 2015.
Harrington, H.J. and Conner, D., Project Change Management and Change Management Excellence.
New York: McGraw-Hill, 2000.

have been complete failures, and the majority wind up in the middle. As quoted in the Ivey Business Journal article *Using A Change Management Approach to Implement IT Programs*, a 2003 revealed that over 60 percent of IT projects failed to meet their stated goals. A contributing factor was poor change adoption fueled by resistance to change. The key to attaining sustainable change is for the organization's leadership to continue the alignment, engagement, and enrollment process, ensuring predictable and measurable (at least more reliable) change based on the following critical success factors for organizational change:

- Leadership and project alignment with organizational strategic objectives
- Enforcement through alignment with individual performance and project results
- Performance enhancement via employee empowerment and information sharing via a variety of media channels, training, and education
- Measurement, reporting (as a form of feedback) and knowledge of results

To build the supporting case for this book, we interviewed several leaders in the field of change management. One of the thought-leaders in OCM, Darrell R. Conner, has completely shifted his perspective from traditional OCM to one of Strategy Execution and knowledge shift. Based on *The Secrets to Successful Strategy Execution* from the June 2008 issue of HBR, this concept shows how any organization can better execute its strategy without making costly, disruptive changes to its core structure. A key aspect of Strategy Execution is to create deep commitment and alignment within senior leadership, then roll out the enrollment plan by empowering change agents to participate in its construction (APQC 2014).

The research from leading organizations and universities demonstrates how project/portfolio and program managers (and their organizations) can move from mere installation into alignment, realization, and repeatability by following a Model for Sustainable Change, such as outlined in our SUSTAIN Lifecycle Model in Chapter 5 and briefly described below.*

Table 4.3 and the model in Figure 4.6 show the seven threads involved in the model for creating a Sustainable Change environment in the organization. Ingraining these seven behaviors enables organizations to realize results

---

* See for details http://www.bain.com/publications/articles/results-delivery-busting-3-common-change-management-myths.aspx; http://www.simplicityhr.com/sustainable-change.

TABLE 4.3

The SUSTAIN Model for Organizational Change Management (OCM)

Definition	Description
S: Start at the top	If behaviors within the organization are to change, accountability needs to begin with the executive sponsor and the executive steering committee. Establishing a crystal clear change agenda sets the foundation for a successful project.
U: Use an enrollment/ engagement plan approach	The change sponsor also has responsibility for using media to create enrollment/engagement plans, which further outline the desired behaviors, actions, accountability/ownership, and targeted completion date.
S: Shift paradigms when needed	What made your organization great in the past may not be the case today, and may not be nearly strong enough amid increasing global competition to sustain investor demands for increasingly stronger profits and performance.
T: Talk and communicate	Once alignment has been attained among the steering committee and within the organization's strategic objectives, conversation can be created to begin the process of enrolling the organization. This requires clearly talking about the shared vision and purpose for the change by honestly outlining the opportunity (or problem), its associated challenges, and the rewards that will come about as the project goals are realized.
A: Assimilate and integrate	With the senior sponsors aligned and committed to and embracing the change, the change agents are typically the ones who know best how the change may impact their people and processes, and plan accordingly to mitigate the risks associated with the change. A balance needs to be struck between the desire for change and the organization's ability to embrace any fundamental changes.
I: Invest in planning for sustained results	Through practice and iterations of change, the investment in change will be realized as true project ROI is attained. As additional capacities become available and the organization becomes accustomed to adapting to change, it yields a well of resources that can be converted into sustaining prior gains, investment in innovation, new capacities, and product and service lines. This leads to competitive market advantage, building further capacity for additional iterations of change and innovation.
N: Negotiate risks with a portfolio approach	The value in negotiating using a portfolio management approach to change is that it directly links the change agenda back to the organization's strategic plan objectives. Furthermore, a portfolio's collective components (programs, projects, or even subportfolios) are a direct reflection of the organizational strategy and objectives.

consistently and predictably. Based on the prior seven threads of change and on our own current research, we've established this seven-step *Model for Sustainable Change* that captures the best available OCM approaches.

The SUSTAIN Model aligns well with the project management body of knowledge (PMBOK) Portfolio Management (Program Management Institute 2013) in that it will benefit organizations by ensuring standardization of the following practices, typically the province of the organization's Project Management Office (PMO), are applied to the change agenda:

- Providing an infrastructure for the management of projects, programs, and portfolios and the execution of individual change agendas
- Supporting review and evaluation of new initiative requests, facilitating prioritization and authorization of new projects, and allocating resources to affect change in alignment with organizational strategy and objectives
- Providing project and program progress reporting of critical success factor metrics, resources, expenditures, defects, and associated corrective actions to the portfolio governance process and the Change Management Committee
- Negotiating and coordinating resources between projects, programs, or other portfolios
- Assisting with risk identification and mitigation
- Communicating risks and issues related to ongoing initiatives
- Monitoring compliance to PMO policies and ensuring ongoing alignment with the organization's strategic objectives
- Mentoring change agents while developing and delivering training in process, project, and change management tools and techniques
- Providing knowledge management resources and archival services, including collection and propagation of lessons learned

For details, see http://www.pmi.org/PMBOK-Guide-and-Standards /Standards-Library-of-PMI-Global-Standards.aspx.

Once the objectives for change have been attained and reported, it's time to close out the project. This last step is very often overlooked as a bit of change exhaustion may have set in during the course of the initiative. Understanding that this dynamic will be present as your project winds down and energy naturally shifts elsewhere, plan up front on documenting the lessons learned at this stage (transition or closure). The importance to the organization is to ingrain what went right and avoid replicating anything that went off course. Focusing and standardizing organizational change approaches across the portfolios of projects over a sustained period of time is crucial to building an organizational culture that is adaptive to change (and improvement) as part of the organization's day-to-day operations.

SUMMARY

Various methods (with varying results) have been used throughout the last 100 years to affect change and deal with the inevitable impacts of conflict management and change (Gelfand, Leslie, and Keller 2008). In the course of our research, we've documented high-performing organizations that have developed cultures in which conflict and change are managed effectively. As the PMI's whitepaper article titled *Pulse of the Profession* points out, to successfully implement OCM strategy, companies require project and program managers with the skills to drive and navigate change, and the insight to ensure those changes are strategically aligned to business goals. All of the change experts agree that the success or failure of a change initiative is not just about initiating, planning, monitoring, executing, and evaluating the project that will drive the change. It also involves preparing your organization for transformation, ensuring stakeholder buy-in, and engaging executive sponsors to champion and support the change before, during, and after its implementation. By following the models, and specifically the Model for Sustainable Change, suggested in this book, organizations will be better positioned to maximize the return on investment placed into their programs, projects, and people. By following these practical methods, your organization will progress from traditional change management (mere installation) by evolving and involving the culture of the organization into a new paradigm of organizational change enrollment and alignment.

5

Sustainable Change Life Cycle

In a Nutshell: This chapter revolves around the Model for Sustainable Change Life Cycle as it is applied in the OCM process, project, and daily work environments, which is how successful OCM interventions should be conducted. In light of what was covered in the preceding chapters, this model is expressed as two related models with the Change Management Planning Checklist as the integrator: (1) as the acronym SUSTAIN, which is both iterative and incremental, (2) as the daily work life cycle of change management, and (3) the 10-component Change Management Planning Checklist. We created SUSTAIN in 2010 as a multistep process revolving around an evaluation phase, while other aspects, such as resolution and verification, must also be considered. The 10-component checklist was added in 2014 to provide for the evaluation aspects, which consist of identifying, submitting, evaluating, and approving the impacts of the change requests on daily operations.

INTRODUCTION

Using the SUSTAIN model ensures that contemplation exists, meaning that there is consideration of the day-to-day operational consequences of the change at hand and a valid reason for making change (Figure 5.1). The point is that the workforce personnel need to take action in order for changes to occur, not a project team, which almost always leads to failure. Once the checklist has been completed, the next step is the verification phase by the management and supervisors involved and impacted. This is where maintenance is done in order for employees to take the time to practice the new processes and procedures. The iterative nature of OCM as

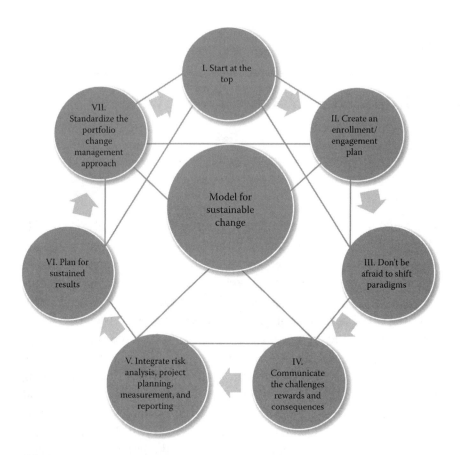

FIGURE 5.1

The SUSTAIN Model for Sustainable Change Management. This figure shows the seven threads involved in the model for creating a Sustainable Change environment in the organization. Ingraining these seven threads as behaviors enables organizations to realize results consistently and predictably. Based on the prior seven threads of change and on our own current research, we've established this 7-Component Model for Sustainable Change that integrates the best available OCM approaches.

a management science enables business representatives to see work under construction, comment on it, and request changes during the development of an increment of the solution. OCM integrates a daily work management life cycle and a process development life cycle into a single process, using daily management as the integrator. For most organizations, change management (coupled with some basic innovation management) is all that is needed, although some gain value from integrating OCM with project and quality management methods, such as Lean Six Sigma, PRINCE2TM,

Initiating Sponsor	Individual/group who has the power to initiate and legitimize the change for all the affected targets
Sustaining Sponsor	Individual/group who has the political, logistical and economical proximity to the targets
Change Agent	Individual/group who is responsible for implementing the change
Impacted Individual	Individual/group who must actually change
Advocate	An individual/group who wants to achieve change but does not have sufficient sponsorship

FIGURE 5.2
Key roles in the change process.

and PMI, or detailed development techniques, such as TRIZ, eXtreme Programming (XP), or other out-of-box practices.

The following are some key terms that will be used throughout the remainder of the book (see Figure 5.2).

Key Roles in the Change Process

There is a lot of learning during the life cycle, and what the change leaders learn they can provide feedback on to make adjustments as well. In addition, those who are embracing change will be far more successful than those who resist it. Those who continue to resist and relapse into the old system will fail. When the change is successful, the employees will think and act along the lines required for the new process to take place to the point where they no longer have to think about it and it then becomes routine. What this means is that the best solution may not be delivered to the business in one go, but in a series of increments that increase the breadth and/or depth of the solution with each delivery. In this way, urgent business needs can be addressed early while less important features are delivered later.

The OCM life cycle process using quality-in-daily-work has five phases: feasibility, foundations, exploration, engineering, and deployment in the business' operational environment.

SUSTAIN MODEL DEFINED

The statistics are undeniable: the fact is that most organizations fail at change management. According to the Wharton School of the University of Pennsylvania Executive Education Program on Leading Organizational Change,* "researchers estimate that only about 20 to 50 percent of major corporate reengineering projects at Fortune 1000 companies have been successful. Mergers and acquisitions fail between 40 to 80 percent of the time." Further, they estimate that "10 to 30 percent of companies successfully implement their strategic plans."

Why do organizations have such a poor track record of managing change? According to the Wharton School, the primary reason is "people issues," coupled with an undue preoccupation on projects versus daily work operations (Leading Organizational Change Course Page). The consulting firm PriceWaterhouseCoopers supports that finding. In a study entitled *How to Build an Agile Foundation for Change*, PriceWaterhouseCoopers' authors noted, "research shows that nearly 75 percent of all organizational change programs fail, not because leadership didn't adequately address infrastructure, process, or IT issues, but because they didn't create the necessary groundswell of support among employees. Without understanding the dynamics of the human transition in organizational change, change initiatives have a slim chance of success. If organizations, whether private or public, cannot change and adapt, they will not thrive or worse, they may not survive in today's dynamic environment." To thrive and survive, your organization needs to abandon the project approach and begin using our SUSTAIN model for organizational change in order to focus on day-to-day work activities.

---

* The Wharton *Leading Organizational Change* program offers valuable insights from research and practice to enrich a leaders view of change. It covers frameworks, models, and perspectives that can be applied immediately, and examine the factors that stall promising change initiatives as well as the strategies that can make them more successful. This program offers specialized approaches designed to enhance a leader's effectiveness as a change agent. See http:// executiveeducation.wharton.upenn.edu/for-individuals/all-programs/leading-organizational -change.

7-CYCLE SUSTAIN MODEL

The 7-Cycle SUSTAIN model is summarized as follows:

S stands for Start at the Top. If behaviors within the organization are to change, accountability needs to begin with the executive sponsor and the executive steering committee. Establishing a crystal-clear change agenda sets the foundation for a successful change intervention.

- Definition: An executive sponsor is a sustaining sponsor that has been selected by the executive team to represent them and to keep them aware of the progress an individual project is making.

U stands for Use an Enrollment/Engagement Plan Approach. The executive sponsor also has responsibility for using media to create enrollment/ engagement plans, which further outline the desired behaviors, actions, accountability/ownership, and targeted completion date.

S stands for Shift Paradigms when Needed. What made your organization great in the past may not be the case today and may not be nearly strong enough amid increasing global competition to sustain investor demands for increasingly stronger profits and performance.

T stands for Talk and Communicate. Once alignment has been attained among the steering committee and within the organization's strategic objectives, conversation can be created to begin the process of enrolling the organization. This requires clearly talking about the shared vision and purpose for the change by honestly outlining the opportunity (or problem), its associated challenges, and the rewards that will come about as the project goals are realized.

A stands for Assimilate and Integrate. With the senior sustaining sponsors aligned, committed to, and embracing the change, the change agents are typically the ones who know best how the change may impact their people and processes, and plan accordingly to mitigate the risks associated with the change. A balance needs to be struck between the desire for change and the organization's ability to embrace any fundamental changes.

I stands for Invest in Planning for Sustained Results. Through practice and iterations of change, the investment in change will be realized as true project ROI is attained. As additional capacities become available and the organization becomes accustomed to adapting to change, it yields a well of resources that can be converted into sustaining prior gains, investment in innovation, new capacities, and product and service lines. This leads to competitive market advantage, building further capacity for additional iterations of change and innovation.

N stands for Negotiate Risks with a Portfolio Approach. The value in negotiating using a daily work focus management approach to change is that it directly links the change agenda back to the organization's operational and strategic plan objectives. Furthermore, a portfolio's collective components (programs, processes, or even subprocesses) are a direct reflection of the organizational strategy and objectives.

SUSTAIN MODEL IN DETAIL*

Start at the Top! You have heard it a hundred times over. "For change to be truly effective, it must be driven from the top" was the conventional wisdom of the majority of traditional top-down change management efforts in the 1950s through the 1990s. This was the time when organizations were still skeptical about the changing tide of participatory change management. For a twenty-first century change effort to be successful—defined as at least 90 of the change goals being accomplished—senior executives must be enrolled first and commit not only to the change, but must embrace and embody the goals of the change effort by enrolling the organization to participate in and truly embrace the change plan.

If behaviors within the organization are to change, accountability needs to begin with the executive sponsor and the executive steering committee. Establishing a crystal-clear change agenda sets the foundation for a successful project, be it the implementation of a new or updated system, a departmental reorg, an organization-wide restructuring, or the creation of a new program or product or service line. To ensure a deep alignment of the change agenda, begin by establishing alignment on the senior team with the business model and strategic plan, and then seek to enroll the people driving and being impacted by the change.

Once you attain leadership alignment, it becomes a powerful force as they ensure alignment occurs below them as well as in parallel interfaces with other areas of the organization. When enforcing the consequences

---

* See Technical Supplement at the end of this book for a more detailed description of the SUSTAIN model and its elements.

of change action, it becomes important for change leaders to back one another as well as leverage interdepartmental cooperation, lest a double standard be perceived, which can drive down adoption rates.

Although the senior leadership team remains the primary and critical drivers for change alignment, other natural leaders will emerge as the organization takes stock and assesses strengths and capabilities and identifies those who can play a key role in the change effort. Starting at the top is evidenced by the change agents and senior management walking the talk and visibly and audibly supporting the goals of the change effort when communicating with their staff. This must also be the case when working across the lines when interacting cross-functionally with other organizational units or departments. One way to assess the impact of the change effort is through the organization's formal and informal social media channels, where the employees, senior staff (and potentially customers) can be observed interacting with and about the change on social media and the senior executives have another chance to interact with employees and customers, not only to demonstrate their involvement but out of a genuine active interest in the change effort borne of their own efforts and engagement.

USE AN ENROLLMENT/ENGAGEMENT PLAN APPROACH

Once the need for change has been identified and communicated, the next critical step is to engage people in planning for the organization's response to the change. Successive levels of the organization must be included in the critical initial dialogue to help design the OCM implementation plan. People within an organization must be allowed an opportunity to involve their IEP: the *intellectual, emotional, and psychological reaction to the desired change.* Providing this opportunity enables people to become accustomed to the idea of change and to align their thinking in ways that will help both identify potential problem areas and contribute substantively to process improvement.

Consider a recent client example. In a complex process change effort, the external consultants developed a new process, down to a very detailed level, with little input from the organization, and many requirements from executives, and proudly handed over the process design and documentation to the team responsible for implementing the new process. The results were not surprising. The user team passively accepted the new process and then aggressively refused to implement it. The user team had neither the energy nor the enthusiasm to implement something in which it had no emotional buy-in. In fact, team members told executives in the project postmortem that they actively sabotaged the new process because "the consultants developed the process, even though we are the experts." The result: we were called in to clean up the mess, and we had three months to do it; we called it the 100 Day Challenge!

The executive sponsor also has responsibility for using an enrollment/ engagement plan approach that further outlines the desired behaviors, actions, accountability/ownership, and targeted completion date. The purpose of the enrollment plan is to drive alignment from the top down through the middle layers of the organization and to ensure the employees being impacted by the change are aware of the purposes and consequences of the change. Informed employees are empowered to help drive change or simply work collaboratively and individually within the project to best assist in the implementation and help to close the gap between mere installation and wider adoption.

In creating the enrollment plan and change plan, consider these four essential factors for sustainable change:

1. Everyone in the entire organization or those who impact or are impacted by the project output knows the purpose of the change agenda and why it is important for their team. Again, this is part of the stakeholder engagement and management process.
2. Everyone receives communication outlining the scope and key milestones of the project.
3. Everyone is enrolled in the essential elements of the change agenda relevant to their roles.
4. Change agents know the critical success factors (CSFs) and potential areas of risk, with reasonable actions assigned to ensure success and mitigate risks (as delegated in the enrollment/engagement plan).

Every person in the organization needs to have their roles clearly defined no matter how great or how small: from project managers, facilitators, team leaders, team members, subject matter experts, end users, and support staff. Everyone in the organization must be enrolled in the change effort—everyone, not just a few project team members. Furthermore, employees must have an incentive to change, a motivation for action, and an understanding of the risks and consequences of both failure and success. To ensure alignment with the change agenda, the enrollment plan should contain a resource matrix consisting of the resources driving and impacted by the change to ensure they are adequately motivated and inspired to act:

a. Dedicated resources are allocated the percent of their time dedicated to the change effort. The resources should consist of change sponsors, change agents, and potential resisters (those who may have previously expressed reservations or exhibited lack of commitment to the change effort).
b. Provisions to charter and train the steering committee.
c. Outline for enrollment session agendas: purpose and benefits, challenges and consequences, roles and responsibilities, peer testimonials, and communication of change agent training.
d. Schedule and guidelines for individual enrollment sessions, information on managing objections, training plan, and next steps.

SHIFT PARADIGMS WHERE NEEDED

General George Patton of the U.S. Army was often quoted as saying: "Never tell people how to do things. Tell them what to do and they will surprise you with their ingenuity to shift paradigms when needed."* Wise leaders know that successful change adoption depends on engaging the hearts and minds, as well as the bodies, of the people facing a changed condition. Organizational leaders need to engage the energy and enthusiasm that comes from people having their own insights, for this is where true commitment to change comes from and where the ownership of results are truly developed.

One technique to encourage people's adoption of a change is to conduct organization-wide facilitated response/adoption alignment workshops. When practiced effectively, these sessions allow people to contribute their own ideas about how a change deliverable should be deployed within the organization. Once these contributions are aligned through multiparty conversations—where much thrashing may occur—an aligned approach for managing and adapting to the change will emerge.

When reactions have been aligned and individuals within an organization are asked to be involved in responding to change, typical human behavior moves to addressing the problem—creating a desired direction

---

* http://www.dtic.mil/doctrine/jfq/jfq-38.pdf.

to facilitate change. Inertia is the force that sustains the status quo, the benign yet catastrophically destructive enemy of change. In a prechange state, many organizations fall into predictable patterns and routines, including those that directly contribute to what made the organization great in the past. However, what made the organization great in the past may not be what is needed for the future, especially given the increasing global competition and shorter change management life cycles.

In many cases, an organization's change management program seeks only to train people and is not concerned with transforming their thinking and behaviors. If your change sponsor is OK with average results (50%–75% of goals realized), then the organization will decide if they can live with that. However, when moving from traditional change management to transformation, your concern evolves past individual behaviors and seeks to change individual and group mindsets. We acknowledge it takes a greater degree of involvement and adds a layer of complexity to get the leadership team aligned, as they may need to change their mindsets before they can expect their staff to embrace change.

First, make the decision for the required mindset shifts, then work on the behavior shifts, and then organizational shifts will occur. You cannot have one without the other, and there are no shortcuts to transformational organizational change. It helps to break the scope of change into manageable segments, identify key behaviors required to sustain the change results, then modify and reinforce positive behaviors by changing the structure of consequence and reward while measuring progress toward the stated goals.

Even though building commitment with all stakeholders is essential for major changes, few people seem to understand how to develop it or how easily it can be eroded. After many years of observing people in all kinds of projects either strong commitment to certain change initiatives or falter during implementation, we have been able to identify three specific phases in the commitment process:

- Phase 1: Preparation
- Phase 2: Acceptance
- Phase 3: Commitment

The vertical axis of the commitment model practices (see Figure 5.3) displays the degree of support for the project and the horizontal axis shows the length of time someone has been exposed to the project. Each of the three phases—Preparation, Acceptance, and Commitment—represents a

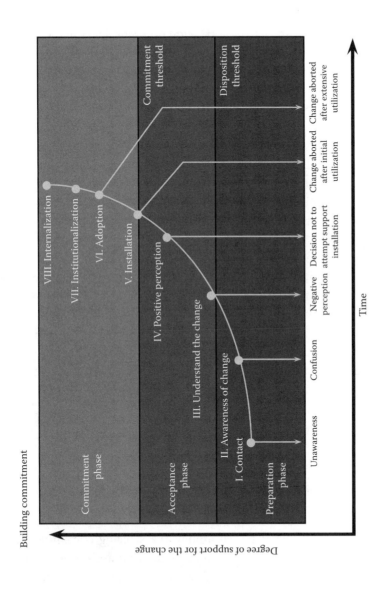

FIGURE 5.3

The eight stages in the change commitment continuum.

critical junction in the commitment process. The model shows how the degree of support for each project can progress or regress as time goes on. You can track the process of building commitment according to the points at which the project can be threatened (indicated by downward lines) or advanced to the next upward states.

As you can see in Figure 5.3, there are eight different stages in the change commitment. They are

- Stage I: Contact
- Stage II: Awareness of change
- Stage III: Understand the change
- Stage IV: Positive perception
- Stage V: Installation
- Stage VI: Adoption
- Stage VII: Institutionalization
- Stage VIII: Internalization

From a change management standpoint you would seemingly think that you would want all employees to reach an internalization stage level on all initiatives. But that is not the case. In some cases it isn't even necessary to expend the cost and effort to bring everyone up to the commitment stage. For example, a change in the way accounting presents the individual's payroll analysis might only require a Stage III change where the individual understands the change. However, the installation of a customer relations management system would require that the salesmen who use it at least reach Stage VII and preferably Stage VIII.

TALK AND COMMUNICATE THE REWARDS, CHALLENGES, AND CONSEQUENCES

Once alignment has been attained among the steering committee and within the organization's strategic objectives, communications can be created to begin the process of enrolling the organization. This requires clearly communicating the shared vision and purpose for the change by honestly outlining the opportunity (or problem), its associated challenges, and the rewards that will come about as the change management goals are realized. When dealing with consequences—and they must be dealt with up front—the communication needs to strike a balance of both positive and negative consequences based on objective measures.

Without this necessary communication, alignment cannot occur, let alone enrollment. Lack of alignment between business units responsible for strategy execution is one of the biggest causes of change management failures. Inadequate information sharing causes that lack of alignment. When you begin at the top, create an enrollment plan, shift people's paradigms toward alignment, and have the leadership team communicate and demonstrate what it will take for everyone (themselves included) collectively and personally to succeed. Accordingly, you begin to create dynamic vertical alignment for the change. Part of the reward will be the organization's investment in the development of new/enhanced skill sets and the consequences can be enforced by tying adherence and adoption directly to individual development plans.

With leaders at the top driving communications and consequences aligned with the change budget, change communication becomes more than a document of intent to explain the project to the rest of the organization. It goes beyond that by articulating that a deep alignment with the organization's strategic plan has already begun and helps the audience understand how they can get on board—to become change agents—in order to go out and enroll their people. By clearly articulating the purpose of the change, the consequences, and the next steps within the enrollment process can be expedited. The stage has been set for the organization to deal with and ultimately embrace change. Helping overcome resistance to change is the fact that the current state has gotten us to where we are today, and if the current state is a burning platform then everything the organization has been working toward could be at risk.

ASSIMILATE RISK MITIGATION USING PROJECT PLANNING, MEASUREMENT, AND REPORTING

With the senior sponsors aligned, committed to, and embracing the change, the change agents are typically the ones who know best how the change may impact their people and processes, and plan accordingly to mitigate the risks associated with the change. A balance needs to be struck between the desire for change and the organization's ability to embrace any fundamental changes. In most organizations, OCM projects are time-bound. One of the goals of many projects is completion within a specific time frame, which begins the negotiation process for allocation of resources. Some of the greatest risks many projects face are slippage and scope creep, both of which are time-constrained. The carpenter's analogy applies to change management: measure twice, cut once. Doing an effective job of risk mitigation up front can save a tremendous amount of time down the road, but you can't measure everything.

The prioritization of change-related risks, ranging from inadequate adoption and knowledge transfer failure all the way to employee exodus and catastrophic system failure, is critical at this juncture during inception. Cisco's (2008) *Change Management Best Practices* adopt an OCM method widely used by many organizations in the utilization of a risk calculation matrix to categorize and prioritize risks associated with the change agenda. High-priority risks do not necessarily translate directly to high-priority changes. There are several factors that the project team uses to evaluate the change including impact, urgency, risk, benefits, and costs. In many cases, change is required immediately or on an emergency basis due to potential risk to life, significant loss of revenue, or the ability to deliver vital public services. From this analysis, values are assigned to prioritize the various risks, and actions are put forth to mitigate higher-priority risks. These risk mitigation actions should be integrated into the overall project plan, the measurement plan, and reporting for the initiative. Project reporting also becomes part of the performance feedback channels that individuals utilize for advancing the aims of the change agenda (as well as their personal and professional development).

The results of the risk analysis, including any tasks tabled for a later phase and especially actions identified to mitigate real or potential risks, should be incorporated into the change agenda, including project planning, enrollment planning, training, and communication. As with all elements of the plan associated with critical success factors, these CSFs (derived from the project's goals and objectives) collectively will become the basis for real-time measurement and reporting, as well as any project/process control measures that will continue past the change completion to ensure ongoing sustainability.

Finally, during the execution of the initiative, the initial goals established (with realistic measurable targets) become the basis for ongoing measurement, as well as the final project report including status on any outstanding risks, tasks, milestones, and deliverables.

INVEST TO PLAN FOR OPTIMUM SUSTAINED RESULTS

Through practice and iterations of change, the investment in change will be realized as true change management ROI is attained. As additional capacities become available and the organization becomes accustomed to adapting to change, it yields a well of resources that can be converted into sustaining prior gains, investment in innovation, new capacities, and product and service lines. This leads to competitive market advantage, building further capacity for additional iterations of change and innovation. During implementation, employees throughout the organization need to remember why they are working so hard on implementing a change. Therefore, change leaders should continually remind people, using multiple media (formal e-mails, progress celebrations, informal conversations) what the change is and why it is so important. Additionally, organizational leaders should ask themselves the following people-related questions to help ensure successful implementation:

- Does the individual have the ability or desire to work in the new environment?
- Are additional skill sets needed to transition to the new job?
- Are changes to job descriptions needed?
- Are job grades or pay impacted by this change?
- Does the change impact short-term productivity? If so, will additional support be needed to ensure business success?

By following the Model for Sustainable Change, plans for near-term enrollment and long-term sustained results are established to address real cultural and perceived barriers to change. By planning to address the human element of change, you help the organization remove resistance to change, which leads to greater stability in the short term and sustainability in the long term (caveat: as long as the efforts to reduce resistance to change are ongoing).

NEGOTIATE THE RESULTS WITH A PROTOTYPING CHANGE MANAGEMENT APPROACH

As previously noted, for change efforts to be successful, the implementation strategies must be fluid. Instead of a grand plan, sufficient flexibility in process and execution tactics must exist to respond to shifting circumstances such as market or business conditions. These midcourse corrections often take the form of rapid prototyping or alternative responses to what-if scenarios— considerations that are not typically included in a detailed master plan.*

Essentially, operational prototyping is another way to get people involved in the change as opposed to being recipients of the change. It gets the change underway, in small increments, rather than waiting for the master plan to be identified. Operational prototyping is critical to successful change management. It is virtually impossible to plan for all contingencies in the development of an overarching strategy, and yet, any successful strategy for change must be able to accommodate unforeseen challenges.

The benefits of prototyping can be seen at every level within an organization. Executives benefit from a greater likelihood of adopting change through incremental buy-in, while staff members benefit because as a result of prototyping, the best approach will likely be used in implementing the change. Overall, an organization's people will have greater ownership of the change because their insights, ideas, and actions are used in building the response to the change. At the very least, an organization should adhere to the spirit, if not the letter, of prototyping to ensure that the organization is adequately equipped to handle new developments and make adjustments on the fly.

The programmed prototype portfolio (3P) is the organization's centralized collection of independent programs grouped together to facilitate their prioritization, effective management, and resource optimization in order to meet strategic organizational objectives. The negotiation value in taking an operational prototype management approach to change is that it directly links the change agenda back to the local organization's strategic plan results and objectives. Furthermore, a prototype's collective components (programs, processes, or even subassemblies) are a direct reflection of the organizational strategy and objectives. Prototyping in OCM involves identifying and aligning the organization's priorities, establishing governance, and a prototype framework for performance management and continuous improvement, if warranted. When taking a prototype management approach to OCM, the organization's projects and programs roll up delivering comprehensive innovative reporting and

---

* Prototyping monitors the thinking and activities of people—both users and implementers—as processes and technology are put into action. Its purpose during the implementation phase is to help organizations avoid getting mired in highly detailed plans that have the potential to stall change efforts.

assessment of value, cost/benefit, and ROI while allowing a broad vantage point for evaluating risk and the allocation of resources across the system.

Once the objectives for change have been attained and reported, it's time to close out the change intervention. This last step is very often overlooked as a bit of change exhaustion may have set in during the course of the initiative. Understanding that this dynamic will be present as your initiative winds down and energy naturally shifts elsewhere, plan up front on documenting the lessons learned at this stage (transition or closure).

The importance to the organization is to ingrain what went right and avoid replicating anything that went off course. Focusing and standardizing organizational change approaches across the portfolios of projects over a sustained period of time is crucial to building an organizational culture that is adaptive to change (and improvement) as part of the organization's day-to-day operations.

DIAGNOSIS AND CHANGE AGENTS

The above treatments and definitions also include advice based on practical experience. As previously mentioned, the preintervention phase ensures that only the right change initiatives are started and that they are set up correctly. The feasibility and foundations phases are completed sequentially. They set the ground rules for the iterative and incremental development of the solution that is to follow, and therefore there is a clear break between foundations and the first iteration of the exploration phase. The feasibility and foundations phases can be merged in small quick hits; the key thing is to understand the scope of the work and how it will be carried out, by whom, when, and where, as well as assessing whether OCM is suitable. The solution's detail should be considered at the appropriate time in the exploration and engineering phases. During the exploration phase, all or part of the problem or opportunity is investigated and a partial solution is created and ultimately rewarded, both incrementally and as a whole.* During the engineering phase, this partial solution is made robust enough for operational use.

---

* B.F. Skinner (1904–1990) expanded the Russian Ivan Pavlov's concept of transmarginal inhibition (TMI), theorizing that we are products of what he called "stimulus/response-driven operant conditioning." His principle: what gets rewarded gets repeated. (Today's field of Performance Management comes directly from this school of thought.)

Usually, the first step in any type of change management intervention is to diagnose the problem or opportunity. Diagnosing an organization takes time to do because it is specifying what the nature of the problem/opportunity is, what the causes are, and providing a basis for selecting strategies. Having a full understanding of what state the organization is in will help alleviate resistance to change. There are two elements of change that have an effect on the organization: change drivers and change agents.

The characteristics that affect change are called change drivers. Employees do not receive change well, so it will help to understand what other issues may be affecting the performance of the company. Elements that can cause a reactionary environment are (a) the nature of the workforce, (b) if there is competition, (c) new technologies, (d) any strong economic issues such as the one we experienced in 2008 with the Bernie Madoff scandal, and (e) if there are social trends occurring. It is important to keep in mind that resistance will most likely happen once change is initiated.

For successful change to happen, change agents are appointed, since they will be the ones who have the capability to alter organizational systems for a much higher and desired level of output (Stevenson 2008) for the organization. As with any kind of change there will be some resistance to it along with fear, uncertainty, and doubt (FUD factor), as Carl Jung liked to call it.* These three things are what determine the decisions that we make in direct correlation to how we react and respond to the given environment. In order to overcome the FUD factor, successful implementation of change using change agents will alleviate resistance. These change agents will need to effectively communicate to the employees in a positive light to convey the level of urgency in the company's future visions, strategies, and goals. In addition, change agents will reinforce and conceptualize the specified values by empowering the current employees and fostering the ideals in new employees. Lastly, change agents must always anticipate change patterns of the drivers and create an embracing culture of creativity and innovation.

---

* Carl Jung (1875–1971) saw the power of archetypes operating in the human psyche and emphasized the role of the Shadow, those aspects of who we are that have not yet been integrated. He also legitimated the world of dreams and intuition and suggested that we were more than rational beings living in a Cartesian or Newtonian world. His concepts on introvertism and extrovertism contributed to the development of the Myers-Briggs Type Indicator (MBTI), a popular personal assessment typology.

THREE COMMON ELEMENTS OF CHANGE

In every organization, regardless of industry or size, there are three organizational elements that both drive change and are affected by change: processes, technology, and people. Technology supports the *processes* designed to respond to changes in market conditions. Ultimately, however, it is the *people* who must leverage these processes and *technology* for the benefit of the organization. Let's look briefly at how each of these elements is affected by OCM.

- *Process.* Business processes are defined by process maps, policies, and procedures, and business rules that describe how work gets done. These processes are redesigned or realigned as new prospective customers or better ways to provide service to existing customers (both internal and external to the organization) are identified. This drives the adoption of new technology.
- *Technology.* Technology ensures greater organizational efficiency in implementing the changes. It is a means to process data with greater accuracy, dependability, and speed. Therefore, essential to any change process is a plan for introducing and systematizing the technology required to execute the intended changes.
- *People.* Generally, organizations excel at designing new or improving existing processes. They also do well at identifying or developing technology to realize the power of new processes. However, most organizations fail to focus sufficient attention on the role people play in the processes and technology used to accomplish the desired organizational change.

As noted in the introduction to this chapter, the overwhelming percentages of organizational change efforts fail either because people are not sufficiently considered at the outset of the initiative or there is an undue reliance on project interventions over a daily-work focus. It is the people within an organization who are responsible for developing and implementing new change methodologies, which will in turn require new technology. It is also the people who must specify, recommend, purchase, and use the new technology. At the most basic level, people must acknowledge and buy into the *need* for change. An organization cannot even begin to introduce change unless its people understand and support the reasons driving the change. This acceptance of change is known as the first step in human transition.

The OCM life cycle process, as shown in the figure above, has five phases: feasibility, foundations, exploration, engineering, and deployment in the business' operational environment. The Development phase is actually a cycle-within-a-cycle, with testing, deployment, support review, and more changes.

Life Cycle Details: Preproject Activities

In some organizations change management life cycle interventions exist as part of a portfolio of projects and sometimes exist as part of a program of projects with a shared business change objective. Regardless of the circumstances, change management interventions need to be set up correctly from the outset to ensure success. The work of the OCM precontext of other potential work or transactions to be done, or already being carried out by the organization, as people were playing out their life scripts.*

The preintervention or opportunity objectives always start at the top in order to

- Describe the business issue to be addressed
- Identify the initiating sponsor
- Confirm that the change being implemented is in line with business strategy
- Scope, plan, and resource the feasibility cycle

The intended work of the preintervention phase should be short, sharp, and ideally restricted to the creation of a short statement issued by senior management that has the purpose of justifying and prioritizing a Feasibility investigation. OCM best practice dictates that the viability of the initiative should be continually assessed throughout the intervention, ensuring that the benefits predicted from the use of end products of the change outweigh the costs of delivery. The feasibility cycle provides the first opportunity for deciding whether a proposed change intervention is viable from both a business and a technical perspective by means of a high-level investigation of the potential solutions, costs, impacts on daily work, and timeframes.

---

* Eric Berne (1910–1970), creator of Transactional Analysis, pioneered the current self-help movement by simplifying the principles of personal effectiveness and making them available to lay people. He saw the role of an internal Adult (our deciding mechanism) mediating between an internal (feeling) Child and overseeing (judging) Parent, and showed people the Games they were playing inside their Life Script in his 1964 runaway best-seller, *Games People Play.*

Life Cycle Details: Feasibility Cycle Activities

The feasibility cycle objectives are

- To establish whether there is a feasible solution to the business problem described in the change management terms of reference defined during preintervention by senior management
- To identify the benefits likely to arise from the delivery of the proposed solution
- To outline possible approaches for delivery, including strategies for sourcing the solution and project management
- To describe the organization and governance aspects of the change
- To state first-cut estimates of timescale and costs for the change overall
- To plan and resource the foundations cycle

The terms of reference for the change have been approved at this point during the life cycle. The required resources are available to carry out the feasibility investigation. The business visionary has sufficient time available to help shape the change initiative. If you are going to stop work on a change, then it is important that you stop the cycle as early as possible. The feasibility cycle should be kept as short and sharp as possible, remembering that its only purpose is to justify progressing to the foundations cycle phase. The detail of the investigation happens in the foundations cycle.

Life Cycle Details: Foundations Cycle Activities

The foundations cycle is aimed at establishing firm and enduring foundations for the intervention. In establishing the foundations, the three essential perspectives of business, solutions, and management need to be combined to provide a clear change focus that is both robust and flexible. To create solid foundations, it is vital that detail, particularly around the solution, is strictly limited so that it does not unnecessarily constrain the way the solution evolves but still clearly demonstrates how it will meet the needs of the business.

The foundations cycle activities objectives include the following:

- To baseline the high-level requirements for the change and describe their priority and relevance to the business need
- To describe the business processes to be supported by the proposed solution, where appropriate
- To identify information used, created, and updated by the proposed solution

- To describe the strategies for all aspects of solution deployment
- To detail the business case for the change
- To start designing the solution architecture and identifying the physical or infrastructural elements of the solution
- To define technical implementation standards
- To describe how quality will be assured
- To establish appropriate governance and organization for the project
- To describe the solution development life cycle for the project along with techniques to be applied in managing the project and for demonstrating and communicating progress
- To baseline a schedule for development along with deployment activities for the solution
- To describe, assess, and manage risk associated with the project

Significant business input will be required during the foundations cycle. The relevant business representatives must be identified early and their level of involvement agreed. Set a time limit for the foundations phase and try to stick to it. The aim of this phase is to create a high-level but sound view of the business and technical aspects of the change without being locked into a bad deal. Only produce the foundation outcomes to the level that allows the project to move into the exploratory development phase. Regardless of whether the formal business case product is created, the justification for the project must be assessed and a conscious decision taken to continue with the work beyond this phase: stopping a project with a poor business case now (too risky, too costly, low benefits, etc.), should be considered a successful outcome of the foundations phase.

Later maintenance activities have a direct impact on determining the appropriate level of quality that is built into all business and technical aspects of the solution and hence the level of quality control and assurance activities needed. Either all the necessary procedures and controls should be in place before leaving the foundations cycle or it should be clear how they will be ready when required. The project manager and the technical coordinator are the roles that are respectively responsible for setting up the management and technical controls.

Life Cycle Overview: Exploration Cycle Activities

The exploration cycle is used to iteratively and incrementally investigate detailed business requirements and translate them into a viable solution.

The preliminary solution created during exploration is not expected to be production-ready but is focused on demonstrating that it will deliver what is needed while fitting precisely with the ever-changing detail of overall need. The end-product of exploration will be refined further during the engineering phase to ensure technical acceptance criteria such as performance, capacity, security, supportability, and maintainability are met.

The exploration cycle objectives are

- To elaborate on the requirements captured and baselined in the Prioritized Requirements List during foundations
- To explore the full detail of the business need and provide detailed requirements for the evolving solution
- To create a functional solution that demonstrably meets the needs of the business
- To give the wider organization an early view of the solution that they will eventually operate, support, and maintain
- Where needed, evolve the business area definition and system architecture definition products of the foundations cycle into models and prototypes that describe how the solution works and how it supports all impacted business processes and systems

Life Cycle Overview: Engineering Cycle Activities

The engineering cycle is used iteratively and incrementally to evolve the preliminary solution created during exploration to achieve full operational readiness. Development effort here is focused primarily on addressing nonfunctional requirements (such as performance, capacity, security, supportability, and maintainability). In addition, the continued involvement from the Business representatives during this phase provides an ongoing opportunity to validate fitness for business purpose from a functional perspective.

The engineering cycle objectives are

- To refine the evolving solution from the exploration phase to meet the agreed acceptance criteria
- To expand and refine any products required to successfully operate and support the solution in live operation

Note that the evolving solution from the exploration phase has been approved. Specifically, the business visionary has acknowledged that the features demonstrated in the Evolving Solution are in line with the vision for the final business solution. The environments (physical, and where appropriate, technical) are in place and adequately set up to support the development of the solution. All required project personnel and stakeholders are engaged as required.

Life Cycle Overview: Deployment Cycle Activities

The primary purpose of the deployment cycle is to get the solution into live use. Where the end-products of the change are to be sold or distributed outside of the organization creating it, the deployment phase is used to get the products ready to ship. A secondary purpose is to act as a key review point prior to deployment or future development work. The number of passes through the deployment cycle will depend on whether it is sensible and feasible for the business to accept delivery of the overall solution incrementally.

The deployment cycle objectives are

- To confirm the ongoing performance and viability of the project and replan as required
- To deploy the solution (or increment of it) into the live business environment
- Where applicable, to train the end users of the solution and/or provide necessary documentation to support the live operation of the solution in the business environment
- To train and/or provide documentation for operations and support staff who will be responsible for supporting and maintaining technical aspects of the solution
- To assess whether the deployed solution is likely to enable the delivery of intended elements of business benefit described in the business case (where created)

And after the final deployment

- To formally bring the change intervention to a close, if desired
- To review overall performance from a technical and/or process perspective
- To review overall project performance from a business perspective

If the solution is being deployed incrementally, it is usually appropriate to formally assess whether the project should continue after each interim deployment. The Pareto Principle (or 80:20 rule) implies that it is possible that the vast majority of the benefit might be enabled by an early interim delivery. It therefore makes sense to check that investment in the rest of the planned project will provide a reasonable return. Justification to continue is likely to reflect the cost of operating the solution as it stands against the cost of operating a more complete solution in the future.

Life Cycle Overview: Post-Initiative Activities

The post-initiative cycle takes place after the last planned deployment of the solution. Its purpose is to reflect on the performance of the change initiative in terms of the business value actually achieved. This assessment should start as soon as the value can be measured, normally three to six months after the completion of the activities.

The post-initiative objectives are to assess whether the benefits described in the business case have actually been achieved through use of the deployed solution. In many cases, the change management intervention will have been over prior to the start of the Post-Intervention phase. In some cases where the overall solution is delivered incrementally, it is often appropriate to start the benefits realization process before the final deployment. Under such circumstances it may be appropriate to feed any proposals for change or enhancement back into the ongoing project. The business sponsor and business visionary have an ongoing responsibility for ensuring that the benefits enabled by the change are actually realized through proper use of the solution provided.

<hr>

CHANGE MANAGEMENT DEPLOYMENT PLANNING CHECKLIST*

See Figure 5.4.

Figure 5.5 shows the SUSTAIN life cycle model in relation to the Prosci Change Management Planning 10 building blocks.

---

* This checklist draws from the Prosci Benchmarking research with over 900 participants, along with the feedback and inputs from hundreds of training participants. According to Prosci, this checklist can be used as an Auditing tool to ensure that you are using a systematic and holistic approach to managing organizational change. Their Change Management Toolkit and Change Management Pilot include complete assessments, guidelines, and templates. They can be reached at 970–203–9332 or at http://www.changemanagement@prosci.com.

☐ 1. Are you using a structured change management methodology for your project?
☐ 2. Are you customizing your change management plans?
☐ 3. Does your approach include a model for how individuals experience change?
☐ 4. Does your project have the necessary sponsorship?
☐ 5. Are your sponsors prepared and able to fulfill the role of sponsor?
☐ 6. Have you created an effective communication plan?
☐ 7. Have you engaged managers and supervisors in the change management program?
☐ 8. Do you have proactive and reactive resistance management strategies and plans in place?
☐ 9. Do you have systems in place to gather feedback and measure change adoption?
☐ 10. Have you implemented reinforcement mechanisms?

FIGURE 5.4
The OCM life cycle using Prosci's Change Management Planning Building Blocks.

The five change management life cycles	SUSTAIN seven elements change management model						
	S	U	S	T	A	I	N
Feasibility cycle	Using structured change management methods		Customizing your change management plans			Approach includes a model for how individuals experience change	
Foundations cycle	Intervention has the necessary sponsorship		Creation of an effective communication plan				
Exploration cycle			Have engaged managers and supervisors in the organizational change management program				
Engineering cycle	Sponsors are prepared, ready, and able to fulfill the role of sponsor				Have proactive and reactive management strategies in place		
Deployment cycle	Have implemented necessary reinforcement mechanisms			Have systems in place to gather feedback and measure change adoptions			
Note: The seven OCM threads that constitute the SUSTAIN life cycle are (1) S = Start with top management, (2) U = Unfreeze-change-refreeze, (3) S = Shifting paradigms, (4) T = Talk and communicate, (5) A = Assimilate and integrate, (6) I = Invest in planning, and (7) N = Negotiate results.							

FIGURE 5.5
The Prosci SUSTAIN life cycle model relationship to the change management planning 10 building blocks.

SUMMARY

Definition: project change management (PCM) is change management as it relates to implementing a specific process.

Project change management just plain does not work—period! The human transition that is required to move from a historically acceptable way of working to one that is completely new or radically different is not to be underestimated. Good leaders will make the reasons for change personal for everyone, not just for executives or shareholders. End-user benefits, down to the day-to-day experience of the individual worker, will create a more receptive environment for fostering new ideas—and a receptive environment is essential to creating any lasting, positive change. Our Sustainable Change life cycle model provides an iterative and incremental implementation framework, with seven life cycle phases occurring during five cycles of development, totaling some 35 possible action items. Each life cycle item has objectives and preconditions. Specifically, each life cycle phase will deliver change, and within OCM, delivery of results to the appropriate and agreed on level of quality is used to assess progress. The acceptance of the prototypes enables agreement that the intervention can move safely from one life cycle phase to another. The framework is highly configurable, depending on the size and formality of the change being delivered.

At the highest level, business leaders are driven by financial goals and government leaders are driven by legislative mandates. Their urgent need to meet these objectives may lead them to impose change unilaterally rather than engaging the people to find the best way to meet a more generally understandable desired future state. Executives who neglect the human transition required in OCM will be less successful at implementing change. Successful OCM boils down to improving the relationships between people in the organization in the attainment of a mutually desirable end state. An organization that is too focused on objectives runs the risk of losing sight of personal relationships.

For a change initiative to be successful, an organization must understand and address the three phases of the change management intervention. To do so, organizational leaders must ask themselves these questions:

- Has the organization thoroughly identified and communicated the impending change? Are disturbances acknowledged and aligned?
- Has the organization engaged all of its stakeholders (at every level of the organization) in the change that will need to be adopted? Is the intent and direction of this change aligned throughout the organization?
- Has the organization developed a flexible plan for implementation that allows for prototyping to move continually toward the desired future state? Are the organizational responses aligned and institutionalized?

The human transition that is required to move from a historically accept-able way of working to one that is completely new or radically different is not to be underestimated. As previously mentioned, good leaders will make the reasons for change personal for everyone, not just for executives or shareholders. End-user benefits, down to the day-to-day experience of the individual worker, will create a more receptive environment for foster-ing new ideas, along with a receptive environment is essential to creating any lasting, positive change.

6

Facilitated OCM Workshops

In a Nutshell: As organizations and information become more complex, it is no longer possible or sensible to rely on project teams or one person to make all the decisions. More and more, organizations achieve success through the behaviors and interactions of other people working together in some sort of facilitated-team-based environment. Understanding or influencing them by exerting hierarchical-type project power is becoming less common than by consultation and direct relationships. As a result, enabling people to interact better in a group through structured facilitated workshops repays enormous dividends in change management implementations.

Facilitation and facilitated workshops will prove to be the most efficient and effective way of achieving change management goals, not the traditional project team approach that we have found simply does not work in most cases. Having facilitated workshops as a specialized type of meeting, with a clear objective (product), a set of people (participants) who are chosen and empowered to produce the product, and an independent person (facilitator) to enable the effective achievement of the objective is a key component of OCM implementations and will replace the failure-prone project mentality. Facilitated workshops are a process in which a neutral facilitator, with no stake in the outcome of the workshop, enables a group to work together to achieve an agreed on OCM goal, whether that be solving a problem, building a plan, gathering requirements, or making a change-based decision. Facilitated workshops ensure a team-oriented approach to rich communication and collaboration, in order to achieve results with speed and commitment and heavy buy-in to the outcome, without having to deal with the ineffective projects-team consequences. Enabling people to communicate and collaborate effectively in workshops pays enormous dividends when it is done properly. Facilitated workshops are an extremely efficient and effective way of achieving this enhanced communication needed in change management interventions. As such, more and more organizations will achieve success through enabling teamwork and interaction through facilitated change management workshops as a viable alternative to project-focus change, which rarely works well, if it indeed works at all.

INTRODUCTION

Facilitated workshop discussion is where a facilitator will guide a group through a discussion keeping in mind the values of the group and what the group wants to achieve. The facilitator provides processes for thinking about the change management issue and processes for creating effective group participation. It is important to note that a facilitator is not the group leader and does not provide her or his own opinions to the discussion.

Stanfield (2000, pp. 34–35) outlines the following qualities of a good workshop facilitator:

- Ensure all participants have their say
- Prevent one or two people from dominating the discussion
- Ensure all topics are discussed
- Emphasize group ownership of the issue
- Trust the wisdom of the group
- Affirm that there are no wrong answers

How this can be achieved is outlined by the facilitative behaviors proposed by many professional facilitators, including Hogan, Voehl, and others, and includes the following:

- Active listening and effective feedback
- Probing for ideas and weak spots
- Opening up change management thinking
- Keeping the conversations on track and focused
- Maximizing participation and minimizing down time
- Listening for common ground among all of the noise factors
- Speeding up and slowing down when needed
- Challenging participants to give more

- Cognitive inputs, such as composing a story or using an analogy to bring an abstract concept to life
- Metaprocessing by remaining aware of group dynamics
- Pinning down the wafflers to give input and make decisions

The main role of the workshop facilitator* is to aid productive and insightful commentary among participants. Problems may arise for facilitating group discussion and expert Brian Stanfield (2000, pp. 32–33) advocates the following resolutions to the four most common difficult situations[†]:

- *Situation 1: Getting off the topic.* Affirm what the speaker is saying, recapitulate what the group has said so far in response to the particular question, and either repeat the question or move to the next question.
- *Situation 2: Long answers.* Ask the speaker for an example; this will help them to clarify what they are saying and ground their ideas. Reaffirm to the speaker that your concern is that their point is understood.
- *Situation 3: Dealing with arguments.* Remind the group to respect and honor all participants' opinions/perspectives. Ask for other viewpoints. If a participant interrupts, ask them to wait until the speaker has finished, then invite them to speak once the speaker has finished. Allow others to speak if they so wish then move on.
- *Situation 4: When participants react negatively to others' answers.* Some participants may be adamant not to let anything pass that they do not agree with. In such cases you can say "I understand your response but I'm not sure how it answers the question/I see you do not agree with Jo's answer, so tell us how you would answer the question."

Facilitated workshop discussions differ from focus groups in that they are less structured. Focus groups have an agenda that is comprised of a

---

* Thirty years of ICA research and training have generated a band of facilitator-consultants around the world who are second to none in their grasp and practice of the dynamics and how-tos of the art and science of group facilitation. In many nations round the world, these practitioners have labored for years facilitating community consultations in the developing nations, assisting major corporations and other organizations to work cooperatively to solve problems, and then trained others in the same art and science.

† Stanfield argues that the facilitator needs to be competent in designing and leading larger or smaller group processes and events: a conversation or discussion, a meeting, a workshop, a design conference, an environmental review, a strategic planning session, or a macro program of consultation. With this comes a complete familiarity with the process of creating and sequencing questions that move the group from surface considerations into the depth implications of any topic.

list of questions, starting with the general and moving to the specific. The overall aim is to get all the questions answered and decisions made. Facilitated discussion is more like a conversation that moves according to its own dynamic and onto topics brought up by the group.*

FACILITATED WORKSHOPS BACKGROUND

Organizational change can sometimes be warranted when the organization's culture has created a negative growth in profits and morale is low. Another reason why change is needed is due to inefficient and ineffective daily work processes, thus creating an entire system that can be bogged down with unnecessary overhead costs, as often happens with project management initiatives. In order for change to happen, an analysis must be conducted in order to diagnose the operational daily work problems that are causing the issues currently faced by the company. As seen on the television series, *House,* the doctors see symptoms the patient is affected with and go through a methodical process to determine what is causing the symptoms. If only the symptoms are treated, there is no resolution because the problem will continue to occur. The same methodology applies to an organization. Most change initiatives fail not because the ideas or concepts were not refined or smart enough, but because (a) the actual implementation was not understood and executed correctly (Clegg, Kornberger, and Ptisis 2009) or (b) there was an undue reliance on a project's approach, which in many cases has failed to maximize participation and deliver on its promise of a better world.†

---

* Stanfield writes in *The Magic of the Facilitator* that facilitators have to be able to care in depth for the client organization. This involves knowing how to customize programs to fit the client's situation and how to close a deal and deliver on the contract. It also presumes the courage to say no to a deal if facilitation is not an appropriate solution or will not work. It means preparing every aspect of the change management program ahead of time. Especially important is getting crystal clear on the specific intents for the workshop (both rational and experiential) and designing the components of the event that will realize those intents.

† Stanfield writes that the facilitator has to be able to elicit the group's best responses to the question, which involves appealing to imagination and encouraging some boldness and even wildness in the responses. This involves giving individuals time to write down their own answers so that people who think a little more slowly, but possibly more surely, than others have time to marshal their input. Then the facilitator has to be able to get all the group's data out through an inclusive brainstorm. Here, maximizing participation is of the essence. The leader has to involve the whole group, find ways to draw out the quieter folks, and push each one in the group to play an active role in organizing the data into bitable chunks and naming it.

GETTING THE PROCESS STARTED

You want to get change going within your organization, and quickly. The question is, how do we get started? Fortunately for change agents, there are multiple ways to facilitate change within your organization.

Create a Change Baseline

Your own assumptions about what motivates people will determine the success or failure of your change program. If your assumptions are incorrect, you may miss a valuable opportunity, that of gaining stakeholder ownership of the change process.*

"Why is this?" you ask. People do what they do for a reason. A person's behavior (what we observe) is an expression of their underlying beliefs and assumptions. To make our desire to facilitate change appealing to others, we must understand why they do what they do.

The baseline is created by identifying the dissatisfaction, vision, first steps, and change resistance for each stakeholder involved with your change program. Using a spreadsheet application, make a table listing the stakeholders and each area of investigation:

- *Who* are the stakeholders?
- What are they *dissatisfied* with?
- How do they *feel* about the planned changes (*Vision*)?
- What *steps* will provide a good ROI?
- What *resistance* must be overcome to succeed?

Define Change Strategies

We now have a baseline of the key issues for each stakeholder. The next step is to select the ones that you can realistically alter and develop targeted

---

* Coming up with a comprehensive group baseline—a documentary record of the group's insights—is the bottom line of facilitation. With the help of an assigned documenter who inputs the group data in tandem with the process, the participants can be handed a hard-copy product before they leave the workshop. Vital to this is the ability to keep track of all the group-generated data and enough versatility in using computer programs to produce data-holding charts to create the desired baseline. Making a powerful verbal report to the client that captures the significance and implications of the change management program, and in certain situations, having the courage to protect the group's conclusions are not insignificant attributes of the facilitator, especially when controversy exists.

strategies to alter them. People won't change unless they feel safe, secure, and in control over the results. You can't just force people to change by management decree. To facilitate change, you must change their underlying assumptions with a credible plan.

List what assumptions need to change. Include a strategy for overcoming the resistance to change identified for each stakeholder group. The strategy should fill the gaps. Increasing dissatisfaction with the status quo should improve motivation. Increasing the vision element will ensure the program is completed. Increasing first steps will make sure the program gets started. Lastly, decreasing resistance will simplify the whole effort.*

Change the Measurements

Measurements define the culture of an organization, so it makes sense they would be a good way to facilitate change. What you measure is what you manage, and the person that does the measuring is the manager. In order to change the outcome, we must change *what* is measured and (possibly) *who* or *what* is doing the measuring.

Think about this a little. The person or thing measuring is receiving feedback, the result of prior changes. This is known as a *control loop* or a feedback loop. If the one measuring can't make changes or the one making changes can't measure the results, the resulting delays are *significant wastes* that cause *serious* trouble.

Leaders define the performance standards, or measures. You can't introduce new measurements into the organization and then continue to ask for the old ones. If a leader keeps *asking* for *old* information, people *give it* to him or her. If a leader seems to counter the aims of your change program, the people being led will respond the same way.

Communicate Change Details

One way to facilitate change is to define what needs to change in as much detail as possible. For example, you can't just say, "Salespeople need to be

---

* Sensing and understanding the diversity of a group as a gift is more than a skill. It stems not only from methodological necessity but from a deep recognition of the wonder of life and the implicit wisdom and greatness of each human being. This involves a foundational affirmation, the constant decision to reference situations positively, and the habit of responding with the "yes" before the "no." The facilitator is aware that the method works best when he or she is able to affirm the wisdom of each person, honor the collective data of the whole group, celebrate the completed work of the group, and at the same time affirm each person in the group individually.

friendlier to customers." You have to define "friendly." You have to communicate the characteristics of friendly behavior, such as "greet customers warmly," "ask about their concerns," or "address them by name." Once you know what the behavior looks like, translate it in detail to employees *and* reward them immediately for doing it.

Communicate Successful Changes

Reward those who change and acknowledge their contributions. In order to facilitate change, you must focus your attention on people who change and ignore those who do not. This will send the message to others that you value the changes made, and in turn, encourage others to participate in the change program. To derive the greatest benefit, the reward—material or not—must be immediate *and public*.*

Measure Change Progress

Make sure you have a regular method to capture where the organization stands with respect to the change program. Are the current dissatisfaction, vision, and first steps level greater than the *resistance to change*? People are not mechanical systems; their behaviors are the result of internal beliefs and assumptions. We must measure and monitor the progress being made to ensure that the change program is having an effect on those beliefs and assumptions. If given the option, most people will opt for the devil they know rather than the one they *don't*.

Ensure Change Lasts

Increasing the values in the change formula will help facilitate change and bring about behavior changes. However, it alone will not make them stick. Organizational culture is far more persistent than many people allow for. Change must be an iterative, interactive, and ongoing *process*. It is definitely *not* an *event*. Go back to the first step and update the change baseline. Discover some new changes that are needed. Develop new change strategies and keep up the change.

---

* The Facilitator must have creative ways to release blocks to the process. This demands a light touch to gently discourage side conversations. It calls for shrewd tactics to discourage speechifying and argumentation, and demands tactful ways to discourage the dominance of particular individuals, to handle difficult people, and to deal helpfully with conflict.

Only the mediocre are always at their best. The rest of us must keep on changing, striving for something better and achieving something more.

Jean Giraudoux, 1882–1944

Facilitated OCM workshops are a proven technique.* They are used successfully throughout the business world and have been used in systems development, in particular, for many years. As one of our suggested core practices, they are a way of making high quality team-based decisions in compressed timescales, which is often needed in organizational change situations. They can be used throughout the OCM Lifecycle wherever embracing several viewpoints at the same time is advantageous, e.g., when capturing and prioritizing requirements, creating plans and strategies, modelling cross-functional business processes, and reviewing an increment. Facilitated workshops are also a useful catalyst for effecting cultural change in an organization. This is because workshops promote buy-in, necessitate empowerment of the participants, and require individuals to take responsibility and honor their commitments.†

BENEFITS OF FACILITATED WORKSHOPS

Using facilitated workshops instead of relying upon project teams alone brings both direct and indirect benefits to a change initiative—rapid, high-quality decision-making. Using facilitated workshops instead of project teams can reduce the elapsed time required to achieve objectives, such as the identification, agreement, and sign-off of requirements. Because all relevant stakeholders are present at the same time and able to communicate and collaborate effectively with each other, they will have greater

---

* Facilitating a process for an organization is much, much more than using a bag of tricks to occupy the audience for a day or two. The facilitator must have the maturity to assume responsibility not only for the process, but also for the overall task, the participants, and the outcome of the event. This assumes the willingness to take on a big load, to take responsibility for every single aspect of the program, to deal successfully with ambiguity, use one's critical intelligence to make hard decisions, and then to take the consequences of those decisions.

† We all know the challenges that come with organizational change. Depending on the source of change, it's well documented that 70%–85% of all projects and programs requiring people to adapt to a new way of doing things fail. Change is constant and organizations will continue to spend millions of dollars on things associated with change only to have change come at them at a higher speed, and the unaccounted cost of poorly managed change is far greater than the direct cost.

confidence in the result, unlike a project team environment, where getting the proper involvement is usually hit or miss.

The workshop group is focused on the objectives to be achieved in the session so that the information gathering and review cycle is performed with greater speed than usually happens with the traditional project team approach. Also, unlike project team work where misunderstandings and disagreements are usually invisible, these are made visible and can be worked out at the time, in a safe environment, managed by the objectivity of the workshop facilitator. Any concerns should therefore have been raised and resolved, or noted for action after the workshop, with appropriate people assigned as owners.*

Greater buy-in from all stakeholders is another benefit. Facilitated workshops lead to participants feeling more involved and committed to the end results due to having an opportunity to participate in, and contribute to, both the content and the decisions that are made. This builds and helps maintain enthusiasm throughout the intervention, unlike project work where involvement is usually left to a few critical staff people. Building team spirit as well as delivering results is often achieved among all of the stakeholders. Facilitated workshops are a managed way of building rapport across the community. The output of the workshop benefits from the participants building on each other's ideas and gaining a better understanding of each other's viewpoints. A successful workshop depends on high levels of synergy being achieved and it is a major part of the workshop facilitator role to ensure that this happens.†

In our experience, building consensus among all relevant stakeholders is a major benefit that does not always happen in a project environment. The facilitated workshop provides an opportunity for participants to discuss the relevant subject matter, including the major issues and problems, and reach a consensus on important decisions. If business procedures and practices are reviewed, participants can gain a greater understanding

---

* A key role of the facilitator is to provide objectivity to the group process. One side of the facilitator is more like an orchestra conductor who wants a first-class product, but the other side is more like the dispassionate referee who knows the importance of maintaining a neutral stance toward what is coming out of the group. To this end, the facilitator has to be able to set aside personal opinions on the data of the group, to be careful not to react negatively to people's insights, and to maintain detachment from the group-generated data.

† In the new normal of rapid change there will be new expectations because the changing nature of change has actually changed the nature of work. Change management is now day-to-day management and knowledge of change management strategies and practices are expected of leaders and facilitators.

of the inputs and implications of their work. This can lead to improved efficiencies led by the participants themselves, giving greater buy-in and commitment and therefore a greater chance of successful implementation than is the case with typical project approaches. Finally, clarification of issues and gaining valuable insights are also vital deliverables of the workshop as they help to minimize ambiguities and misunderstandings. In the facilitated environment, participants can explore and model innovative ideas, which in turn will simplify and accelerate the review and sign-off of the workshop deliverables.

NEUROLOGICAL ROOTS OF RESISTANCE TO CHANGE*

The prevailing contemporary research confirms that, while change is personal and emotional, it is *neurological* as well. Here's what researchers now know about the physiological/neurological response that occurs when an individual encounters change (see Figure 6.1):

1. A new condition (a change) is created, introduced, and transmitted
2. The prefrontal cortex region of the brain receives the transmission through one or more of the physical senses
3. The prefrontal cortex compares the new condition to the current condition by accessing another region of the brain, the basal ganglia, which stores the data we receive and contains the wiring for the habits we have
4. If a difference between the new condition and the existing condition is detected, an error signal is produced and sent throughout the brain
5. The error signal is received by the amygdala, the prehistoric part of the brain that tells us to be wary of a saber-toothed tiger
6. The amygdala places a value to the changed condition and sounds an alarm, producing the emotion of fear

---

* The facilitator is practiced in sensing dynamics in the group. In particular, the facilitator has to be versed in interpreting both the resistance and silence of the group, identifying hidden agendas, and not only sensing the group's uncertainty at particular points but taking steps to clarify it. Deft at picking up nonverbal cues, the facilitator can also listen to the group with the third ear to pick up the significance of what lies behind participants' words. On the more active side, the facilitator is facile in pushing negatively phrased data for its underlying insight and to probe vague answers for their fuller meaning.

INSIGHTS: THE ANTIDOTE TO RESISTANCE TO CHANGE

An important contribution of modern neuroscience to helping us be more effective as leaders concerns the phenomenon of insights, which is sometimes called an epiphany or an ah-ha moment. Here's how insights help overcome resistance to change:

- During change, the disturbance an individual feels is produced by competing mental models (a conflict between various parts of the brain).
- Individuals can either allow the conflict to continue, producing resistance to change (the old model wins out over the new model), or they can take active steps to move past the dilemma.
- If individuals (or their leaders) choose to move beyond resistance, reflection—quieting external stimuli and using the unconscious brain—will help prepare them for insights.
- When an insight occurs, new neural connections are made across the brain and adrenaline is released, producing a surge of energy. This energy creates the momentum to overcome the resistance circuit, and allows an individual to commit more readily to change.

(Rock, 105–107)

FIGURE 6.1
Insights, the antidote to resistance to change.

7. The prefrontal cortex receives the fear signal from the amygdala and creates what it believes to be a necessary response
8. The new condition is resisted by the prefrontal cortex, and by extension, the person

(Schwartz and Rock, 71–80)

MANAGING THE WORKSHOP

It is the responsibility of the workshop facilitator to design and amend the process to assist the group in achieving its objective. There are many great tools and techniques that may be used in workshops. Physically gathering, modeling, and presenting information requires tools to help workshop participants see this information. A whiteboard, flipchart, brown paper, and sticky notes are commonly used tools. Techniques are the practices used to achieve the workshop aims and include such things are brainstorming, storyboards, rich pictures, SWOT analysis, grouping, and diagramming.

The group dynamic is about how people interact together and their relationships and feelings displayed by their behavior. This is the organic part of any group interaction. Systems and procedures do not take account of human beings with their fears, hopes, aspirations, and feelings. The workshop facilitator's role is to manage the people through the process toward achieving the goal. Typically, this will mean making sure that individuals or factions do not dominate, ensuring that shy people with valuable input are heard, ensuring discussion around issues is productive and does not become emotive or personal, and focusing the group on what they should be doing. It is the responsibility of the workshop facilitator to try to create the appropriate dynamic for differing situations, such as problem solving, creativity, conflict resolution, or strategic thinking and to identify and manage the dynamic operating within the group.* Other matters that can affect the dynamic are internal politics, pay and conditions, room layout, length of meeting, refreshments, seating, and lighting. Some are within the workshop facilitator's control, some are capable of influence, but all need to be facilitated.

Facilitation is the key because it is based on the power of the question. And the power of the question is what makes things happen. People can handle change, even if it is thrust upon them, if they can answer fundamental and meaningful questions for themselves:

"What's it all about?" What is the nature of the change; why do we need to change?

"What's in it for me?" How will this affect me; what do you need me to do; what risk do I face and what are the benefits?

"How will you help me?" What do I need to know; how can I get help; how can I be successful?

Through our work with hundreds of organizations around the world over the past 40 years, we have helped many companies navigate through significant change. Below are some essential components of facilitating change management that we have found extremely helpful to the process:

- *Visioning Workshops* with senior leaders to clearly identify both the "things" that need to happen—typically the source of the change—and the potential impact on people in the organization; the visioning session results in a clearly articulated description of the change

---

* There is an old adage that states "organizations don't change; people change and then they change the organization." Facilitation is the key to ensuring that people understand the change, participate successfully to create the desired future, and accept that the real change requires changes in their own thoughts, attitudes, and behaviors.

- *Education and Development Workshops*—facilitating small group education sessions to ensure people understand the nature of the change; this
begins the process of gaining their buy-in through their understanding
of their ability and willingness to move successfully through change
- *Project Planning and Innovation Management Workshops*—sessions
designed to build the project structure around innovation management; developing breakthrough plans to ensure tasks are always
completed on-time, ahead of schedule, and to standard
- *OCM Planning Workshops*—sessions designed to build the people
structure. This includes:
  - Identifying risks and assigning roles such as change sponsors
  and change agents
  - Assessing the impact of the change on processes, staff, customers, and the other stakeholders
  - Assessing the culture and identifying systemic barriers to change
  and the strengths and weaknesses of the culture to navigate
  through the change
  - Developing communication plans for both formal and informal
  communications with a feedback mechanism
  - Individual and team coaching session to continuously increase
  commitment by providing feedback, developing individual
  change skills, and providing encouragement
  - Regular monitoring sessions to ensure both the project plan and
  the people plan are being executed successfully

Change is difficult but in our line of consulting and training work, it really
is the only constant in a sea of turbulence. If we are to navigate the complexity, we need to understand the nature of change, possess effective change
management skills, and make it easy by facilitating people through change.

ROLES AND RESPONSIBILITIES

To successfully move through the OCM process, managers and supervisors need to know how to do the following five things well:

- *Lead change*—understanding both the things that need to get done
and the expected results and the impact on people

- *Facilitate*—a cornerstone skill that increases your ability to lead, plan, communicate, and navigate the culture
- *Plan*—developing both project and change management plans
- *Communicate*—beyond town halls, emails, bulletin boards, Facebook pages, and lunch-n-learns, knowing how to communicate with people; addressing their concerns, responding to questions, and gaining their buy-in
- *Understand the culture*—understanding the unique nature of the culture and the implications for managing change

This section gives some guidance on which OCM roles would fill the roles required during a change management intervention and associated facilitated workshops. Some of the key facilitated workshop roles are defined as being workshop owner, workshop facilitator, participants, co-facilitator, workshop scribe, and observer.

Workshop Owner

The workshop owner is the owner of the objective that the workshop is aiming to achieve and usually the owner of the budget to run the workshop. It is up to the owner to set the objectives and deliverables of the workshop, although the workshop facilitator should help the owner in clarifying and scoping these. The workshop objectives should also be understood and agreed on by the participants at the start of the workshop. The owner of a project kick-off workshop may be the business sponsor, whereas the owner of a timebox planning workshop could be the project manager, team leader, or even the business ambassador. What is important is that the owner is involved in the definition and resourcing of the workshop and retains ownership of the objective throughout the workshop.

Workshop Facilitator

The workshop facilitator manages the process and dynamic of the workshop, enabling the participants to concentrate on the content and the product. The workshop facilitator should be neutral to the workshop objectives, the product (outcome) of the workshop, and the participants. He or she is responsible for helping the group to meet the workshop objectives. Ideally the workshop facilitator should come from outside the project to ensure—and signify—neutrality. Some organizations have internal facilitators

✓	listening effectively and accurately
✓	summarizing
✓	observing and recalling conversation and behavior
✓	communicating clearly
✓	identifying similarities and differences between statements
✓	recognizing and understanding different viewpoints and perspectives
✓	analyzing
✓	identifying assumptions
✓	recognizing effective and ineffective behavior
✓	intervening appropriately as necessary
✓	being a model of effective behavior
✓	providing feedback impartially and tactfully
✓	accepting feedback calmly
✓	being in control of own behavior
✓	developing trust with and within groups
✓	Other related skills as needed

FIGURE 6.2
The top facilitator skills needed for OCM interventions/workshops.

that are allocated to workshops and other organizations employ external consultants.

The workshop facilitator's skills and abilities include the following checklist items, as shown in Figure 6.2.

The Participants' Role

Participants are chosen because they are needed to produce the product or achieve the objectives of the workshop. Participants must add value to the workshop. To do this, they need to have the knowledge, skills, and experience to be able to contribute to the objective of the workshop and be empowered to make decisions if that is what the workshop demands of the group. Group facilitation is a lean process so only the people essential to achieving the objectives and deliverables should be there. A participant could perform one of many roles within the business and may include suppliers or customers from outside the organization. They may be any of the OCM roles, including specialists.

Observers

The observer is a requested role rather than a necessary role for the production of the workshop's immediate product. Examples of the use of the observer role are therefore limited but could include someone auditing the workshop process or the facilitator's ability, a trainee facilitator who wants to observe the group dynamics without being part of the group, or an auditor to the project processes. Observers could also be development or support staff gathering useful background information. In all cases, the observer's presence must be agreed on by the workshop owner and the group. Observers will always affect the dynamic of the workshop, altering the behavior and input of the participants even if they do not speak or interact directly. If it is absolutely necessary to allow an observer to the workshop process, they should not contribute toward the content, process, or deliverables of the workshop. If they need to take an active part, they should be invited and acknowledged as participants.

Co-Facilitators

The co-facilitator works alongside the workshop facilitator, where appropriate, to help record the visible workshop documentation. This may be captured on flipcharts, boards, handwritten notes, or directly onto a computer using standard word processing, graphics packages, or specialist group systems software. The latter enables the involvement of remote participants via tele- or videoconferencing. The co-facilitator also performs the valuable task of monitoring the group dynamic and feeding back any observations to the lead facilitator. The role should be held by another facilitator, or possibly a business analyst, solution developer, or user; in short, someone who has the required understanding of both the workshop issues and facilitation in order to know what to record and what to observe and feed back to the lead facilitator.

Workshop Scribes

The Scribe records and publishes the workshop outcomes and decisions together with any necessary supporting information. The Scribe may also take responsibility for following up on agreed on actions with those who took ownership of these during the workshop itself. The Scribe role may be held by anyone who has the required understanding of the issues in order to know what to record. To support or speed up the process there may be more than one person allocated to this role in a workshop, depending on how the outputs are being documented (for example, sometimes a technical scribe is used where documentation is to be created directly into a specific toolset).

FACILITATED WORKSHOP LIFE CYCLE ACTIVITIES

The key life cycle activities associated with a facilitated workshop are

- Plan the workshop (workshop definition)
- Prepare for the workshop
- Facilitate the workshop session
- Run the workshop
- Review the workshop
- Document the workshop (workshop report)
- Follow-up (postworkshop actions and review)

Plan the Workshop (Workshop Definition)

The workshop owner, with support from the workshop facilitator, defines the objectives of the workshop, nominates the participants, and agrees on, in outline, the form that the workshop should take. It may sometimes be necessary to define several workshops to achieve the objectives. The size of the workshop should ideally be in the range of six to 12 people (more can be accommodated if necessary, but additional planning and structure will be required, which may possibly include the use of extra co-facilitators and the breaking of the workshop into subgroups).

Prepare for the Workshop

In preparation for the workshop, the workshop facilitator or co-facilitator must circulate information to the participants in advance so that they fully understand the objective of the workshop and the background to it. The workshop agenda detailing when, where, and who will be attending, as well as the order of proceedings, will be sent out, together with any preworkshop reading. In particular, individuals will be advised where their input to the workshop is needed so that they may prepare the information to make an effective contribution and where necessary collect the views of those they are representing.

Facilitate the Workshop—Run the Workshop

The tight timescales of an OCM project mean that the workshop needs to maintain its focus and pace. Some workshop facilitators operate on the principle of the five-minute rule wherein any disagreement that cannot be resolved in a period of five minutes is parked as an open issue. Such open issues are documented and deferred to a later session or possibly taken outside the workshop for resolution. For workshops to be effective, there are a few basic guidelines that the workshop facilitator should agree on with the group and remind people of should it become necessary. Typical guidelines (ground rules) are

- Start on time, because timescales are constrained
- Respect the views of others
- Silence may be seen as agreement; if participants do not speak up then they will be assumed to have agreed to the point under discussion
- One conversation at a time
- Each individual in the group has a responsibility to maintain focus

Facilitate the Workshop—Review the Workshop

The effectiveness of the workshop should be examined before the end of the workshop and any lessons learned fed back into the operation of future workshops. In particular, did the workshop meet its objectives fully and did all participants contribute to the process? Most importantly, how effective did the participants feel that the workshop had been and did it run to time?

Document the Workshop

The workshop scribe should produce and distribute a workshop report very soon after the workshop to all participants, and if appropriate, to other interested parties who will be affected by the products of the workshop. The workshop report should be brief and should document

- Decisions
- Actions with action owners
- Open issues
- The product of the workshop itself, as appropriate

It does not record minutes.

Follow-Up

The workshop owner must be consulted to confirm satisfaction with the workshop's results. All actions marked for follow-up activity outside the workshop forum must be addressed, not just documented!

SUCCESS FACTORS FOR FACILITATED WORKSHOPS

The factors that have been found, in practice, to greatly improve the success of a facilitated workshop are

- An effective, trained, independent workshop facilitator.
- Flexibility in the format of different workshops, but with clearly defined objectives.
- Thorough preparation before the workshop by workshop facilitator, co-facilitator, and participants.
- A mechanism for ensuring that the results of previous workshops are built in, where appropriate.
- Decisions and agreements that are not forced. If the workshop participants cannot agree on a point within the workshop (perhaps due to lack of information or time), the workshop facilitator should recognize this and elicit from the group the appropriate action to remedy the shortfall.
- Participants receiving a workshop report, detailing decisions, actions, and the product of the workshop very soon after the workshop (ideally within 48 hours).

Much can be learned by scheduling a short review session just before the end of each workshop and documenting the benefits and concerns from the workshop.

While it seems obvious, identifying the change is an absolutely fundamental first step in successful change adoption. It is important that the changed condition be described in a common, consistent language. However, organizations often fail to identify and communicate the need for change in a way that is understood and embraced by people working at all levels of an organization—from the executive suite to the individual workstation. Many leaders do not adequately consider how a proposed change, or in some cases the rumor of one, may be received—at an intellectual, emotional, and neurological level—by the people it will impact the most. If the disturbance that is produced by a change isn't adequately addressed through some alignment intervention such as a facilitated workshop, this resistance to change is prolonged and can be damaging to the change management initiative.

SUMMARY

Facilitated workshops are one of OCM's key best practices. The skill and independence of the workshop facilitator is important to ensure a successful workshop. This chapter described the workshop roles, together with the workshop activities (before, during, and after the workshop) and the benefits of using facilitated workshops.

7

Culture Change Management (CCM)

In a Nutshell: Up to this point in the book, a great deal of our focus has been on how to apply change management to the successful implementation of projects/programs. In this chapter we are going to discuss and summarize how the operational process and daily management activities need to be aligned with the project change activities in order to create a culture that embraces change as a standard activity, part of the DNA. This is in contrast to resisting and delaying project implementation because it is something new and different that the operational employees and staff are not familiar with. It integrates and reinforces the concept of culture change management (CCM), which is the resulting factor of the harmonizing of the traditional change management activities and the day-to-day management of the organization, and how it impacts the total organization's ability to embrace change rather than resist it.

INTRODUCTION

Since the 1970s, traditional project change management (PCM) has focused on preparing the people impacted by the change initiatives to accept the changes that result from a specific project's activities. Traditionally, PCM has a long history of being used to help project management teams successfully implement projects/programs that involve changing the activities and/or the behavioral patterns of the people within the organization that would be impacted by the change (Campbell 1969). By the early 1980s, project managers were required to have not only an excellent understanding of the technology involved and the processes required to implement the technology, but also awareness that project success was heavily dependent on the degree of acceptance by the people who are using the solutions.

Over the past 20 years alone, there have been hundreds of white papers written and dozens of books published on how to successfully implement projects supported by an aggressive project-change-related methodology. In addition, there have been dozens of different methodologies developed by different consultants and academicians directly aimed at helping organizations implement successful projects through the effective use of other types of change programs that were primarily focused on the use of change management to successfully implement projects and/or major changes in the organization's structure.

Some of the more publicized and implemented project-related change management methodologies that have been discussed earlier in the book include

- The Universal Change Activation Toolkit
- ADKAR Model for Change Management
- Accelerating Implementation Methodology (AIM)
- Beckhard and Harris Change Management Process
- Boston Consulting Group (BCG) Change Delta
- Bridges Leading Transition Model for Change
- The Harrington-Voehl Sustainable Change Model*
- GE's Change Acceleration Process (CAP)
- John Kotter Eight-Step Model for Change
- McKinsey 7S Change Model

All of these approaches were basically directed at ensuring that individual projects/programs were successfully implemented by preparing the affected people to understand, be involved in the development, and accept the proposed project/program when it was implemented. If these approaches were effective after being implemented by thousands of companies, why is it we are still seeing the high failure rates of projects and

---

* This model is based on five books that the authors have written. The first one on project change management (*Project Change Management: Applying Change Management to Improvement Projects* published by McGraw Hill in 1999), the second on change management (*Change Management Excellence: the Art of Excelling in Change Management* published by Paton Press in 2006). Three more have been published since 2007: *Knowledge Management Excellence* (Harrington and Voehl, 2007, Paton Press); *Creating the Organizational Masterplan* (Harrington and Voehl, 2009, CRC Press); and *Making the Case for Change* (Voehl, Harrington and Voehl, 2014, CRC Press).

programs?* According to the Project Management Institute's *Pulse of the Profession® In-Depth Report: Enabling Organizational Change through Strategic Initiatives* (PMI 2014), 48 percent of strategic initiatives are unsuccessful, and as a result, nearly 15 percent of every dollar spent is lost due to poor project performance.

CHANGE MANAGEMENT AND ORGANIZATION DESIGN PROJECTS

Staring out the window at the full moon, Harrington had an aha moment—whether an individual project is successful or fails, it has almost no impact on the change culture within the organization. The greatest impact on change culture is how the organization is managed, not how an individual project/program is managed. As Harrington sat there studying these individual approaches and change tools that should have prepared the individuals impacted by the project/program to accept the outputs in almost all the cases, he questioned if the body of knowledge and methodologies were there—understood and being used—and according to a 2014 McKinsey report, why such a high percentage of the projects are unsuccessful.†

When we compared the percentage of unsuccessful organizational development (OD) projects in the late 1970s to the ones reported in the 2014 study, there was not a statistically significant change in the results regardless of which of the five stems of OD practice were involved. The

---

* This book is the result of an extensive amount of research done analyzing technical papers and studying the methodologies used by 20 of the leading gurus on organization change management. The purpose of this new book is to look at the different methodologies to define similarities and to identify unique strengths in the individual methodologies that should be included in the total body of knowledge related to effective organizational change management techniques.

† According to recent research by McKinsey & Company, about 70% of all changes in all organizations fail. After almost two decades of intense change from corporate reorganizations, new software systems, and quality-improvement projects, the failure rate remains at 70%. As an executive, you know the cost when a major project fails. That's like throwing money away and wasting months of efforts. The creation of knowledge supports McKinsey's core mission of helping clients achieve distinctive, lasting, and substantial performance improvements. They publish their consultants' insights and those of external experts to help advance the practice of management and provide leaders with facts on which to base business and policy decisions.

change management approaches from an OD practice is covered in detail in *Organization Development and Change* by Cummings and Worley.*

The success of organizational change is far less dependent on major changes in the way we run OD projects and much more impacted based on the cultural changes that are occurring in the day-to-day operations. In many cases, an OD project would have a more positive impact on the organization's change culture if it failed than if it was implemented successfully. Culture has more impact on how the organization's change and how the impacted personnel are prepared to accept the output from the project.

It is estimated that the average employee is directly impacted by the output from a project no more than once every five years, and this impacts only a small percentage (estimated to be 10%) of his or her work activities. In addition, the OCM activities impact the affected personnel for only a short period of time while the project is being implemented. As a result, the impact that project management has on developing a culture where change is not just accepted, but also expected, is negligible. This means little or no long-term gain is made as a result of project activities related to organizational change. This results essentially in starting off at zero each time a project is initiated. The starting point may be even lower depending on how the culture within the organization has changed since the last time a project had been initiated. The change directly impacts the same people that are impacted with the new project plan.

With the high turnover in some industries, it means that very few people impacted by a project or program had ever been subjected to a project change cycle before in that organization. As a result, we conclude that the people truly responsible for driving the organizational change are not the members of the project management team but rather the organization's management team and the employees. The individuals who have the biggest impact on organizational change are the operational management team, not the project management team.

We can personally think of a number of very successful projects that resulted in the change culture becoming more negative. The following is

---

* See Cummings and Worley (2015). This fine OD book is intelligently designed to approach and delve into the field of OD smoothly and profoundly. Its first three chapters provide an excellent introduction to OD and how it is differentiated from overlapping organizational dynamics, primarily change management and organizational change. Of particular note is this text's strategic analysis of the OD interventions and the pragmatic models of their implementation. Although developing business organizations sounds theoretical in its conceptual or abstract sense, this text gives you reasonable and sensible tools that help convert the OD theory to a tangible reality.

the general gist of a conversation we overheard after a very successful Six Sigma program had been implemented:

Worker #1: Those black belts are a lot like seagulls—they fly in, dump all over you, and fly away leaving us to live with their droppings.

Worker #2: Yes, they don't understand what it is really like to work here. The flowcharts look impressive but a flowchart doesn't really tell you what it is like to do the job. Both Bob and Marguerite lost their jobs because they put in a continuous flow system. Both of them have families and now they're out of work.

Worker #1: I used to be able to go and get washed up just before the noon whistle blew and could play cards with Bob until the 1 o'clock whistle blew when we returned to work. Not anymore—I have to wash up on my lunch hour and be back at my station when the 1 o'clock whistle blows.

Worker #2: Yes, this used to be a fun and nice place to work but now I dread coming in every day. It's getting to be a sweatshop. I understand the Black Belt got a bonus for getting the line changed over in record time. All we got was the shaft. We can't let them do this to us on that new product that is coming down the line.

Both Workers: They can lead a horse to water, but they can't make us drink! We'll show them a thing or two. We operations people have to stick together.

End of conversation, but not end of story.

Here is another typical conversation in the change story:

Repair Man #1: With the new calibration control software package they installed, I am spending all my time feeding information into the computer. That isn't what I should be doing; I should be out working with the equipment and keeping it running.

Repair Man #2: Those fellows upstairs think they know more about my job than I do and that the computer can tell me what and when I should do something.

Machine Operator: Doesn't it help by letting you know when it's time to calibrate a piece of equipment or to service a machine?

Repair Man: The only use I see is that it lets the people in quality know when I didn't do something on time so they can write me up and then I have to explain it to my manager. I keep everything running in my area better without it.

Repair Man #2: When I walk around the equipment, I can hear if there is a bad bearing in the motor. I stop and grease it to keep it going even though it isn't the right time for maintenance. In the long run they'll be sorry that they installed that computer to check on me.

Machine Operator #2: Last week I heard the motor and the big punch press squealing but I was supposed to be maintaining other equipment so I followed what the computer said and waited. By the next week the motor gave out and the whole line was down for eight days. The company had to order a new $1200 motor.

All: This money didn't need to be spent if they had just let me do what we know how to do best.

The real change impact on the organization is not how well the project team prepared the impacted people to accept the change but rather how well the output from the change fits into the organization's culture and whether it is accepted or rejected. The project manager is given the assignment to help a group to implement a change and get it done on time, at or below estimated costs, and have it function to meet the requirements as defined by the management team. The manager's job is to help the workers move through the eight stages of the culture change management process, as shown in Figure 7.1.

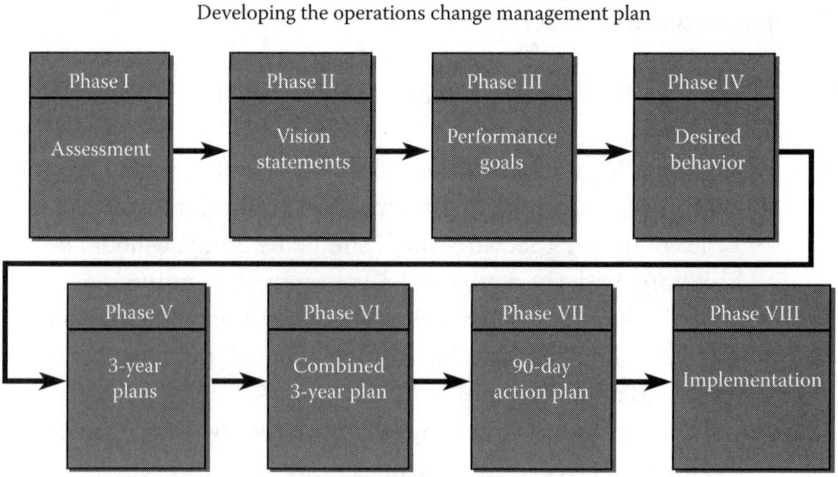

Developing the operations change management plan

FIGURE 7.1
Eight phases to developing a change management plan.

Over our life spans there have been huge changes in the attitudes, behaviors, desires, priorities, and interests of the general population. These changes have forced organizations to drastically change their corporate cultures as well as the way they operate in relation to employees, investors, suppliers, government, and customers. It's hard to say if the 1930s were the good old days or if 2014 was the best year. But we can decidedly say life was very different and has changed drastically in the past 80 years. Many of the things that are accepted as part of our daily life today were nonexistent 80 years ago. Television, computers, iPhones, iPads, fast-food restaurants, and the Internet have brought radical changes to the way we live. It is absolutely essential that both OCM (the way we manage the implementation of projects) and the day-to-day management of change be conducted successfully. If either of these two factors has a negative impact on the organization, the organization's ability to accept change (CCM) will react negatively to the stimuli. The managing of changes introduces foreign elements that result from managerial decisions, business fluctuations, external factors, and the activities that management decides need to be implemented. It reflects changes in behavior, beliefs, benefits, and customers, as shown in Figure 7.2. It includes the makeup of the operational objectives of the output from any project. It also includes the change impact that the various organizational documents have on changing the way the organization functions (e.g., strategic plans, goals and objectives, value statements, and business plans).*

ORGANIZATION DEVELOPMENT AND THE LIFESTYLE EVOLUTION

The purpose of this section is to relate the model of how managers construe organizational development events as a change unfolds to lifestyle

---

* See Weinberg (2011). The premise of the author is that change is inherently dangerous. Moreover, change becomes even more dangerous when we don't know what we're doing insofar as the culture aspects are concerned. Attempts to change organizations commonly fail because of inadequate understanding of change dynamics—the same reason the organizations got into crisis in the first place. Weinberg concludes his series of four stand-alone volumes with this pragmatic, comprehensive testament on the fundamentals of management of culture change. From systems thinking, to project management, to technology transfer, to the interaction of culture and process, this book analyzes change from a broad range of perspectives spanning the spectrum of sources of organizational change. Such breadth of awareness provided by Weinberg is essential for successful management of system evolution and transformation.

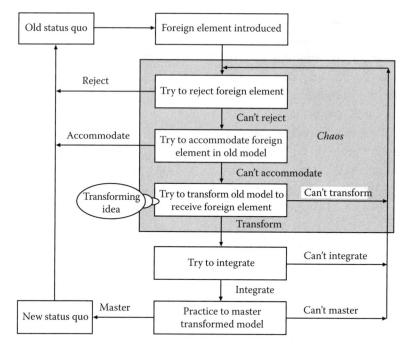

FIGURE 7.2

Weinberg's Model for change management. In his book, *Anticipating Change*, Gerald Weinberg builds maps onto the critical points that can undermine or support the culture change process. He shows that if change is not planned well enough or if the people who receive the change consciously or unconsciously decide to resist it, then the change effort will falter or fizzle.

changes and offer some basic definitions of Organization Development* (see Figure 7.3).

Our CCM model, built from in-depth interviews with many managers, suggests that interpretations of key events unfold in four stages—anticipation, confirmation, culmination, and assessment—that are linked to the process of managing change. The assessments of reality and interpretive tasks at each stage, as well as the triggers that impel managers to move from one stage to another, are important elements of culture change.

Lifestyles of the 1930s were drastically different than those of today. In the 1930s women were expected to stay home, cook, clean, look after the children, and make sure the house was in tip-top shape. They couldn't really

---

* See Cummings and Worley (2015). The 10th edition blends rigor and relevance in a comprehensive and clear presentation. The authors work from a strong theoretical foundation to describe, in very practical terms, how behavioral science knowledge can be used to develop organizational strategies, structures, systems, and processes.

Definitions of Organization Development

Organization development is a planned process of change in an organization's culture through the utilization of behavioral science technology, research, and theory. (Warner Burke)[2]

Organization development refers to a long-range effort to improve an organization's problem-solving capabilities and its ability to cope with changes in its external environment with the help of external or internal behavioral-scientist consultants, or the agents, as they are sometimes called. (Wendell French)[3]

Organization development is an effort (1) planned, (2) organization-wide, and (3) managed from the top, to (4) increase organization effectiveness and health through (5) planned interventions in the organization's "processes," using behavioral science knowledge. (Richard Beckhardo)[4]

Organization development is a system-wide process of data collection, diagnosis, action planning, intervention, and evaluation aimed at (1) enhancing congruence among organizational structure, process, strategy, people, and culture; and (2) developing the organization's self-renewing capacity. It occurs through the collaboration of organizational members working with a change agent using behavioral science theory, research, and technology. (Michael Beer)[5]

Based on (1) a set of values, largely humanistic; (2) application of the behavioral sciences; and (3) open-systems theory, organization development is a system-wide process of planned change aimed toward improving overall organization dimensions as external environment, mission, strategy, leadership, culture, structure, information and reward systems, and work policies and procedures. (Warner Burke and David Bradford)[6]

FIGURE 7.3
Definitions of Organization Development.

express their opinions but in a few countries they were allowed to vote. For men it was bowler hats and classy suits while women wore long dresses that covered 80 percent of their body, while children played hopscotch, stickball, hide-and-seek, king on the hill; football as we know it was just beginning, and Monopoly and Scrabble were new exciting ways to be entertained.

Dinner time was a family gathering. Father carved the meat and everyone sat around the table discussing what they had done during the day. Today you're lucky to have everyone at the table at Thanksgiving. If we measured unemployment the same as we did in the 1930s, unemployment is worse today than it was any time during the Great Depression. In the 1930s the family unit was a strong part of daily life. Today family values are less important than the individual's desires. In the 1930s there was a strong sense of loyalty to the company and lifetime employment with a single organization was more the rule than the exception. Today this is almost nonexistent. Few employees would even consider spending 45 years with one company. People who worked hard were held in high esteem in the 1930s. Children were expected to find work and contribute to the family. Children 12 years of age could get work permits to work in factories. No longer is that the case. The family home was the center of life activities; today the family home is more like a hotel where people come to sleep. In the 1930s people were very concerned about staying out of debt and being personally accountable for themselves and their families. In 2014 personal debts per citizen was $52,307, savings per family was only $8077, and liability per taxpayer was $989,010. The median income in 2000 was $28,822 and during the next 14 years it dropped to $28,606. The U.S. workforce in 2000 was 154,410,867; in 2014, it dropped to 147,414,640. The total number of people within the United States receiving government benefits in 2014 was 158,432,234 more than the total workforce.

During the 1930s anyone who completed eighth grade was considered educated, an individual with a high school degree was very well educated, and very few people got college degrees. There was no such thing as fast food, and eating out was a rare exception for most people. Also in the 1930s, it was not unusual for a family to have little or nothing to eat. The church played a much more important role in an individual's and family's life. People would pressure management to be the one that works overtime; today it's hard to get anyone to work overtime without griping about it. Organizations were more willing to invest in educating employees as it served as a long-term investment; with high turnover rates today, that is no longer the case. And last but not least, friends and family are less important today than personal self-interest.

Today everyone is expected to go to college and prepare themselves for a knowledge-type job rather than a physical job. A BS degree in engineering was a sought-after accomplishment. Today a four-year degree takes an average of 5 to 6 years to get and it is not considered a major accomplishment. You need a master's degree or an MBA; the sought-after professions are lawyers or doctors. Today many children are graduating from college with huge debt hanging over their heads covering many years of education. Television, radio, and the Internet have made more information available in a matter of a few hours than an individual could previously acquire in a lifetime.

THE CULTURAL WEB AND CHANGE AT IBM*

The cultural web is a model initially created by Johnson and Scholtes (2002) and first published in *Exploring Corporate Strategy* (6th Edition),

---

* Author Jim Harrington can personally speak to the cultural change with IBM, one of the great companies within the United States, where he and his father worked for a span of over 50 years or so until the late 1970s.

Pearson, New York. It was applied to organizational culture change in the book *The High-Performance Organization* (Holbeche 2011a). Surveys suggest that trust is perhaps the key component of a high performing organization in that if colleagues trust each other and management, then they are more willing to share information and go the "extra mile" without fear that their goodwill and achievements will be taken advantage of by others around them. However, the surveys seem to indicate that trust is also in decline.* In fact, the way that change is handled today does much to destroy or solidify trust.

In another study by the research firm ISR,[†] they identified a number of key factors that differentiate high-performance organizations from others, including an obsession with quality and innovation. Employees are much more likely to feel that achieving high quality is a priority in their day-to-day work. They also believe that their company outperforms the competition in the rapid development of new products and services and in responding quickly to market changes and adopting technological innovations.

In the cultural web model, the *paradigm* at the heart of Figure 7.4 is a set of core beliefs that result from multiple conversations which maintain the unity of the culture. It suggests that when organizations remain at a firmly embedded state within their own paradigm, they may cease to adapt to the changes in the environment that the new culture demands. Accordingly, a second-order change will be required; otherwise, deteriorating performance will force change due to external pressure. The implications are that if culture change efforts are focused on the outer elements of the web, a ton of effort usually produces limited success.[‡]

In the original 2002 book, Johnson suggests that myths, rituals, and other symbolic aspects of organization do not merely endow and

---

* See Holbeche (2011a); see the Gallup Surveys 2002 through 2014. According to Holbeche (who quotes the Gallup results), these surveys indicate that trust in many key institutions, in large national organizations, and in capitalism in general has fallen to critical proportions, with citizens having as much trust in the media as they do in their national governments.
† International Survey Research LLC operates as an employee research and consulting company. The company engages in designing and implementing employee management and customer surveys. Its solutions include organizational effectiveness, human capital management, employee surveys, benchmarking, advanced analysis, and organizational ethics. The company serves national and multinational companies, not-for-profit organizations, and the public sector. See https://www.linkedin.com/company/international-survey-research.
‡ Ibid.

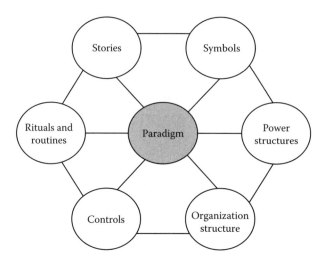

FIGURE 7.4
The cultural web, which is a set of seven core beliefs that result from multiple conversations that maintain the unity of the culture, with the paradigm at the center.

encapsulate meaning on a transitory basis—they are enduring and can be resistant to change.*

The IBM Culture 80 Years Ago

In the 1930s, IBM was an extremely family-focused organization. These observations were made by one of our authors who along with his relatives lived in the IBM environment. The IBM paradigm was as follows:

- Hiring preference was for a Methodist white American with a Western European background/heritage who had a relative already working for the company.
- Marriage between employees was encouraged but as soon as the woman got married she was forced to retire. During the 1940s this was relaxed so that a married woman could work until she got pregnant but then she was required to retire.
- A country club was provided for their employees, and employees' children were encouraged to participate in activities there, which included swimming, golf, bowling, billiards, dancing, and a pistol range.

---

* In effect, says Johnson, they are mechanisms that help preserve the assumptions and beliefs within which the strategy is rooted. Trice and Beyer (1984) view cultures as made up of two components: the network of meaning contained in ideologies, norms, values, and the culture's forms, and practices through which the meanings are affirmed and communicated to the organization's employees.

- Every employee was expected to be actively involved in taking classes at night to better himself or herself. They had special evening education programs for IBM employees, and IBM paid for the cost of outside education whether it was related to work or not.
- The management team worked with every employee to develop career plans for them, since IBM expected their male employees to be with them until they retired at age 65. The open-door policy was practiced all the way up to Thomas Watson Senior, and any employee could request an interview at any level of management to resolve a work situation they were facing. They had apprenticeship programs where they invested 4 years of training before they put an individual to work in regular company job.
- Dress codes were strictly enforced and white shirt, tie, and wing-tip shoes were the expected dress for the men. Work hours were strictly adhered to and people were expected to start work exactly on time.
- Managers were expected to be working before the first employee arrived and stay until the last employee had left the department.
- Any type of alcohol or beer was strictly forbidden from any type of business activity.
- All family activities were centered on the IBM activities and culture.
- The objective of a father would be for his offspring to develop to the point that he or she could get a job at IBM.* It was definitely a status symbol in being an IBMer; it was a sign of stability, reliability, dependability, and honesty that was respected in the community.

Management decisions, not projects, transformed the 1930s culture into what it is today. Some decisions brought about major changes and many others were about little things that had really mattered to employees.

- A big cultural change was the decision to eliminate lifetime employment.
- Typical little things that IBM changed over the years included doing away with giving presents at the children's Christmas party, cutting the 25-year club annual dance to once every two years, and changing the annual IBM picnic annually to every two years. These seem like

---

* Harrington reports that he personally turned down a number of job opportunities at twice his current salary because IBM had invested so much in him. He felt he owed them his loyalty and believed that they were treating him fairly and honestly.

small things on the surface but it is these little changes that management makes on a day-to-day basis that drives the culture of the organization.

As a result IBM has slowly slipped from number one on the Fortune 500 list to 23 in 2015. Their leading edge and innovation has all but disappeared. When we talk about technology leaders today, we cite Google and Apple, not IBM. IBM is no longer the market leader but more of a follower just keeping up with today's trends and needs. We're not saying IBM is a bad place to work—IBM still is a good company—but it is no longer great or the preferred place to work.

Culture Change Management as the Floodgate

The impact made by traditional project-related change management activities is a lot like throwing a pebble into Lake Mead on the Colorado River. It makes a quick splash and a few ripples but does not impact the flow, the depth, or the landmass that the lake covers. If you want to change the landmass covered by Lake Mead, you are going to have to throw in a lot of pebbles before you are going to get any results. Certainly a much better approach is through the control of the floodgates in the Hoover dam. The floodgate in change management is CCM, which helps to mitigate the resistance factors to change.*

We will admit that adjusting the CCM system within any organization is a complex but necessary endeavor. For example, the following needs to be considered:

- Change should be embraced as the all–employees' culture and not only the top management's vision or desire.
- Change should be considered in terms of corporate culture and business needs simultaneously.

---

* Organizations need to change to adapt to external or internal developments, but realizing effective change is very problematic. According to Kanter, Stein, and Jick (1992), change is so difficult that it is a miracle if it occurs successfully. One major barrier for change is resistance of people in organizations according to Bennebroek Gravenhorst, Werkman, and Boonstra (2003) and Heller, Pusic, Strauss, and Wilpert (2000). Resistance is commonly considered to be a standard or even a natural reaction to organizational change. It is often described as an almost inevitable psychological and organizational response that seems to apply to any kind of change, ranging from rather modest and conservative improvements to far-reaching change and organization transformation. Change and resistance go hand in hand, as change implies resistance, and resistance means that change is actually taking place.

- A benchmarking study of the best practices of the participating parties (banks) might be required to achieve the desired change results.
- The core part of any CCM effort is to have a management transformation strategy.
- People will not change unless—and until—they are psychologically ready to withdraw from their current daily habits.
- In any change process people are not being asked to simply learn new ideas; they are asked to break away from their comfortable old habits and align themselves with the new process.

As much as we hate to admit this to our CEO clients, CCM is not a quick-fix program. Leaders looking for that silver bullet are not going to be happy with CCM. It's a thought pattern that must be considered every time an individual makes a decision that impacts other people, and is often reflected in the leadership-manager paradox (see Figure 7.5).

As much as we'd like to think that management dictates and controls the culture within an organization, that is not entirely true. The interface between employees also has an impact on the organization's culture. Many times we've seen key competent people leave organizations not because they're dissatisfied with the organization or the job that they been assigned to but because they feel uncomfortable with the people they work with. Putting that aside, the actions and decisions made by management truly are the single biggest factor that impacts an organization's culture.

- To be able to build a close relationship with one's staff, and to keep a suitable distance.
- To be able to lead, and to hold oneself in the background.
- To trust one's staff, and to keep an eye on what is happening.
- To be tolerant, and to know how you want things to function.
- To keep the goals of one's department in mind, and at the same time to be loyal to the whole firm.
- To do a good job of planning your own time, and to be flexible with your schedule.
- To freely express your view, and to be diplomatic.
- To be a visionary, and to keep one's feet on the ground.
- To try to win consensus, and to be able to cut through.
- To be dynamic, and to be reflective.
- To be sure of yourself, and to be humble.

FIGURE 7.5
The 11 paradoxes of leadership that hang on the wall of every Lego manager.

The real question is: What is the culture within an organization? If the organization's culture really is the single factor that has the biggest impact on how change is embraced within the organization, we have to truly understand what is meant by culture. It is often said that culture is a lot like an iceberg floating in the sea. It is majestic, cold, and beautiful all at the same time. It provides a solid but slippery platform for humans and animals to stand on. The iceberg will quickly disappear if it gets into a current that takes it to a warmer (negative) environment. But when viewed from a boat, how much of the iceberg do you really see?

We all know the answer—only a small portion of an iceberg is visible from the surface of the water. Ninety percent of its mass falls below the water. The same is true of the culture within an organization. Read all you want about the organization—what it does, its values, its goals, its mission, its procedures, and even its strategic plan—and you still don't know what the organization's real culture is.

You have to put on a very good wet suit, swim fins, and diving gear and get into the water and swim down close before you can really see the true mass of the iceberg. The same is true of an organization's culture. No one can see and/or understand an organization's true culture until they get past the superficial publicity and documentation and find their way down to the heart of the organization where the employees work and exist. We don't mean to suggest that things like the organization's vision, values, and strategic plan do not help direct the organization's culture and help lower resistance, but it's only a part of the story.*

It is not what people write about, not what people say, and very often not even what people do; it is what they believe in, what they really value, how they behave, their personal ethics, the standards they set, the judgments they make, what they are expecting, the assumptions they make, and the level of trust the employees have in each other and the management team

---

* Resistance to change often shows itself in different ways. As Coch and French (1948) mention in their studies, grievances, turnover, low efficiency, restriction of output, and aggression against management are common manifestations. Watson (1969) discusses how expressions of resistance alter during a change process. In the early stage, almost everyone openly criticizes the change. In the second stage, the innovators and opponents become identifiable. The third stage is marked by confrontation and conflict. In the fourth stage, innovators become powerful and opponents retreat to latent resistance. In the fifth stage, opponents often become alienated from the organization. Responses to change from individuals and groups can vary from passive resistance to aggressive attempts to undermine.

(immediate manager and upper management) that dictates the culture of the organization.

Even some of the external factors like government regulations, organizational reputation, work locations, work environment, and even the type of output the organization is producing have an impact on the organization's culture. Harrington worked in South Korea, moving Reebok, a major shoe manufacturer, out of South Korea to China. The workers in the shoe factory would gladly have left the organization to go to work in an electronics manufacturing organization even at lower pay because the prestige related to working in the electronic field was much greater. As hard as it is to define it and get your arms around it, the culture of the organization is a single driving factor that either positively or negatively impacts the organization's ability to change and keep pace with the fast-growing external environment.*

WHY FOCUS ON CCM?

We've been in hundreds of companies helping them implement programs like Lean and Six Sigma, establishing a project management office, restructuring the management system, installing a quality management system, upgrading to meet ISO 9000 standards, installing knowledge management systems, developing strategic plans, and so forth. It never ceases to amaze us the difference in resistance we encounter as we move from one company to another. It doesn't matter what the change initiative is directed at. It can be as major as implementing a total organization's operating plan while restructuring the management system or as little as serving as a Black Belt leading a Six Sigma team to solve a manufacturing problem. The degree of resistance and/or acceptance is pretty constant within each organization but differs greatly from organization to organization.

---

* Companies need a particular mind-set for managing change, one that emphasizes process over specific content, one that recognizes organization change as a unit-by-unit learning process rather than a series of programs, and one that acknowledges the payoffs that result from persistence over a long period of time as opposed to quick fixes. This mind-set is difficult to maintain in an environment that presses for quarterly earnings, but the authors believe it is the only approach that will bring about a successful renewal and change of culture.

PSYCHODYNAMIC APPROACH TO CHANGE*

The idea that humans go through a certain type of psychological process during change first became evident due to the research published by Elizabeth Kubler-Ross in 1969.[†] The word "psychodynamic" is based upon the idea that an individual, whenever he or she is facing change in the external world, experiences a variety of internal psychological states. Our investigation into the behavioral and cognitive approaches to change management suggests that research into the psychodynamic approach began not in the arena of organizations, but with Kubler-Ross in the area of terminally ill patients. Later research showed that individuals going through changes in their organizations can have a very similar experience, although perhaps less dramatic and traumatic (see Figure 7.6).

The impact on the organization is based less on how well the change is implemented than on the impact that the implemented change has on the organization. Our analysis of where the unsuccessful projects fail shows that over 75 percent fail prior to the implementation of the change. Our present organizational change strategies/methodologies are all based on maximizing the difficulties in getting the affected employees to accept/support the proposed changes when it should be directed at selecting change initiatives that have the maximum impact on the organization's overall performance.

This doesn't mean that we should drop the emphasis on OCM, but only emphasizes that there are two parts to day-to-day management of change and that OCM is the less important of the two. CCM relates to managing the impact of change on the total organization and it is made up of two parts:

- Organizational change management (OCM): 10% to 20% of the total. This is the needed change that is brought about to have the impacted personnel accept the change. This type of change management is normally included in the project management plan.
- Day-to-day change: 80% to 90% of the total.

---

* The psychodynamic approach includes all the theories in psychology that see human functioning based on the interaction of drives and forces within the person, particularly unconscious, and between the different structures of the personality.

† Elizabeth Kubler-Ross published her seminal work *On Death and Dying* in 1969, describing her work with terminally ill patients and the various psychological stages that they go through in coming to terms with their condition. This research has profound implications and became the basis for people experiencing other types of profound change. The stages are denial, anger, bargaining, depression, and finally acceptance.

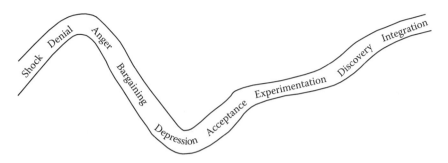

FIGURE 7.6
The Kubler-Ross application of the psychodynamic approach.

CCM MODEL

So far in this book and in most other literature related to change management, the focus has been on organizational project-related change. But the really successful organizations have been able to harmonize their OCM project-related change activities to complement and strengthen their day-to-day management of change. We will call this close harmony among the three parts of the change concept—projects, process, and daily management—culture change management. CCM is taking place today in your organization. You may not realize it. You may not recognize it. And probably you are not managing it, but it is taking place (both positively and negatively) in the day-to-day activities within your organization and at every level in the organization. It means driving a change in the culture within your organization.

There are six elements for driving a change culture associated with our CCM Model, as shown in Figure 7.7.

1. Understand the five principles for conditions involving transformational change
2. Mobilize commitment to change through a joint diagnosis of business problems
3. Develop a shared vision of how to organize and manage for competitiveness, and a plan for dealing with resistance to change
4. Implement a process for fostering consensus on the *desired future state* and the competence and cohesion to move it along

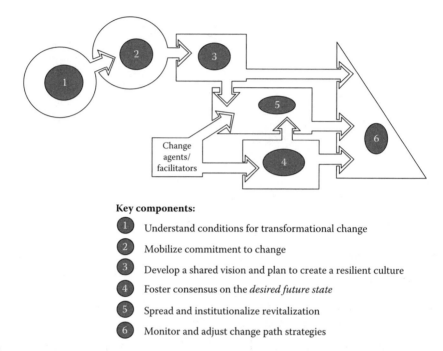

Key components:

1. Understand conditions for transformational change
2. Mobilize commitment to change
3. Develop a shared vision and plan to create a resilient culture
4. Foster consensus on the *desired future state*
5. Spread and institutionalize revitalization
6. Monitor and adjust change path strategies

FIGURE 7.7
The Harrington-Voehl culture change management model.

5. Spread and institutionalize revitalization through formal policies, systems, and structures with a culture of assessment
6. Monitor and adjust strategies in response to problems in the various change paths

Figure 7.7* depicts the six elements of the model according to the usual sequence in the implementation process. We contend that in many cases most efforts in the management of change do not achieve a positive impact on the organization's culture. Our research indicates that most of an organization's culture is spiraling downward. Based on our personal observations as consultants who have looked at many organizations and have been in high executive positions within organizations, we can easily see the negative trends that have developed within the culture for most organizations. These negative trends in culture are not solely driven by business decisions and, in fact, they are often more driven by outside factors

---

* Figure 7.7 was first created by Frank Voehl and Bill Hayes for a handbook and software program about Business Process Management (BPM) that included a component on change management, and has been adapted by Voehl for use in this CCM book.

that the organization has no control over. Accordingly, it is imperative that leaders understand the conditions for transformational change in terms of the five main principles.*

CCM Element One: Conditions for Transformational Change

To start with, employees will alter their mind-sets only if they see the point of the change and agree with it—at least enough to give it a try. There are five or more principles dealing with the surrounding structures (reward and recognition systems, for example) that must be in tune with the new behavior. Often overlooked is the fact that employees must have the skills to do what is required by the changes. Finally, they must see people they respect modeling it actively. Although each of these conditions is realized independently, together they add up to a way of changing the behavior of people by changing attitudes about what can and should happen at the daily work level. The implication of these findings for an organization is that if its people believe in its overall purpose, they will be happy to change their individual behavior to serve that purpose—indeed, they will suffer from cognitive dissonance if they don't.†

But to feel comfortable about change and to carry it out with enthusiasm, people must first understand their roles and their actions in the unfolding drama of the company's future, and—this is key—believe that it is worthwhile for them to play a part. In other words, it isn't enough to tell employees that they will have to do things differently. In addition, anyone facilitating a major culture change initiative must take the time to think through its change-story; that story is what makes it worth undertaking, and needs to be explained to the people involved in making change happen so that their contributions make sense to them as individuals. Many change programs make the error of exhorting employees to behave differently without teaching them the conditions required for transformational change to be effective (see Figure 7.8) and how to adapt general instructions to their individual situation.‡

---

* These five conditions are a blend the ideas of many experts and authors over the years, representing many types of industries. For example, in particular, we like the thinking of Jared Roy Endicott, whose five principles are Have a good reason, the Vision Thing, the Flywheel effect, Direct and Honest Communication, and Establish Trust.

† In 1957, the Stanford social psychologist Leon Festinger published his theory of cognitive dissonance, which is the distressing mental state that arises when people find that their beliefs are inconsistent with their actions. He observed in the subjects of his experimentation a deep-seated need to eliminate cognitive dissonance by changing either their actions or their beliefs.

‡ See the McKinsey Insights study report findings, which can be found at http://www.mckinsey.com/insights/organization/the_psychology_of_change_management.

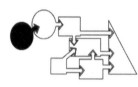

Element One: Conditions for Transformational Change

- Principle 1: *Survival Anxiety* or guilt must be greater than *Learning Anxiety*.
- Principle #2: In order to succeed, Learning Anxiety must be reduced, rather than increasing Survival Anxiety.
- Principle #3: Be concrete in the description of the change goal in respect to the problem or opportunity – not as culture change.
- Principle #4: The new culture elements can only be learned if the new behavior leads to success and worker and management satisfaction.
- Principle #5: Culture Change is always transformative in that it requires a period of learning, which is psychologically painful but rewarding.

Descriptions

- Involves selecting and deploying the right people and projects
- Focuses on issues and opportunities with a high learning impact on operations
- Creates concrete change/ learning goals

- Senior leaders monitor and manage performance
- Participants use measures, indicators, and organizational knowledge to build their culture strategies

- Organize and develop a culture change measurement system that defines quality
- Feedback and adjustment
- Put the engine in place that drives necessary change and facilitates robust feedback and adjustment

Projects Deployment	*Execution Excellence*	*Culture Change Learning*
➤ Visionary Innovation ➤ Systems Perspective ➤ Focus on the Future	✓ Agility in problem solving ✓ Customer-driven Excellence ✓ Valuing employees and partners ✓ Results Focus and Creating Value	❏ Empowering for Innovation ❏ Organizational and Personal Learning ❏ Worker self-control/feedback

FIGURE 7.8

The conditions for transformational change, showing the five principles of CCM, along with some basic descriptions of the outcomes for project deployment, execution excellence, and culture change learning.

CCM Element Two: Mobilize a Commitment to Change

The starting point of any effective change effort is a clearly defined business problem (see Figure 7.9). By helping people develop a shared diagnosis of what is wrong in an organization and what can and must be improved, a general manager mobilizes the initial commitment that is necessary to begin the change process and then helps people integrate the new information. During the 1980s, David Kolb, a specialist in adult learning, developed his four-phase adult-learning cycle. Kolb showed that adults can't learn merely by listening to instructions; they must also absorb the new information, use it experimentally, and integrate it with their existing knowledge.* In practice, this means that you can't teach everything there is to know about

---

* Experiential learning articles and critiques of David Kolb's theory, Active Reviewing Guide. See details: http://reviewing.co.uk/research/experiential.learning.htm by Roger Greenaway.

Component #2: Mobilize a Commitment to Change

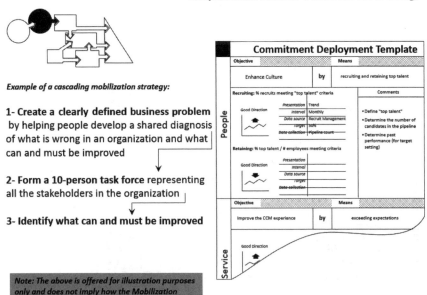

Example of a cascading mobilization strategy:

1- **Create a clearly defined business problem** by helping people develop a shared diagnosis of what is wrong in an organization and what can and must be improved

2- **Form a 10-person task force** representing all the stakeholders in the organization

3- **Identify what can and must be improved**

Note: The above is offered for illustration purposes only and does not imply how the Mobilization Strategy will actually operate.

FIGURE 7.9
Mobilizing a commitment to culture change.

a subject in one session. It is much better to break down the formal teaching into chunks, with time in between for the learners to reflect, experiment, and apply the new principles. Large-scale change happens only in steps. Furthermore, people assimilate information more thoroughly if they have a process to describe to others how they will apply what they have learned to their own circumstances. The reason, in part, is that human beings use different areas of the brain for learning and for teaching.*

CCM Element Three: Develop a Shared Vision of How to Organize and Manage for Competitiveness, and a Plan for Creating a Resilient Organization

Once a core group of people is committed to a particular analysis of the problem, the general manager can lead employees toward a task-aligned vision of the organization that defines new roles and responsibilities. These new arrangements will coordinate the flow of information and work

---

* As the organizational psychologist Chris Argyris showed and reported.

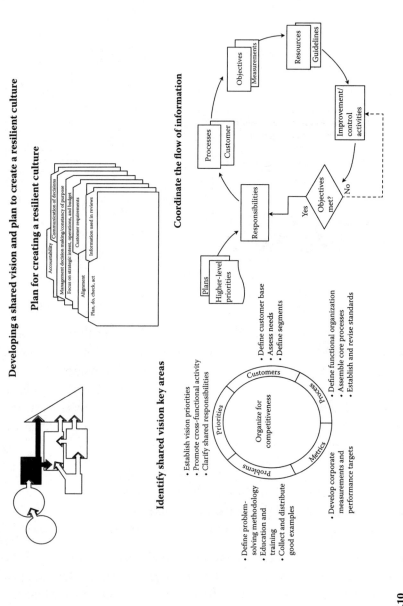

FIGURE 7.10

Developing a shared vision for managing for competitiveness.

across interdependent functions at all levels of the organization. But since they do not change formal structures and systems like titles or compensation, they encounter less resistance (see Figure 7.10).

CCM Element Four: Implement a Process for Fostering Consensus on the Desired Future State and the Competence and Cohesion to Move It Along

The process of simply letting employees help develop a new vision is not enough to overcome resistance to change or to foster the skills needed to make the new organization work. Not all employees and staff can help in the design, and consequently those who do participate often do not fully appreciate what culture change will require until the new organization is actually in place. This is when strong leadership from the managers is crucial. Commitment to change is always uneven—some managers are enthusiastic; others are neutral or even antagonistic.*

In any organization, people model their behavior on significant others: those they see in positions of influence. Within a single organization, people in different functions or levels choose different role models—a founding partner, perhaps, a trade union representative, or the highest-earning sales rep. So to build consensus and change behavior consistently throughout an organization, it isn't enough to ensure that people at the top have developed consensus and are in line with the new ways of working; role models at every level must walk the talk in order to achieve true consensus, as shown in Figure 7.11.†

---

* Change seems to have become one of the few stable factors in the contemporary organization. Almost 70 years ago, Coch and French (1948) stated that frequent changes in people's work was necessary to keep up with competitive conditions and technological development. According to Emery and Trist (1965), the complexity of the environment of organizations increases and its predictability decreases, which makes the study of organizational change more difficult. Kotter and Schlesinger (1979) observed that most organizations need to undertake moderate changes once a year, and major changes every four or five years. Also, change does not always have an external starting point; it can also originate from an internal source (1985). Inefficient organizational processes, problems with coordination, and lack of cooperation are examples of causes for change that lie within an organization.
† The process for building consensus outlined in Figure 8.8 is loosely based on John Kotter's framework. Over decades, Dr. Kotter observed the behavior and results of hundreds of organizations and thousands of leaders at all levels when they were trying to transform or execute their strategies. He identified and extracted the success factors and combined them into a methodology, the Eight-Step Process. He then founded a firm of experts, Kotter International, to implement the approach across a diverse range of organizations. See the website, http://www.kotterinternational.com/the-8-step-process-for-leading-change/.

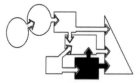

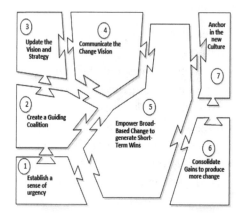

Fostering Consensus on the *Desired Future State*

1. **Establish a sense of urgency**

   Identify opportunities for success and create a fast deployment strategy

   Define the LSS program expectations and metrics

2. **Create a Steering Team/ Guiding Coalition**

   Define projects scope and infrastructure

   Select the right people for training

   Human Resources alignment

   Develop training curriculum

   Define tracking software

3. **Update the Vision and Strategy**

   Focus on alignment

   Commit to projects and chartering

4. **Communicate the Change Vision**

   Workshops for speedy deployment

   Communication plan

5. **Empower Broad-Based Change to generate Short-Term Wins**

   Objectives Deployment

   Client Tiers, Customer Needs, Customer Experience

   Customer Measurements

   Management Reviews

6. **Consolidate Gains to produce more change**

7. **Anchor in the new the Culture**

FIGURE 7.11

Fostering consensus on the desired future state, along with competence and cohesion to move it along.

CCM Element Five: Spread and Institutionalize Revitalization through Formal Policies, Systems, and Structures

There comes a point where senior leaders and managers have to consider how to institutionalize change so that the process continues even after they've moved on to other responsibilities; the new approach has become entrenched, the right people are in place, and the team organization is up and running. Enacting changes in structures and systems any earlier tends to backfire. The revitalization in the new culture needs to be institutionalized through formal policies, systems and procedures, structures and the like. As previously discussed, roles and responsibilities must be updated to reflect the new culture's performance demands, and the performance management system must be strengthened to ensure that the development needs of the organization's people are met. In addition, the

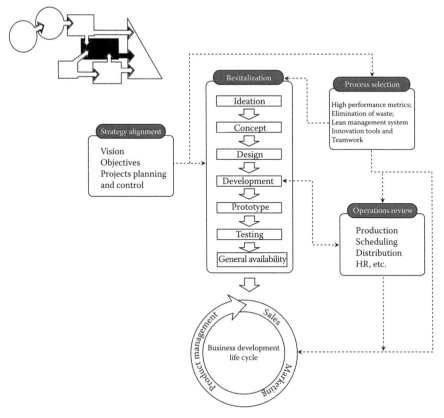

FIGURE 7.12
Spread and institutionalize revitalization through formal policies, systems, and structures.

values, behaviors, and expectations of the new workplace should be clearly defined* (see Figure 7.12).

CCM Element Six: Monitor and Adjust Strategies in Response to Problems

The purpose of change is to create an asset that did not exist before—a learning organization capable of adapting to a changing competitive environment. The organization has to know how to continually monitor its behavior; in effect, to learn how to learn, in order to learn how to become

---

* See Holbeche (2011b). The author explains that there is a need to reinforce any embryonic shifts through closely matched structural changes and then strengthening such changes "through the public use of the organization's reward systems." Finding and using role models who can display key aspects of the new culture through their own behavior helps continue the reinforcement of culture change. As well, "revamping employee communication mechanisms carries the message deep into the organization."

a high-performance organization. Some might say that this is management's responsibility, but monitoring the change process as the organization moves toward high-performance needs to be shared, just as analyzing the organization's key business problem does.

High-performance organizations* can be described as places where the culture

- Is adaptable, flexible, and change-ready
- Has a culture of assessment that is supportive of innovation, knowledge sharing, and knowledge creation
- Is where people work effectively across boundaries and functional departments
- Is values-based
- Is interested in stimulating employees to ever-higher levels of performance
- Is a great place to work

SUMMARY

It is neither easy nor straightforward to improve an organization's performance through a comprehensive program to change the culture and behavior of employees by changing their mind-sets. No organization should try to do so without first exhausting less disruptive alternatives for attaining the business outcome it desires.

Sometimes tactical moves will be enough, as we have seen, and sometimes new practices can be introduced without completely rethinking the corporate culture. But if the only way for a company to reach a higher plane of performance excellence is to alter the way its people think and act, it will need to create the conditions for achieving sustained change using the details of the CCM model that we have outlined in this chapter.

---

* See Holbeche (2011a,b).

Section III

Applying

The ability to use learned material in new and concrete situations. Applying rules, methods, concepts, principles, laws, and theories. Learning outcomes in this area require a higher level of understanding than those under comprehension. Learning objectives at this level can be to apply Change Management concepts and principles to new situations, apply laws and theories of change dynamics to practical situations, solve mathematical problems, construct graphs and charts, demonstrate the correct usage of a change method or procedure.

Collaborative Learning is quite similar to cooperative learning in that the learners work together in small teams to increase their chance of deeper learning. However, it is a more radical departure from cooperative learning in that there is not necessarily a known answer. For example, trying to determine the answer to "how effective is on-line learning?" would be collaborative learning as there are a wide ranges of possibilities to this question, depending upon the learners' perspectives.

Because the collaboration sometimes results from less purposeful and focused activities, some of the learning will be unintentional or perhaps even considered serendipitous.

Applying: Use a concept in a new situation or unprompted use of an abstraction. Applies what was learned in the classroom into novel situations in the work place.

Examples: Use a manual to calculate an employee's vacation time. Apply laws of statistics to evaluate the reliability of a written test.

Key Words: applies, changes, computes, constructs, demonstrates, discovers, manipulates, modifies, operates, predicts, prepares, produces, relates, shows, solves, uses

Technologies: collaborative learning, create a process, blog, practice

This section contains the following chapters:

- Chapter 8: Applying Methods for Deployment
- Chapter 9: Initiatives' Prioritization
- Chapter 10: The Iterative Development Approach

8

Applying Methods for Deployment

In a Nutshell: The methods outlined in this chapter are seen as instrumental for successful CCM initiatives and their deployment. There are 10 critical success factors (CSFs) that are covered in this chapter, along with research findings. Where these factors cannot be successfully deployed (or at least considered), there presents a risk to the change management implementation. Thus, it is important to identify these risks early and consider how they can be eliminated or mitigated. Many organizations successfully use CCM while still identifying that some of these factors will not be in place. These organizations recognize that CCM offers reduced risk yet still offers a much higher probability of success than adopting an approach that statistically often fails to deliver the expected outcomes. For example, if an approach is time-driven, choosing a traditional project approach is very risky since time is not the driving force of such an approach, whereas delivering the 100% solution is. By comparison, choosing CCM facilitated workshops over the project approach means that the entire project will be driven by time and on-time delivery, both of which are managed through the CCM practices of timeboxing and must, should, could, and would (MoSCoW). As part of our research, we interviewed change leaders at various companies over a 12-month period in order to focus on creating a culture for assessment, and the results are outlined in this chapter.

OVERVIEW AND BACKGROUND

The first question that we must answer is: Who needs an internal cultural change management capability? The answer: Any organization that would like to improve the way employees embrace change initiatives minimizing the cycle time to have the change accepted by the affected parties as business as usual. It is important that the senior management team and the change sponsors understand and accept the CCM philosophy. This includes the concept that to deliver the right thing at the right time—and handle change dynamically as well—may result in delivering less than 100 percent of the possible solution. The 10 critical success factors that affect the deployment method need to be agreed on by all parties in advance during the preparation stage, as outlined in our research models and approaches

> Two-thirds of all change initiatives fail to achieve their expected business benefits—a statistic that has stayed constant from the 1970s to the present. This failure rate represents billions of dollars in lost productivity, wasted resources, opportunity costs, and rework—not to mention the negative impact on organizational morale and workforce engagement.

One might conclude that everything we know about change management is wrong and that we need to go back to the drawing board. Instead, we believe that the discipline of change management is reasonably correct, but the capacity to implement the culture change aspects of CCM effectively hasn't been fully developed in organizations. Organizations that invest in an internal CCM capability set themselves apart from their peers. They are able to adapt to the constantly changing business world by virtue of the CCM in their operating methods. They adapt to the environment more easily, they adopt solutions more quickly, and realize change management ROI sooner. Ultimately, it gives those organizations a competitive advantage.

So, who needs an internal CCM capability? Organizations over a certain size that continuously manage a portfolio of multiple, overlapping change initiatives. These are often candidates for an internal CCM capability. These organizations typically display a number of symptoms: a proliferation of change management methodologies and tools, change expertise fragmented across functional areas, underresourced strategic initiatives, and multiple projects that lack a coordinated effort. These symptoms result in the ineffective application of change management and redundant activities, such as multiple communications and potentially confusing engagement initiatives with overlapping stakeholders.

CCM CAPABILITY DESIGN PROCESS

Most often the change management capability is within IT, human resources (HRs), or a project management organization. The right design will vary depending on the needs of your organization. We recommend using a contextual-driven design where a number of factors are considered in determining the optimal capability operating mode for deployment:

- Organization size—the number of people in your extended organization (including employees, contractors, customers, and external partners)
- Geographic distribution—the location of your people (centralized or spread across multiple places, national versus international, remote workers)
- Project pipeline—the number and scope of strategic initiatives undertaken by the organization in a given period of time
- Domain complexity—the inherent sophistication and complexity of your business operations (engineering, manufacturing, store operations, professional services)
- Structure—the current organization and management structure (flat versus hierarchical, collaborative versus command and control, matrix)
- Culture change capability building culture—the organization's values, visions, social norms, working language, systems (current ability to handle and absorb change), and how they are engaged at the workforce level, or in the Lean management parlance called Gemba.*
  The managers at HP would call it management by walking around.

---

* Going to Gemba is a Japanese term meaning "the real place." Japanese detectives call the crime scene Gemba, and Japanese TV reporters may refer to themselves as reporting from Gemba. In business, Gemba refers to the place where value is created; in manufacturing the Gemba is the factory floor. It can be any site such as a construction site, sales floor, or where the service provider interacts directly with the customer. The Gemba walk, much like management-by-walking-around (MBWA), is an activity that takes management to the frontlines to look for waste and opportunities to practice Gemba kaizen, or practical shop floor improvement. In quality management, Gemba means the manufacturing floor and the idea is that if a problem occurs, the engineers must go there to understand the full impact of the problem, gathering data from all sources. Unlike focus groups and surveys, Gemba visits are not scripted or bound by what one wants to ask. Glenn Mazur introduced this term into Quality Function Deployment (QFD), a quality system for new products where manufacturing has not begun, to mean the customer's place of business or lifestyle. The idea is that to be customer-driven, one must go to the customer's Gemba to understand his or her problems and opportunities, using all one's senses to gather and process data.

With a clear understanding of these factors, the design of the change capability can be tailored specifically for the organization's unique characteristics. A suggested change capability blueprint focuses on four building blocks: structure and governance, Methodology, Tools, and resources and competency.

STRUCTURE AND GOVERNANCE FOR DEPLOYMENT

Structure and governance is a critical foundational step that focuses on setting the overall operating model. It defines the structure, where it will reside within the organization, and who will be accountable for it. During this activity, we address the following questions: Does the capability serve the entire organization or does it focus on a particular business unit? In some cases, organizations may find it helpful to distribute change expertise across multiple business units. In other cases, a global and centralized change management center of excellence may be a better short-term approach. The step includes designing the roles and team structure required to support the capability. Ultimately, the overall effectiveness depends on choosing an operating model that is the best fit for the organization, as we have described in this book.*

CHANGE METHODOLOGY

Change methodology defines the change management process that will be used. This may be an off-the-shelf methodology such as Kotter's Eight Steps or Prosci's ADKAR model, or perhaps a homegrown approach like Ernst and Young, GE, or Florida Power and Light (FPL) did in the 1990s. Often, organizations opt for a hybrid or customized methodology since it can be highly tailored to fit the unique characteristics of the organization.

The methodology should address the intake process—how to assess change opportunities and resource them appropriately, as well as the

---

* As we have previously mentioned, the 12 or so Operating Models described in some detail in this book were chosen on the basis of three characteristics: (1) they were effective in deploying to more than 50 organizations, (2) they were recognized as being economical in having a measurable ROI, and (3) they are deemed as long-lasting, as in more than a year or two after deployment.

engagement model—how to work with project teams, executive sponsors, and partners in other functional areas (e.g., HR, OD/learning and development, and communications). Most importantly, this activity should define the set of service offerings that the change management capability has to offer its business customers.

CULTURE CHANGE TOOLS

Culture change focuses on developing a common set of change management tools that map to the culture change methodology phases. Key decisions here include: Which tools to deploy? How many tools should we have? What format should they be in? The tools should have a common look and feel reflective of the organization's brand. Ideally, they'll be stored in an online repository that can be easily accessed by team members. The tools can be homegrown or the organization can leverage an off-the-shelf toolkit, such as Emergent's Change Accelerator (http://www .ChangeAccelerator.com), which can be deployed across the enterprise and customized to the unique needs of the business. (See CSF #10 discussed in the section "CCM 10 critical success factors.")

The major tool that is used is that of defining the desired culture at the organization wants to mature to and then evaluating every decision based upon will it have a negative or positive impact upon the desired future state culture.

RESOURCES AND COMPETENCY

Resources and competency addresses who will fill the change practitioner roles that were designed previously. Do the requisite knowledge, skills, and abilities reside internally or do you need to hire externally? To what extent do you plan to supplement with external consultants?

This activity also involves educating your change practitioners, partners, and business customers about the change management operating model, services, and methodology. We recommend segmenting your organization's key stakeholders based on the level of change management competency required. For example, senior leaders and middle managers should be aware of the change methodology and their roles as sponsors and change agents, respectively. They should have the very best understanding of the desired future culture and be living to it as a role model. They need to understand and consider how their decisions and actions have either a positive or negative impact on the desired future culture. A major part of their performance evaluation should be based on how well their decisions reflect and have a positive impact on the future desired behavior patterns of the organization.

The organization's program and project managers should take a deeper dive into the methodology with an emphasis on partnering with the change management practitioners. The change management practitioners themselves should receive in-depth training focused on how to use the methodology, deploy the tools, and effectively partner with the projects teams and sponsors.

INTERVIEWS AND RESEARCH

We interviewed change leaders at large and midsized companies in order to better understand their internal change management capabilities and state of the culture. While our research does not represent a statistically precise and significant sample size, the various insights that the people provided gave us a valuable perspective on the evolving practice of CCM, as we are calling it in this book.

The organizations range from $500 million to multibillion dollar companies, with employee bases ranging from 1000 to 100,000, and almost all are based in the United States.* They span a variety of industries: health care, financial services, automotive, pharmaceuticals, transportation, and nonprofits and the government sector. The leaders for the most part held positions at one of three levels: vice president, director, and leader/department head/process owner.

The four types of initiative names were (1) change management, (2) transformational change, (3) enterprise-wide transformation, and (4) organizational development/design. Based on the research performed by the authors

---

* See the 2013 Whitepaper by Emergent Technologies titled *Large Company Internal Change Capabilities*, by Jesse Jacoby, Managing Principal. For details, see their website at: http://emergentconsultants.com/about-us/our-team.shtml.

along with that of the change management consultants identified in this chapter, the following 10 critical success factors emerged and are suggested for successful CCM deployment:

1. Establish measurable business goals
2. Align your business and IT operations
3. Get up-front executive management support
4. Let business goals drive CCM functionality
5. Minimize system customization by leveraging out-of-box functionality
6. Use only experienced and trained consultants
7. Actively involve end users in the solution design
8. Invest in training to empower end users and change culture
9. Use a phased-rollout iterative change deployment schedule
10. Measure, monitor, and track culture change and overall results

As part of our research efforts, we came across some interesting findings by Emergent. Their recent research* contained, among other things, the following:

1. Management must agree to delegate decision-making to the design and development team. If this is not possible, they would need to participate in the team themselves (i.e., in this circumstance, the design team member role may need to be taken by a more senior person from the business). Without empowerment, team progress will slow down while awaiting decisions being made elsewhere and to a different time frame. It's important to note that the design and development team is found in areas other than product engineering and R&D. For example, there are design teams that work on designing manufacturing processes and there are similar teams that work

---

* See the 2013 Whitepaper by Emergent Technologies titled *Large Company Internal Change Capabilities* by Jesse Jacoby, Managing Principal. He and his team partner with Fortune 500 and midmarket companies to deliver successful people and change strategies across a range of initiatives including technology deployments, cost-cutting, corporate restructuring, and process improvements. Jesse has led the development of three organizational tools: Change Accelerator, Transformation Ready, and New Leader Accelerator. For details, see their website at: http://emergentconsultants.com/about-us/our-team.shtml.

on developing sales and marketing strategies and campaigns. The design team refers to creation of a usable concept/product.

2. The design team should be empowered to make decisions without referral to higher authorities outside the team. Similarly, the solution developers in the team should also be empowered to make decisions. It is important that the concept of empowerment does not give all solution development team members complete freedom to do whatever they want, whenever they want. In reality, empowerment is within agreed on boundaries of decision-making. When a decision is outside the agreed boundaries, this would still need to be formally escalated. However, this is the exception and the majority of day-to-day decision-making should be within the remit of the solution development team.

3. The business commitment and agreed on participation is critical to successful CCM initiatives, since these roles provide the lowest-level detail and prioritization of the requirements during development time boxes. The level of business commitment for this project should be quantified and discussed in the early stages. Without this commitment, the success of the CCM approach may be limited.

4. Company size does not indicate maturity.

Research revolved around asking questions to gauge the maturity of each company's change management culture and their capability for change as identified by a few key areas, using a scale of 1 to 5, where 5 equals very mature, as follows: (1) demand for change management, (2) integration with a program or project life cycle, (3) internal versus external practitioner mix, (4) experience with change management methods, (5) how change management is valued in the culture, and (6) how change resources are deployed.*

In Figures 8.1 and 8.2, Emergent compares the maturity of the change capability to both revenue and number of employees.

Looking at Figure 8.2, it is apparent that aside from the two organizations with the highest revenue, there is little correlation between an organization's size and the maturity of its change management capability and culture. The one exception is a $21 billion financial services organization

---

* See the 2013 Whitepaper by Emergent Technologies titled *Large Company Internal Change Capabilities* by Jesse Jacoby, Managing Principal.

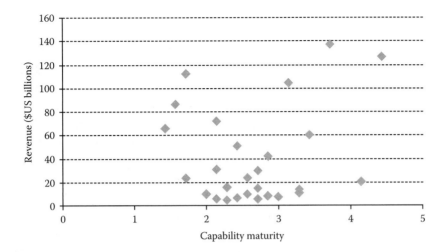

FIGURE 8.1
Change capability relative to revenue.

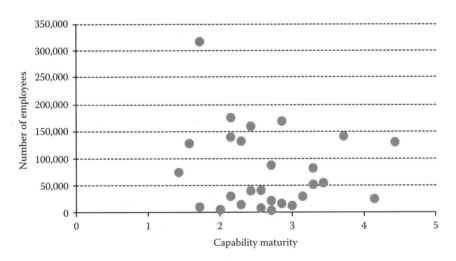

FIGURE 8.2
Change capability relative to number of employees.

with a 4.1 maturity rating. In some companies, their large size was viewed as a hindrance to developing a change management culture and capability. In some cases, the very complexities inherent in large organizations made it difficult for the change leaders and senior management to organize the many disparate teams performing change management along with building awareness for change service offerings and their potential.

CHANGE CAPABILITY BLUEPRINT

Many change capabilities are relatively new and so demonstrating tangible value was deemed a top priority for those change leaders who were trying to change the culture, and the change capability blueprint shown in Figure 8.3 has proven to be helpful. Key decisions here include: Which tools to deploy? How many tools should we have? What format should they be in? The tools should have a common look and feel reflective of the organization's brand.

See the following link for details: http://www.emergentconsultants.com /images/white-paper-change-management-capability-building.pdf. One of the key components shown in Figure 8.3 is that of a CCM toolkit that needs to be used (see Figure 8.4).

The Emergent Toolkit is organized around the following six life cycle phases, which are described in Figure 8.5:

- Plan the Change
- Create a Sense of Urgency
- Lead the Change
- Engage the People
- Align Systems and Structures
- Sustain the Change

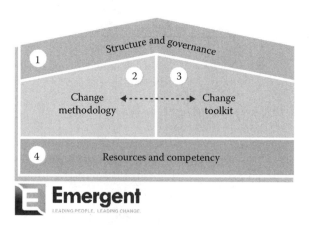

FIGURE 8.3
Emergent change capability blueprint.

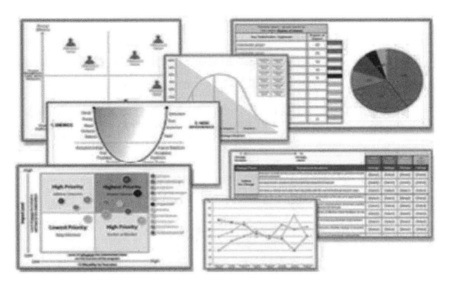

FIGURE 8.4
The Change Management Toolkit.

This Toolkit also has a Dashboard for reporting purposes, as shown in Figure 8.6. The ability to demonstrate progress of your change effort is an important aspect of effective project management. Change Accelerator's Dashboard provides a visual snapshot of each phase's status and progress. On a single page, you will have a comprehensive view of your change initiative's overall health. The Dashboard report is designed to be easily shared with your project team and sponsors, providing them with an update on your change management effort.

Emergent Culture Change Accelerator Tools*

- 4S Realignment
- 7S Analysis

---

* This list of some 60 change management tools and techniques offered by Emergent is by no means exhaustive, but is offered here as an example of the various types of tools available and the need to organize these tools into some type of phased development process. The tools include assessments, templates, models, and checklists in Microsoft PowerPoint, Excel, and Word formats. They can be downloaded, edited, and customized to fit your organization's unique needs. If you already have a corporate culture change management approach—whether you use Prosci's ADKAR, Kotter's Eight steps, or some other model—Change Accelerator will complement your existing approach. Your model will help you know what to do and the change accelerator tools will help you with how to do it. If you don't already have a preferred change model, then simply use the ACTTM model, which is included as part of Change Accelerator. Additionally, with our Change Accelerator–Enterprise License, you have the ability to customize the methodology to suit your organization's preferred approach.

Plan the Change

Plan the Change is about identifying the purpose, scope, and outcomes of the change initiative. The focus is on determining a process that will be used to plan and drive the change effort forward. It's also here that you will assemble a change team and establish the rules by which that team will operate.

Create a Sense of Urgency

Create a Sense of Urgency involves making it clear that the need to change is now and not tomorrow. The focus is on creating a compelling story and building a vision of the future that helps generate excitement and true commitment. It's here you seek to establish a broad desire for change strong enough to overwhelm the collective resistance.

Lead the Change

Lead the Change is about ensuring the business sponsors actively engage in the change effort on an on-going basis. The focus is on equipping team members to be change leaders and advocates who can influence others. It's here that you will align leaders with the what, why, and how of the change initiative.

Engage the People

Engage the People involves informing all stakeholders and engaging priority stakeholders in the initiative. The focus is on reaching diverse stakeholder audiences through multiple communication channels and events. It's here that you will ensure stakeholders have the resources and willingness to successfully change.

Align Systems and Structures

Align Systems and Structures entails establishing reward and incentive systems that promote desired behaviors and actions. The focus is on making sure that management practices are aligned to reinforce the changes. It's here that you will adjust the necessary organizational elements to deliver sustainable results.

Sustain the Change

Sustain the Change is about maintaining a cadence of communications and stakeholder engagement activities. The focus is on highlighting the benefits of the changes and attainment of milestones in highly visible ways. It's here that you will harness the lessons and best practices from this initiative so that they can be applied to future change efforts.

FIGURE 8.5
The Change Management Toolkit organized around the six life cycle phases.

- Action Plan
- Align Systems & Structures: Phase Diagnostic
- Behavior Targeting
- Case for Change
- Change Assessment
- Change Impact Mapping
- Change Leader Assessment
- Change Management Overview Presentation
- Communication Action Plan
- Communication Strategy
- Communications Campaign Planner
- Control-Influence Analysis

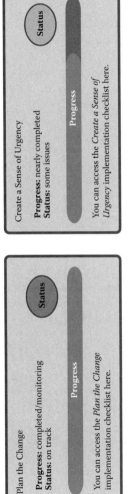
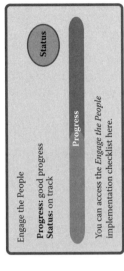
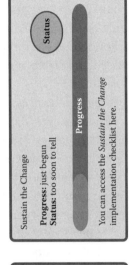

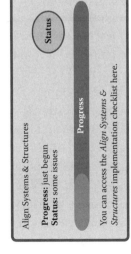

Create a Sense of Urgency

Progress: nearly completed
Status: some issues

You can access the *Create a Sense of Urgency* implementation checklist here.

Engage the People

Progress: good progress
Status: on track

You can access the *Engage the People* implementation checklist here.

Sustain the Change

Progress: just begun
Status: too soon to tell

You can access the *Sustain the Change* implementation checklist here.

Plan the Change

Progress: completed/monitoring
Status: on track

You can access the *Plan the Change* implementation checklist here.

Lead the Change

Progress: good progress
Status: major obstacles

You can access the *Lead the Change* implementation checklist here.

Align Systems & Structures

Progress: just begun
Status: some issues

You can access the *Align Systems & Structures* implementation checklist here.

FIGURE 8.6
The Change Management Dashboard.

- Create Urgency: Phase Diagnostic
- Current-Future State Analysis
- Elevator Pitch
- Engage the Stakeholders: Phase Diagnostic
- Event Planning Template
- Executive Sponsorship Assessment
- Focus Group Process
- Force Field Analysis
- In Frame/Out of Frame
- Influencing Strategies
- Is/Is Not
- Keeping Up the Pressure
- Key Stakeholders Map
- Lead the Change: Phase Diagnostic
- Manager Enrollment Plan
- Measurement Audit
- Measurement-Reward Cycle
- Need-Vulnerability Assessment
- Past Experience Profile
- Phases of Transition Model
- Plan the Change: Phase Diagnostic
- Progress Review
- Project-Change Leadership Matrix
- Responsible, Accountable, Consulted, and Informed (RACI)
- Resistance Profiler
- Reverse Imaging
- Scoping Questions
- Self-Assessment of Personal Change Agility
- Supplier-Inputs-Process-Outputs-Customers (SIPOC)
- Stakeholder Adoption Map
- Stakeholder Analysis
- Stakeholder Interview Process
- Stakeholder Position Map
- Stakeholder Prioritization Matrix
- Stakeholder Role Analysis
- Stakeholder-Specific Communication Action Plan
- Sustain the Change: Phase Diagnostic
- System-Structure Impact Analysis
- Team Capability Assessment

- Team Charter
- Team Effectiveness Assessment
- Team Operating Agreement
- Teamwork Model
- Threat-Opportunity Matrix
- Tracking Progress Checklist
- Visioning Process
- Wordstorming

CCM 10 CRITICAL SUCCESS FACTORS

CSF #1: Establish Measurable Culture Change Business Goals*

It is critically important to define the specific culture-change-related business benefits that you expect your CCM initiative to deliver. This might sound obvious, but many initiatives fail because this "obvious" success factor is not observed. Clarify precisely what you want your change management solution to achieve in terms of culture change at the grass-roots level. Are you trying to help employees change their culture to (a) increase average revenue per sale, (b) improve customer retention rates, (c) lower customer acquisition costs, (d) lower risk of failure for IT systems, (e) improve forecast accuracy, (f) improve customer response times, (g) improve sales close rates, or (I) other.

"You have to know what you're going for, and do it with your eyes wide open," says Francisco Dao, founder and president of The Killer Pitch, a firm based in Tarzana, California, that helps companies and entrepreneurs refine their message, and former business coach and columnist for Inc. "Look at yourself in the mirror and ask yourself what it's going to take in terms of culture change to achieve your goals."

---

* Goal-setting theory was developed and refined by Edwin A. Locke in the 1960s. His first article on goal-setting theory was "Toward a Theory of Task Motivation and Incentives," which was published in 1968. This article laid the foundation for goal-setting theory and established the positive relationship between clearly identified goals and performance.

CSF #2: Align Business Culture and Operations

While CCM is driven by technology, it's not about technology. The point of CCM is to improve your business culture and operations, along with your business processes; technology is only a means to achieving that end. Every successful culture change implementation begins by recognizing this fact and by creating operational culture-change structures that reinforce it. CCM provides a comprehensive system for improving processes, aligning business processes with business goals, and assuring that underlying IT applications, human competency, and organization designs support the culture change management performance objectives. As Figure 8.7 illustrates, in an effective culture change initiative, business goals that are focused on producing meaningful results drive functionality.

Figure 8.7 can be expressed by the equation $R = BG \times (\{Alignment + Measureable\ Objectives + System\ Design\}/3)$, where business goals that are focused on producing meaningful results drive functionality. Information technology (IT) and business managers are aligned in an effective change management initiative behind a well-defined set of measurable objectives, which in turn guide system design. Get the alignment in place before the initiative begins. Jim Burns, vice president for strategic technology at the National Consumer Services group of Chase Manhattan Bank—which has deployed a CRM-based change management initiative system to more than 600 branch offices—offers sound advice on this key point: "Work with business users up front to establish the prioritization criteria for determining which business requirements will guide configuration. This avoids wasting time addressing requirements that are not going to add value to the business."

Bring business culture and IT together, but make CCM the driver, not the project management. However, the more important issue in bringing business and IT together is getting organizations to embrace a process-centric culture change approach to management. To accomplish culture change in a process-centric organization, its leaders need to master and

FIGURE 8.7
Business goals drive functionality.

integrate all of the process elements within the organization and overcome the gap that lies between those interested in the culture change aspects of process change and those interested in the automation of processes. Senior managers need to invest the time in developing the business process architecture. They need to monitor the performance of the processes defined in the architecture and they need to set priorities and manage the processes and the people engaged in all levels of process change. When this occurs, you will have built business culture change right into the fabric of your organization, assuring that your organization's people and processes are aligned for change management to improve organizational performance.

CSF #3: Get Executive Support Up Front

Because CCM consists of strategic initiatives, top management must actively support them. Without executive endorsement—including an explanation of how the new system will support organizational goals— a change initiative might be dismissed as a gimmick or a fad. If change is critical to your company's survival—which is increasingly the case for organizations everywhere—top executives, from the CEO down, must drive that message.

Rob Baxter is vice president and CIO of Honeywell Industrial Control, a $2.5 billion division of Honeywell International (HIC). Reflecting on HIC's recent adoption of a customer-focused e-business solution that provides online service to more than 4000 customers in 60 countries and supports 3600 field engineers, Baxter says: "The senior executives have to get the bug, and it will come in one of two ways. They will see a tremendous opportunity, or they will be scared to death. It doesn't matter which one brings them around, as long as they become the champions of the change management e-business initiative."

Honeywell institutionalizes that imperative by having a vice president responsible for all CCM initiatives in each of its divisions.

CSF #4: Let Business Goals Drive Change Management Functionality

Just as a CCM initiative must be driven by business goals, so must every configuration decision. If a feature doesn't directly help your organization better serve customers, you probably don't need it. Mike Dalton, senior vice president of Marriott Lodging Systems, identifies five criteria against which his organization assesses change management initiatives and their solutions:

1. Improve profitability
2. Enhance customer value
3. Support process integration
4. Reduce technology costs
5. Improve systems performance

It is important to note that every one of the "technology" criteria is driven by business considerations. Follow the IT technology model that enhances the ability of operation's personnel to perform their specific job function. Organizations can also use CCM technology to expand the scope of a functional area. For example, the Belgian bank, Banque Brussels Lambert (BBL), recently used technology to enable agents in its contact center, BBL Direct, to perform outgoing sales calls as well as answer incoming service calls. BBL Manager Catherine deBatty stated: "With this change our employees are able to move from quantity to quality. We can concentrate less on how many calls are being handled and more on gathering information that will improve performance and productivity."

Here the adoption of CRM technology actually changed the job functions, but again, the implementation was driven by business considerations.

CSF #5: Minimize Customization by Leveraging Out-of-Box Functionality

Overcustomization is one of the most common causes of budget overruns and missed deadlines in change management implementations. A team sets out to adopt a just-plain-vanilla application but quickly falls victim to scope-features-creep and ends up with a more specialized product than business functions require. Or the team falls into the trap of customizing the software to mirror the customizations made to legacy systems, resulting in many of these experiments being abandoned or aborted midstream. But even those that succeed do so by straining budgets and obliterating schedules.

These common scenarios are unnecessary if you avoid imitating legacy solutions too closely and carefully select a CCM solution that provides out-of-the-box functionality that meets your organization's needs. Before you start customizing your application, first consider the application's existing functionality. You might find that the plain-vanilla product supports your business requirements much more thoroughly than you had anticipated, eliminating the need for expensive customizations, which are often the most costly, time-consuming, and complex. Staff starts to work more effectively and make better decisions because by using features such as Microsoft Dynamics CRM's search filters, advanced find, and reporting tools, they can quickly and accurately access the precise information they need. Because IT applications keeps all information in one place, there are no more silos of information—everyone has access to all the information they need and they work together more effectively.*

CSF #6: Use of Trained and Experienced Consultants

Change management consultants frequently make bold claims regarding their ability to meet an organization's implementation requirements. To ensure that your systems integrator can actually deliver change initiative on time and on budget, look for consultants who are not only thoroughly trained in implementation methodologies for the applications you are considering, but also have real experience in deploying those applications. How do you know that a potential integration partner meets these criteria? Hire consultants who have been certified by your software provider. It is difficult to overstate the importance of following this practice.

Jim McPeak, a vice president with Nashville-based Envoy Corporation, attests to the value of having used certified professionals for his company's CCM implementation. His advice is[†]: "When you use certified consultants, you know you're working with people who understand the process models inside and out. Certified consultants are able to translate business requirements into change management configurations far more effectively

---

* There are many other specific benefits that IT solutions such as Microsoft Dynamics CRM can deliver to a business. Once you've used IT applications like Microsoft Dynamics CRM for a while, installed an "IT culture" in your business, and started realizing the benefits, then you'll start to appreciate the potential even more. That's when you may start to consider exploiting the flexibility of IT CCM solutions through further development and more advanced configurations for even greater benefits.

† Source: Interview with Jim McPeak. Envoy LLC provides electronic data interchange (EDI) services to participants in the health care market, including pharmacies, physicians, hospitals, dentists, billing services, commercial insurance companies, managed care organizations, state and federal governmental agencies, and others. The company offers health care EDI services on a real-time and batch-processing basis by utilizing proprietary computer and telecommunications software and microprocessor technology. The company was founded in 1981 and is based in Nashville, Tennessee.

than noncertified consultants. They can also provide a much more realistic forecast of what your change management project will entail in terms of time and resource requirements."

CSF #7: Actively Involve End Users in the Design Effort

If you don't have your end users involved in design and deployment of the change management models and applications, you often will not be successful—period! This is a fact for a simple but often overlooked reason: unless you solicit and act on end-user input, you run the risk of implementing systems that confuse and alienate the very people they are meant to help.

Rich Harkwell is vice president of customer experience solutions for Nexstar Financial Corporation, a full-service national mortgage lender that provides residential loans to employees and clients of major corporations and financial service organizations. Nexstar recently completed an effective CCM rollout. When asked what lessons he drew from the experience, Harkwell* replied, "Rely on the invaluable feedback of your end user, in our case the customer care representatives. Once you show them a solution's vanilla capabilities, they will tell you exactly what to do with the change initiative to help them improve their effectiveness."

Take this lesson to heart: incorporate the knowledge of frontline professionals into your change management program's system design. In interface design for a change management application of a customer relationship management (CRM) platform, for example, the goal could be to make the user interface as intuitive and user-friendly as possible. But the only people who can tell a CCM design team what is intuitive are the people who will actually be using the software. This is why, before WorldCom went live with its global accounts call center solution, the design team ran a prototype and involved the company's call center agents in the front-end design, and made adjustments to the screens and the logic based on their

---

* Source: Telephone interview with the author, based on blog information provided during the research for this book. Based in St. Louis, Missouri, Nexstar Financial Corporation is a full-service home finance company. Formed in 1999 by a highly experienced team of mortgage industry professionals in partnership with KKR, Nexstar delivers residential mortgage products to customers nationwide via its website, www.nexstarhome.com, and Customer Care Center, 1–877–363–9782. As a mortgage lender, they provide mortgage outsourcing solutions to banks, thrifts, mortgage lenders, credit unions, and other financial institutions through its Powered by Nexstar program. It also specializes in employee and relocation mortgage programs for corporations and provides home mortgage products to residential customers.

recommendations. The result was a better, more intuitive screen design and a high level of user acceptance. Even when the modifications made in response to user input are relatively minor, the sense of ownership generated by their involvement can significantly boost enthusiasm for the solution.

CSF #8: Invest in Training to Empower End Users

Providing adequate training to end users is critical to the success of a change management intervention. Training should not come as an afterthought. Moreover, training should not merely focus on demonstrating how to use the proposed initiative's features and functionality. Instead, training should teach employees how to effectively execute the business processes enabled by the change. Given that a CCM implementation often entails changes to a company's business processes, end-user training should always focus on change management. Employees need to understand how the new processes and technology will help the company better serve customers. If employees understand how the initiative/system will make them more effective in the long run, they will be eager to adapt. But to garner that degree of employee support and buy-in, the organization must involve end users from the very beginning—both in designing the solution itself and in developing the associated training.

CSF #9: Use a Phased Rollout Schedule with Incremental Delivery

To achieve an early return on investment, the organization needs to be amenable to the incremental delivery of solutions. Another benefit of the incremental approach is a reduction in risk (compared with the big-bang, large drop of a 100% final solution). Delivering a partial solution allows the business to take on the solution in manageable chunks and also ensures that the solution builds on previous increments (i.e., building from a position of confidence). This incremental nature applies both to the business and the development sides of the project. For instance, the business areas may need to handle incremental growth of a solution, retraining, and so forth, and the solution developers will need good configuration management procedures that will not slow down the process of delivery. It is still possible to gain all the project-focused benefits of incremental delivery even if the business chooses not to deploy the solution incrementally: for example, building and potentially accepting the solution incrementally, ahead of a single production release.

Most successful initiatives follow a phased deployment schedule: each phase is focused on a specific change-related objective. Each successive phase leverages the work and experience from prior phases to produce a quick win—that is, meaningful results in a reasonable amount of time (typically three to four months).

A quick win often involves deploying an out-of-the-box, nonconfigured implementation. Australian communications provider Telstra, for example, began its e-business rollout with outbound calling and a lean package of contact, account, and opportunity modules. Within four months, employee productivity tripled. By breaking down a complex project into more easily manageable chunks that produce such quick wins, a phased approach allows project leaders to generate enthusiasm for the new system.

Phased rollouts also provide the advantage of allowing you to learn along the way. They enable you to test new ideas in a low-risk format, to incorporate customer feedback into the developing design, and to avoid repeating errors that you might make early on. At Dow Chemical—which has rolled out a multichannel CRM solution to more than 2000 users— this e-business philosophy is encapsulated in the phrase, "Think big, start small, and scale fast."

Phasing should not be confused with moving back a deadline. Each phase of a multiphase project should have its own tight schedule so that the overall rollout design still hits its deadlines. Most deployments finish the initial phase in one quarter and finish a complete, multiphase rollout in less than a year. No rollout, if properly managed, should exceed six to eight quarters, and the ROI ought to be visible in the first 12 months.

CSF #10: Measure, Monitor, and Accelerate

A Change Accelerator of some kind can be used to integrate the change management tools with the Accelerating Change & Transformation (ACT)* phased-deployment model in order to provide measurements to

---

* For further information, contact Emergent at http://www.EmergentConsultants.com, or see previous footnotes.

monitor and track the initiative's deployment and learnings integration.*
As previously described, the Accelerator Toolkit contains some 60+ tools
with instructions for facilitating each tool as part of our recommended
facilitated workshop approach, along with an ability to configure each tool
to meet your unique needs.

CREATING A CULTURE OF ASSESSMENT FOR CHANGE MANAGEMENT

Organizational culture is stable and difficult to change, as it represents
the accumulated learnings of an organization or a group. The most critical parts of culture—the values, the beliefs, and the principles—are often
invisible because they are under the surface. As the shared mental model
that the members of the organization hold dear and take for granted, it
is difficult for outsiders and even insiders to decipher. The reality is that
there is no right or wrong culture, except in relation to what the organization wants to achieve. Its relative strength is dependent on how well the
employees deal with adaptation and internal integration. For change to
occur, the organization must either recognize a threat to its survival or
encounter a strong positive external pressure that calls for adaptation and
integration of new systems, as such systems provide the means to ensure
the continuation of the organization and its ability to achieve its mission.
Consequently, members must commit to strong organizational values for
it to change effectively.

Accordingly, the institution or organization must learn to prioritize the
various choices involved in the culture change process in order to be effective and succeed. To move to a culture of assessment, the questions shown
in the following list must be dealt with.

Eight questions for a culture of assessment

- Where does the institution focus its efforts and resources to make
the most effective transformation to a culture of assessment?

---

* The ADLI method is often used as the Measure-Monitor-Track CCM tool. Approach, Deployment,
Learning, and Integration = ADLI in Baldrige nomenclature. ADLI is the architecture that
transforms Baldrige Performance Excellence from a set of neat ideas into a powerful tool for
continuous improvement.

- What are the characteristics of leadership that bring about the transformation to a culture of assessment (best practice institutions) when compared with those without?
- How do we sustain a culture of assessment over time?
- How can we balance assessment that stress collaboration with the one-on-one nature of student and faculty relationship? How can we balance the tension between collaboration and one-on-one approaches?
- How do we transform a traditional research culture so that it also values scholarship of assessment?
- What steps are necessary to keep the focus on student learning outcomes?
- How is institutional culture formed/shaped/changed? Who sets the norms and the constructs that define institutional culture? Who are the drivers/definers of culture in an organization? How is culture affected by internal and external forces?
- Given increasing globalization, where can we make international comparisons?

In addition, David Mann describes in his book *Creating a Lean Culture** a vital missing part in many change management implementations: a Lean Management approach to change and create a culture of assessment. Assessment helps leaders and managers learn how to implement a sustainable, successful transformation by developing a culture that has the people throughout the organizational involved and invested in the outcome. A culture of assessment teaches organizations how to successfully navigate the politics in a cross-functional process improvement environment and to engage executives in ways that are personally meaningful to them. If you are a leader at any level in an organization undergoing or considering a change transformation, assessment is where you should consider starting.

Activities considered to bring about organizational culture change are numerous and wide-ranging, and Mann has developed a framework to arrive at a logical and more concise listing of typical generic organizational change activities. This will ultimately serve as the foundation for the

---

* For further details see http://www.panview.nl/en/lean-production/creating-lean-culture-dmann
  -summary, which was the source of the section "Creating a Culture of Assessment for Change
  Management (2nd edition)" and is used with permission by the publisher, CRC Press.

lean organizational culture framework. Allocating specific change activities to broader categories allows for ease of reference. Moreover, it provides a link to the purpose or outcome of each activity within the greater strategy of organizational culture change. This framework is considered both important and relevant to current research.

An examination of the generic organizational culture theories reveals a great deal of culture change synergy between the various findings.* The issues surrounding vision and teamwork, for example, are recurring themes. This lends greater credibility to the activities attributed to causing organizational culture. Multiple sources advocate actions that promote organizational culture, thereby resulting in increased credibility and relevance of such actions. This can be further utilized to develop a credible causal activity framework. The framework developed was based on the causal activities described in the preceding sections.

The resulting framework you begin with (refer to Table 8.1) is developed using a two-stage process. The first stage entailed the selection of a few broad categories that characterize more detailed culture change activities. Key words describing concepts, such as justification, vision, and teamwork, were selected to describe each set of activities involved with culture change management and its related activities. The second stage entailed allocating individual activities to the broader categories.

A culture of assessment reveals for many organizations that the tools and Configuration changes in production include only 20 percent of the potential the respective philosophy has to offer. The other 80 percent are captured in the *Lean Assessment Culture*, which can be facilitated by implementing the right change management systems. A Lean culture change management system consists of three parts: standard work for managers, visual signals, and a defined responsibility structure. Next to these three parts of the Lean management system, Mann describes three strategies to assess the Lean Culture: Gemba walks, an improvement suggestion system, and

---

* Source: "The Development of a Theoretical Lean Culture Causal Framework to Support the Effective Implementation of Lean-in Automotive Component Manufacturers," K.R. van der Merwel, J.J. Pieterse, and A.S. Lourens. Although it is generally accepted that lean manufacturing improves operational performance, many organizations are struggling to adapt to the lean philosophy in the context of change management. The purpose of this study is to contribute to a more effective strategy for implementing the lean manufacturing improvement philosophy. The study sets out both to integrate well-researched findings and theories related to generic organizational culture with more recent research and experience related to culture change management, and to examine the role that culture plays in the effective implementation of lean manufacturing principles and techniques. The ultimate aim of this approach is to develop a theoretical lean culture causal framework.

TABLE 8.1

The Seven Recurring Themes and 25 Related Activities Involved in Assessing Culture Change Management

Category	Culture Change Activities
Justification	(1) Identify the need for need for change, (2) develop a burning platform (justification), and (3) communicate the Justification
Vision	(4) Create the shared vision, and (5) develop and communicate the vision deployment plan
Success	(6) Identify areas for rapid success—the low-hanging fruit, (7) plan interventions for those areas, (8) communicate the ensuing successes, and (9) link the successes to the overall culture change plan
Structure	(10) Identify structures that support the old way, (11) develop alternatives and ways to eliminate, (12) communicate proposed changes, and (13) replace inhibiting structures with enabling structures
Teamwork	(14) Define Team objectives based on the culture change vision, (15) align objectives with culture and skills required, (16) identify optimal Team configurations, and (17) communicate the Team structure
Training	(18) Identify the skills gaps to attain the new culture, (19) arrange for appropriate training, and (20) communicate the training plan
Performance	(21) Develop objectives and goals aligned with the new culture, (22) identify critical processes, (23) define appropriate metrics, (24) link incentives to objectives-aligned performance, and (25) communicate the results via dashboards and visual controls

self-audits. In addition, he suggests standard work and daily responsibility charts, along with the use of visual signals to help reinforce the desired culture change for any type of change management initiative.

Assessing *standard work for managers* (as described by David Mann) is a slightly different form of standard work than the *standard operating procedures* often defined for production operators. One difference is that the amount of work for managers that can be captured in standard work can range from 30 percent to 80 percent, compared to the maximum 100 percent for operators. The culture change management document in which the standard work is defined is a *working document* that lists the tasks or checks the manager has to perform each day and includes a checklist to check whether the task is completed. Some tasks can be part of only one person's standard work, such as "check production capacity for next week," but other tasks can be put to all managers in the organization, such as "Gemba walks." The interval of these tasks can differ between levels of management.

Visual signals are used to assess if a process is running according to plan. The performance of every workstation can be captured in one *A4 tracking chart,* which is preferably filled in by hand. Tasks that can be controlled this way are cyclical tasks, for instance Production Planning, Change over times, and Quality checks. Two guidelines for the charts are: (1) use binary color-coding: green means all is good and red means we have a problem, and (2) be able to react to the possible deviation of the standard; the interval in which the key performance indicator (KPI) is measured should be as short as possible, preferably every (couple of) hour(s).

Noncyclical tasks or tasks with intervals larger than one day, such as preventative/autonomous maintenance or large cleaning activities, can be visualized by using a *T-card system*.* Tasks can be put on the left-hand side of a two-column plan board, while the tasks that are executed are put on the right-hand side. In his lean management culture book, Mann (2014) describes the critical areas to focus on, which are outlined next.

THE MISSING LINK IN CULTURE CHANGE MANAGEMENT: A DAILY MANAGEMENT SYSTEM

When it comes to the *Daily Management Process,* David Mann describes three levels of meetings to follow up on all standard work and discuss (and solve) problems (Mann 2014):

1. The level one meeting takes place every shift, in which a team leader discusses last shift's performance with his or her group and details for the upcoming shift in possible employee input. These meetings should be stand-up meetings and the tool to facilitate these meetings is the *communication cell*.†

2. The level two meeting is the daily meeting between the team leaders and the group leaders, in which the top three problems of different

---

* T-card kanban boards and kanban racks are an efficient way of implementing a lean manufacturing kanban system in pull systems and many other applications for implementing lean.
† The communication cell is used for communication within shifts, between shifts, and between different departments. By visualizing important events of every shift on the cell, one can facilitate information flows and facilitate people from forgetting to share information with peers. The communication cell consists of three parts: (1) People, (2) Performance, and (3) Continuous Improvement.

departments from the previous week are discussed. Improvement activities are defined to prevent these problems from ever occurring again.

3. The level three meeting is the daily meeting between the group leader and the value stream owner, in which the escalated problems for the entire value stream are discussed.

There are three tools that can help to both improve and sustain the processes described above: the Gemba walks, a suggestion system, and mini-audits. According to Mann, there are very few things more important in a Lean Culture than Gemba walks, which are what the name suggests: walks through the Gemba, the place where work happens. These walks give managers the possibility to learn about the processes and encourage colleagues to participate in the improvement programs. When a manager spends all his or her time in the office, how do they know what is really happening on the shop floor? And how can they prioritize among problems if they don't really know what is going on?

Things that should be seen on the Gemba are people processing on their work tasks (of which the previously described A4 tracking charts are an example), a system for improvement suggestions, standard operating procedures that are used by operators, a communication cell where problems and actions from the level 1 and level 2 meetings are published, and a list of 6S actions and agreements. *What people should know on the Gemba* is: How are you performing in comparison with your targets? What are the three major problems preventing you from reaching that target? What kind of improvements are you working on to solve those problems? How do you use your standard work? Are there any excess materials on the shop floor?

A system that will facilitate the culture of continuous improvement is the improvement suggestion system. Problems should be analyzed and solved in a preventative manner so they do not reoccur in the future. A solid suggestion system should include the following four phases: (1) ideas for improvement are handed in, (2) evaluated, (3) implemented, and (4) completed. To make the process as easy as possible, a suggestion board can be divided into four areas, one for each phase, while the suggestions are written on sticky notes and simply placed in the area of the phase of the process.

Finally, in order to sustain the process of continuous improvement, it is also important to measure and verify regularly whether all employees are still as motivated to participate in the improvement program as they were at the beginning. This is what culture change *self-audits* are for. In the audits, T-cards containing 3 to 4 statements are used to ask questions of colleagues. Each statement has three possible outcomes: performance below current standard = 1, on current standard = 2, or better than the current standard = 3. Results of these audits can be visualized in Radar Diagrams, in which the different levels of maturity are plotted in many possible axes. Subjects of the audit cards can overlap with the questions, which can be asked during Gemba walks, making it possible for managers to combine their Gemba walk with a miniaudit. Examples of subjects that are suitable for miniaudits are (1) the use of visual signals, (2) keeping the shop floor tidy and clean, (3) the use of standard work, (4) the participation of employees in the suggestion program, and (5) the skill to perform a root-cause analysis.

Real Lean culture change according to Mann means continuous improvement at the grassroots level. To continuously improve the right things, a Lean change management system is needed. This system will help in implementing and solving the right solutions, fix problems faster, and sustain the culture change itself.

GETTING ORGANIZED WITH A DESIGN TEAM TO-DO CHECKLIST

Progress is significantly enhanced when the design development team contains skilled people, both in terms of business knowledge and technical expertise, including culture change. This does not mean that every design team member needs to be a multiskilled expert; it means that all the core skills for the project must be present within the design development team* as a whole. However all team members must have good communication

---

* The design development team is also referred to as the solution development team, which is part of the culture change planning and design process. Dr. Joseph Juran is considered as one the 4-Horsemen of Quality, a Founding Father. Dr. Juran referred to the design steps as a framework for planning a new culture to create new products and services. Planning an effective solution for a culture change management initiative may require one or more steps of this planning process. New designs or innovations happen when one discovers hidden customer needs. Traditionally, the main activities to capitalize on these insights were executed sequentially. Unfortunately, this approach results in a minimum of communication between the departments, which in turn often leads to problems for the next internal customer department. To prevent this, activities are organized in a design development team framework from the outset.

skills if a team with diverse skills is to function as a coherent unit. As you look ahead to the priority change initiatives in your company's pipeline, it is a good time to focus on culture change success factors associated with CCM. Implement the recommendations using the change management to-do list, an example of which is shown in Figure 8.8, in conjunction with the 10 critical success factors as you start up (or continue) your strategic business initiatives; do so and you will be well on your way to success. Remember, the soft stuff (i.e., people and culture change) *is* the hard stuff.

CCM deployment teams rely on rich communication as their first choice. For this to be effective, we suggest that the optimum solution development team size is seven +/– two people; at this level, the team can communicate with one another with a minimum of formality, management overhead, and risk, and a maximum benefit of ownership. Although smaller and larger team sizes have proven to be effective in a CCM project environment, both have specific risks associated with them. Where the team is very small, (e.g., three or four people) there is a risk associated with not getting "beyond our boxed selves" and creating true innovations.*

When the solution development team is greater than nine, the communications become more complex and cumbersome, daily huddles take longer and may impact productivity, and some of the team communication may need to be managed more formally. Note that the design development team comprises the roles of team leader, business ambassador, business analyst, IT solution developer, and solution tester, if needed. One intervention may have a number of solution development teams but only one design development team. When the team size is going to be greater than our recommended team size, splitting into a number of smaller teams may be a better option, although this in itself will introduce an overhead to manage the various teams. The options, benefits, and risks should be assessed to ensure the most suitable choice for an individual project.

---

* Getting beyond our "boxed" selves is a skill that can be learned and improved with technique, practice, and courage. Letting go requires a systematic methodology. Designing innovative and superior quality services and products requires gaining a clear understanding of customers' needs and translating them into services aimed at meeting them. In competitive business situations, success often comes to the best innovators. To create continuous innovation, an organization must design to meet customers' unmet needs.

- Align leadership behind a clear CCM vision to demonstrate sponsorship and commitment for culture change
- Enroll leaders as sponsors
- Clarify the vision with a compelling argument
- Engage leadership in collectively owning the "how"—the ways we will bring this to life in the business
- Use formal and informal recognition to reward high performance, clarified upfront by the CEO
- Integrate culture change management into program/project management to facilitate organizational culture change
- Design the project team/PMO to promote effective project management, culture change, and decision-making processes
- Use a "stages and gates" approach to ensure that leadership is aligned upfront and ensures and promotes compliance throughout
- Manage global changes from the top; equip process teams with tools to drive culture change at local levels
- Drive ownership and accountability throughout the organization by local DNA of work teams at the local level
- Assign clear accountabilities for discrete initiatives—leaders first, then cascade
- Set clear and ambitious targets/metrics and track and reward performance
- Reinforce expected behaviors through management routines and performance management processes
- Identify cultural barriers and resistance; develop mitigation strategies and build into plans to change the organization's culture
- Promote sustainable culture change results and measure against business outcomes
- Balance accelerated change against impact to outcomes and set reasonable timelines to ensure quality of results
- Track progress against outcomes; reinforce results and culture change efforts
- Align processes and systems (e.g., performance management, HR, IT tools)

FIGURE 8.8

CCM To-Do Checklist. This checklist contains four major areas of focus as the Deployment Team implements the 10 CSFs: (1) align leadership around a vision for culture change, (2) integrate culture change management, (3) drive ownership and accountability into the local DNA, and (4) measure culture change results against the business outcomes. By doing these four things, you will be baking culture change management into the DNA of the organization.

SUMMARY

Understanding and assessing the factors that are instrumental for successful culture change in the early phases of an initiative or intervention can help significantly in addressing and mitigating potential risks to the success of the effort. Having a common understanding of what needs to be in place is a good starting point for any intervention. In this chapter we emphasized five important areas:

- Overview and background
- Culture change management capability design process
- Interviews and research
- Change capability blueprint
- List of the emergent culture change accelerator tools*

Although a portion of the chapter was devoted to discussing change accelerator tools, the reasons behind how and why you should use these tools are extremely important to understand and utilize because they set the foundation for the use of any tools or methodologies. The early part of this chapter made three important considerations. One, there are three very distinct parts of a culture change management methodology. There is project change management that focuses on preparing the affected individuals to accept and use the specific change initiative. The second part is culture change management. CCM is specifically focused on the long-term development of the organization culture to minimize the resistance to change initiatives as a whole and to build resiliency within the organization.

---

* This list of some 60 change management tools and techniques offered by Emergent is by no means exhaustive, but is offered here as an example of the various types of tools available and the need to organize these tools into some type of phased development process. The tools include assessments, templates, models, and checklists in Microsoft PowerPoint, Excel, and Word formats. They can be downloaded, edited, and customized to fit your organization's unique needs. If you already have a corporate culture change management approach—whether you use Prosci's ADKAR, Kotter's eight steps, or some other model—the *Change Accelerator* can complement your existing approach. Your model will help you know what to do and the change accelerator tools will help you with how to do it. If you don't already have a preferred change model, then simply use the CCM model, which can be easily included as part of the Change Accelerator Toolkit. Additionally, with our CCM–Enterprise License, you have the ability to customize the methodology to suit your organization's preferred approach.

Second, concepts such as timeboxing often result in compromises in performance and quality and are becoming more and more important as the windows of opportunity get smaller and smaller. As a result, an organization's success is related more and more to the skills and capabilities of their individual employees than it is to the technologies that are being deployed.

Lastly, there are literally hundreds of tools and methodologies available today to help an organization change its culture and improve its overall performance. Most have proven to be successful when applied correctly with senior management support. With all these approaches available, an organization only gains competitive advantage when it selects the proper combination and sequence of tools and methodologies to meet the unique culture change strategic goals and objectives.

9

Initiatives' Prioritization

In a Nutshell: Much of the recent academic research has shown that it is not the "hard" technology acquisitions by themselves that guide organizational success, but the integration of these assets into organizational change management processes that elevate the importance of the human system. In other words, it is the integration that really makes the difference. In a CCM implementation where time has been fixed, understanding the relative importance of things is vital to making progress and keeping to deadlines. Prioritization can be applied to (a) assessing needs/requirements, (b) design specs, (c) design/develop/testing software, (d) implement systems tasks, products, use cases, user stories, (e) support operations acceptance criteria and tests, and (f) evaluating performance. The MoSCoW method is a time-honored technique for helping to establish priorities in terms of selecting those items that can help identify proper sequencing.

OVERVIEW

The change challenge that faces departments when new technology initiatives are introduced is to engage the staff most impacted, exactly those who often have emotional reactions and feel quite threatened by these kinds of initiatives. They have these emotional reactions because they often have insufficient information about the scope of the change, the training implications, and the potential impact on role changes. The information vacuum is often filled with rumors instead of a carefully orchestrated initiative prioritization plan for integrating and engaging all employees with the technology and business process improvement activities.

To address these challenges, the MoSCoW approach to prioritization is found to be very helpful and a powerful tool for culture change management practitioners. The letters MoSCoW* stand for

- **M**ust Have
- **S**hould Have
- **C**ould Have
- **W**on't Have this time

The reason we use MoSCoW in CCM initiatives is that there is usually a problem with simply saying that requirements are of high, medium, or low importance; the issue is that the definitions of these priorities are missing. The specific use of *Must, Should, Could,* or *Won't Have* implies the result of failing to deliver that particular phase's requirements as the following rules/guidelines suggest:

1. *Must Have*: Requirements labeled as MUST are critical to project success and have to be included in the current delivery time box in order for it to be a success. If even one MUST requirement is not included, the project delivery should be considered a failure (requirements can be downgraded from MUST by agreement with all relevant stakeholders; for example, when new requirements are deemed more important). The word MUST can also be considered an acronym for the minimum usable subset.

2. *Should Have*: SHOULD requirements are important to project success, but are not necessary for delivery in the current delivery time box. SHOULD requirements are as important as MUST, although SHOULD requirements are often not as time-critical or have workarounds, allowing another way of satisfying the requirement, and therefore can be held back until a future delivery time box.

3. *Could Have*: Requirements labeled as COULD are less critical and are often seen as nice but not necessary to have. A few easily satisfied

---

* MoSCoW is a useful technique used in management, business analysis, change management, and business case and software development to reach a common understanding with stakeholders on the importance they place on the delivery of each requirement. This is also known as MoSCoW prioritization or MoSCoW analysis. This use of MoSCoW was first developed by Dai Clegg of Oracle UK Consulting as part of a CASE Method Fast-Track: A RAD Approach. He subsequently donated the intellectual property rights to the Dynamic Systems Development Method (DSDM) Consortium in order to put it into the public domain for universal use.

COULD requirements in a delivery can increase customer satisfaction for little development cost.

4. *Won't Have*: These requirements are either the least-critical, lowest-payback items, or not appropriate at that time. As a result, WON'T requirements are not planned into the schedule for the delivery time box. WON'T requirements are either dropped or reconsidered for inclusion in later time boxes. Doing this does not make them any less important.

MoSCoW RULES FOR CCM

These are some possible definitions of what the different priorities mean. It is important to agree on the definitions with the users. Preferably this is agreed to before the requirements are finalized in order to incorporate it into the change culture.* Jesse Jacoby writes in his blog on culture change about very low success rate "(something like 20% of all change initiatives experience it) has led to an emphasis on methods such as project management (PM). PM is one way of doing it, but even it overlooks a key piece—an assumption that can, and often does, kill attempts to change an organization. That critical piece is culture; and the problem is that all such initiatives assume that it can be changed as needed. The truth of the matter is that it can't; and if you assume that it can, then you're destined to fail before you even begin."†

MoSCoW is often used with timeboxing, where a deadline is fixed so that the focus can be on the most important requirements, and as such is seen as a core aspect of rapid application development (RAD) software development processes, such as Dynamic Systems Development Method (DSDM) and agile software development techniques (see Figure 9.1).

---

* Jacoby writes in his blog that the need for organizational change is ongoing because it never stops. It can't, because just as you get a handle on one thing, something else pops up. He says, "It's like trying to keep flies off your picnic lunch. There's always one. You have to be flexible. You have to be able to not just respond to the market, but also to anticipate it so that you're not caught off balance. You have to watch for new players, too. Not only are entrepreneurs appearing from the most unexpected corners in your own country, but other nations are joining the foray. The West no longer has the influence it once did. Although the pie is bigger and growing, there are more people clamoring for a piece of it."

† http://blog.emergentconsultants.com/2014/12/08/how-culture-kills-change-part-1/.

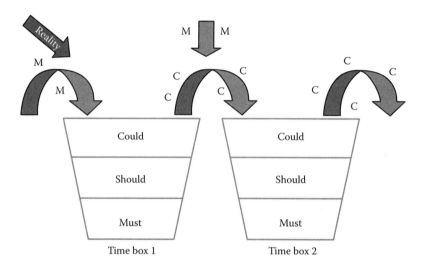

FIGURE 9.1
The MoSCoW Prioritization Method and timeboxing.

Must Have Category

Items in the Must Have category are those that provide the minimum usable subset (MUS) of requirements that the project guarantees to deliver, as defined by the following criteria:

- Cannot deliver on target date without this
- No point in delivering on target date without this; if it were not delivered, there would be no point deploying the solution on the intended date
- Not legal without it
- Unsafe without it
- Cannot deliver the business case without it

Ask the question, "What happens if this requirement is not met?" If the answer is "Cancel the project—there is no point in implementing a solution that does not meet this requirement," then it is a Must Have requirement. If there is some way around it, even if it is a manual workaround, then it will be a Should Have or a Could Have requirement. Downgrading a requirement to a Should Have or Could Have does not mean it won't be delivered, simply that delivery is not guaranteed.

Should Have Category

Items in the Should Have category are

- Important but not vital
- May be painful to leave out, but the solution is still viable
- May need some kind of workaround, such as management of expectations, some inefficiency, an existing solution, paperwork, and so forth
- A Should Have may be differentiated from a Could Have by reviewing the degree of pain caused by it not being met, in terms of business value or numbers of people affected

Could Have Category

Items in the Could Have category are

- Wanted or desirable but less important
- Less impact if left out (compared with a Should Have)

Won't Have This Time

Items in the Won't Have this time category are requirements that the project team has agreed it will not deliver. They are recorded in the prioritized requirements list where they help clarify the scope of the project and to avoid being reintroduced via the back door at a later date. This helps to manage expectations that some requirements will simply not make it into the delivered solution, at least not this time around.

USING A STANDARD BODY OF KNOWLEDGE

The ISO/IEC 12207 standard establishes a process of life cycle for software, including processes and activities applied during the acquisition and configuration of the services of the system. Each process has a set of outcomes associated with it. There are 23 Processes, 95 Activities, 325 Tasks, and 224 Outcomes—the new "ISO/IEC 12207:2008 Systems and Software

Engineering—Software Life Cycle Processes," defines 43 system and software processes. See Figure 9.2.

ISO/IEC 12207:2008 establishes a common framework for systems-related and software life cycle processes with well-defined terminology that can be referenced by the change management community. It contains processes, activities, and tasks that are to be applied during the implementation or acquisition of software, products, or services and during the supply, development, operation, maintenance, and disposal of change management systems.

The standard has the main objective of supplying a common structure so that the buyers, suppliers, developers, maintainers, operators, managers, and technicians involved with systems and software development use a common language. This common language is established in the form of well-defined processes and subprocesses, as shown in Figure 9.2. The

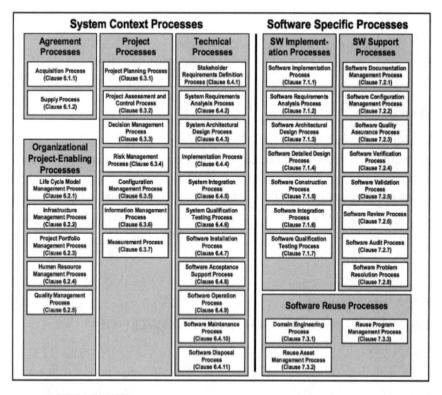

source: ISO/IEC 12207-2008

FIGURE 9.2
ISO/IEC Schemes.

structure of the standard was intended to be conceived in a flexible, modular way so as to be adaptable to the necessities of whoever uses it. The standard is based on two basic principles: modularity and responsibility. Modularity means processes with minimum coupling and maximum cohesion. Responsibility means to establish a responsibility for each process and subprocess, facilitating the application of the standard in change management initiatives where many people can be (legally) involved.

Agreeing How Priorities Will Work

During the requirements building process the definitions of *Must Have, Should Have, Could Have,* and *Won't Have* need to be agreed on. Some examples are described above. However, the Must Have definition is not negotiable. Any requirement defined as a Must Have will have a critical impact on the success of the project. The project manager or business analyst should challenge requirements if they are not obvious Must Haves; it is up to the business visionary or their empowered business ambassador to prove a requirement is a Must Have. If he or she cannot, it is a Should Have at best. At the end of each increment, all unsatisfied requirements are reprioritized in the light of the needs of the next increment. This means that, for instance, a Could Have that is unsatisfied in an increment may be demoted subsequently to a Won't Have because it does not contribute enough toward the business needs to be addressed next.

THE BUSINESS SPONSOR'S PERSPECTIVE

The MoSCoW rules have been cast in a way that allows the delivery of the MUS of requirements to be guaranteed. A rule of thumb often used is that Must Have requirements do not exceed 60 percent of the effort. If this rule is followed, then that ensures contingency represents at least 40 percent of the total effort.

So is this all that the business sponsor can expect to be delivered? The answer is an emphatic "No." While understanding that there is a real difference between a guarantee and an expectation, the business sponsor can reasonably expect more than this to be delivered except under the most challenging of circumstances. This is where the split between Should Haves and Could Haves comes into play. If the Should Haves and Could Haves are split evenly with 20 percent of the total effort associated with each, then the Must Haves and Should Haves, in combination, will represent no more than 80 percent of the total effort. The remaining 20 percent of effort associated with the Could Haves is now the contingency available to protect the more important requirements. By most standards this is still a very reasonable level of contingency and rightly implies that the business sponsor can reasonably expect the Should Have requirements to be met. It is just that, quite understandably, the team does not have the confidence to make this a guarantee. So sensible prioritization combined with time-boxing leads to predictability of delivery and therefore greater confidence. Keeping project metrics to show the percentage of Should Haves and Could Haves delivered on each increment or time box will either reenforce this confidence if things are going well, or provide an early warning that some important (but not critical) requirements may not be met if problems arise.

MoSCoW AND THE BUSINESS CASE

The best way to address prioritization initially is with a quantified business case. If a business case does not exist, the business sponsor and business visionary need to articulate the business drivers, preferably in a quantified form. Some practitioners believe that any requirement contributing to the business case should be defined as Must Have; others accept that a small reduction in benefit is unlikely to make a project completely unviable and desire a more pragmatic solution. These practitioners believe that it is sensible to allow the requirements contributing to the business case to span Must Have and Should Have requirements. It is likely that contractual relationships, whether formally between organizations or informally within an organization, will influence the decision on this issue one way or the other.

ESTABLISHING LEVELS OF PRIORITY

MoSCoW prioritization is really only meaningful in a specified time frame and the same requirement may have a different priority in that context.

A Must Have requirement for the project as a whole may not be a Must Have for the first increment. For example, even if a Must Have requirement for a computer system is the facility to archive old data, it is very likely that the solution could be used effectively for a few months without this facility being in place. In this case, it is sensible to make the archive facility a Should or a Could Have for the first increment even though delivery of this facility is a Must Have before the end of the project. Similarly, a Must Have requirement for an increment may be included as a Should or a Could Have for an early development time box. Many consider this approach to be sensible as it allows the more important requirements to be addressed earlier rather than later, but if taking this approach, beware the risk of confusion. Each deliverable effectively has two or even three priorities in different time frames and the project manager needs to ensure that the team does not lose sight of the real business priorities. The best way to deal with this is to create a time box prioritized requirements list (PRL), a subset of the project PRL that is specifically associated with a time box and leave the priorities unchanged on the main PRL for the project.

Every item of work has a priority. Priorities are set before work commences and kept under continual review as the work is done. As new work arises either through introduction of a new requirement or through the exposure of unexpected work associated with existing requirements, the decision must be made as to how critical they are to the success of the current work using the MoSCoW rules. All priorities should be reviewed throughout the project to ensure that they are still valid. When deciding how much effort should be Must Have requirements, bear in mind that anything other than a Must is, to some degree, contingency. The aim is to get the percentage effort for Must Haves (in terms of effort to deliver) as low as possible and to be wary of anything above 60 percent; that is, 60 percent Must Haves, 40 percent Should Haves and Could Haves. Won't Haves are excluded from the calculation, as they won't be part of this project/increment/time box. Levels of effort above 60 percent for Must Haves introduce a risk of failure, unless the team is working in a project where estimates are known to be accurate, the approach is very well understood, and the environment is understood and risk-free in terms of the potential for external factors to introduce delays.

Requirements are identified at various levels of detail, from a high-level strategic viewpoint through to a more detailed, implementable level. High-level requirements can usually be decomposed and it is this decomposition that can help resolve one of the problems that confront teams: all requirements appear to be Must Haves. If all requirements really were Must Haves, the flexibility derived from the MoSCoW prioritization would no longer work. There would be no lower-priority requirements to be dropped from the deliverables to get the project back on time and budget. In fact, this goes against the whole CCM ethos of fixing time and resources and flexing features (the triangles diagram).

Believing everything is a Must Have is often symptomatic of insufficient decomposition of requirements. A high-level Must Have requirement frequently yields a mix of subrequirements, each with a different priority. Flexibility is once more restored and some of the detailed functionality can be dropped from the delivered solution so that the project deadline can be met. Where a requirement has a Must Have below a Should Have, for example, this would signify that if this requirement were to be delivered, it must have the lower-level requirement to be acceptable.

CHECKLIST OF TIPS FOR ASSIGNING PRIORITIES

- ✓ Work closely with the business visionary to ensure they are fully up to speed as to why and how CCM prioritizes requirements.
- ✓ Start all requirements as Won't Haves and then justify why they need to be given a higher priority.
- ✓ For each requirement that is proposed as a Must Have, ask: "What happens if this requirement is not met?" If the answer is "Cancel the project. There is no point in implementing a solution that does not meet this requirement," then it is a Must Have requirement.
- ✓ Ask: "I come to you the night before deployment and tell you there is a problem with a Must Have requirement and that we can't deploy it—will you stop the deployment?" If the answer is "Yes" then this is a Must Have requirement.

✓ Is there a workaround, even if it is manual? If there is, then it is not a Must Have requirement. Compare the cost of the workaround with the cost of delivering it, including the cost of any associated delays.

✓ Ask why is the requirement needed—both for this project and this increment.

✓ If there is a business case in sufficient detail, can it be used to justify the intended priority? If not, create one.

✓ Is there more than one requirement implied in a single statement? Are they of the same priority? Decompose the requirement!

✓ Is this requirement dependent on any others being fulfilled? A Must Have cannot depend on the delivery of anything other than a Must Have because of the risk of it not being there.

✓ Allow different priorities for levels of acceptability of a requirement. For example, "The current back-up procedures will be followed to ensure that the service can be restored as quickly as possible." How quick is that? Given enough time and money, that could be within seconds. They may say that it Should happen within four hours, but it Must happen within 24 hours, for example.

✓ Can this requirement be decomposed? Is it necessary to deliver each of those components to fulfill the requirement? Are the decomposed elements of the same priority as each other?

✓ Tie the requirement to a project objective. If the objective is not a Must Have, then probably neither is the requirement relating to it.

✓ Remember that team members may cause scope creep by working on the fun things rather than the important things. MoSCoW can help to avoid this.

✓ Does the priority change with time? For example, for an initial phase, it is a Should Have but it will be a Must Have for the second increment.

✓ Prioritize defects/bugs using MoSCoW.

✓ Prioritize testing using MoSCoW.

✓ Use MoSCoW to prioritize your To-Do list. It can be used for activities as well as requirements.

SUMMARY

A more systemic, engagement-oriented and process-focused approach to the management of organizational change enables collaboration between leaders, managers, and staff in the implementation of technology and business process changes and the MoSCoW tool is primarily used to prioritize requirements, although the technique is also useful in many other areas. CCM recommends no more than 60 percent effort for Must Haves for a project, with 40 percent Shoulds and Coulds. Anything higher than 60 percent poses a risk to the success and predictability of the project, unless the environment is well understood, the team is established, and the external risks are minimal. The top prioritization tips are (1) agree what the priorities mean early in the iterative development life cycle, (2) use all the priorities, (3) challenge Must Haves, (4) control the number of Must Haves, and (5) prioritize everything, as it helps the iterative development and deployment concept become deeply ingrained in the team's approach. The commonality of the MoSCoW language, its mental model, and the prioritization approach it brings is guaranteed by ensuring that staff, management, and leaders work in an integrated and collaborative fashion. This also ensures an understanding of the intricacies of leading and participating in a culture-related system change effort and contributes in a significant way to the return-on-investment (ROI) of the change initiative.

10

The Iterative Development Approach

In a Nutshell: Iterative development is the key technique used by a design and development team to evolve solutions from a high-level idea to a delivered product. The so-called evolving solution is the main CCM product that is subjected to the iterative development process, although it is expected that the concepts associated with the technique will be applied to most project deliverables. As such, this approach is a life cycle within a life cycle. Iterative development is a way of breaking down the solution development of a large change management intervention into smaller chunks. In iterative development, the basic approach is designed, developed, and tested in repeated cycles. With each iteration additional features can be designed, developed, and tested until there is a fully functional application already being deployed to customers in three- to six-month cycles. Iterative development contrasts with change management traditional methods in which each phase of the development life cycle is a gated one. If software is involved, then coding doesn't begin until design of the entire proposed application is complete and has gone through a phased gate review. Likewise, testing doesn't begin until all production and coding is complete and has passed necessary phase gate reviews. The purpose of working iteratively is to allow more flexibility for changes. When requirements and design of a major application are done in the traditional method, there can be unforeseen problems that don't surface until development begins. By working iteratively, the change management team goes through a cycle where they evaluate with each iteration and determine what changes are needed to produce a satisfactory end product.

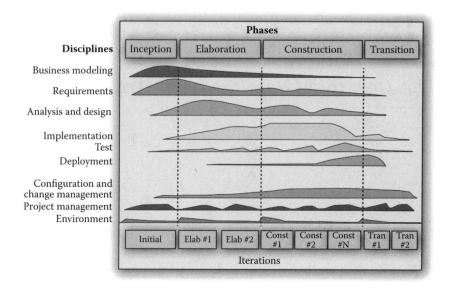

FIGURE 10.1
CCM phases, iterations, and disciplines.

OVERVIEW

Iterative development follows a fundamental cycle of inception, elaboration, construction, and transition, which is embedded in the CCM process, as shown in Figure 10.1. In particular, this process is an intrinsic component of timeboxing,* ensuring both that the time box is controlled and that a feedback loop is built into the evolution of the solution. At the time box inception and elaboration level, the iterative development cycles are short, typically a matter of days or weeks. However, this cycle may also be applied outside an inception/elaboration time box, for example to create a CCM product, such as a document or an increment of the solution, and in

---

* In time management, timeboxing allocates a fixed time period, called a time box, to each planned activity. Several project management approaches use timeboxing. It is also used for individual use to address personal tasks in a smaller time frame. It often involves having deliverables and deadlines, which will improve the productivity of the user. With timeboxing, the implementation deadlines are fixed, but the scope may be reduced. This focuses work on the most important deliverables. For this reason, timeboxing depends on the prioritization (with the Chapter 9 MoSCoW Method, for example) of deliverables, to ensure that it is the project stakeholders who determine the important deliverables rather than the business case or change management developers.

these circumstances the iterative development cycles will typically be longer. Wherever it is used within CCM, the feedback afforded by the cycle ensures that the right solution evolves over time in a controlled manner.

The CCM iterative development approach defines four phases for iterative development. Each phase provides the team with a specific focus to support the continuous and controlled refinement of the requirements, architecture, design, and code. These phases are

- *Inception*: Define the scope and life cycle of the project
- *Elaboration*: Mitigate risks and create a stable baseline architecture
- *Construction*: Develop the remainder of the system as efficiently as possible
- *Transition*: Train users to be self-sufficient; get customer acceptance of the product

The CCM approach advocates two levels of granularity for planning: a coarse grain for the four phases of the project (outlined in the CCM development plan), and within each phase, a fine grain called an iteration (detailed in the iteration plan) consisting of the eight disciplines shown in Figure 10.1: Business modeling, requirements, analysis and design, implementation testing, deployment, configuration and change management, project management, and environment. Within any phase, there will typically be one or more iterations of a manageable duration (e.g., one week to many months), depending on the size of the project.

In every iteration relevant disciplines, such as project management, requirements, analysis and design, coding, integration, and testing, are performed. The degree to which any one of these disciplines is performed will vary according to the current phase of the project. The key goal of every iteration is to produce an executable version of the system that is tested and measured against the defined evaluation criteria. Every iteration is planned in sufficient detail to ensure that all team members have a clear and unambiguous understanding of the iteration's objectives, scope, and evaluation criteria. This is so that only essential activities are addressed. The transition phase review may conclude that the objective has been fully achieved. If this is the case then the changes that are made are accepted and a new baseline of the deliverable is agreed on. If required, the cycle starts again with a new evolutionary objective. If the review concludes that the objective has not been met, the team has a choice of either (a) discarding the changes made (reverting to the last baseline—rolling back to the last agreed version) and possibly planning a new approach to achieving the objective, or (b) identifying remedial work required for the objective to be achieved in a new pass through the iterative cycle.*

Applying Iterative Development to the CCM Solution[†]

In many cases the CCM solution is developed over time to accommodate specific functional and nonfunctional requirements captured in the requirements list, which then must be prioritized. Whereas functional requirements tend to deal with specific objectives, nonfunctional requirements tend to deal with more generalized objectives. At any given time, the iterative development cycle may be applied to the many evolutions of the solution from a three-perspective vantage point:

- *Functional perspective*: Demonstrating how a specific business objective has been achieved by the CCM evolutionary step
- *Usability perspective*: Demonstrating how the user of the CCM solution interacts with it to achieve the business objective
- *Nonfunctional perspective*: Demonstrating how general issues related to performance, capacity, security, or maintainability have been accommodated by the CCM solution

Sometimes it is necessary to make fundamental, strategic decisions related to how the overall CCM solution is going to evolve into the desired future state. These may relate to options for achieving the related business objectives, or options around how the objectives can be achieved from a technical perspective. Under such circumstances, a proof of concept

---

* Within each of the four phases, the CCM Design Team defines clear objectives and follow a development life cycle that includes requirements, analysis and design, develop and test, subsystem integration, implementation, and other disciplines, such as configuration management. The outcome of each phase is a tested product of known maturity. In their implementation, however, these four phases allow for many variations. For example, take the Product Development Phase, for which the following questions may be considered: What is the expected duration of this phase? Weeks, months, quarters (three months), years, tens of years? Also, does the result of the proof-of-concept Phase form part of the final product, or is it to be scrapped and redeveloped?

† The important consideration here is not whether the technique described above is the so-called ideal or right way, but rather whether it will assist you in taking another step toward effectively managing a project and communicating the scope of an iteration to the entire team. Like any artifact in an iterative life cycle that matures over time, the processes and techniques you use to manage and communicate across the team should evolve as well.

prototype may be required in order to explore those options and work out the best way forward to accomplish the desired culture change.*

Managing the Iterative Development Process When Software Is Involved in the Deployment†

Management of the iterative development process as a whole is achieved through the detailed management of various aspects of the project that underpin it in the form of a spiral—thus it is called the Spiral Model, as shown in Figure 10.2. This model was first described by Barry Boehm in his 1986 paper "A Spiral Model of Software Development and Enhancement" (Boehm 1986). In 1988, Boehm published a similar paper to a wider audience. These papers introduce a diagram that has been reproduced in many subsequent publications discussing the spiral model.

Sequentially defining the key artifacts for an intervention often lowers the possibility of developing a system that meets stakeholder objectives and constraint conditions. In situations where these assumptions do apply, it is a change risk not to specify the requirements and proceed sequentially. Boehm itemizes these assumptions as follows:

- The requirements are known in advance of implementation
- The requirements have no unresolved, high-risk implications, such as risks due to cost, schedule, performance, safety, security, user interfaces, or organizational impacts

---

* Systems engineering specialists sometimes calls these demos capability/technique prototypes. Like all change management approaches, the CCM approach prefers that culture change practitioners keep the work they do on demos to a minimum. A prototype in CCM is defined as a piece of work that demonstrates how a given culture-related objective can be or has been achieved—thus the term "demo." In one sense all evolutionary development on a particular deliverable, carried out in accordance with the iterative CCM development cycle, can be considered a prototype, right up until the point that the elaboration review step accepts that the changes made have met, or are at least demonstrably moving toward, the agreed on objective. For this reason, the iterative development technique is sometimes known as prototyping. In this context, the prototype is evolutionary rather than throwaway.

† A major issue that CCM interventions sometimes face is that a requirement cannot be fully implemented in a single iteration. If a system must support 10 different technology devices, for example, most likely a subset of these devices can be incorporated in any given iteration. There are two ways to deal with this situation. The preferred technique is to create separate requirements for each iteration and then manage these like any other requirement. A second technique can be used when it's either not possible to rewrite the requirements or there is resistance to rewriting them. In such cases, the attributes planned iteration and actual iteration are modified so that a requirement can be assigned to multiple iterations. The status attribute has two new values added: Partially incorporated and partially tested. To enable testers to define in which iteration(s) the requirement will be tested, a new attributed test iteration is created. To define the scope of each iteration, a notes attribute may be created if a single notes attribute is insufficient.

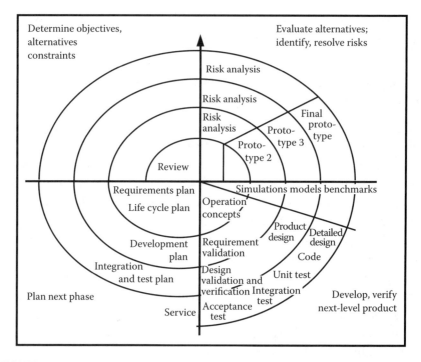

FIGURE 10.2

Boehm Model for Iterative Development Spiral. (Image courtesy of Dr. Barry Boehm.)

- The nature of the requirements will not change very much during development or evolution
- The requirements are compatible with all the key system stakeholders' expectations, including users, customers, developers, maintainers, and investors
- The right architecture for implementing the requirements is well understood
- There is enough calendar time to proceed sequentially

The Boehm Spiral Model is a risk-driven process model generator for all types of change management software-related projects. Based on the unique risk patterns of a given program or project, the spiral model guides a team to adopt elements of one or more process models, such as incremental or evolutionary prototyping. Early papers on the subject used the term "process model" when referring to the spiral model as well as to incremental, waterfall, prototyping, and other approaches. Successful iterative development is very dependent on continual and frequent involvement of business roles (specifically business ambassadors and advisors) and on the concept of applying what has been learned on one iterative cycle through feedback from the Review step to the next cycle. When applying iterative development in the context of a change management development time box, many experts strongly recommend three iterations.

The research identifies the four basic activities that must occur in each cycle of the spiral model:

1. Consider the win conditions of all success-critical stakeholders
2. Identify and evaluate alternative approaches for satisfying the win conditions
3. Identify and resolve risks that stem from the selected approaches
4. Obtain approval from all success-critical stakeholders, plus commitment to pursue the next cycle

Development cycles that omit or shortchange any of these activities risk wasting effort by pursuing options that are unacceptable to key stakeholders, or are sometimes too risky. Some iterative processes violate this concept by excluding key stakeholders from certain sequential phases or cycles. For example, system maintainers and administrators might not be invited to participate in definition and development of the system. As a result, the system is at risk of failing to satisfy their win conditions.

EVOLUTIONARY DEVELOPMENT STRATEGY

The final consideration in planning an iterative development approach is to formulate a strategy to guide the evolution of the solution overall. This strategy is established as part of the solution foundations and is a key factor influencing the delivery plan. In an iterative model, iterative process starts with a simple implementation of a small set of the software requirements and iteratively enhances the evolving versions until the complete system is implemented and ready to be deployed.

An iterative life cycle model does not attempt to start with a full specification of the culture change requirements. Instead, development begins by specifying and implementing just part of the culture change pathway, which is then reviewed in order to identify further requirements. This process is then repeated, producing a new version of the model at the end of each iteration. The iterative process starts with a simple implementation of a subset of the software requirements and iteratively enhances the evolving versions until the full system is implemented. At each iteration, design modifications are made and new functional capabilities are added. The basic idea behind this method is to develop a system through repeated cycles (iteratively) and in smaller portions at a time (incrementally). Iterative and incremental development is a combination of both iterative design or iterative method and incremental c model for development. During software development, more than one iteration of the software development cycle may be in progress at the same time.

In an incremental approach model, the whole culture change requirements package is divided into various builds and modules. During each iteration, the development module goes through the requirements, design, implementation and testing phases, just as one would with software deployment and implementation. Each subsequent release of the culture change module adds functionality to the previous release. The process continues until the complete system is ready as per the requirements. The key to successful use of an iterative culture change development life cycle is rigorous validation of the new-culture requirements and verification and testing of each version of the deployment against those requirements within each cycle of the model. As the new culture evolves through successive cycles, tests have to be repeated and extended to verify each version of the new desired future state.

The advantage of this approach is that there is a working model of the desired future state of the new culture at a very early stage of development, which makes it easier to correct functional or design flaws and poor assumptions. Finding issues at an early stage of culture change development enables you to take corrective measures within a limited budget. The disadvantages with this approach is that it is applicable mostly with a project approach, which we have argued is not the most favorable or successful method of culture change. Table 10.1 lists the advantages and disadvantages of the iterative/incremental development approach.

Like other approaches, iterative and incremental development has some specific applications in the software industry that have been historically demonstrated and can also be applied to CCM. This approach to CCM is most often used in the following checklist of potential scenarios:

✓ Requirements of the complete desired future state system are clearly defined and understood

✓ Major requirements must be defined; however, some functionalities or requested enhancements may evolve with time

✓ A new technology is being used and is being learned by the culture change development team while working on the rollout

✓ Resources with needed skill sets are not available and are planned to be used on a contract basis for specific iterations in the future

✓ There are some high-risk features and goals that may change in the future

TABLE 10.1

Advantages and Disadvantages of the Iterative/Incremental Development Model

Advantages and Strengths	Disadvantages and Shortcomings
1. Some working functionality can be developed quickly and early in the CCM life cycle.	1. More resources may be required.
2. Results are obtained early and periodically, and parallel development can easily be planned.	2. Although the cost of change is less, it is not very suitable for changing CCM requirements.
3. Progress can be measured in a staged manner.	3. More management attention is required.
4. It may be less costly to change the scope/requirements.	4. System architecture or design issues may arise because not all requirements are gathered in the beginning of the life cycle.
5. Testing and debugging during smaller iterations may be done more easily.	5. Defining increments may require definition of the complete system.
6. Risks are identified and resolved during iteration, while each iteration is a more-easily managed milestone.	6. Not suitable for smaller projects.
7. The often easier-to-manage risk, high-risk parts can be done earlier or first.	7. Management complexity is often more.
8. With every increment, an operational outcome is delivered.	8. End of project may not be known, which can be considered a major risk.
9. Issues, challenges, and risks identified from each increment can be utilized/applied to the next increment.	9. Highly skilled resources are required for risk analysis.
10. It supports changing CCM requirements.	10. The new culture solution's progress is highly dependent on the ongoing risk analysis.
11. It may be better suited for large and mission-critical solutions.	11. It may take longer to accomplish.
12. During the CCM life cycle, new culture design solutions are produced early, which can facilitate customer evaluation and feedback.	12. It may be harder to measure specific components and their contribution to the success, or lack thereof.

SUMMARY

One of the most important and significant outcomes of culture change efforts that are coupled with culture change initiatives and their implementations is the demonstration of the power of community and community action involved with iterative development approaches. Also, the creation of change agent roles, which are populated by organizational members, bringing all staff together to engage one another and the leadership in dialogue about the vision going forward in an iterative manner—all bring out the pride and commitment of employees. Furthermore, it then becomes clear that everyone in the organization has great ideas about how the organization can improve itself in a systematic fashion. Employees often are just waiting for the opportunity to be invited to contribute. The creativity and innovation that is available but untapped can be an encouraging message to senior management because it says that they do not have to take full responsibility for the progress of the organization by themselves alone.

Section IV

Analyzing and Evaluating

Analyzing and Evaluation sharpens critical thinking by involving logical thinking and reasoning. This includes skills such as comparison, classification, sequencing, cause/effect, patterning, webbing, analogies, deductive and inductive reasoning, forecasting, planning, hypothesizing, and critiquing.

Creative thinking via analyzing and evaluating involves creating something new or original. It involves the skills of flexibility, originality, fluency, elaboration, brainstorming, modification, imagery, associative thinking, attribute listing, metaphorical thinking, and forced relationships. The aim of creative thinking is to stimulate curiosity and promote divergence. While critical thinking can be thought of as more left brain and creative thinking more right brain, they both involve "thinking." When we talk about "higher-order thinking skills" (HOTS) we are concentrating on the top three levels of Bloom's taxonomy: analysis, synthesis, and evaluation.

This section contains the following chapters:

- Chapter 11: Gathering, Analyzing, and Prioritizing Requirements
- Chapter 12: Using Estimates and Time Boxes

11

Gathering, Analyzing, and Prioritizing Requirements

In a Nutshell: This section explores what culture change requirements are, and how important a set of well-developed and agreed-on prioritized requirements lists is to the culture change approach. The CCM approach to requirements involves establishing the requirements early, at a high level, during the feasibility and foundations phases, negotiating these with the business sponsor and relevant stakeholders, and establishing the detailed requirements, both iteratively and incrementally during later life cycle phases. It describes the purpose of following a structured requirements' management process, which is to ensure that an organizational culture change initiative documents, verifies, and meets the needs and expectations of its customers and internal or external stakeholders. Change management begins with the analysis and elicitation of the objectives and constraints of the organization.

WHAT ARE REQUIREMENTS?*

At its simplest, a requirement consists of a service, feature, or function that the user wishes the solution to perform or exhibit. Different users may have diverse, even conflicting, perspectives on which requirements should be included and their relative priorities. Most culture change

---

* The gathering of Requirements is an essential part of any initiative and change management. Understanding fully what a desired future state culture will deliver is critical to success. This may sound like common sense, but surprisingly it's an area that is often given far too little attention in the arena of culture change management, which is why we have included this chapter.

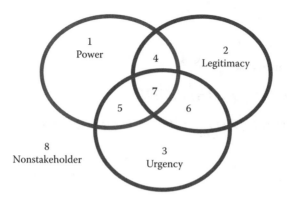

FIGURE 11.1
Organization development and culture change areas.

initiatives specify a phased plan for deployment and business roles to identify who is responsible for defining, agreeing on, and prioritizing requirements. Facilitated workshops are used to define and gain buy-in to requirements and to aid resolution of conflicting requirements. The prioritized requirements' list is created to document agreement and assist in the management of the requirements throughout the project. By using the MoSCoW prioritization method, we allow for consistent, agreed-on levels of priority.

At the more complex organizational level, CCM requirements involve a six-phase, general process for managing cultural change, as shown in Figure 11.1, including requirements for

1. Motivating change (power)
2. Creating vision (legitimacy)
3. Developing functional requirements and political support (urgency)
4. Managing the transition (power and legitimacy)
5. Sustaining momentum (power and urgency)
6. Action Learning (legitimacy and urgency) (Cummings and Worley 1995)

A structured requirements' process and related software seems suitable for organizing and describing general guidelines about managing change.*

---

* The software for culture change management consists of a collection enterprise technology (such as C++, Java Enterprise Edition) organized around structured query methods to create a relational database using the Agile approach. The developer is Edge Software, Inc., and they can be contacted at 925–462–0543. More information is available at workdraw.com.

Whatever model you choose to use when deploying organizational change, that model should include the requirements, priorities, and areas of emphasis described in the following five phases of change. The CCM collaborative consulting model integrates highlights from all of the six phases around power, legitimacy, and urgency.

REQUIREMENTS FOR MOTIVATING CHANGE (POWER)

The motivating change (power) phase requirements include creating a readiness for change in your client organization and developing approaches to overcome resistance to change. General requirements for managing this phase include

- Enlightening members of the organization about the need for change.
- Expressing the current status of the organization and where it needs to be in the future.
- Developing realistic approaches about how change might be accomplished.
- The need for the organization's leaders to recognize that people in the organization are likely to resist making major changes for a variety of reasons. Typical reasons are fear of the unknown, inadequacy to deal with the change, and the belief that the change will result in an adverse effect on their jobs.
- The need for people to feel that their concerns are being heard.
- Leaders must widely communicate the need for the change and how the change can be accomplished successfully.
- Leaders need to listen to the employees, who need to feel that the approach to change will include their strong input and ongoing involvement.

CREATING VISION (LEGITIMACY)

Leaders in the organization must articulate a clear vision that describes what the change effort is striving to accomplish along with the desired culture that will be created to support it. Ideally, people in the organization will have strong input into creating the vision and the basic requirements of how it can be achieved, and the following guidelines are useful:

- The vision should clearly depict how the achievement of the culture change vision will improve the organization.*
- It is critically important that people believe that the vision is relevant and realistic.
- Research indicates that cynicism is increasing in organizations in regard to change efforts. People do not want to repeatedly hear about the need for the latest silver bullet that will completely turn the organization around and make things better for everyone.
- People want to feel respected enough by leaders to be involved and to work toward a vision that is realistic yet promising for the long run.
- Often the vision is described in terms of overall outcomes (or changes) to be achieved by all or parts of the organization, including associated goals and objectives to achieve the outcomes.†
- Sometimes, an overall purpose or mission is also associated with the effort to achieve the vision.‡

---

* Vision can provide both a corporate sense of being and a sense of enduring purpose. While incorporating a measure of today's success, vision transcends day-to-day issues, and by providing meaning in both the present and the future, vision can empower and encourage leaders and followers to implement change (Sullivan and Harper 2007).
† Change is about survival. Change is especially necessary in organizations that wish to prosper in a volatile, uncertain, complex, and ambiguous environment. If changes rocking the external environment were *temporary*, the slow and uncertain pace at which organizations change would matter less. But, the reverse is true. Powerful forces in the environment are pressuring public and private organizations to alter *permanently* existing structures, policies, and practices (Bolman and Deal 2013).
‡ Change is absolutely necessary for the survival of individuals and organizations. The question isn't whether or not to implement change. Over the long run, you have no choice unless you are willing to become irrelevant. The strategic environment, over which you have little or no control, is in a state of constant change and it's your job to sense when changes in the organization are going to be necessary. Therefore, the first real question is: What role are you going to assume? Domain defender? Reluctant reactor? Anxious analyzer? Or, enthusiastic prospector? If you choose to play only one role in a fixed manner over time, then you and your organization will survive for as long as the environment tolerates that role. A successful culture change leader knows which role to play at what time, and he or she knows when to change roles. Once the role is sorted out, you can ask the other really important questions: What changes are necessary and desirable? How do you go about managing change?

DEVELOPING FUNCTIONAL REQUIREMENTS THAT BUILD ON POLITICAL SUPPORT (URGENCY)

The Functional Requirements Phase of change management is quite often overlooked, unfortunately, since it is the requirements contained in this phase that often stops successful change from occurring. Politics in organizations are about power. Power is important among members of the organization when striving for the resources and influence necessary to successfully carry out their jobs. The power of politics is also important when striving to maintain jobs and job security. Power usually comes from credibility, whether from strong expertise or integrity. Power also comes from the authority of one's position in the organization.

Some people have a strong negative reaction when talking about power because power often is associated with negative applications and even manipulation, abuse, or harassment. However, power, like conflict, exists in all human interactions and is not always bad. It is how power and conflict are used and managed that determine how they should be perceived.*

Organizational politics is a controversial subject. Advising managers on how to become better organization politicians may not be widely regarded as a legitimate activity. This book adopts a different stance, however, arguing that political behavior is inevitable and even desirable, as political exchanges generate the dynamic and drive the debate behind organization culture change and development initiatives. Most managers are likely to find the implementation of innovation and change challenging unless they possess political skills. Therefore, requirements surrounding matters of power and politics are critically important to recognize and manage during organizational change activities, as the following checklist suggests:

- Change requirements often mean shifts in power across management levels, functions, and groups.

---

* Organizational politics are a reality in most organizations, and while game-playing might outwardly appear to be wasted time, it is necessary in order to secure resources, progress ideas, achieve personal goals, and often to enhance one's standing. It is naive to realistically expect to be able to stand aloof from organizational politics. You may be respected for doing so, but your progress will be limited and you will be seen as an easy target. (Told to us by a middle manager, private sector manufacturing company, male.)

- To be successful, the change effort must recruit the support of all key power players; for example, senior management, subject matter experts, and others who are recognized as having strong expertise and integrity.*
- Requirements for a strong mechanism for ensuring alignment of power with the change effort is needed to develop a network of power players who interact and count on each other to support and guide the change effort.
- Means to manage power can include ensuring that all power players are involved in recognizing the need for change, developing the vision and methods to achieve the vision, and organization-wide communication about the status of change.
- Any recommendations or concerns expressed by those in power must be promptly recognized and worked through.
- As the objective is analyzed, more requirements emerge, clarifying what is required. These may be expressed in terms of a more detailed business function, feature, or service.
- Once the problem is understood a little more, it may be expressed in terms of a feature that the solution is expected to have. Features can evolve out of requirements. Eventually, there is a need to delve further into the requirements.
- As the level of detail increases, the requirement begins to describe how something will be achieved.
- At the lowest level of detail, there will be a point where the requirement does not need to be written down—rather, it is simply evolved with input from the business champion and built directly into the solution.

From a global culture change perspective, current organizational trends have reinforced the significance of political skill. The stable, ordered, bounded, predictable, rule-based hierarchical organization today seems

---

* My view is that organizational politics are almost inevitable, but they can be constructive or destructive. The best management skills would seek to ensure that constructive uses, such as attraction of resources or changed working practices, are delivered through using supportive political skills. The worst skills are tantamount to bullying and dishonesty, which should not be condoned. (Told to us by a middle manager, public sector hospital, female.)

to be a dinosaur and thing of the past.* The twenty-first century dynamic organization is characterized by fluidity, uncertainty, ambiguity, and discontinuity. Organization boundaries are oftentimes blurred with the development of partnerships and joint ventures, subcontracting and outsourcing, peripheral workforces and virtual teams, and social media networking and technology-based collaborative networks. Hierarchy is replaced, in part, by reliance on expert power and in this context, those with the best understanding of the issues make the better decisions.†

Many managers and especially those with roles that include responsibility for innovation and change have no direct line authority over those on whose cooperation they must rely. In this context, those with the best political skills attract more resources and support.

MANAGING TRANSITION REQUIREMENTS (POWER AND LEGITIMACY)

Transition requirements occur when the organization works to make the actual transition from the current state to the future state. In consultations, this phase usually is called "implementation of the action plans." The plans can include a wide variety of interventions or activities designed to make a change in the organization; for example, creating and/or modifying major

---

* Like the dinosaur, culture change can be evolutionary or revolutionary. It can take place gradually within an existing paradigm or it can be a dramatic shift to an entirely new paradigm. In addition to being gradual, evolutionary change usually is linear and sequential. The downside of evolutionary change is that it is predictable. Competitors can figure out what your organization is doing and where it is going. Revolutionary change is about transforming the organization. The revolution can be small or it can be sweeping. The path of transformational culture change, while not linear and sequential, can be made predictable to people inside the organization through proper planning and communication. Both evolutionary and revolutionary culture change can be legitimate strategic choices under the right environmental conditions. Environmental conditions can be defined by velocity, mass, and complexity. The velocity of change is the rate change takes place. The mass of the change is how widespread it is. The complexity of change means that change never occurs in isolation. Each change affects other changes in often unseen, unanticipated, or misunderstood ways that lead to unintended second- and third-order cultural effects (Sullivan and Harper 2007).

† In the modern-day organization, individuals are stripped of the luxury of a stable position and are deprived of a predictable vision of their future. This fluid context implies an increased dependence on personal and interpersonal resources, and therefore on political skills to advance personal and corporate agendas. There is clearly enhanced scope for political maneuvering in a less well ordered and less disciplined organizational world, and hence the need for a critical understanding of the nature, shaping role, and consequences of political behavior requirements.

structures and processes in the organization, and the following general requirements are usually involved:

- These changes might require ongoing coaching, training, and enforcement of new policies and procedures.
- In addition, means of effective change management must continue, including strong, clear, ongoing communication about the need for the change, status of the change, and solicitation of organization members' continuing input to the change effort.
- Ideally, the various actions are integrated into one overall change management plan that includes specific objectives, or milestones, that must be accomplished by various deadlines, along with responsibilities for achieving each objective.
- These plans are rarely implemented exactly as planned. Thus, making the many ongoing adjustments to the plan with key members of the organization while keeping other members up to date about the changes and the reasons for them is just as important as developing the plan itself.
- Transition requirements documentation should be maintained to the level that is sufficient to track the requirements and enable them to be tested.
- As a requirement is established, its test acceptance criteria also need to be defined.
- In the case of IT initiatives, when it comes down to defining exactly what a piece of software may need to do and what the customer wants the software to do, there are often misunderstandings due largely to a gap in the understanding of technology.
- The customer is not expected to understand how the software gets the job done, just that it gets it done correctly.
- The programmer needs to understand exactly what end result the customer expects and write the program accordingly.

Figure 11.2 has been around for many years and illustrates how elusive and changeable the understanding of requirements can be, depending on where you sit in the organization.

As the illustration shows, the process of developing and translating requirements into user-oriented terminology is often misapplied and is fraught with error. The six-phased model previously described can be helpful in resolving these conflicts and misunderstandings.

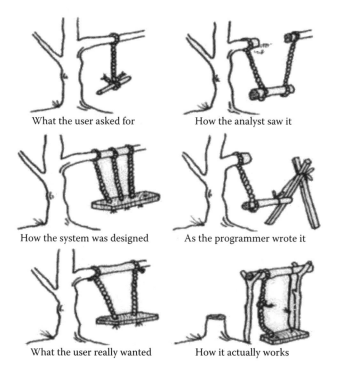

What the user asked for

How the analyst saw it

How the system was designed

As the programmer wrote it

What the user really wanted

How it actually works

FIGURE 11.2
The ambiguity of understanding requirements.

SUSTAINING THE CULTURE CHANGE MOMENTUM (POWER AND URGENCY)

Quite often, the most difficult phase in managing culture change is when leaders work to sustain the momentum of the implementation, and at the same time previously unknown factors require adjustment to the plan. Change efforts can encounter a wide variety of obstacles* for which requirements are needed:

---

* How can we anticipate the generalized effects of change on people? Within the domain of human behavior, the answers revolve around four main effects: self-confidence, confusion, loss, and conflict. Change can cause people to feel incompetent, needy, and powerless; in short, to lose self-confidence. It is essential for the people in the organization to be involved in planning and executing change, to have opportunities to develop new skills required by the change, and to depend on psychological support mechanisms put in place before, during, and after the change is implemented. Change can create confusion throughout the organization. Change alters the clarity and stability of roles and relationships, often creating chaos. This requires realigning and renegotiating formal patterns of relationships and policies.

- Strong resistance from members of the organization, sudden departure of a key leader in the organization, or a dramatic reduction in sales
- Strong, visible, ongoing support from top leadership is critically important to show overall credibility and accountabilities in the change effort
- Those participating in the change effort often require ongoing support, often in the form of provision of resources, along with training and coaching
- The role of support cannot be minimized and is often forgotten despite its importance during organizational change
- At this point in a CCM project, it may be wise for you to ensure you have ongoing support (including from other consultants) that can provide you with some ongoing objectivity, affirmation, provision of resources, and other forms of necessary support and foundation
- Employee performance management systems play a critical role in this phase of organizational change, including (a) setting goals, (b) sharing feedback about accomplishment of goals, (c) rewarding behaviors that successfully achieve goals and accomplish change, and (d) addressing performance issues

ACTION LEARNING* AND OTHER REQUIREMENTS CONSIDERATIONS (LEGITIMACY AND URGENCY)

Action learning is an approach to changing the culture involving solving real problems that includes taking action and reflecting on the

---

* Professor Reginald Revans is the originator of action learning. His formative influences included his experience training as a physicist at the University of Cambridge. In his encounters with this talented group of scientists—several went on to win Nobel prizes—he noted the importance of each scientist describing their own ignorance, sharing experiences, and communally reflecting to learn. He used these experiences to further develop the method in the 1940s while working for the Coal Board in the United Kingdom. There, he encouraged managers to meet together in small groups, to share their experiences and ask each other questions about what they saw and heard. The approach increased productivity by over 30%. Later, working in hospitals, he concluded that the conventional instructional methods were largely ineffective. People had to be aware of their lack of relevant knowledge and be prepared to explore the area of their ignorance with suitable questions and help from other people in similar positions. Action Learning is being applied using the Action Learning Question Method (Hale) to support organizational development/change management capability development across the central government in the UK Civil Service supported by OD specialists Mayvin (Hale and Saville 2014). As such, this is combining action learning with organizational change management, as reported at the 2014 Ashridge Action Learning Conference and Action Learning: Research and Practice, October 2014.

results. The learning and culture change that results helps improve the problem-solving process as well as the solutions the team develops. The action learning process includes (1) a real problem that is important, critical, and usually complex, (2) a diverse problem-solving team or set, (3) a process that promotes curiosity, inquiry, and reflection, (4) a requirement that talk be converted into action, and ultimately, a solution, and (5) a commitment to learning. In many, but not all, forms of action learning, a coach is included who is responsible for promoting and facilitating learning as well as encouraging the team to be self-managing. In addition, the learning acquired by working on complex, critical, and urgent problems that have no currently acceptable solutions can be applied by individuals, teams, and organizations to other situations. The theory of action learning and the epistemological position were developed originally by Reg Revans (1982) who applied the method to support organizational and business development, problem solving, and improvement.

There is another type of requirement (called nonfunctional requirements in various types of initiatives and projects) that describes how well, or to what level, something is to be done or carried out. These requirements are specified in terms of any restrictions that need to be considered and are therefore built into the design of the solution (e.g., security) or specific attributes that the solution will demonstrate (e.g., speedy or quick performance). Some will be global and apply across the whole set of requirements and some will be specific to an individual requirement. For instance, high levels of security may be needed for the entire solution or it could be that only part of the solution requires such rigor (e.g., one small business process handles information that is particularly sensitive so it requires extra controls). Just like functional requirements, nonfunctional requirements should be prioritized using the MoSCoW technique and be visible to all stakeholders.

So how does a major change take hold and become infused throughout the organization? The answer comes from being broad-minded rather than narrowly focused. A strategic culture change leader must

- Develop sensing networks and expand the target audience
- Gather and broaden the power base
- Alert the organization that change is coming
- Actively manage the planning and execution processes by linking every day-to-day action to the vision for change

- Continually communicate the vision for change to key internal and external constituencies
- Know about and plan for overcoming resistance
- Be prepared for unexpected but necessary midcourse corrections

GATHERING AND PRIORITIZING REQUIREMENTS

A number of techniques are commonly used to gather requirements for an initiative. Examples include observation, interviews, focus group sessions, brainstorming, joint application development (JAD) sessions, sampling, research, and administration and analysis of questionnaires and surveys. Asking questions such as the following will help to foster the requirements gathering:

Who does it now?
Who is perceived to do it in the future?
What is done now?
What is perceived to be done in the future?
Where is it done now?
Where is it perceived to be done in the future?
When is it done now?
When is it perceived to be done in the future?
How is it done now?
How is it perceived to be done in the future?

Fulfilling some requirements requires much more effort and cost than others. Therefore, it is important to prioritize the requirements after they are gathered. This could be as simple as classifying the requirements as high, medium, and low priority, giving the business customers and the project team the information they need to ensure that the most important requirements are incorporated into the final solution. In general, all of the high-priority requirements should be accommodated. As many medium requirements should be included as possible and as many of the low priority requirements should be accommodated as time and resources permit, which usually isn't very many.

If you could ask your customers what their requirements were and have them respond with everything they needed, the analysis phase would be an easy process. However, that is rarely the case. A number of requirements gathering challenges must be overcome:

- No single customer normally knows all of the requirements up front.
- You should do a proper follow-up with a number of customers and stakeholders to make sure that you have as complete a picture as possible as to what is needed.
- Different customers have different visions of what the business needs are.
- Gathering requirements requires consensus building so that you can reconcile differing and conflicting requirements.
- Requirements are vague. This requires good follow-up and probing skills to obtain the correct level of detail.
- Many statements are not requirements. Be careful to recognize when you are receiving a valid business requirement and when you are getting statements of scope, risk, approach, or simply opinion.
- When customers tell you they think the project should have all the funding it needs, they are giving you an opinion, not a business requirement.

Many initiatives start with the barest headline list of requirements, only to find later the customers' needs have not been properly understood. One way to avoid this problem is by producing a statement of requirements. This document is a guide to the main requirements of the initiative and includes

- A succinct requirement specification for management purposes
- A statement of key objectives—a cardinal (key) points specification
- A description of the environment in which the system will work
- Background information and references to other relevant material
- Information on major design constraints

The contents of the statement of requirements should be stable or change relatively slowly. Once you have created your statement of requirements, ensure that the customer and all other stakeholders sign up to it and understand that this and only this will be delivered. Finally, ensure you have cross-referenced the requirements in the statement of requirements with those in the project definition report to ensure there is no mismatch.

GUIDELINES ON REQUIREMENTS GATHERING

Gathering and managing requirements are important challenges in CCM. Solutions succeed or fail due to poor requirements at any time throughout the life cycle. Thus, the continuously evolving baseline of requirements needs to be managed effectively, and the CCM design development team needs to assess and understand the uniqueness of the requirements gathering process for his or her individual project.

Preliminary scope statements are the beginning of the requirements gathering process. They are high-level and are designed to initiate progressive elaboration, where that preliminary scope statement is expanded into the detail that makes up the complete requirements baseline. The CCM Design Team must get their hands around how that progressive elaboration process will take place as part of the project. Two points of focus can help:

1. Requirements definition
2. Requirements management

Requirements definition refers to the details that make up the actual requirements or description of the product of the project. The key is to understand the reason for the project: the underlying problem to be solved or opportunity to be seized. It entails discovering the underlying problem or opportunity. This involves distinguishing what might be symptoms and possible solutions. Often someone might state something like: "What I need is a…" The individual is acutely aware of a problem and often focuses on a narrow set of possible solutions, mistakenly stating the problem as one of these solutions. The Project Manager (PM) or requirements analyst needs to gain control of the conversation and by engaging stakeholders and to identify the root causes. Once the root cause is identified, many problems become very simple. Other situations may be more complex, may demand coordination among stakeholders, or will require collaboration to discover and document the requirements definition.

Putting Together Requirements Definition and Requirements Management

Here is what can be done to effectively manage the requirements process on any CCM Intervention using an iterative development approach, such as the three time boxes shown in Figure 11.3.

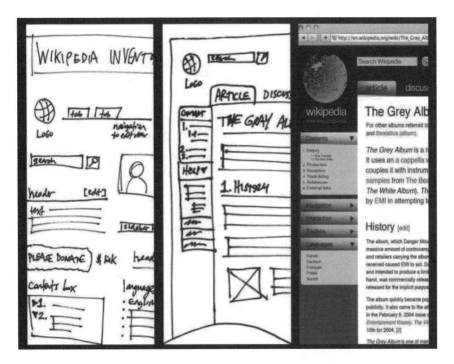

FIGURE 11.3

The requirements development prototype shown for a Wikipedia inventory item. Time Box 1: rough design; Time Box 2: preliminary time box; and Time Box 3: final design.

Requirements configuration management with time boxes is sometimes needed to manage an expanding and changing set of prototype details that make up that requirements definition. Usually in the beginning of the culture change initiative, there may be little apparent need for sophisticated requirements management. Often it can be assumed that there will be a need, or that need will become apparent as the new culture unfolds. The more the requirements are elaborated, the greater is the need to organize requirements definitions for each part of the culture change initiative. The more parts, and the more in-depth the definitions, the greater is the need for a more sophisticated requirements management system.

The process for requirements development is as follows:

1. Identify *all* stakeholders. Develop categories for types of stakeholders, such as users, support, interfacing in certain areas, managers affected by the project, and more.
2. Make sure that all areas that the culture change initiative will touch are represented by a stakeholder.

3. Determine a communications strategy for engaging with your stakeholders.
4. Begin to build bridges to the stakeholders and you will ideally be able to establish at least one face-to-face meeting with each stakeholder and ideally at least one face-to-face meeting among all stakeholders.
5. Develop Time Box 1 with a list of questions organized around various facets of the problem to be solved by the project. This list should provide clarification to both you and the stakeholders on the issues to be addressed. Make sure they address a clear understanding of the problem, as opposed to specifying a solution. Thoroughly vet the questions within the team and with the project sponsors.
6. Determine how much time will be needed in terms of both sessions and overall duration for the project requirements gathering. Develop a schedule for meetings and other engagements as developed through your communications strategy.
7. Do Time Box 2 with initial requirements gathering by obtaining answers to the questions you have developed. Whether by survey, face-to-face meetings, online meetings, or one-on-one meetings, you will need to establish a set of raw data addressing your questions.
8. Document answers to the questions in an initial requirements document draft and proceed to Time Box 3 (final design). Review this thoroughly with all key stakeholder representatives and revise accordingly. Make sure all stakeholders buy into these answers.
9. Move into stakeholder focus group sessions. This is where you will likely also engage developers, and some iterative solution development will take place. One of the keys to this process is that you will be able to show stakeholders what is possible. You will also be able to put something concrete out there that will provide a greater point of focus to smoke out remaining requirements and clarify understanding.
10. Get formal sign-off from all major stakeholder groups. This is an important process, as it forces some attention by the stakeholders to assure there are no hidden doubts or caveats.

The requirements definition is the continuous process of fleshing out and refining the baseline description of the product of the project. Requirements management is how the flow of information in these steps is organized and configuration managed. Be wary of moving too quickly from the what (the requirement) to the physical how (the solution). It is common for both business and technical sides of the culture change initiative to jump into solutions much too soon. Requirements should clarify

- *Functionality*: Describing clearly and unambiguously what the end product (solution) is supposed to do, in business terms.
- *External interfaces*: Defining how the solution needs to interact with people, processes, technology, and other business areas and projects.
- *Performance and attributes*: Giving expectations of the volumes, resilience, reliability, and response times needed. Solution aspects such as portability, accuracy, maintainability, disaster recovery, and security should be considered.
- *Design constraints imposed on an implementation*: Certain standards may be required to be met, both internal and external to the organization for which the solution is being developed. These may impose implementation constraints or they may be associated with policies, resource limits, or operating environments.

In CCM, functional requirements should be specified at a high level during the earlier phases of the life cycle and decomposed into lower-level requirements that are more specific in later phases. This integrates well with the exploratory nature of the CCM life cycle, where a deeper understanding of the desired future state evolves and deepens as the initiative progresses. A word of caution here: nonfunctional requirements that are missed or discovered too late can be a major source of failure. If discovered too late, it may be difficult or impossible to accommodate them* (see Figure 11.4).

Initially, the customer will have an idea of what they need. As they gain a better understanding of their needs, they gain a better understanding of how they will achieve it, as it is shown in the Rangaswami example in Figure 11.4. The nonfunctional requirements (performance attributes and constraints) may also emerge throughout the life cycle. Some of the more critical ones may be evident at the outset, when the objective is established. Others should be actively sought alongside the functional requirements when they are captured during facilitated workshops to establish the requirements list and plan.

---

* Research on organization change has generated important insights for both managers and consultants. Five conclusions are particularly relevant to the work of organizational culture change capacity building: (1) underlying issues must be recognized, (2) the difficulty of change needs to be understood, (3) client readiness should be evaluated, (4) the culture change process should be managed, and (5) active leadership is crucial.

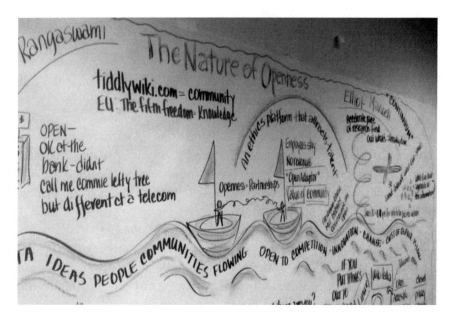

FIGURE 11.4
Example of an unfolding nature of openness.

Change Management Requirements Plan Template
Introduction
Provide background, link to strategic goals and other changes.

CCM Sponsor
This person leads the change project and is accountable for ensuring the project and change plan are implemented.

CCM Objectives
Detail what the desired future state will look like and achieve.

Culture Change Objectives and Requirements
Provide details of

- What the culture change process will achieve (e.g., information sharing, engagement, input into system changes)
- Principles that underpin the culture change plan (e.g., inclusiveness/consultation, timeliness)

- New employee skill sets that are or might be required
- Ethical issues that need to be considered and how the change plan will address them
- Any related computer software that may be needed

Change Plan Elements

What are the main requirements elements in the change plan? (e.g., people/culture, systems and technology, documentation, positions/roles, process, skills). Each of these elements may require a particular focus in the change plan.

Rationale for the Change

List the drivers and constraints for change.
What are the risks for the change process?

Key Stakeholder Analysis

Identify the key stakeholders (consider staff, other work units, management, unions, customers, and other clients) and

- Analyze their response to the change (e.g., what will be their main concerns/fear, where there is likely to be support for the change)
- Identify their requirements in terms of change management and consider the style of communication required (language style and level)
- Identify the preferred media for communicating or consulting with them about the change (e.g., sessions involving dialogue about the changes, newsletters, and briefings from project team members; frequently asked questions)

Assessment of Readiness to Change

Comment on the status of the change so far (e.g., is there a high-level strategy in place that stakeholders are already aware of and committed to that provides a framework for the change?).

What elements might support the change requirements? (e.g., dissatisfaction with current processes; a workplace culture that supports change and innovation).

Is there strong senior management support for the change?

Key Change Messages

Identify about six key messages to convey about the change process, being upfront about gains and losses. Consider

- What will be gained/lost for the key stakeholder groups in the change process
- The messages from the stakeholder perspective
- What their main concerns will be
- Presenting changes in a positive light even while acknowledging loss

Identify Change Elements

Structures/Processes/Responsiblities/Resources/Timeframes/Performance Measures

Consider the need for particular change support structures (e.g., a change team, superusers/specialists who are trained first and can support people in the workplace, involvement of users/key stakeholders at various stages, change champions in the workplace).

Consider if there is a need for transitional arrangements to support and whether the introduction of the change process needs to be staged.

What will be the impact on workloads and how will these be managed?

Develop Change Plan

Develop a change plan including performance measures (how will you know the change plan is effective?). Ensure that the plan is adequately resourced.

Actions	Who	When	Performance Measures

Consolidation

Ensure policies, procedures, and performance measures reinforce the requirements for change.

Remove organizational barriers to the change.

Reinforce how change requirements will/have provided benefits.

Evaluation

How will the requirements be evaluated in relation to the achievement of the planned objectives?

How will the change management requirements processes be evaluated? Consider summative as well as final evaluations; how can you assess your change management requirements and strategies as you implement them?

How will the evaluation outcomes be circulated and promoted to stakeholders?

How will evaluation outcomes be used in other organizational processes?

━━━━━━━━━

THE STRUCTURE AND HIERARCHY OF REQUIREMENTS

In the early developmental phases, requirements are captured at a very high level (the highest level requirement being a statement of the objective of the project) defining the main features of the solution for the culture change desired future state. Whatever the solution being developed, in feasibility there should be a small number of clear statements that are just sufficient to scope the project and make some rough estimates of its duration to identify whether it is worth proceeding further and to establish rough costs and benefits achievable.

A useful approach to prioritizing requirements, the Kano model is a theory of product development and customer satisfaction developed in the 1980s by Professor Noriaki Kano that classifies customer preferences into five categories.* These categories have been translated into English using various names (delighters/exciters, satisfiers, dissatisfiers, and so forth) (see Figure 11.5).

---

* Dr. Kano was one of the JUSE Counselors to FPL during the Deming Prize Challenge, and the Lead Reviewer for FPL QualTec Quality Services, of which I was the general manager. The Kano analysis model was developed to identify and contrast essential customer requirements from incremental requirements and initiate critical thinking. In the real world, we will not always have the precise data that allows us to quantitatively identify the Pareto optimal point on the cost-benefit curve. It is important to understand the fundamental principles of the requirements trade-offs so that we can make informed decisions and judgment calls. Some analyses will be relatively easy, as our development curves are usually discrete data points based on estimates of the work required to implement particular future state designs. Also, we won't have access to the full spectrum of design choices because we will be limited by other constraints on the culture change initiative as well as the creativity and capabilities of our development teams in proposing alternatives. For further details, see http://ayushveda.com/blogs/business/kano-model-tool-for-measuring-consumer-satisfaction/.

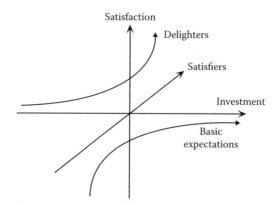

FIGURE 11.5
Kano model of prioritizing requirements.

1. *Must-be Quality*: These attributes are taken for granted when fulfilled but result in dissatisfaction when not fulfilled. An example of this would be a carton of milk that leaks. Customers are dissatisfied when the carton leaks, but when it does not leak the result has not increased customer satisfaction. Since customers expect these attributes and view them as basic, it is unlikely that they are going to tell the company about them when asked about quality attributes.
2. *One-dimensional Quality*: These attributes result in satisfaction when fulfilled and dissatisfaction when not fulfilled. These are attributes that are spoken of and ones that companies compete for. An example of this would be a milk package that is said to have ten percent more milk for the same price will result in customer satisfaction, but if it only contains six percent then the customer will feel misled and it will lead to dissatisfaction.
3. *Attractive Quality*: These attributes provide satisfaction when achieved fully, but do not cause dissatisfaction when not fulfilled. These are attributes that are not normally expected; for example, a thermometer on a package of milk showing the temperature of the milk. Since these types of attributes of quality unexpectedly delight customers, they are often unspoken.
4. *Indifferent Quality*: These attributes refer to aspects that are neither good nor bad, and they do not result in either customer satisfaction or customer dissatisfaction.

5. *Reverse Quality*: These attributes refer to a high degree of achievement resulting in dissatisfaction and to the fact that not all customers are alike. For example, some customers prefer high-tech products, while others prefer the basic model of a product and will be dissatisfied if a product has too many extra features.

During CCM development, more understanding of the requirements is needed that is sufficient to understand the scope of the initiative and prioritize, estimate, and formulate a realistic timeboxed plan. During development, high-level requirements established in the feasibility stage are broken out into more detailed requirements (functional and nonfunctional). It would be reasonable to expect requirements in double figures here (e.g., 40, 60, or 80 separate requirements, perhaps, but not several hundreds). If hundreds of requirements are found at this point, it may mean that the scope of the increment is too large and the increment should be refocused and some requirements descoped. Alternatively, it may mean that too much detail has been elicited for this phase of the life cycle. If this is so, it will restrict the project's later innovation, or it may simply be time wasted, since some requirements could be dropped and all the effort in the detailed investigation will have been wasted. Another risk is that it introduces waterfall-style practices and thinking into the project. At foundations, the concentration of work on the requirements should be to specify what is needed and not how they will be physically realized. The foundations phase provides a broad idea of the structure; the detailed solution focus must come later.

A good requirement needs to be clear, concise, and complete. It should not be combined, overlap, or conflict with other requirements. For certain types of culture change requirements (functional requirements), it is helpful to think of the phrase "the solution will have the ability to..." before writing the requirement. When considering how well a requirement should perform, it can be helpful to think about how the requirement could still fail even though the functional requirement is met. Avoid using the words "must" or "should" in the wording of a requirement, as this may be confused with its priority. Use neutral words such as "will" or "shall" (e.g., "The customer will have the ability to enter a postcode").

LIFE CYCLE OF A REQUIREMENT

Any requirement passes through four life cycle phases*:

- *Elicitation*: The requirement is identified, for example during facilitated workshops in the foundations phase, with more detail being elicited throughout the life cycle.
- *Analysis*: The requirement is analyzed to determine whether it is realistic, ambiguous in any way, or conflicting with other requirements. This will happen during the foundations phase, with more detailed requirements being analyzed throughout the life cycle.
- *Validation*: The requirement is validated by review and by examination of models of the solution whether in diagrammatic or physical form. This will happen during the foundations phase, with more detailed requirements being validated throughout the life cycle.
- *Management*: The requirement is documented in the prioritized requirements list (PRL) and any modifications or further subdivisions of the requirement should be traced back to the higher-level requirement they support. This will happen from the point where the highest level requirements are discovered and continue throughout the life cycle.

It is important that the team is aware that there is more work to be done once a requirement has been identified. Requirements capture at a facilitated workshop is not the entire job. Each requirement must be worded clearly, simply, and unambiguously. Its dependence on, and potential conflict with, other requirements must be identified and resolved as necessary. The requirement must also be testable. Even at the early stage of identifying the requirement, the team needs to be thinking about testing the requirement so that they can confirm both that a requirement has been met and that it is successful in operation. When defining a requirement,

---

* In the final analysis, change sticks when it becomes part of the organizational culture; when it becomes part of "the way we do things around here." There are two techniques for institutionalizing change. First, show people how the change has helped improve performance and competitive advantage. Helping people make the connections between their efforts and improvements requires communication. Second, the strategic leader makes sure that the next generation of top leaders personify the vision. If requirements for promotion and advancement do not change in a manner consistent with the vision, the change rarely lasts. Bad succession decisions can undermine years of hard work (Kotter 2007).

the team should simultaneously determine its acceptance criteria as measurable targets. This will provide a means of testing that the requirement has been satisfied. Once a requirement has been identified, it must be managed so that its eventual inclusion within the solution (or its fate if it has been descoped) is traceable along with the rationale and authority for this. This is where the role of Business Analyst within the team, as the guardian of the requirements, is essential.

PRIORITIZING REQUIREMENTS USING MoSCoW

While prioritizing requirements using MoSCoW is a fundamental part of the CCM philosophy, it is important that the essential work is done and that it is only noncritical = Should Have and Could Have requirements that are omitted. The key to ensuring this is the clear prioritization of the requirements using the MoSCoW rules. The MoSCoW rules provide the basis for decisions about what the culture change management team will do

- During a time box within an increment
- Within an increment of the deployment to the desired future state
- Over the whole deployment process

The gathering of functional and nonfunctional requirements starts during the early deployment phases in order to form the prioritized requirements list that is agreed to. The requirements here are necessarily high-level but they need to have sufficient substance to enable an informed judgment on how realistic the culture change is and to allow planning of timeboxed increments.

As shown in Figure 11.6, the very nature of some type of decomposition can help resolve one of the problems that may confront the team: when all the requirements seem to be Must Haves. However, the assertion that all requirements are Must Haves is, in fact, often symptomatic of insufficient decomposition of the higher-level requirements. A high-level Must Have requirement frequently yields a mix of subrequirements, some with lower priorities. Flexibility is once more restored. New requirements will often emerge as existing requirements and are defined in more detail and as the project progresses. All requirements need to be prioritized using the MoSCoW rules, no matter when in the project they are defined. All

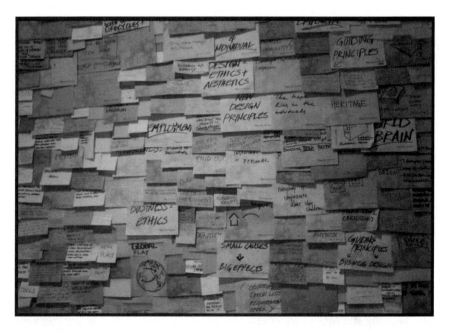

FIGURE 11.6

A requirements brainstorming session before consolidation. Requirements can be identified at various levels of detail from a high-level, strategic viewpoint through to a more detailed, deployable level. High-level requirements can often be decomposed into sub-requirements that can be further subdivided into detailed requirements.

priorities should be reviewed throughout the project to ensure that they remain valid. The team has the authority to descope Should Have or Could Have requirements by agreement of the team, including solution developers and business champions. However, the change of priority of a Must Have requirement in the PRL has to be referred to the business visionary and possibly a wider group of stakeholders.

Some culture change projects are, by their very nature, highly exploratory. For these initiatives, the level at which it is possible or desirable to specify requirements in the early stages may be limited. However, value for money from the culture change is a consideration and must be maintained, and exploration must not be unbridled. In such cases, objectives should be clearly stated and agreed to during the early parts of feasibility. Then the team should establish a timeboxed plan for work on specific aspects of the objectives, with goals and outcomes as requirements. CCM's strength is in the adaption and application of the timeboxes to maintain control of the rollout that is in line with its culture change objectives.

THE PRIORITIZED REQUIREMENTS LIST (PRL)

The PRL authorizes and documents what is to be included in the culture change deployment plan, together with the priorities. The PRL is an integral planning tool that allows the team to

- Establish the basis for agreement between the customers and the suppliers on what the outcome of the culture change will be
- Provide a basis for estimating costs and schedules to attain the *desired future state*
- Provide a baseline for validation and verification
- Facilitate transfer from old to new working culture
- Control and enhance the culture change requirements
- Indicate which requirement is anticipated to be in which time box

The PRL should contain all the requirements that the new culture needs to address, and must be reviewed throughout the design and rollout and updated and reprioritized whenever a new requirement is identified or an existing requirement's priority changes. The requirements in the PRL should be agreed on by the Sponsor and the appropriate stakeholders from the business. By the end of the design planning, the requirements should be baselined (agreed on and signed off) in order to avoid and mitigate scope creep. This does not mean that the requirements cannot be changed, only that change is under control and the requirements agreed on at the outset are clear, together with their priorities.

SUMMARY

Requirements can be obtained through a mix of facilitated workshops and model-building sessions, decomposing from high-level to detailed requirements. Focus groups of end users of the solution being developed, with significant input from the business roles, can supplement this work. Models built during exploration can be used to demonstrate the solution and clarify the business rules and functionality required. Elements of the solution built iteratively during the Engineering Phase allow usability and performance to be checked and refined along with other nonfunctional requirements.

CCM advocates the inclusion of multiple roles in a development project. The culture change manager (CMA) is the guardian of the requirements plan, with a responsibility to ensure clarity and completeness of the requirements within it. Often there is a communications gap between the business and technical roles due to a difference in language or culture or a lack of appropriate analytical skills. The CMA facilitates communication between such roles but it is important not to replace the true business roles, separate them from the CCM developers, or act as a barrier to direct communication between them. It is equally important to recognize that the individual champion will usually have neither the specific analysis techniques and skills nor the perspective of other business areas to see the full implications of their requirements. A CMA is there to help users think through the full implications of their ideas until they are complete. The CMA has specific techniques and skills to enable them to identify the dependencies, overlaps, and conflicts between requirements and the effect of project level requirements on the corporate objectives and direction.

Requirements always evolve and emerge in any CCM initiative. Detailed analysis of the requirements is deliberately done as late as possible to avoid unnecessary rework and to manage complexity. It is important to obtain agreement to a high-level baseline set of prioritized requirements in the PRL from the champion and key stakeholders. This allows change to be embraced and controlled. Another essential point is to identify the nonfunctional (performance attribute) requirements; these are a vital part of the success of the project. In summary, it is important to follow the guidelines for requirements success.

To be successful at requirements gathering and to give your initiative an increased likelihood of success, you should try to follow these 10 rules:

1. Don't assume you know what the customer wants; ask
2. Involve the users from the start
3. Define and agree on the scope of the solution
4. Ensure requirements are specific, realistic, and measurable
5. Gain clarity if there is any doubt
6. Create a clear, concise, and thorough requirements document and share it with the customer
7. Confirm your understanding of the requirements with the customer and play them back

8. Avoid talking technology or solutions until the requirements are fully understood
9. Get the requirements agreed on with the stakeholders before the initiative begins
10. Create a prototype if necessary to confirm or refine the customers' requirements

Finally, focus on the objective: if the project objective is to support sales operatives in the field, then speeding up invoicing is not likely to be a Must Have, but information on customers' past payment records probably is. Keep a record of requirements: the priorities list includes functional and nonfunctional requirements, functions, features, constraints, and progress. Keep the list in a form that is useful for both business and technical staff.

12

Using Estimates and Time Boxes

In a Nutshell: A time box is a somewhat controversial time management technique involving a fixed period of time that is established to accomplish a task. As such, timeboxing* is a key technique in CCM: it is more than just setting short time periods and partitioning the development work. It is a well-defined process to control the creation of low-level products in an iterative fashion, with several specific review points to ensure the quality of those products and the efficiency of the delivery process. By managing on-time delivery at the lowest level, on-time delivery at the higher levels can be assured. Initial MoSCoW prioritization of the work within the time box—and continual reassessment of what can be achieved in the agreed on time frames—ensures that time boxes finish on time, every time, even at the expense of features.

OVERVIEW

Estimates can be used for several purposes: to evaluate a business case, to assess feasibility, to plan project costs and schedules, and to communicate with stakeholders. An estimate is a forecast of how much it will take to deliver a specified requirement in terms of cost, effort, skills, and duration

---

* The date is usually set in stone and does not change. When timeboxing is utilized in change management, a team estimates the scope of the task, and then they estimate how much of the scope can be accomplished within the time frame, just as they would in a project management environment. This way, the deliverables come in on the scheduled dates, hopefully without fail. The scope of the project can be adjusted and reduced accordingly, but the deadline never changes. The deadline is one of the most important aspects of timeboxing. Many of us want to finish a task within a certain time, but we refuse to change the scope of the task to facilitate its completion.

or, conversely, how much functionality can be delivered for a given cost, effort, set of skills, or duration. Associated with these is a definition of assumptions and risks. Estimating in CCM can use any of the techniques used in other projects but there are four key points:

1. Estimates need to include a level of contingency to cover the risk associated with unknown factors. In CCM, contingency is placed in the scope of features to be delivered by applying the MoSCoW prioritization.
2. Estimates are only as precise and accurate as is necessary for their purpose at a given point in the life cycle.
3. Where possible, the people delivering the project carry out the estimate.
4. Estimates are expected to be revalidated throughout the project as the understanding of the requirement deepens and as the team's actual velocity is proven.

THE ESTIMATING CYCLE

Estimates are carried out at all stages of a project, initially to help with planning. Throughout the project, these initial estimates should be validated and revised to give increasing precision based on emerging detail, the validation of assumptions, and actual measures of project performance. CCM expects early estimates to give a broad picture that is sufficient only to support the decision on whether to proceed. They are not expected to lay down a precise shape for the project and estimates are expected to change as more information becomes available. Initial estimates during feasibility will be based on the limited information known about the project at this stage, but also on experience of similar solutions in different projects. In foundations, as more becomes known about the detail of the project, the estimates can be refined based on that knowledge. Later, as some of the solution starts to be developed (during exploration and engineering), actual results and measures of velocity can be used to refine estimates even further.

Estimates are not static. They should always be reviewed at intervals throughout a project to reassess their validity based on actual events and experience, such as further detail being elicited, risks manifesting or going away, velocity (speed of delivery) being higher or lower than expected, assumptions proving valid or invalid, unexpected events occurring, team availability changing, change requests being formally raised, and so forth. In CCM, the effort and duration are fixed so the focus is on validating what will be delivered.

PROJECT VARIABLES AND CONTINGENCY

The single biggest difference in estimating for CCM projects comes from the CCM approach to project variables. This is described in more detail elsewhere and the following summary is intended only to explain its impact on estimating. Most projects have four factors that can vary: time, cost, features, and quality. It is not possible to fix every one of these as this would allow no contingency for the inevitable unknowns and changes that happen during the life of a project. In traditional project management, the features are fixed and time and cost are allowed to vary (e.g., extra resources are added or the delivery date is postponed) so that quality may inadvertently be compromised. In a CCM project, time, cost, and quality are fixed by the end of foundations and it is the amount of features that is allowed to vary by applying MoSCoW prioritization. Thus contingency in a CCM project is managed within the prioritization of the features rather than by adding extra time or cost. The impact of this on estimating is that the overall estimate for the work in a given time frame must include enough lower priority features to provide the necessary level of contingency. This enables the guaranteed delivery of the Must Have features to be confidently predicted. Contingency is built into the estimate and not an additional percentage, which means driving down the Must Haves to as small a set as possible. A rule of thumb is that Must Haves should not be more than 60 percent of project effort, but the aim is to build in enough contingency to cover the perceived risk. For example, you may need to keep the effort in fulfilling Must Haves to less than 50 percent where risk is very high or the project is more exploratory. Early project estimates during feasibility and foundations are based on less detailed information with higher levels of risk and uncertainty and it is therefore important to take account of these factors when producing such estimates. Assessments of project risk must be considered within context, for example: size of project, experience of team, technologies, knowledge of client, locations, and so forth.

Top Tips

- Use early estimates to support decisions—don't expect them to be definitive and unchanging.
- Ensure there are sufficient lower-priority requirements to provide contingency.
- Estimates should be carried out by, and belong to, those who will be doing the work.
- Use a collaborative approach to produce estimates.
- Challenge all estimates, either by using more than one approach to give comparison or by taking input from a range of individuals.
- Estimate based on the knowledge available at the time. The estimate will be at the same level of precision as the requirements.
- Estimates should be directly related to business requirements.
- Document all estimates together with their associated scope, assumptions, calculations, and risks.
- Collect metrics to validate and improve estimates.
- Learn from experience.

ESTIMATING DURING THE LIFE CYCLE

- *During Feasibility.* This early in the project, the requirements are high-level and few in number, and estimating is done top down and so the estimate cannot be precise. Its purpose is to support the business case and to give outline costs and timescales for the project. At this stage there is a high degree of uncertainty and the estimate is by no means accurate. It can easily be half or twice the figure quoted and so will typically be quoted as a range. Very often the prioritization within requirements is not enough to allow for this level of uncertainty and it is more useful to present the estimate as a range of values for both cost and duration; for example, a figure of between 100 and 200 days/\$100,000 to \$200,000. Ideally, the lower end of this range should be enough to guarantee delivery of the Must Have requirements. A detailed estimate for the work of the next phase (foundations) is also produced.
- *During Culture Change Design.* During this phase, more detail is known about the requirements as the level of detail increases. This additional detail provides more information for estimating and

reduces the range of uncertainty in the estimate, but the estimate is still typically top down. Now the estimate is likely to be accurate to plus or minus 50 percent, which should be covered by the prioritization of the requirements in scope. Some projects may be able to be more precise depending on the size of project, the experience of the team, and the client. The purposes of estimating at this stage are to revisit the business case and to produce the delivery plan.

- *During Exploration and Social Engineering.* During these phases the purpose of estimating is to define exactly what will be delivered within the coming Development Time Box and to review and validate the estimate for the whole project. There is much more information available on which to base estimates as the requirements are being refined to a greater level of detail, the solution is more detailed, the assumptions become validated, and actual progress and speed of delivery are measured. This means that the estimates are much more accurate and precise and contingency is completely covered within the prioritization of requirements. Estimates are generally based on the tangible deliverables of the time box and are therefore created bottom-up. As the project progresses through repeated development time boxes the estimates become more accurate. The estimating workshop for a development time box takes place at the start of the time box. The requirements need to be understood and refined to more detail so that the solution components can be identified. These provide the basis for the time box estimate and hence the Time Box Plan. In more exploratory development time boxes, this may happen iteratively throughout the time box, with initial component estimates based on assumptions and refined as understanding develops. Each time a time box estimate is produced, the impact on the whole project estimate is reassessed based on the actual rate of delivery. After a couple of time boxes within an increment, the team's actual speed of development (their velocity) should emerge. If the velocity of a team is shown to be slower or quicker than originally envisaged, all estimates for the current increment should be revisited.

The timeboxing technique is based on the premise that it is better to have a working system with limited functionality than to wait for months and even years to have a complete system. With this technique, the project team can guarantee the delivery of the most important requirements on specific dates, with other requirements scheduled for release on successive dates. Timeboxing is considered a technique for delivering prioritized requirements based on the work the project team can deliver within a set period, period! It is typically used on Agile development efforts characterized by fixed deadlines and solutions that require frequent enhancements.

According to Miranda* in 2002 (see Miranda 2011), timeboxing requires that

- Features/user requirements be grouped into functionality or complete subsets
- Subsets be prioritized so that the team knows which requirements should be implemented first
- Each time box begins with a kickoff session and ends with a closeout session that involves reviewing what was achieved in the time box
- Work stops when the time box deadline is reached to review progress and prepare for the next iteration (time box)
- Timeboxing requires a fixed schedule and team size
- The normal completion effort is that which, in the knowledge of the estimator, has a fair chance of being enough to develop the estimated feature while the safe estimate is that which will be sufficient to do the work most of the time except in a few truly rare cases

The team focuses on value so that the most valuable work is delivered after each iteration. Each iteration delivers working software that is an addition to the previous version. Not all requirements will be implemented, but the ones that are implemented are the result of prioritization and perceived customer value. Finally, the project team works with the customer to select the requirements to be included after which each identified and prioritized subset of requirements is completed for each iteration. With this technique, requirements do not need to be fully understood before each iteration and can evolve over time. With timeboxing, scope can be reduced but the deadline never changes. If all the deliverables cannot be met within the set time, the scope of work is reduced. Timeboxing can be combined with the MoSCoW technique for increased effectiveness.

---

* Timeboxing is a management technique that prioritizes schedule over deliverables but time boxes, which are merely a self-imposed or outside target without agreed on partial outcomes and justified certainty, are at best an expression of good will on the part of the team. This essay proposes the use of a modified set of MoSCoW rules that accomplish the objectives of prioritizing deliverables and providing a degree of assurance as a function of the uncertainty of the underlying estimates (Miranda 2011).

Time boxes are used as a form of risk management* to explicitly identify uncertain task/time relationships (i.e., work that may easily extend past its deadline). Time constraints are often a primary driver in planning and should not be changed without considering project or subproject critical paths. That is, it's usually important to meet deadlines. Risk factors for missed deadlines can include complications upstream of the project, planning errors within the project, team-related issues, or faulty execution of the plan. Upstream issues might include changes in project mission or backing/support from management.

A common planning error is inadequate task breakdown, which can lead to underestimation of the time required to perform the work. Team-related issues can include trouble with interteam communication, lack of experience or required cross-functionality, or lack of commitment, drive, and motivation (i.e., poor team building and management). To stay on deadline, the following actions against the triple constraints are commonly evaluated to reduce scope: (a) drop requirements of lower impact (the ones that will not be directly missed by the user), bearing in mind that time is the fixed constraint here, or (b) increase cost (e.g., add overtime or resources).

There are advantages and disadvantages of timeboxing. The advantages include the following:

- It helps prevent feature creep, which is what happens when teams add features to software applications without scrutinizing their relevance
- It is a way of focusing on achieving what needs to be done without delay or procrastination
- It speeds up development time and ensures that the most value is delivered within the shortest possible time
- It facilitates quick feedback from customers and reduces communication overhead due to the small team size

The disadvantages of timeboxing include the following:

- Quality may be sacrificed due to the high priority placed on achieving deadlines
- It does not work well for many types of large interventions; it's usually suitable for those that can be controlled and completed within 90–120 days or less

---

* See the Wikipedia notation on timeboxing.

Controlling a Time Box*

Every time box can be considered as beginning with a kickoff and ending with a closeout meeting. The time box itself is comprised of main stages or iterations, such as investigation, refinement, and consolidation, each reflecting a pass through the iterative development cycle. (See Chapter 10 on *The Iterative Development Approach* for a description of the various life cycle approaches that may be suitable for your organization at the present moment.) See Figure 12.1 for an example.

Traditionally, these constraints have been listed as scope (quality), time, and cost. These are also referred to as the project management triangle, where each side represents a constraint. One side of the triangle cannot be changed without affecting the others. A further refinement of the constraints is to separate product quality or performance from scope, and turn quality into a fourth constraint.† The old adage still holds: Do you want it good? Fast? Cheap? Pick any two and one has to suffer. You are given the options of fast, good, and cheap, and are told to pick any two. In this instance, fast refers to the time required to deliver the outcome, good is the quality of the final outcome, and cheap refers to the total cost of designing and building the solution. This trilogy reflects the fact that the three properties of a culture change initiative are interrelated, and it is not possible to optimize all three—one will always suffer. Thus, in the final analysis you have three options:

1. Design the desired future state quickly and to a high standard, but then it will not be done cheaply
2. Design it quickly and cheaply, but it will not be of high quality
3. Design it cheaply and with high quality, but it will take a relatively long time

---

* For all project types, timeboxing ranked 23 and was rated "Very Good Practice"; for small or culture change interventions it ranked 7 and was rated a "Best Practice" by the survey in Jones (2010).
† The time constraint refers to the amount of time available to complete a project or change initiative. The cost constraint refers to the budgeted amount available for the initiative. The scope constraint refers to what must be done to produce the end result. These three constraints are often competing constraints: increased scope typically means increased time and increased cost; a tight time constraint could mean increased costs and reduced scope; and a tight budget could mean increased time and reduced scope. The discipline of CCM is about providing the tools and techniques that enable the project team (not just the project manager) to organize their work to meet these constraints, as shown in Figure 12.1.

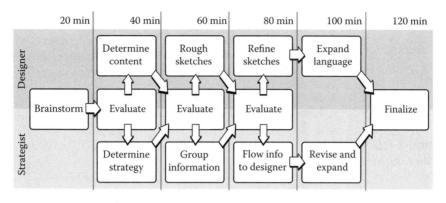

Time box	Nature of the work done	Suggested timescale
Kickoff	Short session for the solution development team to understand time box objectives and accept them as realistic	1–2 hours
Investigation	The initial investigation of the detail of all the products to be delivered by the time box including agreement on the time box deliverables and quantitative measures that will prove success	10%–20% of time box
Refinement	The bulk of the development and testing of the time box products in line with agreed priorities	60%–80% of time box
Consolidation	Tying up of any loose ends related to development and ensuring all products meet their acceptance criteria	10%–20% of time box
Close-out	Formal acceptance of the time box deliverables by the business visionary and technical coordinator	1–3 hours

FIGURE 12.1
A time box for a 2-hour segment.

Many executives have a hard time making the trade-off between meeting the schedule and cutting back on the deliverables, suggesting that such a thing is an erosion of quality. However, many things never come to fruition because of the quest for perfection—for that one last requirement. The real value of this kind of thinking is to show the complexity that is present in any culture change initiative. By acknowledging the limitless variety possible within the triangle, using this graphic aid can facilitate better culture change decisions and planning to ensure alignment among team members and the outcome owners (see Figure 12.2).

FIGURE 12.2
The Good-Fast-Cheap Euler diagram.

Euler diagrams consist of simple closed curves (usually circles) in the plane that depict sets. The sizes or shapes of the curves are not important: the significance of the diagram is in how they overlap. The spatial relationships between the regions bounded by each curve (overlap, containment, or neither) correspond to set-theoretic relationships (intersection, subset, and disjointedness).

An Euler diagram is a diagrammatic means of representing sets and their relationships. The first use of Eulerian circles is commonly attributed to Swiss mathematician Leonhard Euler (1707–1783).

GETTING STARTED WITH A TIME BOX KICKOFF

The aim of the time box kickoff is to

- Review the time box objectives to gain a common understanding of what is to be achieved.
- Ensure that it is still feasible to deliver in the time box what was expected at the Foundation stage and to replan accordingly if not.
- Agree on the acceptance criteria for each product to be delivered. If it is not possible to do this in detail at this point, such agreement can be deferred to the end of the investigation iteration, but in this case, high-level acceptance criteria should be agreed on until the additional detail is available.
- Review the precise availability of team members to participate in timeboxed activities. Remember that commitment to delivery is based on a preagreed and fixed minimum resource levels.

- Ensure that any dependencies on teams working in other time boxes or elsewhere in the business are understood.
- Analyze risks associated with the above, and on that basis ensure an acceptable balance of requirements of differing priorities in accordance with the MoSCoW rules.
  - The kickoff should be attended by all of the solution development team members (including business champions) who will be working in the time box, the CCM Design Team, the technical coordinator, and if needed or interested, the business visionary.

INVESTIGATION ITERATION

The aim of investigation is to provide a firm foundation for the work to be carried out during refinement. For time boxes focused on Exploration activity, this will entail the solution developers and business champions jointly investigating the detail of requirements and agreeing how these requirements will be met as part of the evolving solution. This detailed information may be captured as part of a formal product description or as an embellishment of the Prioritized Requirements List. Ideally, an initial prototype of the solution will be created to demonstrate both an understanding of the requirements and provide an early impression of the solution for assessment. During investigation, the entire team should work together on the full set of requirements agreed at the kickoff. It is necessary to understand the full detail of all the work intended for completion in the time box if informed decisions are to be made later on about what lower priority requirements may be dropped if necessary.

REFINEMENT ITERATION

The aim of refinement is to complete as much of the development work as possible including testing the deliverable(s). Development is carried out iteratively, with the primary objective being to meet the detailed acceptance criteria previously agreed on, at the latest, by the end of Investigation period. Refinement should start off with a quick and informal planning session, focused on determining which members of the team will be working on what products and in what order. The order of the work should be driven by the MoSCoW priorities for the time box but should be pragmatically influenced by other factors, such as a sensible development order from a technical perspective, availability of specific resources such as specialists or business advisors, and any known cross-team dependencies. Refinement ends with a review with the business champions, and where appropriate, other stakeholders. The review should determine what actions are necessary to achieve completion of the work according to the acceptance criteria. No new work should be started after this point. Final changes requested at this time should be carefully considered and prioritized. Significant demand for change at this point often exposes a lack of appropriate involvement of business representatives through the time box to date, a lesson to be learned for the future.

CLOSEOUT

The primary aim of the closeout is to record formal sign-off or acceptance of all the culture change outcomes delivered within the time box. An important secondary aim is to determine what is to be done about work that was initially part of the time box but was not completed. Such work may be considered for the next time box, scheduled for some point further into the future, or even dropped from the increment or initiative completely. It is important to avoid the situation where unfinished work simply passes without thought into the next time box if overall timescales are to be met. A final aim of the closeout is to look back on the time box to see if there is anything that can be learned to make the development and/ or time box management process (TMP) more effective in the future. This could be classed as a miniretrospective and is useful to provide information for the later, formal retrospective, or else the formal retrospective will be reliant on attendees' abilities for recollection. If the time box has been well controlled, this session should be very short and documented, and can be run back-to-back with the kickoff session for the next time box.

Changes are natural during any culture change initiative. When a change occurs, it should be ranked against current priorities, and if accepted, it will be at the expense of an already planned requirement or by changing the time box itself. With respect to defects, a sensible strategy is to fix all critical and major defects within the time allocated at the subset in which they are discovered, postponing minor defects to the end of the initiative and giving the customer the choice between fixing the problems and developing additional functionality. It is obvious that acknowledging from the very start that the customer might not receive everything requested requires a very different communication, and perhaps a different marketing strategy, than that of a solution that promises to do it even when nobody believes it will do it.

The premise on which the method is based is that businesses are better off when they know what could realistically be expected than when they are promised the moon, the sun, and the stars, but no assurances are given with respect as to when they could get it. To be workable for both parties, including the developer and the sponsor, a charter (contract) must incorporate the notion that an agreed partial delivery is an acceptable, although not preferred, outcome. A charter that offloads all risk in one of the parties would either be prohibitive or unacceptable to the other.

RELATIONSHIP WITH OTHER METHODS

Timeboxing acts as a building block in integrating with other personal time management and culture change intelligence-building methods, with the consideration of The Chinese Room concept especially useful for learning to think in an out-of-the-box fashion in terms of learning about different cultures*:

- The Pomodoro Technique is based on 25-minute time boxes of focused concentration separated by 5-minute reflection and dialogue, followed by short breaks allowing the mind to recover (Nöteberg 2009)
- Andy Hunt gives timeboxing as his "T" in SMART (Schwaber 2009)

---

* Timeboxing is a simple time management technique that is used often in software development. Let's say you have a fixed deadline for a new product you need to release, such as an annual upgrade to software for calculating state and local taxes. You must have a new version ready by a certain date. So you'll probably use timeboxing for your development cycle, meaning that you do the best job you can within the time available. What new features you can implement are totally determined by the time frame. Slipping the schedule is simply not an option, so if you get behind, you must choose to cut features. As this section indicates, it is often helpful to use timeboxing in conjunction with other techniques, such as The daily huddle and The Chinese Room.

- The chartering process for CCM Teams
- The daily huddle for CCM teams
- The chinese room concept

THE TEAM CHARTER AND THE DAILY HUDDLE

A team charter is a document that is developed in a group setting that clarifies team direction while establishing boundaries. It is developed early during the forming of the team. The charter should be developed in a group session to encourage understanding and buy-in. The team charter has two purposes. First, it serves as a source for the team members to illustrate the focus and direction of the team. Second, it educates others (for example the organizational leaders and other work groups), illustrating the direction of the team, as shown below.

On a daily basis, the team working in a time box gets together for a huddle meeting. Normally run by the team leader, it is a daily opportunity to understand progress against the chartered objectives at a detailed level and expose issues that may be getting in the way. It is important that the daily huddle session is used to identify problems and to agree who needs to participate in solving any problems that arise. It should not attempt to solve problems if reaching the solution will take any more than a minute or two. The stand-up provides the primary mechanism for the CCM team leader to track progress and exert the necessary control over the work of the team to ensure on-time delivery of the agreed on products of the time box. A potential useful side effect of this daily huddle is that people often end up working much longer than originally intended. If they commit to working on a tedious task for just 30 minutes, it's easy to get started because you have given yourself permission to stop after only 30 minutes. But once you have overcome that inertia and are now focused on the task, 90 minutes may pass before you feel the desire to stop (see Figure 12.3).

The hypothetical example above shows that all the elements can come together to create a highly useful document that boost the team's success. The charter also provides the information needed to reduce the risk of rework, enabling the team to get it right the first time. Investing the required time to develop a charter reduces confusion about the group's objectives. An example is provided by Joe Mikes, CMRP, who is a Senior

---

TEAM CHARTER

Team Purpose

This team will improve delivery time of finished goods. Ideally 75% of our current late orders will be completed on time in the future.

Duration and Time Commitment

The team has been commissioned to work together for three months. The daily efforts will average 50% of the team members' time.

Scope

Activities that happen within the factory are all in scope. Decisions and activities that are outside the physical factory that have an effect on late orders will be document but not pursued at this time.

Members

Connie Smith – Team Leader
Dave Smith
Susan Smith
Roger Smith
Debbie Smythe – Smith
Carlos Eduard Smith – Team Sponsor

Desired End Result

This team will identify, price, and prioritize activities that will change the current situation of late deliveries. The team will be expected to drop our late finished goods delivery rate by 75%. Over the last six months there have been 82 orders on hold due to a variety of reasons. The average per month is 14. A 75% improvement will be equivalent to only allowing three per month on average.

Supporting Resources

The team will need access to: Production planning SME, historical records of production holds, downtime records for all feeder departments, change manager, VP of Ops, VP of engineering, 3–5 Year Facility Strategic Plan, on-going use of the west boardroom for a permanent working space, travel budget for the whole team to see Winterville Plant.

Reporting Plan

The team leader will provide a weekly report that outlines participation, past-due supporting documents, availability of supporting resources, progress of primarily tasks, documenting any past due tasks. There will also be a monthly leadership review of progress and hurdles.

Deliverables

The team will deliver a series of A3 documents outlining the current status of the different variables, desired changes, and projected benefits that will drive down late orders. The team will also quantify what percent of the total change each variable represents to make up the whole 75% improvement.

Links

This team effort will link to the 6-Sigma project, the CORE Safely program, and the internal vendor alignment approach.

FIGURE 12.3
Example of a team charter.

Consultant with Life Cycle Engineering. He has helped numerous companies launch and sustain continuous improvement culture change initiatives and can be reached at jmikes@LCE.com.

The Huddle has the following characteristics*:

- Is attended by all members of the development team
- Runs to a strict format in which each team member in turn describes:
  - What they have been doing since the last stand-up
  - What they will be doing between now and the next stand-up
  - Any problems, risks, or issues they are encountering that are slowing progress
- Has a short and fixed duration—normally no longer than 15 minutes (2 minutes per team member + 2 minutes is a good guide)
- Is ideally held with all participants standing in a circle in their normal workplace (reenforcing the desire to keep the session short and informal)
- May be attended by other roles, such as
  - The CCM Design Team, in order to observe progress and pick up escalated issues
  - The technical coordinator, in order to keep abreast of technical decisions and pick up escalated technical issues
  - Specialists, to participate as transient team members

Let's take a moment to look at the three elements that make up a powerful huddle: vision, unity, and clarity (see Figure 12.4).

Businesses can take a page out of the football playbook and start using the huddle in their regular CCM development process on a daily basis; this will help to begin the culture change by creating a similar experience that football players experience with their team, as Figure 12.4 illustrates.

- *Communicate vision.* There is nothing more important in business today than communicating the shared vision of a team and ensuring

---

* An interesting element of American football is the team huddle. This is the point of the game where the team members responsible for running the play circle up for dispensing information regarding how the series is to play out. It isn't a time for conversation or discussion; it is about the leader sharing a play that everyone is familiar with, understands, and knows their individual roles. The coach sends in the play, the quarterback reiterates it, the team hears it and prepares to act accordingly, they break (generally with a clap and as a unit), and they go make it happen. In some cases, the quarterback decides to ignore the coach's play and call a play of his own—an audible.

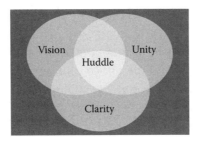

FIGURE 12.4
The three elements of a powerful huddle.

that you support that vision regularly. Too many businesses write out a vision or value statement and display it somewhere on the wall for all to see. Many times these posters get lost with all of the other artwork that is hanging around the office. In order to ensure that a vision statement makes it from the head of the employees to the heart of the employees, that statement must be communicated on a regular basis. The huddle is a great place for the leader to speak to the existing vision, to cast new vision, and to inspire the team to embrace the journey ahead. This can be done intentionally by using the huddle as an opportunity to directly speak to the various aspects of the vision *or* by simply using vision language throughout the huddle.

- *Provide clarity.* Many times teams get sidelined or derailed because there is confusion regarding the individual roles and how those roles play out to accomplishing the vision. Having a regular time for the team to huddle provides clarity on who's doing what and how that responsibility is adding value to the larger picture; unclear expectations and unclear directives will destroy a team and will kill productivity, creativity, and innovation. A way to make this efficient and effective is to allow each team member the opportunity to share what they are working on and what obstacles they may be experiencing. This allows for exposure, accountability, and the opportunity for members to help each other accomplish tasks that may require extra support.

- *Demonstrate unity.* The basic structure of a team assumes unity but oftentimes this unity gets lost as star performers begin to do their part to make the business better and further their personal careers. To ensure that everyone on the team understands the importance of the team, regular huddles where everybody speaks to their part of the team becomes an invaluable resource. A leader can also use this time as an opportunity to recognize those team members that have gone above and beyond in their efforts. In today's working environment employees enjoy recognition and often leaders take too long to recognize their star performers. The huddle provides an opportunity for consistent recognition, support, and direction.

Timeboxing's ability to circumvent perfectionism and avoid procrastination makes it a useful time management technique as part of the daily huddle.

A regularly scheduled team huddle can go far in your efforts to enhance a company's new CCM culture as long as they're done with intentionality and design. Don't feel that you can simply throw something together at the last minute and have an impact. Leverage this time to build your team and add value to the culture that exists within your organization.

Here are some other tips for conducting successful huddles:

- Huddles have the most impact when they are a regularly scheduled part of the day; whether that is daily, every other day, or at the least, weekly.
- Make the huddle interactive where every team member is responsible to share with the rest of the team. This may be difficult for some at first but it has great advantages.
- Put a time limit on the huddle and on how much each individual shares with the team.
- Allow different team members to lead the huddle and discover your up-and-coming leaders.
- Create spontaneity in the huddle by having guest speakers or special events; for instance, breakfast, watch a TED Talk, show a YouTube video, or play a game.
- Huddles are usually most effective when they are scheduled first thing in the morning. It is a great way to discuss the various elements of the day and how the team may be impacted.
- To insure the proper communication of a thought or idea, have a talking stick or other item that gets passed around so that the only person speaking is the person holding that item.

THE CHINESE ROOM

Most people have never heard of American philosopher John Searle's Chinese Room.* Here is the essence of it: Searle's Chinese Room is a thought experiment devised as an out-of-the-box experiment against "strong artificial intelligence," the school of thought maintaining that machines can meet and exceed human cognitive capabilities. Searle argues that, given sufficient processing horsepower, proper architecture, and the right software, a computer can not only do some of the things that the mind can do, it can actually be a mind of its own kind, and thus enjoy all the rights and responsibilities we reserve for humankind thinking and minds.

In the Chinese Room, a person sits isolated, locked in, possessing nothing but the clothes on his or her back and a collection of rules written in English. These rules are simple "if-then" statements that tell the person what to do when presented with patterns of ink on slips of paper, which can be passed one at a time through a small slit in one wall of the room. As it turns out, those patterns of ink on paper represent questions posed in Chinese. And as it also turns out, the person in the room, who doesn't know a scintilla of Chinese, can correctly answer those questions, in Chinese, simply by manipulating the symbols according to the rules. The system works so well, in fact, that those asking the questions believe they're getting answers from a Chinese-speaking person, instead of an English-speaking person robotically manipulating Chinese symbols. Assuming that's true, the question is: Does the person sitting in the Chinese Room understand Chinese or not? Certainly, the person seems to behave intelligently, but does he or she have any sense of what's really going on?

The parallels of the Chinese Room contrasted to many modern business situations, where there are many rules about how to enact a change but little or no understanding of what's really going on, should be obvious. But does all that really matter, argues Searle and others, given that the outcome

---

* The argument and thought-experiment—now generally known as the Chinese Room Experiment—was first published in a paper in 1980 by American philosopher John Searle. It has become one of the best-known and controversial argument/experiments in the recent philosophy and culture change. Searle imagines himself alone in a room following a computer program for responding to Chinese characters slipped under the door. Searle understands nothing of Chinese, and yet, by following the program for manipulating symbols and numerals just as a computer does, he produces appropriate strings of Chinese characters that fool those outside into thinking there is a Chinese speaker in the room. The narrow conclusion of the argument is that programming a digital computer may make it appear to understand language but does not produce real understanding. Hence, the Turing Test is inadequate.

is the same regardless? As authors of this book, we would argue that it does indeed matter for understanding the concept of CCM, if we consider a concept at the heart of computer science: GIGO, or garbage in, garbage out. GIGO means that nonsense fed into a rule-based system will be nothing but garbage when it exits the system. This is one of the biggest reasons that top-down, authoritarian, because-we-say-so-change-processes usually always fail, because they fail at changing the culture. Rules-based systems behave intelligently as long as the inputs make sense. When those inputs—competitive changes, organizational changes, random fluctuations in the Matrix—stop making sense, the outputs also stop making sense. It's as if you asked the fellow in the Chinese Room, What's the color of funny? The answer: Why sky-blue-Swiss cheese, of course.* For another interesting perspective involving the parallels with CCM and the Chinese culture, see Tanaka, 2004.†

A second component (or antecedent) to the Chinese Room influencer is the idea of a paper machine, a computer implemented by a human. This idea is found in the work of the little-known Alan Turing, the so-called father of the modern computer, who wrote about it in his report *Intelligent Machinery* in 1948 (Turing 1948, 1950). Turing writes that he designed a program for a "paper machine" to play chess. A paper machine is a kind of program, a series of simple steps like a computer program, but written in natural language (e.g., English), and followed by a human. The human operator of the paper chess-playing machine need not know how to play chess. All the operator does is follow the instructions for generating moves on the chessboard. In fact, the operator need not even know that he or she

---

* The Chinese room argument has had a remarkable history since it was first published in 1980. The original article was published in at least 24 collections and translated into seven languages. Subsequent statements of the relevant argument in *Minds, Brains and Science* (The 1984 Rath Lectures Pelican, 1989) were also reprinted in several collections and the whole book was translated into 12 languages. There have been hundreds of renditions of the publication and reprinting and translations of other statements. Two decades after the original publication of the article, a book came out called *Views into the Chinese Room* edited by John Preston and Mark Bishop. As well, a website currently cites 137 discussions on the argument: http://consc.net/mindpapers /search?searchStr=chinese+room&filterMode=keywords.

† The paper is concerned with John Searle's famous Chinese room argument. Despite being objected to by some, Searle's Chinese room argument appears very appealing. This is because Searle's argument is based on an intuition about the mind that we all seem to share. Ironically, however, Chinese philosophers don't seem to share this same intuition. The paper begins by first analyzing Searle's Chinese room argument. It then introduces what can be seen as the implicit Chinese view of the mind. Lastly, it demonstrates a conceptual difference between Chinese and Western philosophy and culture with respect to the notion of mind. Thus, it is shown that one must carefully attend to the presuppositions underlying Chinese philosophizing in interpreting Chinese philosophers.

is involved in playing chess—the input and output strings, such as "N–QB7" need mean nothing to the operator of the paper machine.

Turing was optimistic that computers themselves would soon be able to exhibit apparently intelligent behavior, answering questions posed in English and carrying on conversations. In 1950 he proposed what is now known as the Turing Test: if a computer could pass for human in on-line chat, it should be counted as intelligent. Or, instead of becoming omnipotent or rebooting every time a glitch comes along, you could endow the system with strong artificial intelligence (AI), the capacity to actually understand what it's doing and why it's doing it, as opposed to just following orders.*

Perhaps these two methods—the Chinese Room and the paper machine—are a bit too abstract, but this is why we focus so much on learning, and by extension, communication in the culture change management process.† It is why it's so important that everyone in your organization understand the motives and meaning of change, as well as the method, in order to begin to understand and change the culture and seek a better way. And that's why, when it comes right down to it, every change initiative is a learning initiative. Or as Edison used to say: "There is a better way, find it!"‡ (See Figure 12.5.)

---

* Hauser, Larry (online) on the Chinese room argument. The Chinese room argument—John Searle's (1989) thought experiment and associated (1984) derivation—is one of the best known and widely credited culture change counters to claims of artificial intelligence (AI) (i.e., to claims that computers do, or at least can, think. According to Searle's original presentation, the argument is based on two truths: brains cause minds, and syntax doesn't suffice for semantics. Its target, Searle dubs "strong AI," which (according to Searle) "the computer is not merely a tool in the study of the mind, rather the appropriately programmed computer really is a mind in the sense that computers given the right programs can be literally said to understand and have other cognitive states" (1980a, p. 417).

† Culture change communications suggest that good is the enemy of great. Good gets in the way of doing our best. Good holds us back from tapping into our true potential. Many people accept the status quo and misguidedly believe that thinking, creativity, and innovation is someone else's job. Some people have literally turned off their curiosity. They have become apathetic, hopeless, and indifferent. During a recent culture change workshop we asked the participants: "How many of you are excited about coming to work every day?" Not surprisingly, no one raised their hand. For them, work is a means to an end. Work is just something they have to do to provide for their families, to pay the bills, and to live a half-decent life. Why do people settle for a "half" decent life? What would a "full" life look like? Is there a better way?

‡ The sign above Edison's door in his office in Menlo Park, New Jersey, and in Fort Myers, Florida, as well, bore this famous inscription. This quote by Thomas Edison reminds us that we should never be satisfied with the status quo and that we need to strive to improve not only ourselves but those things around me that we can impact, such as processes, work cycles, and mentoring other people. More often than not, the better way is not clear or easy to locate, and sometimes you have to do a little digging and seek guidance and feedback from others.

Thomas Edison   **Menlo Park Laboratory**

FIGURE 12.5
Thomas Edison.

PLANNING AND SCHEDULING TIME BOXES

A primary purpose of the delivery plan is to provide a schedule of the increments, and within them, the time boxes that make up the project. The schedule should reflect the likely number and duration of each time box in a current or imminent increment and also states, at the highest level, the planned focus for each of those time boxes. Application of the timeboxing technique (described above) in conjunction with the MoSCoW prioritization technique will ensure on-time completion of each time box and the delivery of a fit-for-purpose product in that time frame. If each time box completes on time, then each increment will complete on time and thus the project as a whole will complete on time.

Although they are not controlled in the same way, an increment and a project can also be considered as time boxes because they share the characteristics of delivering a fit-for-purpose solution in a preset time frame. For this reason, it is sometimes convenient to refer to these as project time boxes and increment time boxes. When creating a schedule of time boxes, the primary driver should always be the business priority. However, it is advisable to consider other factors when working out a delivery order. Such other factors will include

- Business and technical risk
- Solution architecture and external dependencies
- Ease of implementation and the drive for an early return on investment

- Availability of critical or specialist resources
- Constraints associated with business process or corporate policy
- Quick wins

SUMMARY

Timeboxing is one of CCM's key practices to ensure on-time delivery. At the lowest level, the Development Time Box maintains focus on delivery in the short term (weeks or even days). It also provides control at the lowest level, as well as a clear indication of the health of the project. If development time boxes are delivering at least the Must Haves on time every time, then the estimating process is working, the team is working, the delivery plan is being validated, and the risks should be reducing. This low-level confidence feeds upward to instill confidence at the increment and the project levels.

Section V

Creating

Creation and creativity involve all of the other facets of taxonomy. In the creative process, the change masters remember, understand, and apply knowledge and analyses, and evaluate outcomes, results, successes, and failures—as well as processes to produce a final product. The following are some of the key terms for this aspect of the taxonomy:

1. Designing
2. Constructing
3. Planning
4. Producing
5. Inventing
6. Devising
7. Making

This section contains the following chapters:

- Chapter 13: Modeling and Simulation
- Chapter 14: Measurement and Appraisal
- Chapter 15: Risk Management Considerations
- Chapter 16: Deploying and Implementing CCM

13

Modeling and Simulation

There is nothing more difficult to take in hand, more perilous to conduct, or more uncertain in its success, than to take the lead in the introduction of a new order of things; because the initiator has for enemies all those who have done well under the old conditions, and only lukewarm defenders in those who may do well under the new.

Niccolo Machiavelli (The Prince, 1532)

In a Nutshell: Modeling and simulation are about getting information on how something will behave without actually testing it in real life. Ultimately, any organization's culture is developed on a daily basis by a complex interplay of organizational values, reward, and recognition— formal and informal and personal behaviors. This process continues whether an organization is aware of its culture or not. Advancements in computing power, availability of PC-based modeling and simulation, and efficient computational methodology are allowing the leading edge of prescriptive simulation modeling, such as optimization, to help in pursuing investigations in systems analysis, design, and culture change management processes that were previously beyond the reach of the modelers and decision makers. The use of modeling and simulation to depict the future that the CCM wants to achieve the organization and its leaders to become more aware of the desired future state, which this Chapter on modelling attempts us to help clarify and envision.

INTRODUCTION TO MODELING

A model can be defined as

- A description or analogy used to help visualize something that cannot be directly observed
- A small but exact copy of something
- A pattern or figure of something to be made

Modeling and simulation (M&S) involves using models, including emulators, prototypes, and stimulators, either statically or over time, to develop data as a basis for making managerial or technical decisions. The terms "modeling" and "simulation" are often used interchangeably. The use of M&S within engineering is well recognized. Simulation technology belongs to the tool set of engineers of all application domains and has been included in the body of knowledge of engineering management. M&S has already helped to reduce costs, increase the quality of products and systems, and document and archive lessons learned.

Modeling is a discipline on its own. Its many application domains often lead to the assumption that it is pure application. This is not the case and needs to be recognized by change management experts who want to use simulations. To ensure that the results of simulation are applicable to the real world, the practitioners must understand the assumptions, conceptualizations, and implementation constraints of this emerging field.

WHAT IS A SIMULATION MODEL?

Dynamic simulation modeling in organizations can be defined as the collective ability to understand the implications of change over time. This skill lies at the heart of a successful strategic decision process. The availability of effective visual modeling and simulation for culture change enables the analyst and the practitioner to boost their dynamic decisions by rehearsing strategy to avoid hidden pitfalls. System simulation, in reality, is the mimicking of the operation of a real system, such as the day-to-day operation of a bank, the value of a stock portfolio over a time period, the running of an assembly line in a factory, the personnel assignments of a hospital, or a security company using a computer. Instead of building extensive mathematical models by experts, the readily available simulation software in the past 10–20 years has made it possible to model and analyze the operation of a real system and its culture by nonexperts who are managers and not programmers.

A simulation is the execution of a model represented by a computer program that gives information about the system being investigated. The simulation approach of analyzing a model is the opposite of the analytical approach, where the method of analyzing the system is purely theoretical. The analytical approach can sometimes be considered as more reliable, but the simulation approach offers more flexibility and convenience. In the arena of CCM, the activities of the model consist of planned events that are activated at certain points in time and in this way affect the overall state of the culture being emulated. The points in time that an event is activated are treated in a random manner, so that input from outside the system is not usually required. Events exist autonomously and are discrete, so that between the execution of two events, nothing happens.

In the field of simulation, the concept of the principle of computational equivalence has beneficial implications for the decision maker.* Simulated experimentation accelerates and replaces effectively the wait-and-see anxieties in discovering new insight and explanations of future behavior of the real system. The 2006 National Science Foundation (NSF) report, *Simulation-based Engineering Science*, showed the true potential of using simulation technology and methods to revolutionize the engineering science. Among the reasons for the steadily increasing interest in simulation modeling applications are the following (National Science Foundation Blue Ribbon Panel, 2007).

Using simulation models is generally cheaper and safer than conducting experiments with a prototype of the final product. One of the biggest computers worldwide is currently designed in order to simulate the detonation of nuclear devices and their effects in order to support better preparedness in the event of a nuclear explosion. Similar efforts are conducted to simulate hurricanes and other natural catastrophes.

Simulations can often be even more realistic than traditional experiments, as they allow the free configuration of environment parameters found in the operational application field of the final product. Examples

---

* SIMSCRIPT provides a process-based approach of writing a simulation program. With this approach, the components of the program consist of entities, which combine several related events into one process.

are supporting deep water operation of the U.S. Navy or simulating the surface of neighboring planets in preparation of NASA missions.

Simulations can often be conducted faster than experiments done in real time. This allows using them for efficient if-then-else analyses of different alternatives, in particular when the necessary data to initialize the simulation can easily be obtained from operational data. This use of simulation adds decision support simulation systems to the toolbox of traditional decision support systems.

Simulations allow setting up a coherent synthetic environment that allows for integration of simulated systems in the early analysis phase via mixed virtual systems with the first prototypical components to a virtual test environment for the final system. If managed correctly, the environment can be migrated from the development and test domain to the training and education domain in follow-on life cycle phases for the systems (including the option to train and optimize a virtual twin of the real system under realistic constraints even before the first components are being built).

Many organizations seeking to change their culture in most industries benefit from the use of models, prototypes, and mock-ups to establish requirements, confirm expectations, and test the achievability of objectives. These can be as diverse as a Storyboard to represent an advertisement, or a computerized scale model of a proposed hospital. They can be temporary, transient, or throwaway. Harrington Management Systems advocates the use of models to improve communication and to create or challenge ideas by making developing culture change, ideas, and products visible (Tolk 2014).

Social scientists try to explain aspects of the real world by comparing them with models that are based on familiar mechanisms. When using models to explain cultural change phenomena, social scientists tell us that models must be testable and that they are acceptable only after they have been tested in the real world.

Models may be physical (e.g., a built version of some part of an eventual solution, such as working software) or they may be expressed in a language (e.g., a diagramming convention) with its own rules and symbols.

MODELING AND PROTOTYPING

The most common misunderstanding about science is that scientists seek and find truth. They don't—they make and test models. Making sense of anything means making models that can predict outcomes and accommodate observations.

Modeling and prototyping are often linked concepts. While a prototype is a type of model a model is not necessarily a prototype. For example, we can model an existing situation: a building, a staffing structure, or an IT data structure, without intending to change it. It becomes a prototype when we use it as the basis on which to build a new structure. For example, in science a good model should include a mechanism. When scientists construct a model, they are hypothesizing that some poorly understood aspect of the real world can be compared—in some respects—to a mechanism that is well understood. In software engineering, the term "model" has traditionally been used to refer to a set of diagrams formulated in a diagram-based language, such as the Unified Modeling Language (UML), describing an aspect of a solution (e.g., data, objects, processes, states) through the help of various diagram types.

WHAT TO MODEL OR PROTOTYPE

Every culture change model is built up through the collaboration of the community that advances the body of knowledge (BoK). Those models that survive do so because they not only fit into but also consolidate the fabric of the particular BoK. In other words, CCM is a collective enterprise and its models are cumulative, interconnected, and coherent. CCM practitioners and behavioral scientists need to construct new models in such a way that they fit into the fabric of existing specialized knowledge whenever applicable. In CCM (as in science itself), there are usually different teams working on the deployment and testing of any change model, and they need to communicate their findings through conferences and reports.*

No single study should be viewed as the final word on any particular issue. Rather, it should be seen as a contribution to the discussion. Eventually, as a BoK on a topic accumulates, the community and its researchers form a consensus about the correct model or models. Some implementations and

---

* Social scientists are expected to publish the results of their research in associated journals so that others are informed and can give feedback. They need to cite previous research that is relevant to their study so that others can see how the work fits into the existing picture and BoK.

studies will have made significant contributions to the consensus, others only minor ones, and still others may have been totally wrong.*

We may model the following areas involving organizational culture:

- Current situation, often known as the As Is state
- Prototype of the future, desired situation—the To Be state

We may model either of these states physically.

We may also find it useful to model them conceptually or logically, just focusing on the aspects that are of interest to the culture change. Some models are just snapshots in time: they capture a single configuration of a highly dynamic system. Models may also be used to capture the properties of the "type" of something. Such models can be used to document and collect concepts and to draw conclusions about universal properties of the eventual solution.

A typical example of a combination of both static and dynamic models is the map in a car's satellite navigation system, which captures the roads and junctions (static information), but also the position and speed of the vehicle at this moment in time (dynamic information). Some of the detail in such a snapshot will change quite frequently but it may often be found to be useful and insightful to model a sample situation at a point in time.

MODELING AND ABSTRACTION

Modeling usually incorporates some degree of abstraction, which involves omitting certain details from the model to allow clearer focus on another particular aspect. For example, the map of the sub-way system in a city shows just what it needs to in order to communicate specific information to its target audience,† which is the traveler. It is intended to allow travelers

---

* Occasionally, the links binding a model into the interconnected web of scientific knowledge begin to break down because new discoveries have weakened them. This is a sign that the model is in trouble and it may end up being replaced by a new model that meshes better.

† See http://www.dsdm.org/content/12-modelling for more details. The DSDM Consortium was formed out of the RAD movement. DSDM has continually evolved through practice, maintaining a whole-systems development effort perspective and key principles. In 2001, Arie van Bennekum represented the DSDM Consortium at the drafting and signing of the Agile Manifesto in Snowbird, Utah. It has been suggested that the Manifesto has influenced the way that software is now developed to a far greater extent than any new technology has done, and Agile is now the preferred way of working in many organizations including government departments.

to move from one railroad station to another. To do this, it needs to illustrate the stations and the links between them, while omitting the power cables, the mechanisms to change tracks, and the signals followed by the driver. Also, very often it doesn't itemize the true distance. Another model of the same sub-way system, created for a different purpose or target audience, may show these details.*

An important principle to remember in CCM is that models should be valid in all contexts in which they are relevant. This means that irrespective of the specific discipline, geographic location, or culture they are used in

- The same models should apply; the science of change management is consistent and integrated
- There are no areas of the culture change management practice whose models clash violently with the models proposed in other areas
- The same should be true of CCM, which is why interconnectedness is an important feature†
- Bogus science often relies on models that clash with those of real science, and in some cases, there are even internal inconsistencies within a branch of bogus science itself

TARGET AUDIENCE FOR THE MODEL

The following are the four targets for a model:

- A model provides information about something (the content or meaning)
- A model is created by someone (the sender)
- A model is for someone (the receiver)
- A model is for some purpose (the usage context)

---

* Physicist James Trefil has composed a list of the interlocking "grand ideas" that scientists use to make sense of nature. Homeopathy uses a model which proposes that the effect of a solution increases as it becomes more dilute. This model is not scientific because it is completely at odds with other models in chemistry and biology. Acupuncture uses a model in which a type of energy, called qi flows in the body, are helped by channels known as meridians. This model is not scientific because there is no real-world evidence for the existence of either qi or meridians and they do not fit with other biological models.
† For example, biology uses the same atomic model as chemistry and the models that explain gravity at any place on Earth also explain the gravitational interactions between galaxies.

It is important that the level of detail and the language used is appropriate for the target audience (the receivers) of the model. At the Harrington Institute and Harrington Group Software, models are used to communicate between teams of mixed specialties, including system designers and analysts, users, technologists, and solution developers.

VIEWPOINTS FOR MODELING

Modeling should be used to facilitate understanding and communication of the business area and testing the developing solution. A coherent picture of the whole solution area can be gained by considering each of the perspectives: what, where, when, how, who, and why, and the relationships between them. For example, who performs which processes or what data is needed to support each process. Matrices can be helpful in drawing these relationships.*

However, it is worth checking whether the development effort omitted a particular perspective intentionally. If we take each of the four quadrants in the Schneider culture change model shown in Figure 13.1, and use the interrogative method of the 5W and 1H, we can develop quite a large database of information concerning the culture change that we are involved with.[†,‡]

The Schneider culture change model shows four areas of focus: collaboration, control, competence, and cultivation, which we call the 4Cs of culture change. According to the principle of the Five Ws, a report can only be considered complete if it answers these questions starting with

---

* From 1986–1991, Jim Harrington developed the Total Improvement Management approach. (Reference: His first document published for general public release was Ernst & Young's Technical Report TR91.002 and then in his book, *Total Improvement Management—The Next Generation in Performance Improvement*, published by McGraw-Hill in 1995), Harrington and Voehl started developing the approach to prepare a Strategic Improvement Plan in 1987 and 1988 (Reference: The first document published for general public release was Ernst & Young's Technical Report—TR91.002) and another was FPL Qualtec Technical Report on Strategic Quality Planning (see QQS88.003).

† Schneider's Culture Model is—like all models—flawed. However, we think it still tells us something of value about the organization we are looking at or attempting to change. If you look at Figure 13.2, you should be able to map your company's footprint on the various quadrants. Ask questions such as: How much focus do people put on the various areas? How much are they discussed? What attitudes do you notice?

‡ The Five Ws, and one H, or the Six Ws are questions whose answers are considered basic in information-gathering. They are often mentioned in journalism (cf. news style), research, and police investigations. They constitute a formula for getting the complete story on a subject. Source: Journalism website. Press release: getting the facts straight. Work by Owen Spencer-Thomas, D.Litt. URL initially retrieved 24 February 2012.

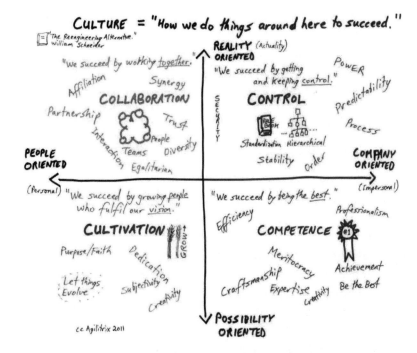

FIGURE 13.1
Modeling perspectives using Schneider culture change model—the 5Ws and 1H.

an interrogative word: (1) Who is it about? (2) What happened? (3) When did it take place? (4) Where did it take place? (5) Why did it happen? Some authors have added a sixth question—How?—to the list, although "how" can also include how to measure, and by what means.

The following approach is suggested and is based on the 5Ws and an H that should come after every news story*:

- *What*: The information within the solution area, relationships, and business rules
- *Where*: The locations at which the business operates in relation to the solution area
- *Who*: The people: customers, users, stakeholders
- *When*: The events of importance to the business (times and scheduling)

* See footnote ‡ on p. 284. Source: Journalism website. Press release: getting the facts straight. Work by Owen Spencer-Thomas, D.Litt. URL retrieved 24 February 2012. Also see the DSDM website at: http://www.dsdm.org/content/12-modelling for more details. The 5Ws and 1H is one of the classic quality and innovation interrogatory tools.

- *Why*: The business objectives and strategy, as related to the development effort
- *How*: The functions, features, and processes within which the solution area operates; also, How to measure + How much $

USING THE CULTURE CHANGE MODELS

The CCM framework has identified a number of outcomes that may need to be generated by the end of each phase of the life cycle. Of necessity, these outcomes may be a robust combination of technical information, culture change objectives, and constraints. Models and prototypes will help to analyze and present some of the required technical information for culture change to succeed in manageable increments and to test the developing models or prototypes. context diagrams of the whole solution area (the big picture) at early stages in the life cycle are invaluable as a guide to the scope and dependencies within the solution space and as an unambiguous communication of these elements to the stakeholders within and outside the development effort.*

The Context Diagram shows the system under consideration as a single high-level process and then shows the relationship that the system has with other external entities (systems, organizational groups, external data stores, etc.). Another name for a context diagram is a context-level data-flow diagram or a level-0 data flow diagram. Since a Context Diagram is a specialized version of a Data-Flow Diagram, understanding a bit about Data-Flow Diagrams can be helpful. A Data-Flow Diagram (DFD) is a graphical visualization of the movement of data through an information system. DFDs are one of the three essential components of the structured-systems analysis and design method (SSADM).

A Context Diagram is process-centric and depicts four main components:

- Processes (circle)
- External Entities (rectangle)
- Data Stores (two horizontal, parallel lines or sometimes an ellipse)

---

* A Context Diagram (and a Data Flow Diagram for that matter) does not provide any information about the timing, sequencing, or synchronization of processes such as which processes occur in sequence or in parallel. Therefore, it should not be confused with a flowchart or process flow, which do show these things.

FIGURE 13.2

A sample Context Diagram. The best context diagrams are used to display how a system interoperates at a very high level or how systems operate and interact logically. The system context diagram is a necessary tool in developing a baseline interaction between systems and actors, actors and a system, or systems and systems.

- Data Flows (curved or straight line with arrowhead indicating flow direction)

A sample Context Diagram is shown in Figure 13.2.

A culture model tells us about the values and norms within a group or an organization, regardless of the type or complexity. It identifies what is important to the organization and its leaders, as well as how people approach work and each other; how "we do things around here." For example, one culture may value stability and proper order. In this case clearly defined processes will be very important and there will be a strong expectation of conformance rather than of innovation and creativity, which can often be a problem when trying to change the culture toward more creativity. The Schneider Culture Model* defines four distinct cultures:

---

* See http://www.methodsandtools.com/archive/agileculture.php. The Schneider book, *The Reengineering Alternative*, was first published in 2001. The premise is that every business has its own particular kind of corporate culture. Before you sink a lot money, time, and effort into a reengineering/culture change initiative, you will need to know if and how your organization would benefit from such a program. The Reengineering Alternative explains how companies can develop effective culture change improvement plans based not on some cookie-cutter notion of change management, but on that organization's unique strengths and corporate objectives. This book will be especially valuable to managers who recognize the need for organizational change, but either haven't found an appropriate improvement program or can't fit an outside program into their own particular budget.

- *Collaboration* culture is about working together
- *Control* culture is about getting and keeping control
- *Competence* culture is about being the best
- *Cultivation* culture is about learning and growing with a sense of purpose

Figure 13.1 summarizes the Schneider Culture Model. Each of the four cultures are depicted—one in each quadrant. Each has a name, a descriptive quote, a picture, and some words that characterize that quadrant. Please take a moment to read through the diagram and get a sense of the model and where your company fits.

An important aspect of the Schneider model is the axes that indicate the focus of an organization:

- *Horizontal axis*: People-Oriented (Personal) versus Company-Oriented (Impersonal)
- *Vertical axis*: Reality-Oriented (Actuality) versus Possibility-Oriented (Visionary)

This provides a way to see relationships between the cultures. For example, control culture is more compatible with collaboration or competence cultures than with cultivation culture. In many cases, cultivation culture is the opposite of control culture in that learning and growing is the opposite of security and structure. Similarly, collaboration is often seen as the opposite of competence.

All models are wrong, some are useful.

George Box
Statistician

All models are an approximation of reality and it is important to remember that we are ignoring minor discrepancies so that we can perform analysis and have meaningful discourse. Also, we may wish to consider other models such as spiral dynamics if we wanted to understand cultural evolution (Beck and Cowan 1996). In the Schneider model, no one culture type is considered better than another. Please refer to the book for details on the strengths and weaknesses of each. Depending on the type of work, one type of culture may be a better fit.

Companies typically have a dominant culture with aspects from other cultures. This is fine as long as those aspects serve the dominant culture. Different departments or groups (e.g., development versus operations) may have different cultures. Differences can lead to conflict.

USING SYSTEMS THINKING MODELS

Systems thinking takes the position that organizations are dynamic systems whose parts impact and are impacted by both external and internal influences. Taking a systems thinking perspective is a conceptual framework that has been developed by a number of academics (e.g., Merrelyn Emery, Peter Senge) and practitioners to help understand that organizations are made up of highly interdependent processes that are also impacted by the environment. This means that the smallest intervention will have unanticipated influences on other parts of the organization. This in turn means that there will be situations that require tools, methods, and techniques that are more group-focused rather than individual-focused (e.g., a group visioning process has the impact of increasing participants' awareness of other parts of the organization and how the parts influence one another). This would not happen if an individual intervention occurs.

In the development phases, models from a previous solution in the same space may be a useful shortcut to understanding the problem and clarifying the objective. A very rough prototype of the initial ideas may help stakeholders to understand what is being proposed. In the design phase, the communication is with planners, owners, and stakeholders, and the level of the model is a simple big-picture view in order to convey scope. This view could incorporate models of the current situation in addition to proposed solution options. The definition of "why" (business objectives and rationale for the solutions—the terms of reference) is paramount here and will guide the rest of the development effort. The outline solution could include models/prototypes to convey the different options being considered. All throughout the culture change life cycle, the teams are beginning to work in more detail on the definition and prioritization of the requirements. The Schneider modeling approach from the perspectives of what, where, when, how, who, and why can be useful, along with the iceberg model for systems thinking shown in Figure 13.3.

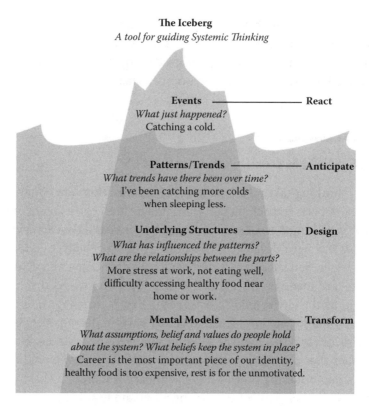

The Iceberg

A tool for guiding Systemic Thinking

Events ———————— **React**
What just happened?
Catching a cold.

Patterns/Trends ———————— **Anticipate**
What trends have there been over time?
I've been catching more colds
when sleeping less.

Underlying Structures ———————— **Design**
What has influenced the patterns?
What are the relationships between the parts?
More stress at work, not eating well,
difficulty accessing healthy food near
home or work.

Mental Models ———————— **Transform**
What assumptions, belief and values do people hold
about the system? What beliefs keep the system in place?
Career is the most important piece of our identity,
healthy food is too expensive, rest is for the unmotivated.

FIGURE 13.3

The Iceberg Model shows the four levels involved in Systemic Thinking using a simple example of catching a cold and also shows the countermeasure for each of the four levels: Events = React, Patterns = Anticipate, Structures = Design, and Mental Models = Transform.

THE ICEBERG MODEL

One systems thinking model that is helpful for understanding global issues is the iceberg model. We know that an iceberg has only 10 percent of its total mass above the water while 90 percent is underwater. However, scientists will tell us that 90 percent is what the ocean currents act on and what creates the iceberg's behavior at its tip. culture change organizational issues can be viewed in this same way as Levels of Thinking*:

- *The Event Level.* The event level is the level at which we typically perceive the world. While problems observed at the event level can often

---

* See more at http://www.nwei.org/resources/iceberg/#sthash.gtCZWpRe.dpuf.

be addressed with a simple readjustment, the iceberg model pushes us not to assume that every issue can be solved by simply treating the symptom or adjusting at the event level. For example, we are catching a cold.

- *The Pattern Level.* If we look just below the event level, we often notice patterns. Similar events have been taking place over time—we may have been catching more colds when we haven't been resting enough. Observing patterns allows us to forecast and forestall events.
- *The Structure Level.* Below the pattern level lies the structure level. When we ask, "What is causing the pattern we are observing?" the answer is usually some kind of structure. Increased stress at work due to the new promotion policy, the habit of eating poorly when under stress, or the inconvenient location of healthy food sources could all be structures at play in our catching a cold.*
- *The Mental Model Level.* Mental models are the attitudes, beliefs, morals, expectations, and values that allow structures to continue functioning as they are. These are the beliefs that we often learn subconsciously from our society or family and are likely unaware of. Mental models that could be involved in us catching a cold could include a belief that career is deeply important to our identity or that rest is for the unmotivated.

High-level system thinking models in many cases can be sufficient to understand dependencies and to estimate well enough for planning. Models will also communicate the scope of the system and highlight areas that are out of scope. High-level models can be used to analyze the whole breadth of the solution space, to communicate ideas, and to identify inconsistencies, dependencies, and omissions. End-to-end diagrams of the solution will be useful. Again, the current situation could also be modeled; such models drawn here can be invaluable as an aid to deployment. Solution options may result in several sets of high-level models. These may be from a logical perspective (showing what is proposed, but deliberately omitting how, when, where, and who). Later models will show different technical options.

---

* According to Professor John Gerber (2006), structures can include the following: (a) physical things, like vending machines, roads, traffic lights, or terrain, (b) organizations, like corporations, governments, and schools, (c) policies, like laws, regulations, and tax structures, and (d) ritual, habitual behaviors so ingrained that they are not conscious.

During exploration stages, detailed solution models, business models, and the design models help to analyze the culture change and solution system in detail in order to communicate ideas and to further analyze increments of the solution. Various types of end-to-end diagrams and single-user perspectives may be useful here. Models will be high-level models of the big picture plus incrementally delivered detailed models as each increment is undertaken. During the deployment stage, component models of the existing situation will be useful along with detailed models of the deployable solution and models from the user perspectives of how the solution will be used. These should link users to the elements of the solution related to them, thereby easing deployment planning. The Deployed Solution is the working, implemented version of the final prototype. The nonimplementable models, such as diagrams, can provide user and support/maintenance documentation, as shown in Figure 13.4.

Whatever the culture change that is desired or business solution being developed, the authors recommend an iterative, incremental, and collaborative approach following the CCM life cycle. This approach places

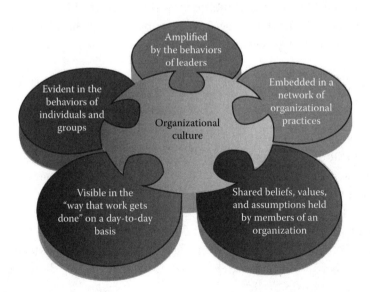

FIGURE 13.4

The Organizational culture influence areas. Organizational culture change is a large puzzle that is influenced by at least five major factors: behaviors of leader, individuals, and groups; a network of organizational practices; shared values and beliefs held by members; and evident in day-to-day visibility in the way "work gets done around here."

a high emphasis on communication—and calls for clear and continuous communication, using rich communication techniques—of which the development of models and prototypes is a key element. These should be developed iteratively, taking a top-down approach to detail and modeling from different perspectives using the guidelines discussed in this chapter and summarized below.

SUMMARY

As part of the CCM approach to drive for clear and continuous communication, modeling can offer significant benefits in making ideas, situations, and options visible. Modeling can range from very informal models (Post-It notes on a table) to very detailed, complex models using specific notations. The emphasis remains on ensuring that any models used enhance communication and are clearly understood by the intended audience, as well as by the creators, as follows:

- Models should be developed iteratively, taking a top-down approach to detail and modeling from different perspectives.
- Models should always be an aid and looked at as a bureaucratic overhead.
- There should always be a clear focus on using languages and terminology that are easily understood by the intended audience for the models.
- There must always be emphasis on using models to enhance the effectiveness of communication for all members and levels of the development process.
- The use of models and their degree of formality will depend on the nature of the culture change initiative, along with the skills and experience of the team in the use of particular modeling techniques.
- The simplest rules are to do what works for the initiative and the organization.
- You will need to capitalize on the skills that exist within the organization and use diagrams and models to establish a common language between the functional work areas/teams.

- Models should be used to see the overall picture at a high level and then to help identify how to break down the development effort into comprehensible chunks that are easier to manage than the whole and can be handled incrementally.
- Modeling is to help people to visualize complex things. Used as such, they can then be used as a basis for incremental development and time box planning for culture change.

We've all heard the saying, "A picture is worth a thousand words" and we fully concur with that statement. But if a picture is worth a thousand words, a three-dimensional model is worth one million words. Today we are able to generate three-dimensional models quickly and easily electronically. This allows us to look at the output from all angles—to feel it, to touch it, and to provide a full degree more critical evaluation of the object. The cost to do modeling has been cut to about 10 percent of what it was just 10 years ago. Taking advantage of this technological breakthrough has saved organizations millions of dollars.

When it comes to simulation, what can we say (in summary) to the organization that is using them? The information and skills that individuals acquire from using a simulation model that simulates unusual and worst-case conditions has saved thousands of lives. Without a simulation model of our key processes, we would never be able to do effective Monte Carlo analysis of the process to optimize the total performance and to simulate the various conditions that the process is subjected to.

14

Measurement and Appraisal

To every person there comes in their lifetime that special moment when they are figuratively tapped on the shoulder and offered the chance to do a very special thing, unique to them and fitted to their talents. What a tragedy if that moment finds them unprepared or unqualified for the work which could be their finest hour.

Winston Churchill

In a Nutshell: Measurement and appraisal are powerful tools to help change culture develop successfully because using appropriate measures improves understanding and control and hence boosts confidence in the delivery. Measurement of effort versus progress achieved enables the culture change development effort to refine its estimates regularly and be able to predict the final outcome a little more effectively. Often measurement is considered relevant only to software-based initiatives, but it can apply equally to change efforts with a purely business content. While techniques may differ, the principles remain the same. This chapter gives an overview of why you should attempt to measure culture change initiatives and outlines where the approaches used in CCM vary from more traditional measurement efforts. It is not the intention of this chapter to describe in detail measurement techniques, since there is already a wealth of information available in published sources.

INTRODUCTION TO CCM MEASUREMENT

CCM measures can be used at all levels within an organization. This chapter is concerned with those that directly relate to delivering the culture change initiative and then evaluating its impact and progress. The key thing to note about measurement in CCM is that the intervention gets an immediate payback because of the iterative structure used in development. In a traditional development effort, each stage (such as analysis) is carried out only once. By the time the measures from each stage are available, it is generally complete and will not be repeated. Therefore, the measures do not help with reestimating the rest of that development effort—they will only be of use to future development efforts of a similar nature. In CCM development efforts, time boxes are repeated, so the measures collected for each time box can often be very relevant to later ones. For example, the actual time taken to accomplish a particular component of the intervention outlined in the first time box can often immediately be helpful to validate the estimates for the next time box, and so forth during the remainder of the development effort. In actuality, such measures will also be relevant for future development efforts. The principles of measurement, however, remain the same whether the development effort is OCM or traditional, software development or business. Although it sounds obvious, the crucial factor in any measurement is to have a reason for it (e.g., knowing how productive the solution development team actually is). Once the reason for the measurement has been decided, the method of measurement is chosen (e.g., through analyzing timesheet information). In some very small development efforts, there may be no need to measure anything.*

USING THE OUTCOMES' APPRAISAL PURPOSE

Although there are various objectives and drivers of workplace change, the common objectives are to reduce costs and to increase efficiency. The changing organizational and external contexts, such as the increasing demand for talented knowledge workers and changing work patterns, have led to the development of new offices that can promote social networks and interaction among employees. The new workplace does not only aim at achieving cost

---

* In actuality, this applies to very few development efforts, such as those internal ones that are unlikely to be repeated. For all others, there will be some level of measurement that is essential to control the outcome, to demonstrate culture change value, and to improve change management performance over time.

efficiency, but it should also support employee satisfaction and productivity.* The most common purpose for measuring and appraising within development efforts is to understand enough about progress to allow the outcome to be controlled and continued. At times, you may also want to know whether some technique or practice is effective (i.e., whether the process is working).

The change management focus is to bring communities of people together within the organization to find opportunities for cooperation, agreement, and problem solving in improving their organization's culture and natural environment. Using the lens of organizational well-being and health to achieve social change, Change Agents work within the organization's communities to develop and sustain democratically based, participatory decision-making that promotes involvement of a diverse segment of the culture in ways that empower the organization and its workers. This is accomplished by facilitating and providing assistance in the following areas:

1. Skills training and leadership development that enhances each individual's talents and expertise to its fullest potential in order to expand the voice and influence of community-based groups
2. Research, information, and public education on issues impacting local communities
3. Community organizing and strategic planning to address these issues
4. Advocacy for changes in public policy that are community-driven, protective, and enhance local resources

Accordingly, measurement can be for two purposes—progress and process—and each gives rise to a different set of measures. Process measures are less used in agile development efforts but can prove valuable. Questions need to be specific to be used to define actual measures. Examine the question

---

* Based on literature review, an overview of performance measurement systems and measures has been developed. The list of corporate culture change performance measures has been classified into six categories according to Bradley (2002) and subsequently compared with the findings from the case studies. The six categories include (1) stakeholder perception, (2) financial health, (3) organizational development, (4) productivity, (5) environmental responsibility, and (6) cost efficiency. The impact of workplace change was examined using the work environment diagnosis instrument (WODI) questionnaire, which evaluates employees' responses to the changed work environment in three areas: employee satisfaction, perceived productivity support, and prioritized aspects (Maarleveld et al. 2009). The Organisational Culture Assessment Instrument (OCAI; Cameron and Quinn 2006) was used to assess organizational culture. See https://doaj.org/article /3dc43814ebd94ef3900d90397beafcb9; article Performance Measurement of Workplace Change: In Two Different Cultural Contexts, by Chaiwat Riratanaphong (Thammasat University Thailand, Faculty of Architecure), Architecture and the Built Environment, Delft University of Technology.

until you understand exactly what it is you need to know and can define specific measures that will provide the relevant answers. Measures can be defined as quantitative (numerically based) or qualitative (based on observation combined with some interpretative understanding). There are some key quantitative metrics for development efforts: effort, cost (or value), duration, and defects. These can be measured at various levels of detail and can be combined in various ways to provide the information required. Wherever possible, metrics should be quantitative rather than qualitative as their analysis is more easily understood and justified. Keeping the purpose in mind, the aim should be to identify the simplest set of measures that will answer the defined questions. Using too many measures is a waste of time and effort and is generally a result of giving insufficient thought to their purpose.

Although you don't have to write a book about defining each of the needed measures, there are certain facts that are useful to record about each; for example, the purpose, what the measure is, the cost of the measurement, where the data comes from, who measures it, when is it measured, how is it interpreted, and what behavior might this measure cause. Even the seemingly simplest measure may require definition. The six standard categories for measuring the impacts of culture change on outcomes are (1) stakeholder perception, (2) financial health, (3) organizational development, (4) productivity, (5) environmental responsibility, and (6) cost efficiency.

Take cost efficiency; for example, what should be included in the cost of a development effort? It could be resources, cost of office facilities, tax, and so forth. The outcome of a development effort is the business value to the organization requesting the work to be done. Outcome refers to more than just the initiative and products. It may be that the product has to achieve a certain state before it starts to have any value. For example, a software component of a development effort does not start earning value until it is put into operation. So, in this case, you would have to define completion for the software components as the point at which they go live.

The primary reason for measuring business value is to demonstrate progress and return on investment. To assess progress during a development effort, the delivery of outcomes is of more real value than the amount of effort spent. In OCM development efforts, there is usually an early delivery of business value and development efforts may start earning value before they finish. It can help the development effort's business case to be able to assess this value and demonstrate when it starts accruing. While measures of outcome are the best and preferred means to represent the real progress of the development effort in business terms, it is not always appropriate or possible to use these with empirical studies. In individual development time boxes, which are not directly delivering business value, it is necessary to measure output to statistically assess progress and help maintain progress and control.*

COMBINE, COMPARE, AND INTERPRET MEASURES

Based on anecdotal views, conceptual frameworks and empirical studies, it has been suggested that culture change management initiatives and engagements that possess the following factors will lead to more favorable outcomes:

- An emphasis on results versus consultant deliverables
- Clear and well communicated expectations and outcomes
- Visible executive/senior management support
- An adaptation to organizational readiness
- An investment up front in learning the organizational environment
- Defined in terms of incremental successes
- Real partnership with consultants and employees

A single measure means very little on its own. Looking at trends over time during the development effort gives a better understanding of progress and better ability to predict what will happen in the future. For instance, if the number of negative comments raised in the review at the end of Refinement in a particular time box is looked at in isolation, it has little meaning. However, if the number of negative comments being raised in Refinement reviews decreases over time, the development effort is clearly improving. When this is combined with other metrics, the development effort can show what has caused the observed improvement: increased productivity, more rigorous testing, and so forth. The development effort may decide to change a technique to improve performance.

---

* The empirical studies include a combination of both qualitative and quantitative methods. The qualitative data from the case studies that were analyzed inductively helped to understand workplace change phenomenon, to clarify the relationships between the variables in the conceptual framework of workplace change, and to answer the research questions formulated at the beginning of the thesis. So far, the quantitative data from questionnaire surveys was used to explore the relationships between employees' responses to workplace change and organizational and national culture in a qualitative way. The collected data can be used for further exploration of complex relationships by statistical analysis.

Comparing performance (e.g., average effort to deliver a requirement) before and after the change will let the development effort assess whether the change was worthwhile.

If something is measured, then generally people will strive to achieve the best measurement results. This often skews behavior. For instance, a metric used in the IT world is the number of lines of code created in a certain time frame. Its aim is to measure productivity of individual programmers: more lines of code mean more working software. Unfortunately, it is all too easy to spread one line of code over several lines so that the program resembles a long thin poem rather than a piece of prose. This unwanted effect can be minimized by being more specific about the meaning of "line." The bottom line is that care should always be taken when defining measures. It is useful to consider the behavior that any measure might cause. It should then be adapted to avoid any unwanted behavior, or if this is impossible, another measure should be chosen.*

MAKING THE COLLECTION OF MEASURES EASY

Collecting measures can be time-consuming and costly so the aim should always be to automate as much as possible. This has the added benefits of minimizing human error and allowing more flexibility in later analysis. If measurement activities are too costly in terms of either time or money, their value to the development effort is minimized. If automation is not possible, the measures should be defined so that they are created during normal work (i.e., keep the measuring processes as light as possible). For instance, in a software development effort, it is standard practice to record defects as they are found during testing. This defect log can be used as a measure of the robustness of the solution and adds no extra effort to the work of the Development Team.†

---

* Triangulation of data collected from different sources (documents, surveys, interviews) helps to validate the findings through cross verification (i.e., reduce weakness or intrinsic biases from the researcher's background knowledge). The assessment of both tangible (physical characteristics) and intangible components (perceived quality) of the office environment can help to validate the findings from the empirical research.

† The Defect Log for small businesses can be applied to the four perspectives of the Balanced Scorecard (financial, customer, internal business process, learning and growth) and can be applied in many situations, with different points of focus regarding their business types.

For small culture change efforts, there is probably only one set of measures, but in a longer one, there may be a different focus and the development effort should therefore drop measures that are no longer relevant or add new ones to meet a new purpose. Similarly, not all development efforts require the same measures. Don't assume that what you used in the last development effort is automatically relevant to the next. This relates to estimating—estimates may be based on measures from previous development efforts. During a development effort the estimate to complete should be updated according to current delivery rates (e.g., use of velocity). See Chapter 12, "Using Estimates and Time Boxes," for more information.*

EXAMPLES OF CULTURE CHANGE MEASURES

Barrett's Seven Levels of Consciousness provides the measure of value of human needs and motivations being delivered from and to the business (i.e., when the customer is able to start earning value or reducing cost from the deliverables of the employee efforts and vice versa), as shown in Figure 14.1. An example of this would be when a new business process is implemented or when a new service is launched on the market.

The power and impact of an organization's culture is often only felt when it is challenged; for example, when you merge two organizations requiring different teams of people to work together, or when you seek to lift business performance with your existing workforce requiring a change in how the work is done. The measurement of both human needs and human motivations is shown by Barrett's diagram in Figure 14.1.

The Seven Levels of Consciousness model was conceived in 1997 by Richard Barrett, founder and chairman of the Barrett Values Centre. The distinguishing feature of the Seven Levels of Consciousness model is that it is evolutionary in nature. It provides a framework for understanding the stages in the development of both individual and group consciousness. The model covers both the internal dimensions of consciousness—our inner journey into self-knowledge and meaning, and the external dimensions of

---

* Today, organizations must cope with the pressure of cost reduction and efficiency in order to succeed in a highly competitive business environment. However, drivers to improve social interaction and employee's performance and as such to contribute to organizational goals and objectives make it necessary to be concerned with other performance criteria as well, such as effectiveness, flexibility, employee satisfaction, productivity, and creativity.

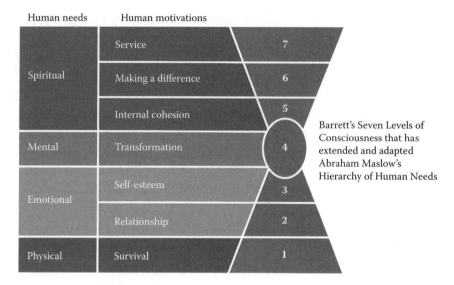

Human needs   Human motivations

Barrett's Seven Levels of
Consciousness that has
extended and adapted
Abraham Maslow's
Hierarchy of Human Needs

FIGURE 14.1

Barrett's Seven Levels of Consciousness, which is an extension of Maslow's Hierarchy of Needs as applied to culture change. Barrett realized that with some minor modifications Abraham Maslow's Hierarchy of Needs could be turned into a model for mapping the evolution of consciousness in individuals and all forms of human group structures, such as organizations, communities, and nations.

consciousness—the gradual expansion of our sense of identity in terms of who and what we care about in our lives.

By 1998, the model was complete and was being used as the foundation of the cultural transformation tools (CTTs) to map the values of organizations and their leaders.

Barrett made three changes to Maslow's model and created a way of using the new model to measure the consciousness of individuals and organizations by mapping their values:

1. Changed the model from needs to consciousness
2. Expanded the concept of self-actualization
3. Relabeled the basic needs
4. Developed a way of using the model as a measurement instrument

An overview of the first three changes is shown in Table 14.1.

Barrett changed the names of the basic needs by grouping "physiological" and "safety" needs into survival consciousness, and relabeling "love and belonging" as Relationship Consciousness.

TABLE 14.1

Hierarchy of Needs Comparing Barrett's and Maslow's Levels

Maslow		Barrett
Hierarchy of Needs		Levels of Consciousness
Self-actualization	7	Service
	6	Making a difference
	5	Internal cohesion
Know and understand	4	Transformation
Self-esteem	3	Self-esteem
Belonging	2	Relationships
Safety	1	Survival
Physiological		

USING EARNED VALUE ANALYSIS

Earned value analysis is a rather routine measure used throughout industry to control development efforts. Its basis is on measuring the value that has been earned to date in the development effort. This can then be compared with planned value and with expected and actual costs to gain an understanding of progress. While full earned value analysis may not be appropriate for fast-moving agile development efforts, there are many aspects of agile development efforts that give a good basis for some forms of this technique. The business focus of development efforts means that all activities are directly related to the business value. The timeboxed approach means that there are frequent deliveries of product to the customer. The total business value is stated in the business case and may be broken down into different elements. However, to be able to use a form of earned value to control development efforts, this business value must be split down to a further level of detail; that is, to assign a value to each requirement or feature of the solution. This may be done either by assessing each one or by splitting the total value evenly or *pro rata* across requirements. Thus the value at any stage of the development effort can be assessed by adding up the value of all completed requirements. This value can be used to demonstrate the point at which the development effort starts to deliver business value, the break-even point (i.e., when value gained equals cost of delivery), and it can be used to judge whether the development effort will meet its goals.

This is the broad outline, but there are various factors that must also be considered to gain a more exact specification of the measures. For example, what is meant by "complete"? Most development efforts have activities that are not directly associated with any business value, such as setup. How are these to be taken into account? One approach is to allocate these a zero business value. This approach is particularly appropriate to CCM increment time boxes.

There are a number of factors that can act as obstacles to successful cultural change and are good candidates for both soft and hard measurement techniques:

- The value of promised extrinsic rewards (such as pay and bonuses) might not be developed to accompany change
- Key management supporters of the change effort might resign or be transferred with a resulting backslide
- Environmental pressures, such as decreased sales or profits, can cause management to regress to more familiar behaviors and abandon change efforts
- Initial changes may provide intrinsic (e.g., psychological) rewards that create higher expectations that cannot be fulfilled (e.g., early involvement of broad stakeholders in decision making may not continue, and so employees lose trust that the organization legitimately wants to change traditional practices)
- New hires and/or newly introduced employees and management are not socialized to understand the new environment, and so act inconsistently with change expectations

Some of these factors are controllable while some are not. The challenge is to focus attention on those issues over which influence can be exercised. In addition, the following questions form a sample of the issues that must concurrently be considered and determined how to measure (if at all):

- How serious is the executive/senior management about measuring the newly instituted change-friendly culture?
- Is there a committed guiding coalition that measures how the organization talks the talk and walks the walk?
- Is the organizational culture evolving to one that is consistent with one that deals with change effectively? How is this being measured?

- Is there a substantial and measurable budget allocated to address change issues like development of change support resources?
- Is the focus on CCM only politically expedient? How do you know?
- Has there been a concerted effort invested in identifying alternative performance measures as part of a broad-based culture change scorecard?
- Have the issues of employee acceptance and resistance been integrated into an overall change measurement plan?
- Is there a network of change resources to support organizational initiatives?
- Are the new change behaviors being integrated and measured into all employees' roles, and especially those of managers?
- Has a CCM plan been created that will extend beyond the end of the project and address sustainability issues?

Although output measures are not the preferred option for demonstrating progress to the culture change initiative, they are often used to define the objectives for development time boxes and hence to demonstrate control. Output measures may include solution components that are completed and delivered internally. Because they are not yet in operational use, such components are not yet delivering any value to the business, but they are contributing to the progress of the development effort. As an example, a series of development time boxes within an increment time box each deliver a set of features that are delivered to operational business use only at the end of the increment. The final delivery is a measurable outcome of business value, but the individual time box outputs are important for measuring progress and maintaining control. When using output measures, it is important to focus always on product delivered rather than tasks completed. Such measures may be used at any stage of a CCM development effort, but would typically be used during the main exploration and engineering time boxes.

QUALITY METRICS

At the very broadest level, it has been discovered that attention to organization development and change management has resulted in a positive impact on productivity, job satisfaction, and other work attitudes. Thus, there is justification for the pursuit of change management effectiveness in most organizational interventions, and particularly in initiatives that traditionally tend to turn the organization into which they are introduced upside-down. The number of CCM defects* is one of these quality indicators that could be measured and is also useful both in measuring progress and in the decision about the organization's readiness for the embracement and delivery of new products and services. The earlier in the development effort a defect is identified, the cheaper it is to correct; the general aim is to correct as many as possible before the product is delivered. When recording defects—for example, during a prototype review or testing—it is important to classify them according to severity or priority, and also for process improvement purposes, to record enough information to analyze their origin and cause. The FASTBREAK Strategy Execution† may be used to bring more focus and effort. This will enable defect categorization to be built into the normal time box processes for strategy planning and execution. In this approach, a showstopper defect is a Must Have and so it must be fixed before the next stage, whereas another that is an improvement might only be classified as a Could Have. These measures are of most value during development time boxes and may be used in deployment. However, too many companies that are full of good ideas, good products, and great people flounder due to a lack of focus, spreading themselves too thin, wasting time, effort, and money chasing too many shiny objects, having lots of projects in the pipeline but not getting traction on any. Lack of focus and effort are the biggest speed bumps on the road to success. Too many businesses lack focus and alignment and wind up wasting time and energy.

What are the two or three critical culture change areas your organization is focused on? If you don't have a sharp focus, your change management effort is in trouble. Effort is a fundamental measure of most development efforts and is used throughout to assess progress and to validate estimates.

---

* A culture change defect is where the individuals and the systems do not perform as required and applies in both IT and business contexts. Human defects can be identified during prototype reviews, during testing, and in the delivered solutions.

† See *FASTBREAK: The CEO's Guide to Strategy Execution*, December 2012 by John R. Childress. *FASTBREAK* is a unique synthesis of how-to, philosophy, principles of effective leadership, and case studies to help the CEO and business leader improve their organization's ability to deliver on their strategy and culture change promises. *FASTBREAK* is filled with breakthrough thinking that is practical and applicable in any industry and any organization, private or public. Organizations operate in a world where both the pace of change and customer expectations are rising inexorably. This means the cycle time for strategy development, execution, and culture change needs to move from typically an annual intervention or process to near real-time.

As a basic measure, effort has to be compared with others to be useful (i.e., it is compared with the delivered product (output) to assess the team's velocity). Assessing velocity is useful within the development time boxes, particularly during the first few. The effort for a time box is fixed and it is expected to deliver a number of prioritized features. An early confirmation of the velocity can give confidence (or otherwise) that the time box objectives can be achieved. Understanding the reasons for slower-than-expected velocity can highlight other issues, such as lack of effective challenge on the prioritization of features or overoptimistic estimates.

This assessment of progress in the sense of delivery capacity or speed can also be used to check the estimate for the whole development effort. It also forms the basis for estimating and planning future development efforts of a similar nature. Effort should be recorded at the lowest level of granularity that is practical and that meets the purpose. Very detailed measurements can be time-consuming and should be used only where necessary and only until sufficient data has been collected. For example, the first engineering time box might include detailed measures of the effort to deliver individual components, which can then be used to confirm the estimates. For process improvement and future estimating a less detailed measure would generally be good enough; for example, the total effort per person for the whole time box. Higher-level measures such as these are less labor-intensive to collect and so are more likely to be accurate and can be carried out throughout the development effort.

EMPLOYEE INVOLVEMENT METRICS

Employees' expectations about their continued involvement in any intervention tend to be raised significantly by empowerment efforts. However, this kind of raised expectation is a double-edged sword. While the benefit to management is a workforce that is ready to partner going forward and to use all their creativity to contribute to the improvement of the organization, there is a pitfall to be aware of—the failure to follow through on the progress that has been achieved or unreasonable delay has the consequence of creating cynicism or reinforcing the cynicism that already may exist.

Cynicism is the enemy of trust and empowerment; a cynical workforce will demonstrate either ambivalence or resistance. It will become even more difficult to overcome during subsequent culture change efforts. To offset cynicism, management can help by

- Continuing to focus explicitly on the change process, thereby establishing it as a norm
- Identifying key individuals to support the change initiative and using them to promote a combined shared organizational understanding throughout any transition
- Providing employee training on the newly developed business processes and technology
- Actively leveraging the findings of the culture change through leadership commitment and implementation
- Establishing an accountability framework for continuing reviews of the organizational change progress on a semiannual basis
- Establishing a way-forward empowerment culture that would include employees in planning and decision making
- Establishing a culture change process that would empower the employees more closely with the external contributors; together, they can identify opportunities to realize the responsiveness and efficiencies of the new technology/business process solution

Empowerment is defined in terms of developing the organizational conditions that support high staff involvement in change initiatives, sharing appropriate decision-making responsibilities among management, supervisors, and staff, and sharing of power as appropriate for the circumstances. The applications of empowerment in North American organizations have suffered from a lack of definitional rigor and this has resulted in different consultants defining it differently. Ultimately, this has resulted in much inconsistency in how it has shown up in organizations. This lack of definitional clarity could have contributed to outcomes that were less than satisfactory. Nonetheless, the core of empowerment is employee involvement, shared decision making, redistributed authority and control, and increased organizational flexibility and adaptability.

COST METRICS

Cost may be derived from effort or may be assessed separately. In all commercial development efforts, cost is a fundamental measure: the Business

Case is based on the balance between cost and business value. During the development effort the cost generally has to be monitored to ensure it is within expectations. On the other hand, the contribution of effective change management/leadership to the achievement of positive results cannot be ignored. For example, Statistics Canada has reported that Canadian firms have achieved performance improvements of 46 percent for process innovation, 32 percent for product innovation, and 25 percent for productivity improvement, when combining high usage of innovative human resource management (HRM) practices with high usage of information and communication technologies in change initiatives.*

Burn rate is often used for this (e.g., the daily or weekly running cost of the development effort). In a CCM development effort, this is less likely to change as the resource is fixed, but as with effort, if it is different from the expected, it can highlight other issues. Another use of this measure is to assess the cost of delivering each requirement or feature to allow comparison with their value to the business. As well as resource costs, there are likely to be other costs associated with the development effort, including hardware and software, buildings and facilities, or third-party services. Refer to the following criteria:

- Keep the purpose in mind—define measures to answer specific questions
- Keep it simple—use the fewest and simplest measures that answer your questions
- Be specific—define measures accurately
- Evaluate the ROI of a given measure to be sure that it is worth collecting the data
- Automate collection as much as possible
- Measure outcomes, not outputs
- Combine, compare, and interpret measures to answer the defined questions
- Be aware that measures drive behaviors—understand the likely effect on the measures
- Change the measures as required during the development effort

---

* When firms do not include or use only low levels of culture change practices and only rely on high technology for benefits, the resulting productivity improvements were noticeably smaller: 24 percent for process innovation, 14 percent for product innovation, and 9 percent for productivity improvement. These findings have served to reinforce the importance of engaging employees in any change initiative, to establish alignment through an industry best-practice change process, to establish a common vision for the end-state, and to maximize the benefits derived.

CREATING A CULTURE CHANGE WEB INDEX

Don't base the success of your culture change on gut instinct alone. Instead, use these tools to measure exactly how effective your culture change is. You've gone through a lot of trouble to make your culture change effort the best it can be, and in most cases you'd like to think you've been successful. But to really know, you need to choose objectivity over subjectivity. True culture change requires radical behavior shifts over a period of several months or years. The new behaviors have to be ingrained in the culture so that most of your leaders and employees are demonstrating them readily and consistently. Although you can usually sense when this is happening, it is always helpful to rely on facts rather than intuition—especially if your change management program costs a lot of money!

Our advice is to get help from an established tool. Dan S. Cohen, the author of *Make It Stick: Embedding Change in Organizational Culture* (Harvard Business Review 2006), offers an easy and effective way to assess the uptake of culture change initiatives. His tool, appropriately called the Make It Stick Diagnostic (MISD), determines the extent to which new behavior has been adopted, and as a result, the probability that a new culture is emerging.

The MISD tool presents 15 statements (Harvard Business Review 2006), including

- As a member of this organization, I believe that the new behaviors will stay, even if key leaders involved in the effort leave.
- As a member of this organization, I believe that new practices resulting from the change effort are superior to old ones.
- As a member of this organization, I agree that leadership spends a lot of time promoting new attitudes and behaviors.
- As a member of this organization, I see my peers exhibiting new behaviors.
- As a member of this organization, I see new behavior becoming a part of the way we operate.

To use the tool, make sure everyone is clear on the change behaviors you want to measure (e.g., making stellar customer service our No. 1 priority). Then, issue the questionnaire to people whose perspective you desire. Respondents should assign a value of 1 to 6 to each statement, with 1 indicating that they strongly disagree with the statement and 6 indicating that they strongly agree with the statement. After all of the questionnaires have been returned to you, tally the results. The farther they are from the maximum score possible, the more work you need to do to get your changes to stick. The Culture Change Web by Johnson, Whittington, and Scholes (2012) is a useful model on which to build a culture change index, as shown in Figure 14.2.

The Cultural Web identifies six interrelated elements that help to make up what Johnson and Scholes call the Paradigm, or what is called the pattern or model, of the work environment. By analyzing the factors in each of the six key areas, you can begin to see the bigger picture of your culture along with what is working, what isn't working, and what needs to be changed.

The six elements of the culture web paradigm are

1. *Stories*: These are the past events that people talked about inside and outside the company. Who and what the company chooses to glorify and immortalize says a great deal about what it values and what it perceives to be classified as great behavior.

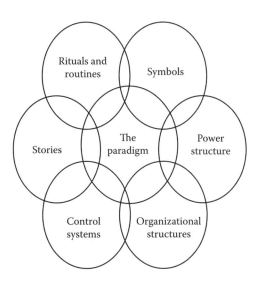

FIGURE 14.2
The Johnson and Scholes Culture Change Web, developed by Gerry Johnson and Kevan Scholes in 1992, provides an approach for looking at, changing, and measuring your organization's culture impact areas. Using it, you can expose and begin to measure cultural assumptions and practices and set to work aligning organizational elements with one another and with your strategy.

2. *Rituals and Routines*: These are the daily behaviors and actions of people that signal what the organization considers to be acceptable behavior. This determines what is expected to happen in any given situation and what is valued by management and workers alike.

3. *Symbols*: These are the visual representations of the organization, including logos, the physical environment (how plush the offices are), along with the formal or informal dress codes in each of the work areas and locations.

4. *Organizational Structure*: This includes both the structure defined by the organizational chart and the unwritten lines of power and influence that indicate whose contributions are most valued.

5. *Control Systems*: The ways that the organization is controlled. These include financial systems, quality systems, and rewards (including the way they are measured and distributed within the organization).

6. *Power Structures*: The pockets of real power in the company. This may involve one or two key senior executives, a whole group of executives, or even a department. The key is that these people have the greatest amount of influence on decisions, operations, and strategic direction.

Cohen suggests that after uncovering objective results of positive change, you publicize them—taking advantage of any opportunity to link well-known organizational successes to the change initiative. And don't be discouraged if your change efforts aren't quite there yet. True culture evolution takes a great deal of diagnosis, patience, and persistence, and by continuing to spotlight what's working and what still needs to be done, you will eventually get where you want to be, perhaps with the aid of some online diagnostic tools.*

SUMMARY

The challenge for organizational leadership is to continue the momentum generated in any change initiative in establishing a highly responsive

---

* The authors have read about the Artifacts of Culture Change, an online diagnostic tool developed for public use by the Centers for Medicare & Medicaid Services and Edu-Catering LLP. Designed to assist in individual eldercare providers' culture change implementation and ongoing sustainability efforts, the administration process involves assembling a Culture Change Leadership Team and having members talk through the online questions in small groups. The groups eventually come back together for an all-hands discussion that establishes an immediate action plan and future change goals.

organization. It is critical that management follow through on the key change enablers: organizational structure, policies, information dissemination, training and development, performance evaluation, and recognition. Measurement activities can enable CCM estimates to become increasingly accurate. They also allow key questions about the current and future state of the development effort to be answered based on fact rather than opinions. The information needs of the individual development effort determine what to measure, while the method of obtaining the data should be cost-effective.

In today's information-rich environment, too many executive and management decisions are based on fiction, not fact. All too often we are flooded with analysis that is performed by conscientious professionals that use sample sizes that do not provide meaningful results. They're presented as sound fact, when in reality they turn out to be best guesses. A good rule is to measure just what you need and measure enough so your decisions are sound.

We believe strongly in appraisals of systems and people. Edward Deming took the position that it is wrong to appraise individuals. We have had discussions with him personally and his position was based on his belief that he had never seen an effective personnel appraisal system. We believe that the only people that don't like to have their output measured are the individuals who are poor performers. People who are performing well are proud of what they do and they like to prove it. Organizations that do not have effective appraisal systems are doing everyone an injustice. They do not help the person who is a poor performer and they do not recognize the individual who is outstanding.

Don't be afraid to set stretch targets/goals for your organization and your employees. Too often management views failure to reach a target or goal as a bad thing, and as a result, punishes the individual or group for failing. This results in a continuously decreasing efficiency and effectiveness throughout the organization. People will estimate that a project they think can get done in two months will take three months; by doing this they feel confident they can meet their goals. Unfortunately, this leads to just the opposite results. The employee feels no pressure to get the job done so the project keeps slipping and being put off for tomorrow. All of a sudden the three months are up and the job is not done. Next time a similar job comes along they estimate that it will take four months because that's what it took the last time. Each time you cycle through a similar process or activity, you should be looking at improving the efficiency and effectiveness of the operation by 5 to 10 percent. Look at your own self and the work you're doing. Are you 10 percent more effective and efficient this year than you were last year? If not, it indicates that you are not learning and finding better ways to do your assigned task. John Young, when he was president of Hewlett-Packard, set a goal for all parts of the organization to improve by 10-fold in a matter of 10 years. People said it couldn't be done the way they were working. John's reply was simple, "Now you understand my message."

If you are a runner and you are running a mile in 8 minutes and 10 seconds, you might decide to set a goal to run a mile in 6 minutes and 20 seconds within the next 12 months. At the end of the 12 months, you find you're able to run the mile in 5 minutes and 50 seconds. This is much better than if you had just set your target to run the mile in 7 minutes and you had just met that target.

15

Risk Management Considerations

In a Nutshell: Traditional change management has been around for decades, but is the same old approach really enough to make a difference? More than 70 percent of major change efforts typically fail, and a key reason is that the old culture remains unchanged. Our approach to deploying and obtaining the CCM results outlined in this book has the promise to help clients overcome the odds. Our approach to results-delivery focuses on predicting, measuring, and managing risk associated with the change from day one. The result is typically a considerable increase in the odds of success and the support of experts and dedicated partners within the client's organization who are focused on achieving it. Change management studies report that it is possible to establish leadership, direction, policies, and risk processes relatively quickly, but that embedding risk management into core business processes (such as business planning or performance management) can sometimes take 12–18 months, and full culture change is expected to take several years (estimates of 5 to 7 years are common) and some suggest even as long as 10 years.

INTRODUCTION

The key issue for the CCM risk management program is: How do we make as much progress as possible with culture change, as quickly as possible, and sustain the momentum in a positive direction?* A development effort

---

* See the Culture Change Study Report, *Creating a Risk Management Culture*, at http://www.sgvw .ch/d/dossiers/Documents/dossier_22_rm_culture.pdf.

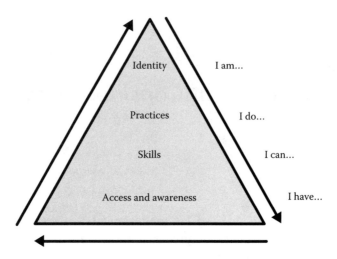

FIGURE 15.1
Beetham and Sharpe Pyramid Model.

risk is something that may happen, and if it does, it will have a detrimental effect. Figure 15.1 shows a typical risk management process and how to treat the risk with countermeasures.* The nature and extent of the countermeasure will depend on the nature of the risk and on the impact assessment carried out. Countermeasures need to be noted in the risk log and included in the delivery plan and/or time box plans, either as specific actions to prevent or reduce the risk or through rebalancing the priorities in order to deal with risk. Contingency plans should be linked to specific risks, so in a time box where significant risk has been identified, it is advisable to increase the proportion of Should Have and Could Have requirements providing additional contingency for the guaranteed delivery of the Must Have requirements.†

---

* The field of risk management as it applies to culture change consists of a group of actions or countermeasures that can be taken to resolve identified sociotechnical risks. The countermeasure activities include five major areas to consider: (1) Risk avoidance, accomplished by eliminating the source of the risk, (2) Risk Reduction, characterized by the implementation of actions that lower the risk to the agency, (3) Risk Spreading, through the distribution of risk across various program areas or activities, (4) Risk transfer, by the use of insurance to cover costs that would be incurred as the result of a loss, and (5) Risk acceptance, which is necessarily based on the knowledgeable determination that a risk is best managed by taking no action at all.

† There is a clear, widespread view that visible commitment to risk management from the very top is "a critical condition precedent to its adoption" (see, e.g., the report of comments from James Colica, Senior Vice President at GE Capital, and others in the series of international risk management Reports from Felix Kloman at http://www.riskreports.com).

There is a perception that risk management is a culture change manager's responsibility. However, in reality, the whole team should be aware of the risks, even though the Manager may drive risk management. Since the focus of the initiative is on delivering a business solution and the risks could affect the success, a decision to cancel, especially during the early stages, is sometimes made based on an unacceptably high level of risk and lack of readily available countermeasures. Take opportunities presented by changes of personnel at the top level to get their commitment to the risk agenda. Be ready to present them with evidence of success while training your leaders to lead the culture change in the following ways:

- Explain how risk management helps to deliver results, succeed with innovation, improve resource allocation, and reduce failure/crises.
- Explain how good risk management is a requirement for them to be able to sign a satisfactory statement on internal control. Good risk management is a requirement for CFOs/accounting officers.

THE CULTURE CHANGE RISK LOG*

An essential tool in any CCM methodology is the use of a risk log or risk register. This tool provides a means of recording the identified culture change risks, the analysis of their severity, and the necessary management actions to be taken. The risk log can be a simple checklist or spreadsheet, and as a general guide any risk log should contain the following fields:

- *Unique ID*: This may be simply a title but some kind of alphanumeric coding may be useful where you are dealing with a large number of risks.
- *Risk (description) presented in a structured format*: Condition—"There is a risk that"/Cause—"Caused by"/Consequence—"Resulting in."
- *Likelihood (probability)*: What is the likelihood of the risk occurring? It would be helpful to record the justification behind this analysis.

---

* The risk log described here is loosely based on the risk log described at JISC INfonet. http://www .jiscinfonet.ac.uk/infokits/risk-management/identifying-risk/risk-log/.

- *Impact*: What will the impact be if the risk occurs? It would be helpful to record the justification behind this analysis.
- *Red, Amber, Green (RAG) status*: RAG status, based on the product of the probability and impact.
- *Timescale/time box*: What is the risk window when this risk may occur and when do you start to scuttle certain culture change options as to how you respond?
- *Cost*: What will the risk cost if it does occur? You can't assess this unless you know what your response action will be.
- *Risk Owner*: There should be a person nominated to own the risk, which means monitoring the situation and ensuring that necessary management actions are carried out. In a project situation this should be somebody within the project team and in all cases it should be somebody who will be impacted by the risk and who has a vested interest in addressing it.
- *Risk Avoidance or Mitigating actions*: What are the agreed-on response actions? These may be broken into preventative actions to mitigate the risk and the response action if the risk actually occurs; sometimes known as the culture impact plan.
- *Residual cultural risk*: This is the expected level of risk once all the mitigating actions are complete.
- *Early warning signs*: What culture artifact or trigger might alert you to the fact that the risk is about to occur? In some cases you may only choose to spend money on a response action once the activity has been triggered and actually occurs.

ON DIGITAL LITERACY AND CCM

Culture change risks often revolve around the need for developing digital literacies and data visualization. Accordingly, management needs to provide ideas and resources to inspire the strategic development of digital literacies (i.e., those cultural and technical capabilities that support living, learning, and working in a digital society). Data visualization is an integral part of data analysis and business intelligence. Culture change practitioners need to learn how to explore the most effective type of charts and good design tips to help you create powerful and persuasive graphs for culture change decision making. Literacy is about culture development, so understanding digital literacy in this way is important; we acquire language and become increasingly proficient over time and eventually reach a level of fluency.*

The Beetham and Sharpe framework shown in Figure 15.1 describes digital literacy as a development process from access and functional skills to higher-level capabilities and identity. However, this will change depending on the context so it also reflects how individuals can be motivated to develop new skills and practices in different situations.

You may also want to note any interdependencies between risks (i.e., where one risk occurs that will impact on another risk). This is sometimes known as risk coupling. This cross-reference alerts you to the fact that when one risk occurs, a related risk also requires reviewing.

USING CROWDSOURCING AND WIKIMEDIA FOR CULTURE CHANGE†

Crowdsourcing is not the best way to do everything, but crowdsourcing offers huge efficiency gains for certain kinds of large, complex change management initiatives. Managing it requires a different way of thinking that accepts unpredictability, imperfection, and diminished control. Crowdsourced effort is hard to control, but the absence of central control gives it its efficiency and strength.

> There is something fundamentally appealing about the notion that out of millions of heads can come information ... larger than the sum of its parts. Imagine if the world's people could write poetry or make music together; these are unbelievable ideas.

Mahzarin Banaji (2010)

---

* JISC Infonet has four InfoKits to assist organizations with their culture change management practices and developing digital literacies. Their InfoKits contain a wealth of self-help material, from simple methodologies to manage projects, risks, change, and processes, to image galleries of technology-rich spaces and reflections from leaders to learners showcasing the inspiring use of technology across the sectors. See http://www.jiscinfonet.ac.uk/infokits/risk-management /identifying-risk/risk-log/.

† The *Crowdsourcing JISC Infokit* will explain an approach to culture change work that is in some ways the opposite of traditional planning and management. It will draw out some lessons from the most visibly successful crowdsourcing projects that support education and research, including Wikipedia. It will show how these community-based projects, despite their unorthodox methods, share educational and scholarly objectives with more traditional institutions and projects. It will suggest ways in which those institutions and projects can benefit from working with Wikipedia and the wider Wikimedia community.

Wikipedia is one of a suite of crowdsourced, free sites for education and reference, which include Wikiversity, Wikidata, Wiktionary, and others. They are hosted in the United States by the nonprofit Wikimedia Foundation. The term "Wikimedia" encompasses

- The suite of resources mentioned above
- The volunteer communities that maintain them
- National and regional organizations that support them
- Related work including research, software development, and outreach

CHANGE MANAGEMENT RISKS

Much of the recent academic research has shown that it is not the "hard" technology acquisitions by themselves that guide organizational success, but the integration of these assets into CCM processes that elevate the importance of the human system. It is the integration that really makes the difference. For example, in 2003 a Standish Group International survey showed that an astounding 66 percent of information system (IS) projects failed/were canceled or were challenged.* The frequent use of a standard with common language, mental model, and approach is helpful in reducing risks by ensuring that staff, management, and leaders work in an integrated and collaborative fashion, as shown in Figure 15.2.

The Standard provides a generic framework for managing risks. The framework is intended to enable organizations to achieve an appropriate balance between realizing opportunities for gain while minimizing losses. This process ensures that all change management risks are identified, assessed, and managed. It also helps to manage culture change risk by reducing the probability of a risk occurring, identifying contingency plans where needed and at times justifying that a risk is accepted. Countermeasures should be considered for every risk uncovered during the monitoring and review process.

---

* Standish is a market research and advisory firm that regularly tracks the success of IT projects around the world. It maintained that a significant contribution to this poor showing was the failure of most IS/IT interventions to effectively integrate employee adoption issues (including how to effectively resolve resistance to change).

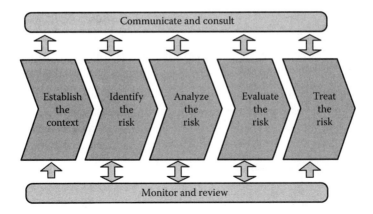

FIGURE 15.2
The AS/NZ 4360:2004 typical risk management process.

Another approach to managing the risks associated with culture change is Wikipedia. Wikipedia is one of a suite of crowdsourced, free sites for education and reference, which include Wikiversity, Wikidata, Wiktionary, and others. They are hosted in the United States by the non-profit Wikimedia Foundation. The term "Wikimedia" encompasses

- This suite of resources mentioned above
- The volunteer communities that maintain them
- National and regional organizations that support them
- Related work including research, software development, and outreach

Despite the popular notion of speaking with facts, data and numbers cannot always speak for themselves. Sometimes, too much time can be spent on struggling to understand the data presented in lengthy reports and numerical tables. This time could be better spent on making evidence-based decisions. Large amounts of data are hard to wade through, but data visualization can make that data easily digestible. Data visualization* can help with the analysis of that information and present it in a

---

* The JISC Data Visualization infoKit is not intended to be an exhaustive guide to the subject in hand as there are too many good sources of information (specialist books, blogs, and publications dealing with the topic of data visualization for us to recreate it all. Even among the experts, the opinions vary on what should be the gold standard and best practice in this area. Instead, the JISC guide intends to be a distillation of these opinions and advice—many of which have been tried and tested by us in practice—and to bring many useful resources together into one place.

way that allows viewers to discover patterns that might otherwise be hard to uncover. During the past two decades, we have seen amazing progress in technologies enabling us to collect and process huge amounts of data. This vast data availability has driven the interest in data analysis and visualization. This in turn has led to visualization methods being constantly updated and developed as new evidence about the effectiveness of visualization methods emerge. The use of infoKits for CCM helps to focus on business intelligence to explore this essential element of decision making based on accurate data about the state of your organization and the environment in which it operates.

Modern organizations require access to accurate, timely, and meaningful information about their core businesses culture and the environment in which they operate if they are to adapt and thrive during times of great uncertainty, which will prove to be the norm during the next 10 years and beyond. This also ensures an understanding of the intricacies of leading and participating in a large-system change effort, and contributes in a significant way to the return on investment. However, in order for an organization to see long-term benefit, it is necessary that it be prepared to devote ongoing energy and resources to maintaining innovations and to transform itself by adopting practices that appear to have not been previously utilized (e.g., continued development of the change agents and more consistent information exchange with all staff).* The CCM team should use a risk management assessment tool (see Figure 15.3)† coupled with these criteria and 30 possible associated impacts for consideration to help estimate the degree of change risk involved in the initiative.

It is based on a strategy designed to shift embedded organizational beliefs, values, and attitudes at every level of the organization to support the implementation of the business transformation initiatives (Table 15.1).

Too often, many projects involving the implementation of enterprise-wide information technology neglects the human factor. Many research authors attempt to demonstrate that attention to organization development and

---

* This strategy involves alignment between impacted personnel and facilitates strong partnerships among those taking responsibility for any cultural change initiative. This strategy is designed to shift embedded organizational beliefs, values, and attitudes at every level of the organization to support the implementation of the business transformation initiatives.

† For details see https://www.gov.uk/government/uploads/system/uploads/attachment_data/file /191516/Risk_management_assessment_framework.pdf.

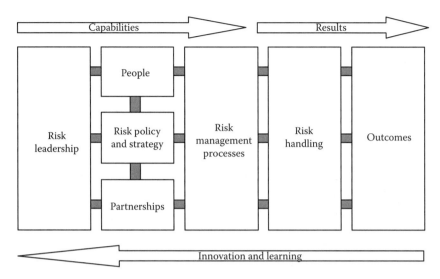

FIGURE 15.3
Risk management assessment. (Adapted from the EFQM Excellence Model.)

change management in technology implementation has resulted in a positive impact on productivity, job satisfaction, and other work attitudes, in the end, justifying the pursuit of change management effectiveness in most organizational interventions, particularly in IT initiatives, that traditionally tend to turn the organization into which they are introduced into an upside-down state of chaos and dysfunctionality.

Individual psychology and organizational roles will influence how people perceive these risks. Professor John Adams' work in this area, drawing on key works in cultural theory, may help us to understand how unhelpful standoffs can result. Adams has developed a model of how people respond to risks (see Figure 15.4). This is represented in the diagram of the Adams Risk Thermostat, and postulates that (a) everyone has a propensity to take risks, (b) this propensity varies from one individual to another, (c) this propensity is influenced by the potential rewards of risk-taking, (d) perceptions of risk are influenced by experience of "accident" losses—one's own and others', (e) individual risk-taking decisions represent a balancing act in which perceptions of risk are weighed against propensity to take risk, and (f) accident losses are, by definition, a consequence of taking risks; the more risks an individual takes, the greater, on average, will be both the rewards and losses he or she incurs (Adams 2000).

TABLE 15.1

Potential Risk–Impact–Change Solution Matrix

Potential Risk Area	Impacts on Organizational Culture	Major Issues and CM Solutions
Value Proposition benefits realization outcomes	1. Benefits realization—achievement of results and outcomes—often will depend on individuals embracing, adopting, and utilizing a change initiative.	*The business doesn't know exactly what it wants.* Being unsure of the solution detail in the early stages of the intervention is seen as normal.
	2. If individuals do not change how they do their daily work (e.g., use the new technology; adhere to the new systems and/or processes, or exhibit the new behaviors) then the change will not have a high likelihood of success and the many benefits will not be realized.	From the high-level baseline created during the Value Proposition, the detail emerges through Iterative Development.
	3. Need to deal with the reality of change. Change management is a solution to the reality of change, not an add-on.	Supporting this emerging understanding, CCM life cycle's focus on continuous and clear communication (workshops, modeling, prototyping) allows the team (including the Business roles) to work together to agree on the detail.
	4. Culture Change Management provides a structured approach to enabling and encouraging the individual transitions required by a new value proposition, opportunity, and initiative.	
Proposed Likelihood of success parameters	5. There is a direct and distinct correlation between the effectiveness of Business case implementation and the likelihood of meeting objectives, staying on schedule, and staying on budget.	*The business changes its mind.* Change is seen as a fact of life and the power of change is harnessed by the team to ensure the solution is correct at the point of delivery.
	6. Harrington Institute's research over the last three decades has shown that development efforts with excellent parameter change management met or exceeded objectives a high percentage of the time, while development efforts with poor parameter change management met or exceeded objectives a lower amount of the time.	In other words, the solution works the way the business needs it to work.
		Since there is no detailed signed-off specification and the lowest level of detail is only agreed to as late as possible, many "changes" do not affect the initiative at all.

(*Continued*)

TABLE 15.1 (CONTINUED)

Potential Risk–Impact–Change Solution Matrix

Potential Risk Area	Impacts on Organizational Culture	Major Issues and CM Solutions
People parameters that define development effort ROI	7. Any time a change impacts how employees do their jobs, there are three people side factors that define or constrain return on investment.	*Not having all the detail agreed to at the start.* The CCM life cycle's principle of Build from a Firm Foundation' ensures Enough Design Up Front is done to allow the development effort to move safely forward. It also ensures that a clear high-level baseline is created to enable control of scope.
	8. The ROI of the Business Case Change Management Model proposed by many experts identifies these three factors as: speed of adoption (how quickly employees and their management make the change), ultimate utilization (how many affected people in total make the change), and proficiency (how effective they are when they have made the change).	
	9. When the people parameters of change is not managed effectively, employees are slower to make the change, fewer of them make the change, and they are less effective once they have made the change.	
	10. Each of these factors directly impacts development effort ROI. Effective change management results in faster speed of adoption, higher ultimate utilization, and greater proficiency, which all drive higher ROI.	

(Continued)

TABLE 15.1 (CONTINUED)

Potential Risk–Impact–Change Solution Matrix

Potential Risk Area	Impacts on Organizational Culture	Major Issues and CM Solutions
Costly redesign activities in implementing the Value Proposition	11. When the people side of change is ignored or addressed late in a development effort, the result is a number of wasteful, nonvalue-adding, costly, and discouraging rework and solutions redesign. 12. Business case Development Teams absorb these costs in terms of budget impacts and schedule delays. When the people side of change is addressed up front, these negative consequences can be avoided. 13. Effective change management helps eliminate many unnecessary redesign costs that can derail a development effort and evaporate ROI.	*Unwillingness to commit to final sign-off.* Using CCM life cycle's Development Time Boxes, the business accepts the evolving solution incrementally. Therefore, achieving final sign-off poses very little risk, since this is simply the final step in a gradual process.
Avoiding costs and minimizing risks	14. Poorly managing the people side of Value Proposition implementation often adds excessive costs and risks at two levels: the development effort value proposition level and the organizational level as well. 15. The negative consequences for the Business Case implementation may often include numerous delays, excessive budget overruns, loss of momentum by the Business case team, active resistance, passive resistance, and resources not being made available.	CCM life cycle relies on having appropriate input from the Business Ambassador during evolution of the solution detail. If the Business Ambassador regularly misses sessions, the rest of the Solution Development Team are unlikely to deliver the right solution. This will lead to the need for late rework and hence time and/or cost overruns.

(Continued)

TABLE 15.1 (CONTINUED)

Potential Risk–Impact–Change Solution Matrix

Potential Risk Area	Impacts on Organizational Culture	Major Issues and CM Solutions
	16. The degree of change negative consequences for the organization include productivity plunges, loss of valued employees, reduced quality of work, morale declines, stress, confusion, and fatigue.	
Ignoring the people-side consequences	17. The people side of the changing resources factor can be quantified: you can calculate the impact of speed of adoption, ultimate utilization, and proficiency.	Changing resources sometimes results in a situation where the newcomer to the team does not understand the background to the decisions that have been made, nor will he or she have the necessary depth of information.
	18. Furthermore, there are countless anecdotes and examples of the costly nature of ignoring the people side of change.	
Using weak or ineffective decision support tools	19. The Business Development strategies to enable change must be planned, tested, refined, and monitored to ensure success.	CCM life cycle uses Iterative Development, MoSCoW, and Timeboxing to converge on and strengthen a more accurate solution.
	20. However, conventional decision support tools lack the necessary horsepower to address these needs effectively. Spreadsheets and other simulators excel at manipulating numerical data and development *efforting* quantitative trends, while falling short in modeling and reasoning about qualitative factors and interactions.	Where a fully detailed specification already exists, the benefits of the CCM life cycle approach with its inherent flexibility may be very useful.
	21. This often leads to uncertain and rapidly changing information and disruptive events.	In reality, it may be possible to deliver all requirements at the high level and to achieve contingency within the lower levels of each feature (i.e., all high-level features will be delivered, but the depth of some features may be limited).
	22. More importantly, business case developers fail to provide insight into personal and social dynamics of how people and groups are likely to perceive and respond over time to alternate change initiatives.	

(Continued)

TABLE 15.1 (CONTINUED)

Potential Risk–Impact–Change Solution Matrix

Potential Risk Area	Impacts on Organizational Culture	Major Issues and CM Solutions
Estimating costs for each change parameter	23. Estimating costs for change management can be very complicated and oftentimes tricky. 24. Several approaches include (a) allocating as a percentage of total development effort budget, (b) allocating as a percentage of development effort full time equivalents (FTEs), (c) adding in the nature and complexity of the change to scale resource requirements (i.e., a small, incremental change does not require the same change management resources as a large, dramatic change), and (d) estimating work required to complete change management activities (i.e., creating a work breakdown structure of the activities in the methodology and estimating time for completion). 25. Drawing on previous experience and examples in your organization can also be very helpful in estimating the degree of change that will be brought about for each development effort parameter.	Where possible, try to introduce the concept of a CCM life cycle before time and effort is spent producing a detailed specification (many business do this because they did not realize that other options are available). Also, it is important to consider the risk associated with the accuracy of the specifications—unchanged, it will rarely reflect the true business need. The CCM life cycle approach can still be used for the various parameters, effectively validating the specifications costing through delivery-focused Development Time Boxes.
Linking to the expected results and objectives of the Business case Proposal	26. When articulating the degree of change, it is essential to begin and end with one concept: *achievement of the results and objectives of the development effort or initiative.*	CCM life cycle's approach is based around the idea that Time, Cost, and Quality are fixed and contingency is built around the prioritization of Features. If the business needs all features to be delivered, then contingency must be built in to Time and/or Cost instead.

(Continued)

TABLE 15.1 (CONTINUED)

Potential Risk–Impact–Change Solution Matrix

Potential Risk Area	Impacts on Organizational Culture	Major Issues and CM Solutions
	27. There are numerous benefit perspectives for estimating the degree of change, but to make a compelling case that wins the hearts and minds of your audience, the Business Development Team must connect each of these benefits back to the intended outcomes of the development effort or initiative.	The combination of CCM life cycle's groups/teams and the use of rich communication means that a great deal of the team information is known and shared informally rather than being formally written down, which requires sound documentation practices.
Preparation for change readiness	28. A key question remains: What is required to prepare the people affected for the transition the organization needs them to make?	When you focus on building readiness rather than managing resistance to change, you can help more people move through the change continuum and to more correctly estimate the degree of change for each parameter involved.
	29. This key question focuses your organizational change efforts on the activities needed for people readiness, as resistance to change cannot coexist with readiness. Staff that are ready for change don't resist change.	Where a team change is unavoidable, try to ensure this happens at the end of an increment, since this is a natural partial closure during the development effort.
	30. Increasing readiness for change requires two things: (1) knowledge of the way people naturally move through the change process, and (2) an understanding of the fundamental elements that create change readiness.	The risk of more frequent change than the cases cited above can be mitigated to an extent by the use of diagramming and modeling techniques.
		It is still possible and valuable to deal with detail as it emerges during the Iterative Development process, and in this scenario the models and their review records provide a visible and useful mapping of group knowledge.

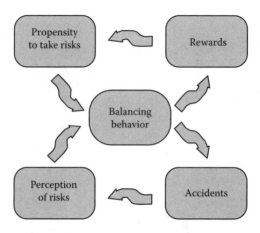

FIGURE 15.4
The Adams Risk Thermostat.

USING THE CCM APPROACH TO REDUCE RISK

There are some common factors that will make CCM life cycle the most appropriate approach in order to reduce risk. Following the wrong or inappropriate approach can dramatically increase the risks. For example:

- Adopting a traditional approach where a development effort must deliver on a fixed date adds a risk since a traditional approach expects to use time as a contingency
- Adopting one of the agile approaches that promote No Design Up Front (NDUF) can introduce significant risks when delivering a solution into a complicated corporate architecture
- Adopting a traditional approach that mandates big design up front (BDUF) can restrict flexibility and creativity

Professor John Adams basically argues that rewards and accidents/losses are consequences of risk taking. Rewards influence the propensity of a person to take risks. Risk propensity varies from one person to another. On the other hand, failures and losses influenced the perceived danger. Both influence what Adams calls balancing behavior. Using this model, John Adams argues that today's institutional risk management is only focusing on the lower part—the accident-reducing loop.

On an ongoing basis, the whole team should be ensuring that the CCM life cycle principles are being complied with. Since these typify the behavior needed, breaking any of the principles will immediately put the CCM life cycle approach at risk. The CCM life cycle provides a development effort approach questionnaire that can help identify potential risk areas.

The questionnaire should be completed initially during Feasibility and then revisited during foundations to see whether the risk profile for the development effort has changed. The risks identified should then be kept visible and reviewed for every Development Time Box. It is usually appropriate to run a risk analysis workshop early on in the development effort but the same technique can be used at any appropriate time.

ON DEVELOPING A RISK-ORIENTED CULTURE

How well organizations develop a risk-oriented culture can vary greatly, but among organizations that excel at it, there are certain common features. "When I'm assessing how strong a company's risk culture is, I start by understanding how an organization allows and responds to challenge in general—whether it's a challenge to a policy, an action taken by the organization or other aspect," says Eddie Barrett, a director in the Deloitte Consulting LLP's Human Capital practice, who presented during a webcast.* Whether senior people are comfortable with being challenged and how they respond to being challenged, especially in a group environment, can reveal important aspects of organizational culture. So do what consequences and outcomes occur for those who raise challenges, Bartlett postulates. In some cases, people who have challenged others have lost their jobs or have been penalized as a result and that's clearly not the sort of culture that you want to encourage if you want to build an organization with a strong risk culture.

According to the Deloitte approach to establishing a risk-oriented culture, positive attributes of a strong culture include the following four key characteristics:

1. *Commonality of purpose, values, and ethics*: The extent to which an employee's individual interests, values, and ethics are aligned with the organization's risk strategy, appetite, tolerance, and approach
2. *Universal adoption and application*: Whether risk is considered in all activities, from strategic planning to day-to-day operations, in every part of the organization

---

* See the webcast at http://www2.deloitte.com/us/en/pages/dbriefs-webcasts/upcoming-webcasts.html.

3. *A learning organization culture and mentality*: How and if the collective ability of the organization to manage risk more effectively is continuously improving
4. *Timely, transparent, and honest communications*: People are comfortable talking openly and honestly about risk, using a common risk vocabulary that promotes shared understanding

During the webcast, participants were asked a series of polling questions, including, "To what extent does your organization's risk culture influence how your people behave day to day?" Of more than 1700 respondents, 32.4 percent answered "to a great extent," 41.3 percent said "somewhat," and 13.6 percent answered "a little."

There are three stages of continuous improvement of an organization's risk culture, each with its own components: cultural awareness, cultural change, and cultural refinement.* An organization's initial focus should be on building cultural awareness, predominantly through communications and education. Cultural improvement will likely require meaningful changes to established ways of operating, as Deloitte outlines in their webcast on risk and culture change.

Stage 1: Building Cultural Awareness. In the cultural awareness stage, companies are establishing their risk management expectations for the organization and defining roles and responsibilities around risk. "Companies at this stage are communicating clearly and continuously to their employees what their expectations are," says Kevin Blakely, senior advisor to Deloitte's Governance, Regulatory and Risk Strategies group, who also presented on the webcast. "Such companies are taking the time to educate their employees either through communications or through formal training, so they understand how to meet the organization's cultural expectations," adds Mr. Blakely, who spent two decades as a senior regulator with the Office of the Comptroller of the Currency.

The components of building cultural awareness include

- Delivering communications from leadership using a common risk management vocabulary, and clarifying risk management responsibilities and accountabilities

---

* See the webcast at http://www2.deloitte.com/us/en/pages/dbriefs-webcasts/upcoming-webcasts .html. After attending the Deloitte webcasts, participants can download their CPE certificate immediately following the live webcast. Participants will also receive the CPE certificate within 24 hours via email at the email address used to register for the webcast.

- Conducting risk management general education and customized training programs based on employees' roles
- Embedding risk management into induction or onboarding programs
- Refining recruitment methods to include risk management capabilities

Stage 2: Changing an Organization's Culture. The Deloitte approach details that at a more advanced level, organizations approach and embrace the cultural change stage, where they foster an environment that both recognizes and rewards people for paying attention to risk, including knowing how to challenge the status quo constructively. "It's at this stage where organizations develop motivational systems, both positive and negative, to reward the right kind of behavior or to penalize the wrong kind of behavior," says Mr. Blakely. "We see a keen focus on talent management trying to get the right people into the right positions to drive the right results." Another hallmark of this stage is the emphasis on the ethical and compliance standards that are important to the organization.

There are essentially five key components of changing an organization's risk culture according to the experts that we have talked with, although many use different terms than the ones outlined here:

- Creating a culture of constructive and beneficial challenge
- Embedding well-defined risk performance metrics into the organization's motivational systems
- Establishing risk management cultural considerations in talent management processes
- Position individuals with the desired risk orientation in roles where effective risk management is critical
- Reinforcing behavioral, ethical, and compliance standards

Stage 3: Refining the Organizational Culture. In the third stage, organizations are getting more experienced and mature at their cultural development, trying to monitor cultural performance versus expectations. And those expectations can be set by various stakeholders, including employees, management, board of directors, investors, and analysts.

At this stage, companies are engaging in adjustments of people, strategies, and communications in order to produce the cultural outcomes that they desire. Companies that can demonstrate that they are both learning and have the ability to adjust and move on are fairly far down the path of the cultural change timeline and road map similar to the ones that are outlined in this book. Steps that are typically taken to change and reinforce risk as part of the culture change process enacted during this stage include*

- Integrating risk management lessons learned into communications, education, and training
- Holding people accountable for their actions
- Refining risk performance metrics to reflect changes in business strategy, risk appetite, and tolerance associated with the culture change initiative
- Redeploying and retraining individuals to reflect changes to business strategy and priorities

THE TEAM SPIRIT ENVIRONMENT†

Executives and leaders who are undertaking culture change understand the value of creating a work culture that fosters teamwork and enhances team spirit. The potential effect of both factors on the efficiency and productivity of a culture change initiative can be very substantial. A number of steps can be taken to cultivate teamwork within an organization to help facilitate culture change, and the basic transformational idea is to create a team spirit environment. Karen Gately writes about the CEO being the guardian of the team spirit‡: "The culture of a business directly and sub-

---

* Once the desired risk culture for the change management intervention has been established, the organization should continually refine it to reflect ongoing changes in business strategy, since anticipating tomorrow's complex issues and new strategies is a challenge. The Deloitte Dbriefs and their live webcasts can offer valuable insights on important culture change developments. Deloitte offers complimentary live webcasts featuring practical knowledge from Deloitte specialists, while you earn CPE credit from the convenience of your team spirit room or desk.

† Adapted from "Create a Work Culture that Facilitates Teamwork, team spirit," by Stephen Tharrett and James A. Peterson, October 2008. For complete details, see http://www.athleticbusiness .com/staffing/create-a-work-culture-that-facilitates-teamwork-team-spirit.html.

‡ Karen Gateley's philosophy is both holistic and comprehensive, with a strong focus in helping leaders to realize the goals and objectives of their organization through awakening the discretionary effort and creativity of their teams. Karen's approach does away with ambiguous HR concepts and advocates the harnessing of the human spirit and effort through inspiring, results-based leadership. See Gateley's article *The CEO—Custodian of the Team Spirit* at https:// karengately.wordpress.com/2011/10/13/the-ceo-custodian-of-team-spirit/.

stantially impacts team spirit and is therefore a critical tool and priority for every leader. I often meet HR leaders and executives striving to improve culture who are frustrated by a lack of ownership and support from their CEO. The CEO's focus on the spirit of the team is crucial to improving staff engagement, shifting corporate culture, or influencing performance standards." Gately goes on to say that the CEO is "responsible for ensuring the executive team understand and are committed to achieving business results through people. Together they must understand and commit to dealing with the reality of the organization's current culture and team spirit." The key message here is that as a team it is critical that they adopt a determined, focused, and courageous approach, or in Gately's terms, "to consistently mandate and endorse agreed strategies, programs and policies aimed at building team spirit."

For any culture change initiative, one of the measures of success is determined by the extent to which each CEO holds themselves—as well as the other leaders—accountable. There are at least 10 strategic CCM actions that revolve around creating a sense of organizational team spirit:

1. *Create and cultivate a team spirit.* The first step to create teamwork is to establish a team spirit mission, vision, and values that serve as the heart and soul of the culture change within your organization. This could then be followed with a centrally located team spirit room.*

2. *Avoid hoarding important information.* Power comes from having something someone else does not have, and this includes information. In business, having information that others don't can result in an environment that is counterproductive to teamwork. This does not mean that managers must share confidential information; it does mean that any information that would drive the performance of the organization should be made available to everyone.

---

* The notion of a team spirit room has its roots in the Empowerment Room concept, which first emerged about 20 years ago and was documented in *Global Quality* by Richard Tabor Greene, ASQ Press. Also see the paper covering the primal objective of innovation and culture change, which is to create and grow real wealth. The focus is on the long-term, net cash flows of companies that develop, apply, and bundle technological and other innovations with the products and services they take to competitive global markets. It is critical to put this hard cash flow metric of success on innovation and culture change management and to conceptualize it as a tough set of specific, well-defined strategic choices for culture change practitioners and managers. See *The Philosophy to Succeed: Team Spirit, Innovation, Research, and the Creation of Technological Competitiveness*, by Lamia Atma Djoudi and Rome of Synchrome Technologies for a detailed treatment of this subject. See http://www.iaria.org/conferences2014/filesBUSTECH14/ThePhilosophyToSucceed.pdf.

3. *Cross-train everyone.* One of the pitfalls to a team environment is the evolution of the superspecialist. While employees can have a specialty, they must also be cross-educated so that they can also perform other roles, when necessary, and they understand how difficult other jobs can be.

4. *Eliminate the prima donna attitude.* Prima donnas can compromise every effort to create a teamwork-oriented culture change environment because they feel they deserve special attention, often because of a special skill or talent they possess. In most cases, prima donnas don't start off that way, but along the way either society or the organization creates them.

5. *Pass the trophy.* In their book, *Walk the Talk,** Eric Harvey and Alexander Lucia comment wisely, "Let everyone hold the trophy." This phrase refers to the fact that success must be a team celebration. In other words, success is not about MVPs (most valuable players); it's about TEAM (together everyone achieves more). As such, "Praise loudly and blame softly," say Harvey and Lucia.

6. *No finger pointing.* Finger pointing refers to a strategy of blaming someone else for organizational mistakes. Normally, when a mistake occurs or a goal is missed, it's a multilevel issue, not an individual one. When facility managers allow fingers to be pointed, it sends a message that if employees take a risk and fail, the organization will make sure everyone knows about it. Instead, focus on solutions that everyone needs to take part in.

7. *Encourage connections.* Encourage employees to establish trusting relationships with other employees. Fostering relationships requires that an organization provide opportunities for employees to connect socially without the burdens of professional responsibilities.

---

* *Walk the Talk*, by Eric Harvey, Steve Ventura and Michelle Sedas, co-published by Simple Truths, 2007, Naperville, OH is a short book with one central idea: that you should do what you say you are going to do and practice what you preach. This concept is presented throughout in a story about how an elderly janitor takes the CEO of a company on a tour (similar to the TV show *Undercover Boss*) that covers three areas: the value of values, the conflict of contradictions, and the wonder of walking the talk. Along the way, there are a number of points that are emphasized for each topic. For example, "Values are the gold that is within each of us. They are the real fortune of an organization. We judge ourselves mostly by our intentions; but others judge us mostly by our actions. If you can't do it don't say it." The book ends with a speech given by the CEO to company employees after he has been exposed to these ideas by the janitor and people he meets on this journey. For example, we meet Golden Rule Mike O'Toole who, of course, practices the Golden Rule as follows: (a) Give whatever you expect, and (b) have great expectations. The focus on these concepts is a business environment, although in reality anyone could benefit from following these ideas.

8. *Eliminate politics.* Office politics are the enemy of teamwork. Politics represent behavior designed to gain power and exhibit control. Politics are based on who a person knows and who an individual owes versus what and how a person contributes. Organizations can create a nonpolitical environment when they measure individual and team performance through results that are based on the fulfilment of the organization's mission and achievement of business goals.

9. *Don't be judgmental.* Teams are successful when no one is judged as an individual but rather as part of a team. Human tendency is to pre-judge people and treat them according to how they perceive them. The only judgments a team should make are those that pertain to the performance of the team itself and how all the parts of the team mesh.

10. *Accept apologies and offer forgiveness.* The hallmark of a teamwork-oriented environment is when employees are willing to apologize for their own mistakes and forgive others. Great relationships are rooted in the ability to forgive and move on.

Fostering a work culture that facilitates teamwork and team spirit is a significant challenge. Fitness managers can start by hiring the right people who can become teamwork-oriented. It is this process of creating a team-work environment that can ultimately determine the level of greatness a team can achieve.

SUMMARY

The CCM life cycle directly addresses many of the common risks for development efforts—missing fixed deadlines, having unclear or volatile requirements, and many others. Using the CCM life cycle ensures on-time delivery of a fit-for-purpose solution. Choosing the right approach is a key factor in reducing development effort risks in the early stages. CCM life cycle's development effort approach questionnaire provides a good starting point for creating a clear understanding of development effort risks and their mitigation. It also helps highlight where the CCM life cycle approach should be scaled (up or down) and where tailoring is appropriate, in order to gain the maximum benefit from using the CCM life cycle.

In today's innovative culture employees at all levels are encouraged to take risk. 3M actually gives positive recognition to individuals that have noble failures. To fail, at least once, is looked at as a learning experience, not an error, as long as the same reason for failure is not repeated. While this is true to a limited degree (no organization can afford to have every employee learning by failing in every potential way), the key is to take reasonable risk. The plan is to understand these risks more clearly so that mitigation plans are effective at limiting the costs related to risk that turn out to be failures. Much better than learning from failing, it is far less costly for everyone to learn from failures that occur throughout the organization. We call this proactive risk results in that if no one learns from the failure, that is bad. If one person learns from the failure, that's costly. If everyone learns from the failure, then that's wise.

The CCM methodology is designed to minimize risks that can result in failures as it's based on the experience, both positive and negative, that organizations have had around the world related to successful and failed culture change initiatives and programs. By following the guidance provided, you may not be able to eliminate all of the risks, but the risks you take should be fewer and less costly to the organization. Someone once said that very few people, if any, have made it to a position of responsibility and got there because of the failures they created as their careers developed.

16

Deploying and Implementing CCM

In a Nutshell: Statistics show that the vast majority of organizational change initiatives underperform, or even worse, significantly fail to produce their intended value, and the situation is getting more challenging all the time as changes come more rapidly and have longer-term impacts. Organizations are typically managing not just one initiative, but a complex portfolio of change as part of a larger, enterprise-wide transformation. This complex portfolio of change programs creates a complex ever-expanding impact on the enterprise, leading to change resulting in even more change, and often requires implementation and deployment approaches and tools beyond traditional change management. CCM, when it is successfully planned and implemented, has been shown to increase the certainty of reaching desired business goals at the right pace and with fewer risks. It also creates an organization that is more resilient and change-capable, with an ongoing ability to adapt to and capitalize on transformational change.

INTRODUCTION

Managing change is often made more difficult because employees often work across multiple functions, and in such a matrixed organizational structure a manager may have direct responsibility for a handful of employees, but only indirect influence over the others. As work processes increasingly cross multiple functions, resulting in the sharing of applications and tools, better transparency and stricter controls over the deployment and use of change-related information is important. Leaders need to see to it that not only the portfolio of change programs progresses successfully, but also that the work of the organization gets done at the same time.

Customers need to be served, products made and shipped, and operations and the supply chain kept moving smoothly. The CCM deployment process outlined in this chapter will help the organization to stay agile and flexible even while it is reconfiguring parts of the enterprise.

Also, overlaps or touchpoints between the different change initiatives need to be carefully managed so that the organization as a whole is not tripping all over itself and delays in one program do not hold up progress in another within the broader CCM transformation. As we all know, time marches on for each component of the culture change portfolio, and if one grinds to a halt waiting for another to catch up, then a great deal of waste and dissatisfaction can occur.

Also, our research shows that change fatigue can set in for a workforce that is buffeted by the demands made on them by successive or disconnected changes thrown at them over a period of time. The organization needs to be able to assimilate the scope and breadth of the culture change required across the multiple change programs at a personal employee level; organizational culture change affects people both professionally and emotionally. All things considered, this helps to explain why the track record on the delivery benefits from long-term change management programs is often bleak. Organizations can increase their success rate for CCM and improve their organizational resiliency by using a systematic approach, such as the one outlined in this chapter.

Let's look at two different kinds of organizations and how they accept or reject any change initiative. For example, in one organization (Company A), a change initiative is viewed as an exciting opportunity to work with something different and to learn something new. In this type of organization a change initiative is looked at as a learning experience, an opportunity to break out of the rut of what they're doing. This type of organization sees every change initiative as an opportunity to improve the way the organization is performing.

On the other hand, employees in another organization (Company B) implementing these same projects as Company A had done will view these change initiatives as threatening their existence. They are viewed as a disruption in the normal flow of activities that will in the long run do nothing but distract from the job they need to get done. To these types of organizations, these change initiatives are viewed as someone upstair's dumb idea of what needs to be done—decisions by those who don't understand what's going on down where the real work is accomplished. They will do something that they have to but don't expect them to like it. We have seen situations where we installed a customer relation management system and the sales group reluctantly accepted it and agreed to use it because they were forced to record the information. However, this sales group continued to keep their own records just as they did in the past because that's the information they depended on to do their job.

Now why do we see these massive differences and so much difficulty with implementing change initiatives? Why is it so much more costly, more time-consuming, and require so much more effort to install the change solution in Company B than in Company A? And why are these change initiatives' impacts/results so much less successful in Company B? Certainly it isn't that the employees in Company A are all more intelligent and better educated than those in Company B. Nor is it that they are more dedicated and hard-working. And it isn't because the project team did not try to involve the employees in the change initiative, nor was it because management did not show interest and commitment to the change initiative. The difference rests solely with the basic culture differential within the two organizations. Company A's culture evolved to the point that their employees trusted the executive team and felt that they had their best interests at heart and understood the difficulties and opportunities that existed at the various levels within the organization.

In the case of Company B, the culture of this organization reflected the employees' lack of trust in the management team. They felt that business decisions were being made to benefit the highly paid people without regard to the negative impact those decisions would have on middle management, first-line supervisors, and the employees. In this organization there was a feeling that the change initiatives were experiments being run by management and driven by unproven theories that someone learned about in college or at a management conference.

> The culture in Company B has more impact on the success of changes within the organization than the way changes within the organization are implemented by the project team.

INSTALLING AND IMPLEMENTING A CCM SYSTEM

Now, as difficult as it is to define what the organization's culture is, you may think it's difficult to install an organization's CCM system. Well, it

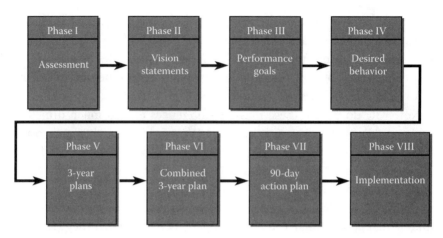

FIGURE 16.1
Developing the CCM Implementation Plan.

isn't impossible but it does take some concentrated effort. The following are the steps that an organization should go through in implementing a CCM system. We use an eight-phase plan as outlined in Figure 16.1.*

CCM can be successful only when you have a good understanding of the difference between the culture you currently have and the culture you are trying to build. Clear and objective staging into phases along with good solid measurement is one of the common features of successful culture change programs.

---

* The CCM Eight-Phase Implementation Plan we profile at the end of this chapter is based on the one we offer to our clients, and identifies who fulfills the role of *change strategists*, *change implementers*, and *change recipients*. Generally speaking, the CEOs and the management teams were the strategists, the line managers were the implementers (or were supposed to fulfill this role), and the employees were the recipients of the change in most cases. Three remarks must be added to this general classification. First, the members of the management teams who were responsible for a division of their organization also fulfilled the role of implementers together with the line managers. In fact, these members of the management team were the leading implementers. Also, in many cases, the employees also fulfilled the role of implementers; as well, line-managers and employees sometimes work together in translating the consequences of focusing on demands of clients to changes in the work of the teams. In other unique situations, we have found that everyone in the organization was involved in the change implementation process from the start. In a sense, all members of the organization fulfilled each of the three roles. However, the CEO, management team, and line managers were the most important strategists. Employees fulfilled this role to a lesser extent. Line managers and employees contributed equally to the implementation.

Start with an organizational assessment to determine the most critical change areas to focus on first

FIGURE 16.2
Defining how to change.

THE EIGHT-PHASE IMPLEMENTATION PLAN

Phase I: Perform a Current State Assessment (See Figure 16.2)

Definition: Key business drivers (KBD) are things within the organization that management can change that control or influence the organization's culture and the way the organization operates (also called controllable factors)

- Define the KBDs. Typical KBDs would include
  - Management leadership and support
  - Product types
  - Processes
  - Employee interface
  - Knowledge management
  - Innovation management
  - Customer interface
  - Cultural development
- Perform a current state assessment. Typical surveys that would be used to identify current state are
  - Cultural assessment analysis
  - Employee opinion surveys
  - Customer opinion surveys
  - Should be assessments
  - Change history implementation assessments
  - Implementation problem assessments
  - Sponsor evaluations
  - Change agents evaluations
  - Personnel resistance questionnaire

- Landscape surveys
- Influence style surveys
- Key business drivers maturity grid assessment
- Develop a current state paragraph related to each KBD. The following is a typical example of a current state paragraph for business processes.
  - The key business processes are flowcharting and a few of the major ones have been optimized to meet business needs. None of them have been reviewed to ensure that they are being followed or have been evaluated from the users' and the employees' standpoints

Phase II: Develop Vision Statements

- Develop a vision statement for each of the KBDs. The following is a typical vision statement for business processes (see Figure 16.3):
  - Major processes are documented, understood, followed, easy to use, prevent errors, and are designed to be adaptable to our stakeholders changing needs. Staff uses them because they believe they are more effective and efficient than the other options. Technology is effectively used to handle routine, repetitiveness, time-consuming activities, and remove bureaucracy from the process.

Phase III: Prepare Performance Goals

- Compare vision statements to the strategic plan
- Set 5-year performance goals for each of the key business drivers

FIGURE 16.3
Get a clear view of where you need to go.

Phase IV: Define Desired Behavioral Patterns for Each of the KBDs

- Review organization's value statements to be sure they are in line with desired behaviors. Typical behavioral patterns for empowered employees would be
  - Wild ideas are encouraged and discussed
  - Unsolicited recommendations and suggestions are often turned in
  - Business information is readily available to all employees
  - Management defines results expected, not how to get them
  - Decisions are made at lower levels
  - Less second-guessing

Phase V: Develop a 3-Year Plan for Each of the KBDs

- Evaluate each recommended improvement initiative to define its impact upon desired future behaviors and culture in conjunction with the four key change factors shown in Figure 16.4.

Figure 16.4 depicts the process, people, technology, and knowledge change factors as they relate to the CCM model.

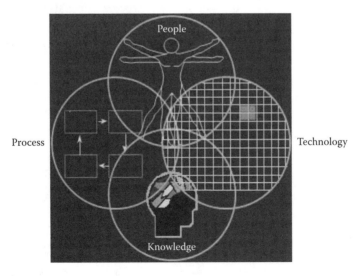

FIGURE 16.4
The four key change factors.

Phase VI: Combine the Individual 3-Year Plans into One Masterplan*

- Ensure there is a higher level of positive cultural impacts than negative cultural impacts.
- Plan for early positive impacts on culture to establish the initiative as having a positive impact early in the initiatives activity.
- Ensure proper cultural training is given to team members assigned to implement activities. Specific emphasis should be given to all project managers.

Phase VII: Develop in Detail the First 3 Months of the Master Plan

- The 3-month plan is broken down by week with individuals assigned to each task by name.

Phase VIII: Establish a Team to Implement the Action Items Defined in the 3-Month Breakout

- Every initiative should have a change plan that positively impacts the desired future culture.
- Both cultural and project change management training should be given to all individuals assigned to any project/initiative.
- All management and/or personnel affected decisions should be evaluated in light of their impact on the desired future culture. Any decision having a negative impact on the desired future culture should be reviewed and approved by a CCM committee.
- The CCM Committee should meet frequently to evaluate and/or measure the impact the CCM initiative is having on the culture of the organization.
- For the first 2 years, a representative sample of the organization's employees and managers should take a cultural assessment survey every 3 months.

---

* See *The Organizational Masterplan Handbook*, by Harrington and Voehl, Productivity Press, Boca Raton, FL, 2012. This book defines the makeup and highlights the differences in the operating plan, strategic business plan, strategic improvement plan, and the organization's business plan. It defines each and explains how to link them to reduce costs and cycle times. Describing how to use controllable factors as the foundation for constructing your Organizational Master Plan, it demonstrates how the plan fits into organizational alignment activities.

- At least every 18 months a total employee opinion survey should be conducted to identify negative and positive trends within individual functions, departments, and/or natural work teams. Negative trends at the individual level should have corrective action programs generated by the employees within those operating units. Negative trends in the organization's total population should have corrective action developed by the executive team.

The most important features of successful cultural change programs are, on the front end, trust, and on the back end, follow-up. Without good follow-up, all the effort put into the earlier stages can be lost, and the organization may revert to its original state or worse. It will also build cynicism that makes it difficult for management to implement future programs. The positions and roles of management teams, line managers, and employees in the changing organizations often explain the differences that we found in the degree to which each group was willing to trust in the change. In all cases, CEOs and the other members of the management teams in the organizations were the strategists. As strategists they initiated the changes, defined the goals, and decided the change approach.

In addition, some of the members of the management teams fulfilled a leading role in the implementation. It is hardly surprising that they fully supported the changes they started themselves and that their expectation of the outcome was positive. In all cases, line managers were the implementers. This meant that they had a lot of influence on the translation of the changes in their departments and teams. Thus, their close position to the change strategists was reflected in their positive expectations of the outcome of the change processes and high support for change. In almost all cases, employees were merely recipients of the changes that the others invented. Their role was limited to carrying out the instructions of management teams and line managers. This can explain the relatively higher percentage of individual resistance in this group. Nevertheless, a large majority was willing to change.

CEOs, top managers, and consultants do not have to overcome the resistance of the employees. Their challenge is to design change processes and improve the organizational culture's capacity to trust in such a way that groups can work together and realize a shared goal: improving the organization and their work. This asks for a change approach in which strategist, implementers, and recipients come from all departments and hierarchical levels of an organization.

ACTIONS TO IMPROVE ORGANIZATIONAL CULTURE OF TRUST

Now we could write a book on all the things any organization can do to improve and internalize the organization's culture. In fact, we probably will. Due to restrictions on the length of this book, we will just present you with a very few typical examples.

Employment Security

Employment security is one of the most critical and complex political and economic issues facing top management as a result of outsourcing and improvement initiatives that have been initiated within most organizations.

Management must determine

- Is the employee an investment or a cost?
- How much improved performance and flexibility would be generated if the organization provided employment security?
- Is it better to retrain or relocate employees or hire new ones?
- Should the organization look at other ways of handling surplus employees besides layoffs?

The employee must determine

- What impact will the organization's change initiatives have on my employment security?
- Will the organization's change activities jeopardize or improve my standard of living?
- Would I be willing to change jobs or move to another location?
- Will I be more valuable as a result of what I'm learning during the change process?

How can we expect our employees to give freely of their ideas to increase their productivity and minimize waste if it means that their job or the job of their friends will be eliminated? The answer is *trust*. If you start a continuous improvement process and then have layoffs, what you are going to end up with is a continuous sabotage process (Hardy and Klegg

> **FOCUS: How eBay Created a Trust Bandwagon**
>
> The online auction site eBay.com has succeeded in persuading millions of rational human beings to send money to total strangers, for goods, sometimes quite expensive goods, they have never seen. The strategy, premised on eBay's ability to use technology to build a trust-based brand, originated with company founder Pierre Omidyar. Believing that democracy should be the core principle of the company, Mr. Omidyar came up with the idea for a "feedback forum" through which individuals (suppliers or purchasers) would earn a reputation based on their trading habits. The concept is simple: If we do business together on eBay and if I am happy with the merchandise that you sold me and you are happy with how rapidly I paid you and how I treated you in the e-mail discussion that we had, then we give good feedback on each other for everyone else to see. This serves to enhance our reputations as users. Too many negative comments and you are banned as an eBay seller forever. The feedback forum is particularly critical for sellers, the vast majority of whom are small retailers or individuals who rely on eBay exclusively.
>
> To ensure even higher professional standards by its seller, eBay recently announced that it will offer low-cost premium health insurance to "Power Sellers," those who sell at least $2,000 a month via eBay and achieve 98 percent positive feedback ratings. Not every seller on eBay reaches that level; in fact, established companies appear to have the most difficulty meeting the feedback criterion. As of 2003, both IBM and Ritz Camera had positive feedback levels of only 93 percent; Disney's feedback was labeled "private," indicating that bidders could not view comments left by previous buyers. This seems to show that the huge shipping and handling fees and slow turnaround times that go along with the large companies' direct marketing efforts do not work on eBay.
>
> Although eBay relies mainly on buyers and sellers to police themselves, it does investigate fraud claims when required to ensure that confidence and trust in its service is maintained at all times. The company is aware that even a handful of unhappy users could damage its reputation. Although its technology and tactics are specific to its industry, the principle is universal—to scale up a market, consolidators must invest in reducing the customer's perceived or real risk of adopting a new product or service.

FIGURE 16.5
eBay FOCUS Profile. (Profile by Frank Voehl, Strategy Associates.)

1996). See the FOCUS Profile in Figure 16.5 on how eBay created a culture of trust between its vendors and its customers and made trust part of the eBay core brand.*

---

* The question is: Why should organizations care about maintaining and increasing employee trust? There are a number of answers: wanting to avoid having employees "quit and stay" (according to Gallup Research, disengagement costs corporations up to $300 billion per year), to prevent a culture rife with office politics, back-stabbing, excessive red tape, information hoarding, hidden agendas, and manipulation—all of these things are expensive for organizations. But none of these reasons carry as much impact as this one: trust. Trust is a key indicator of an organization's overall financial performance, playing a significant contributing factor to the bottom line. According to the Great Place to Work Institute, trust is the "primary defining characteristic," accounting for a full 60 percent of the criteria used to identify *Fortune Magazine's* 100 Best Companies to Work For. Of particular interest are the companies comprising the 2007 *Fortune* list who achieved an 18.1 percent return to shareholders over 3 years, compared to only a 10.5 percent return earned by companies comprising the S&P 500. And, over the prior 5 years, the Fortune Top 100 earned an average of 15.7 percent, while the S&P returned only 6.2 percent. Even more convincingly, global performance consulting experts Watson Wyatt found that high-trust organizations had over the long term a total return to shareholders that was almost 300 percent higher than comparable low-trust organizations.

DOWNPLAYING DOWNSIZING

Corporate America has been on a downsizing bandwagon since the late 1980s. It supposes that the answer to business pressure is to slow down and lay off, with the hope of rising stock prices, but that does not work. In an analysis published by *U.S. News and World Report*, the stock price of organizations that went through a major downsizing in the last half of the 1980s were compared with those within the industry group. On average, the organizations that downsized saw a 10 percent improvement in stock prices over the first 6 months after the downsizing occurred. Six months later, stock values went negative by about 1 percent. Three years after the downsizing, they were negative on average of 25 percent (Harrington 1995).

Layoffs produce sudden, substantial stock gains. These gains occur because the impact of removed employees has not reached the customer and the competition has not been removed from the bottom line, making organizations appear to be more profitable than they really are. But in the long run, the downsizing had a negative impact. CEO Frank Poppoff of Dow Chemical put it this way, "Layoffs are horribly expensive and destructive of shareholder value."

The cost of layoffs and replacement is growing all the time. Dow Chemical estimates that it costs between $30,000 to $100,000 to replace technical and managerial personnel. Layoffs not only cost organizations money and some of its best people, but when it comes time to hire, the best people do not trust the organization and will not come to work for them (Harrington 1995).

An alternative approach of a golden parachute or early retirement is equally bad. The people who leave are all the best performers who will not have problems finding a new job. The deadwood, who barely meet minimum performance, stay because they know it will be hard to find an equally good job in today's job market.*

Employees can understand that organizations need to cut back when demand for their products fall off, and they can accept that (Emery and

---

* One of the key aspects of successfully leading any type of change is to understand that people's reaction to change is based on emotion, not logic. Many times, leaders analyze the information gathered, think about the appropriate solution, and then launch into the answer that will be the new change paradigm, all without taking into account the people factor, including the deadwood that is often left standing after the high performers have long gone.

Enlightened Layoff Policy

No employee will be laid off because of improvements made as a result of the change process that is going on within the organization. People whose jobs are eliminated will be retrained for an equally or more responsible job. This does not mean that it may not be necessary to lay off employees because of a business turndown, but sufficient notice will be given and adequate compensation packages will be provided.

FIGURE 16.6
No-layoff policy example.

Trist 1965). The problem we face is what happens to an employee whose job has been eliminated due to an improvement initiative. We know that programs like Six Sigma, lean, and reengineering are designed to improve productivity. But if our share of the market does not keep pace with our productivity improvements, what will management do with surplus employees? (See Figure 16.6.) To cover this scenario and to alleviate employee fears, top management should consider publishing a "no-layoff policy." A typical no-layoff policy would state.

You will note that the policy does not guarantee the employees will not be laid off as a result of a turndown in business. It only protects the employees from being laid off as a result of the change initiative. These are people who would still be working for the organization if the change initiative had not been implemented.

We know of one organization that was able to eliminate 200 jobs as a result of their change initiatives. As they started their change initiatives, they put a freeze on new hiring and used temporary employees to cover workload peaks. This was reviewed with the labor union leaders and they concurred with the use of temporary employees to protect regular employees' jobs. As a result, attrition took care of about 150 surplus jobs. The organization then held a contest to select 50 employees who were sent to a local university to work toward an engineering degree. While at school, they received full pay and their additional expenses were paid for by the organization. The results were phenomenal. Everyone within the organization started looking for ways to eliminate their job so they could go to school.

Alternatives to Layoff

Just having a no-layoff policy is not enough. Just having and practicing a no-layoff policy isn't even enough. Management has to put in place a series of alternate activities where laying off an individual is a last-resort measure. Enlightened organizations should be able to say to their employees who are losing their jobs that they have looked into at least 12 alternatives that didn't result in creating value-added activities to the degree necessary so that we had to resort to laying an individual off. The following are some of the alternatives to layoffs that we have found to be effective. With a little brainstorming on your part you may be able to come up with your own additional alternatives.

1. Increased customer demands
2. Deadwood removal
3. Overtime reduction
4. Skills training
5. Attrition
6. Train-the-trainer
7. Increased marketing and sales efforts
8. Voluntary leaves
9. Job rotation
10. Incentive retirement programs
11. Shorter work week
12. External schools
13. Civic programs
14. Employee relocation
15. Job sharing
16. Contract workers

Note: Whenever you have a layoff, be sure that the conditions you used to select the individuals who would be losing their job is well-defined, documented, and explained to the organization. Of course, the most easily defined and best accepted practice is layoff based on seniority. Probably a more logical approach, but harder to justify, is a combination of seniority and skills.

Employee Involvement in Their Jobs

The second approach that we would like to highlight is involving the individual in designing and improving the way they work within the organization. Too often we rely on the industrial engineer to design the workflow and write the work procedures that are used throughout the organization.

We will agree that this is an excellent starting point but it should be considered only a starting point. Once a person is assigned to do a particular job, he or she becomes the individual who has the most knowledge and skill related to improving the way the work is performed. We want the employee to feel that he or she is the owner of the job that they are performing. We want them to feel and believe that they not only are allowed, but are responsible for looking for ways to improve the efficiency and effectiveness of the way their job is performed.*

Management needs to encourage and empower their employees to be creative related to their assignment. We hire engineers, accountants, MBAs, and so forth to help improve the quality and productivity of the total organization. They are expected to do their part of their assignment. Some of these employees do an outstandingly creative job. Others do a good job, while others do just enough to get by. For years management has relied on the theory of "cream floats to the top" to help them identify and promote the best candidate. This is an excellent theory if the milk is not homogenized and the management's ranks are expanding to make room for those high-potential employees. The problem is that this is not the case in most organizations today. As a result, we need to search for ways to motivate our employees by allowing our professionals to compete, and for organizations to develop a database that encourages the very best candidates to be identified for each promotional opportunity.

An effective way to motivate our employees is by implementing an improvement effectiveness program (IEP). This program should be available to all individuals and teams alike. It's a way to recognize employees for improving the things they are responsible for. In this program, the employees, after they have implemented a suggestion that is within their job scope, make an estimate of the first year's net savings that result from the suggestion (savings minus implementation costs). These estimates should be reasonably accurate (about plus or minus 10%). This individual who made the suggestion should then fill out a form documenting the idea and the savings.

---

* Worker self-improvement begins by involving and successfully engaging and enabling the organization as a whole by communicating directly and openly. In order to achieve buy-in, leaders should engage in a continuous dialogue that tells a compelling story with all key employee groups. This strategy also focuses on empowering employees, which requires removing barriers, enhancing team member's skills, and realigning business performance measurements. Meaningful and timely short-term wins need to be created. They should be planned, visible, and unambiguous. These short-term wins start a successful execution path forward.

The next step of the IEP program is for the department manager to review the document and sign it if he or she concurs with the estimate and can verify the change was implemented. This form is then sent to personnel where the information is added to the employee's personnel file. The improvement effectiveness ideas that have general and/or multiple applications will be noted at this point. These multiuse ideas are then documented in a quarterly report that is circulated to management. This report provides a stimulus for many spinoff improvement effectiveness ideas.

At IBM, the ideas that generated the most added value to the organization from each functional unit within the organization are recognized. This individual who made the suggestion is invited to a luncheon with the president of the division where the idea is discussed and he or she is presented with an appropriate gift. These individuals and ideas are also highlighted in the division's monthly newsletter. Everyone is expected to participate in this activity as everyone is expected to be creative in looking for ways to improve the way they work. During the past 10 years, a best-practice criterion was set for employees generating ideas to improve the way they work. In some companies, every employee from the CEO down to the newest intern is expected to turn in an average of two implemented ideas per month on how to improve the way they work. Dana Corporation asks each employee to submit two ideas a month in writing. During the first year they received 2 million ideas and 80 percent of them were implemented.*

At Southwest Airlines, the Employee Suggestion System has been very effective for over 20 years and in 1991 the $58.5 million in savings for suggestions implemented produced enough savings to pay for a new Boeing 757.† Of course, success depends on follow-through on the suggestions in a timely manner—days, not months. The studies show that employees will offer many ideas if they know that their ideas will receive a timely and fair hearing and that the good ones will be quickly implemented. A survey of 6000 by the Employee Involvement Association shows that the responding

---

* Most great corporate innovations come from front-line workers and not the managers, according to Teitelbaum, Matthis and Jackson, among others. In fact, over 75% of product improvements and money-saving ideas come from workers who deal with the products and their problems each and every day. The reasoning is simple: the individual closest to the problem is the most likely to recognize the symptoms and envision the possible solutions. As early as 1995, Dana Corp.'s 48,000 employees submitted an average of 1.22 ideas a month, or "666,120 nuggets of labor-saving, cost-cutting productivity-increasing wisdom." And some 70% of all suggestions are used (Teitelbaum 1997).

† For details, see the 1994 report by Matthis and Jackson.

businesses have saved an average of just over $6000 for each suggestion implemented.*

Best Practice Benchmark: Two Accepted Ideas per Month per Employee

Dr. Kaoru Ishikawa, the father of the Japanese quality process and the quality circle concept, stated, "In Japan, only 10% of the quality improvement comes from teams. The remaining 90% come from individual suggestions."

You can't expect to get the kind of results Dana Corporation or the Japanese industry is getting without investing some creative training in all of the individuals within the organization. In addition, their job descriptions and evaluation performances need to reflect that it is their personal responsibility to be creative by making suggestions on how to improve the job they are assigned to. Before Technicolor Inc. trained and set creativity expectations for their employees, they received an average of 13 employee suggestions per year. The first year after the employee creative training was conducted, they received 1320 employee ideas.

Frank K. Sonnenberg, in his article entitled, "It's A Great Idea, But" wrote, "an idea, like a human being, has a life cycle (Sonnenberg and Goldberg 2015). It is born. If properly nurtured, it grows. When it matures, it becomes a productive member of society." He points out that at 3M, some people claim the company's 11th commandment is, "Now sell—not kill—an idea."

SELECTING THE RIGHT PROJECTS

The best time to stop a project that is going to fail is prior to starting it!

Jim Harrington

We have attended dozens of executive meetings where the major question is: "Why did we ever approve this project?" Literally billions and billions of dollars is wasted every year on projects that never delivered value to

---

* See Allerton, page 80.

the organization that initiated them. Many of them get started because the executive team just rubberstamps an idea that one of them strongly supports. Probably more are approved based on value propositions that were prepared by an individual or a team that came up with a concept and prepared the value proposition that presented a false picture of the risks that were involved in the project. And then the team or individual that was assigned to prepare the business case blindly accepted the assumptions and the data that was included in the value proposition, allowing the business case to present a very false picture of the value that the proposed project would bring to the organization. All too often the data that is presented to the executive team is based on false information or irrelevant or statistically unsound data that is often made up rather than being factual. We believe that one of the biggest factors that cause projects to fail is not the way they are managed; it is caused by the executive team being provided with faulty information when they approved the project, making it near impossible for the project team to be successful. We estimate that if the value propositions were prepared correctly, 30 percent of projects would never be approved. A properly prepared business case would then exclude almost 20 percent of the value propositions that were proposed to become active projects.

Definitions

- A value proposition is a document that defines the net benefits that will result from the implementation of a change or the use of an output as viewed by one or more of the organization's stakeholders. A value proposition can apply to an entire organization, part thereof, or to customer accounts, products, services, or internal processes.
- A business case captures the reasoning for installing a project, program, or tasks.* The business case builds on the basic information included in the value proposition by expanding it to focus on the total organizational impact and the quantification of the accuracy of the

---

* See Voehl, Harrington, and Voehl (2014). The premise of the book is that the best time to stop projects or programs that will not be successful is before they are ever started. Research has shown that the focused use of realistic business case analysis on proposed initiatives could enable your organization to reduce the amount of project waste and churn (rework) by up to 40 percent, potentially avoiding millions of dollars lost on projects, programs, and initiatives that would fail to produce the desired results. This book illustrates how to develop a strong business case that links investments to program results, and ultimately, with the strategic outcomes of the organization. In addition, the book provides a template and example case studies for those seeking to fast-track the development of a business case within their organization.

data and estimates used in the analysis and recommendations. Often outcomes are expressed in worst case, best case, and most probable values, and the final decision is made on combinations of worst-case conditions while the budgeting is usually based on best-case conditions. (This is sometimes referred to as minimum maximum and average values.) The objective of the business case evaluation is not to get the project/initiative approved or disapproved. The objective is to fairly evaluate, with a high degree of confidence, the value-added properties the proposed project/initiative will have on the organization's stakeholders. Then, based on this evaluation, it recommends the management action that should be taken related to the proposed project/initiative. The logic of the business case is that whatever resources, such as money or effort, are consumed, they should be in support of a specific business need. A compelling business case adequately captures both the quantifiable and intangible characteristics of a proposed project. The business case evaluation should be conducted by an independent individual or group that is not involved in the initial creation of the project/proposal.

All too often the value proposition is created by the individual or group that originally conceived the idea/concept. As a result, the value proposition turns out to be a document directed at selling the ideas/concepts rather than evaluating the risk and advantages related to the idea/concept. It typically presents the idea/concept without considering the other ideas/concepts that are consuming resources or considered for consuming resources within the organization. As a result, the value proposition which presents an idea/concept that looks very attractive from the presenters' point of view may not be approved because it does not represent the best way to utilize the organization's limited resources when the organization's total operation is considered.* This is the very reason why a very effective business case analysis should be conducted to be sure that the organization's resources are used in the most effective manner and the decision to authorize the formation of a project as part of the organization's portfolio

---

* See Harrington and Brett (2014). This book illustrates the role of the opportunity center in capturing new ideas, describes how to present value propositions to management, and includes an example of a new product value proposition. Detailing a method for continuous review of the improvement process, it will help you foster an entrepreneurial mind-set within your employees and encourage them to actively search and document value-adding ideas.

of projects is not based on the charisma of the individual that is presenting the proposed project/initiative.

Based on this, it is absolutely essential that a very effective business case analysis be performed by an independent group. Unfortunately this is usually not the case. Accuracy of projections, costs, risk, and value added is not quantified. The complexity of the development, documentation, implementation, and sustaining the project/initiative often is not thoroughly analyzed. In addition, the scope and breadth of the proposed project/initiative is not thoroughly understood and as a result, there are a number of scope changes implemented after the project is approved, greatly increasing the time and resources required to complete the project. We're constantly amazed at the lack of statistical capabilities on the business case analysis team that are required to make accurate projections or at a minimum to quantify the accuracy of projections. If the true costs, time requirements, and benefits were understood when the business case was presented to the executive team for approval, between 25 to 35 percent of the projects that are presently being approved would be rejected. When an organization invests $3 million and 2 years in developing a project and a project manager comes back and says they require an additional $500,000 to complete the project and 6 more months, it's hard, if not impossible, for the executive team not to approve the additional expenditures in order to salvage the project. Time spent in doing business case analysis can save the organization millions of dollars and may provide one of their biggest returns on investment.

SUMMARY

We agree with all the work that the OCM gurus have publicized and promoted for the last 25 years related to the importance of preparing the individuals that are affected by the output from a project to accept and embrace the project output. But we feel that too little emphasis has been placed on the importance of how the content of these change initiatives impact the organization's culture and how the day-to-day decisions made by managers that does not trigger a project impacts the culture and performance of the organization. We believe that improving the resiliency factor within the culture of the organization has a bigger impact on the ability for the organization to change and operate in a turbulent economy that exists today than changing the degree of acceptance of individual project outputs. PCM has a relatively short time and little impact on how the organization functions.

In the more successful organizations, cultures act as reinforcers for productive behavior in that they assist employees in coping with the environmental uncertainties and in coordinating their activities. According to Wilkins, Dyer, and Burrell, cultural roadmaps are made up of general and specific frames of reference that allows individuals to define situations they encounter and develop the appropriate response (Buchanan and Bryman 2009).* Mottoes, visions, and mission statements add to an organization's ability to shape its own culture. For example, in 1912 the following words were inscribed on the walls of the New York City Post Office: "Neither snow nor rain nor gloom of night stays these couriers from the swift completion of their appointed rounds." Although this pledge was never intended to be the official motto of the U.S. Post Office, such is the power of words to shape belief that millions of Americans still take this pledge to be the motto of the postal service and infuse the words with an almost sacred trust.†

People need to be both empowered and motivated in order for real change to take place; that is, you need to achieve a situation where management and staff are both able and willing to change, as outlined in the checklist below:

- A cultural audit will in itself facilitate change: if you measure it, you change it. A very powerful form of measurement is to obtain customer feedback on the service provided; this provides a significant motivation for change across all levels of management and staff.
- The behaviors and attitudes in the department often reflect those exhibited in the management team. Undertake some management

---

* In *The Words We Live By*, Brian Burrell, a lecturer in mathematics at the University of Massachusetts at Amherst, turns his father's passion for words into a spirited study of the ideals and principles recorded in America's key texts. While Brian Burrell was growing up, his father began collecting mottoes, oaths, and creeds from around the country in a notebook titled "The Words People Live By," which takes its reader on a tour of America through the phrases of belief, duty, and community that offer ready-made opinions and profess values for everyday life in the United States.

† CMM has a much bigger impact on the way the organization operates and its attitude related to embracing and accepting change initiatives. It brings about a basic change in the attitude and the way the organization operates on a day-to-day basis. CCM also has a major impact on the content of the individual change initiatives and management decisions. Comparing the results between CCM and Organizational (project) change management, the latter has a relatively minor impact on how the organization brings about fundamental changes in the way it reacts.

team building and it will have a knock-on effect throughout the whole organization.

- Changing people in influential positions can have an effect on the culture, but their personalities and approach need to be different from the existing culture. They also need to be encouraged in bringing a fresh approach, or else it might be their behavior that changes (by conforming) rather than the culture.
- A well-designed organizational change can also change the culture. But beware; as Caesar first observed, reorganization can simply be a substitute for achievement.
- A bottom-up program is more pragmatic—trying to change the culture in a few parts of the organization and hoping it will spread out from there. These are generally cheap programs, but not that effective.
- A well-designed mission, vision, or set of objectives will also facilitate change, but simply having a mission is not good enough—it has to be a motivating mission that inspires people and makes them feel good about coming to work.

Finally, we outlined the eight stages involved in implementing a CCM program and covered the following major considerations involved in changing an organization's culture:

- Before an organization can change its culture, it must first understand the current culture, or the way things are now.
- Once you understand your current organizational culture, your organization must then decide where it wants to go, define its strategic direction, and decide what the organizational culture should look like to support success. What vision does the organization have for its future and how must the culture change to support the accomplishment of that vision?
- Next, the management team needs to answer questions such as
  - What are the most important values you would like to see represented in your organizational culture?
  - Are these values compatible with your current organizational culture? Do they exist now? If not, why not?
- However, knowing what the desired organizational culture looks like is not enough. Organizations must create change management plans to ensure that the desired organizational culture becomes a reality.

In reality, the individuals in the organization must decide to change their behavior to create the desired organizational culture. This is often regarded as the hardest step in CCM, and the most rewarding.

- But even that is not enough; the cultural impact must be considered in every decision and action that is considered for implementation. It doesn't matter how small or how big that decision is. The cumulative impact on the culture of many small decisions/actions can often have a bigger impact on the organization's culture than a reorganization has on it.

In the final analysis, there are lots of resources out there on leading culture change, but none will likely help unless you are truly willing to ask yourself these four fundamental questions (Beer, Eisenstat, and Spector 1990):

1. Do we know how to lead culture change?
2. Have we developed the skills to put that knowledge into action?
3. Are there any hidden conflicts that stop us from using what we know?
4. Are there unwritten rules in our culture that inhibit our well-intended plans?

Three Absolutes of CCM

1. Cultural change management changes the way the organization operates, reacts and functions.
2. Project change management improves the way affected parties except an individual change.
3. The ability for an organization to accept change is driven by the cumulative effect of the decisions that are made and the ability to reduce learning tension, not on the individual change initiatives themselves.

Bibliography

A brief review of alternative models of organizational change can be found in B. Schneider, Organizational Behavior, *Annual Review of Psychology*, Vol. 36, pp. 573–611, 1985.

A comprehensive treatment of the organizational culture concept can be found in H. M. Trice and J. M. Beyer, *The Cultures of Work Organizations*, Englewood Cliffs, NJ: Prentice-Hall, 1993.

Adams, J., 2000, *Risk*, Boca Raton, FL: Routledge Press/Taylor and Francis.

An introduction to the history of the study of organizational climate can be found in A. E. Reichers and B. Schneider, Organizational Climate and Culture: Evolution of Constructs, in B. Schneider (ed.), *Organizational Climate and Culture*, San Francisco: Jossey-Bass, 1990. Much of the material on climate in this chapter can be found in more detail in this book.

APQC, 2014, *Transformational Change: Making It Last*, Houston, TX: American Productivity and Quality Center.

Argyris, C., 1973, *Intervention Theory and Method*, Reading, MA: Addison-Wesley.

Argyris, C., 1976, Single and Double Loop Models in Research on Decision Making, *Administrative Science Quarterly*, 21(3): 363–375.

Argyris, C. and Schon, D. A., 1989, Participative Action Research and Action Science ComparA Commentary, *American Behavioral Science*, 32: 612–623.

Baggini, J., 2009, Painting the Bigger Picture, *The Philosopher's Magazine*, 8: 37–39.

Bain & Company, 2013, Bain Brief: Insight on Management Tools and Trends 2013, retrieved from http://www.bain.com/publications/business-insights/management -tools-and-trends.aspx.

Beck, D. E. and Cowan, C. C., 1996, *Spiral Dynamics: Mastering Values, Leadership, and Change*, Victoria, Australia: Blackwell Publishing.

Becker, B., Huselid, M., and Ulrich, D., 2001, *The HR Scorecard; Linking People, Strategy, and Performance*, Boston: Harvard Business School Press.

Beckhard, R. and Pritchard, W., 1992, *Changing the Essence: The Art of Creating and Leading Fundamental Change in Organizations*, San Francisco: Jossey-Bass.

Beer, M., 1980, *Organizational Change and Development: A Systems View*, Santa Monica, CA: Goodyear Publishing Co.

Beer, M., Eisenstat, R. A., and Spector, B., 1990a, *The Critical Path to Corporate Renewal*, Boston: Harvard Business School Press.

Beer, M., Eisenstat, R. A., and Spector, B., 1990b, Why Change Programs Don't Produce Change, *Harvard Business Review*, November–December, 68(6): 158–166.

Beer, M. and Walton, E., 1987, Organization Change and Development, *Annual Review of Psychology*, 33: 229–272.

Bennebroek Gravenhorst, K. M., Werkman, R. A., and Boonstra, J. J., 2003, The Change Capacity of Organisations: General Assessment and Five Configurations, *Applied Psychology: An International Review*, 52(1): 83–105.

Block, N., 1978, Troubles with Functionalism, in *Perception and Cognition: Issues in the Foundations of Psychology*, Savage, C. W. (ed.), Minneapolis, MN: University of Minnesota Press. (Reprinted in many anthologies on philosophy of mind and psychology.)

Block, N., 1986, Advertisement for a Semantics for Psychology, in *Midwest Studies in Philosophy*, French, P. A., Uehling, T. E., Jr., and Wettstein, H. K. (eds.), Minneapolis, MN: University of Minnesota Press, Vol. X, pp. 615–678.

Block, N., 2002, Searle's Arguments against Cognitive Science, in *Views into the Chinese Room: New Essays on Searle and Artificial Intelligence*, Preston, J. and Bishop, M. (eds.), New York: Oxford University Press.

Bloom et al.'s *Taxonomy of the Cognitive Domain* (Dr. William G. Huitt, Valdosta State University).

Bloom's Digital Taxonomy by Andrew Churches is a thorough orientation to the revised taxonomy, with practical recommendations for a wide variety of ways mapping the taxonomy to the uses of current online technologies; and associated rubrics.

Bloom's Taxonomy—An Overview and *Bloom's Taxonomy—Designing Activities* (Colorado Community College System Faculty Wiki).

Boden, M., 1988, *Computer Models of the Mind*, Cambridge: Cambridge University Press, pp. 238–251 were excerpted and published as Escaping from the Chinese Room, in *The Philosophy of Artificial Intelligence*, Boden, M. A. (ed.), New York: Oxford University Press, 1990.

Boehm, B., 1986, A Spiral Model of Software Development and Enhancement, *ACM SIGSOFT Software Engineering Notes*, ACM, 11(4): 14–24.

Boeker, W., 1989, Strategic Change: The Effects of Founding and History, *Academy of Management Journal*, 32: 489–515.

Bolman, L. G. and Deal, T. E., 2013, *Reframing Organizations: Artistry, Choice, and Leadership*, 5th Edition, Hoboken, NJ: Wiley/Jossey-Bass.

Boonstra, J. J. and Bennebroek Gravenhorst, K. M., 1998, Power Dynamics and Organizational Change: A Comparison of Perspectives, *European Journal of Work and Organizational Psychology*, 7: 97–120.

Bostick, J. and Freeman, J., 2003, No Limits: Doing Participatory Action Research with YOUNG People in Northumberland, *Journal of Community and Applied Social Psychology*, 13(6): 426–436.

Brown, L. D. and Tandon, R., 1983, Ideology and Political Economy in Inquiry: Action Research and Participatory Research, *Journal of Applied Behavioral Science*, 19(2): 277–294.

Buchanan, D. and Bryman, A., 2009, The Sage handbook of Organization Research Methods, Los Angeles, CA: Sage Publications, Chapter 19, p. 329.

Burgelman, R. A., 1991, Inter-organizational Ecology of Strategy Making and Organizational Adaptation: Theory and Field Research, *Organization Science*, 2(3): 239–262.

Burke, W. W., 1976, Organization Development in Transition, *Journal of Applied Behavioral Science*, 12: 22–43.

Burke, W. W., 1982, *Organization Development: Principles and Practices*, Boston: Little, Brown.

Burke, W. W., 1993, The Changing World of Organization Change, *Consulting Psychology Journal*, 45(1): 9–17.

Burke, W. and Litwin, G., 1992, A Causal Model of Organizational Performance and Change, *Journal of Management*, 18: 523–545.

Burke, W. W., Lake, D. G., and Paine, J. W. (eds.), 2009, *Organization Change: A Comprehensive Reader*, San Francisco: Jossey-Bass.

Burrell, B., 2011, *The Words We Live By*, New York: Free Press, Simon and Schuster Canada.

Cam, P., 1990, Searle on Strong AI, *Australasian Journal of Philosophy*, 68: 103–108.

Campbell, D. T., 1969, Variation and Selective Retention in Socio-cultural Evolution, *General Systems*, 16: 69–85.

Chalmers, D., 1992, Subsymbolic Computation and the Chinese Room, in *The Symbolic and Connectionist Paradigms: Closing the Gap*, Dinsmore, J. (ed.), Hillsdale, NJ: Lawrence Erlbaum.

Champy, J., 1997, Preparing for Organizational Change, in *The Organization of the Future*, Drucker Foundation Future Series, Hesselbein, F., Goldsmith, M., and Beckhard, R. (eds.), San Francisco: Jossey-Bass Publishers, pp. 9–16.

Church, A., 2001, The Professionalization of Organization Development, in *Research in Organization Change and Development*, Woodman, R. and Pasmore, W. (eds.), Oxford, UK: JAI Press.

Church, A. and Burke, W., 1995, Practitioner Attitude about the Field of Organization Development, in *Research in Organization Change and Development*, Pasmore, W. and Woodman, R. (eds.), Greenwich, CT: JAI Press.

Churchland, P., 1985, Reductionism, Qualia, and the Direct Introspection of Brain States, *The Journal of Philosophy*, LXXXII: 8–28.

Churchland, P. M. and Churchland, P. S., 1990, Could a Machine Think? *Scientific American*, 262(1): 32–37.

Clark, A., 1991, *Microcognition: Philosophy, Cognitive Science, and Parallel Distributed Processing*, Cambridge, MA: MIT Press.

Clark, T. R., 2008, *EPIC Change: How to Lead Change in the Global Age*, Hoboken, NJ: Jossey-Bass.

Clegg, S. R., Kornberger, M., and Pitsis, T., 2009. Managing and Organizations: An Introduction to Theory and Practice, Los Angeles, CA: Sage Publications.

Cobb, A. T., Wooten, K. C., and Folger, R., 1995, Justice in the Making: Toward Understanding the Theory and Practice of Justice in Organizational Change and Development, in *Research in Organizational Change and Development*, Woodman, R. and Pasmore, W. (eds.), Greenwich, CT: JAI Press, Vol. 8, pp. 243–295.

Coch, L. and French, Jr., J. R. P., 1948, Overcoming Resistance to Change, *Human Relations*, 1(4): 512–532.

Cole, D., 1984, Thought and Thought Experiments, *Philosophical Studies*, 45: 431–444.

Cole, D., 1990, Functionalism and Inverted Spectra, *Synthese*, 82: 202–222.

Cole, D., 1991a, Artificial Intelligence and Personal Identity, *Synthese*, 88: 399–417.

Cole, D., 1991b, Artificial Minds: Cam on Searle, *Australasian Journal of Philosophy*, 69: 329–333.

Cole, D., 1994, The Causal Powers of CPUs, in *Thinking Computers and Virtual Persons*, Dietrich, E. (ed.), New York: Academic Press.

Cole, D. and Foelber, R., 1984, Contingent Materialism, *Pacific Philosophical Quarterly*, 65(1): 74–85.

Collier, J., 1945, United States Indian Administration at a Laboratory of Ethnic Relations, *Social Research*, 12: 275–285.

Conner, D. R., 1992, *Managing at the Speed of Change*, New York: Random House.

Conner, D. R., 1998, *Managing at the Speed of Change. How Resilient Managers Succeed and Prosper Where Others Fail*, Chichester, UK: Wiley.

Copeland, J., 2002, The Chinese Room from a Logical Point of View, in *Views into the Chinese Room: New Essays on Searle and Artificial Intelligence*, Preston, J. and Bishop, M. (eds.), New York: Oxford University Press, pp. 104–122.

Crane, T., 1996, *The Mechanical Mind: A Philosophical Introduction to Minds, Machines and Mental Representation*, London: Penguin.

Cummings, T. and Worley, C. G., 2015, *Organization Development and Change*, 10th Edition, Stamford, CT: Cengage Learning, Chapter 1, p. 7.

Davis, L., 2001, Functionalism, the Brain, and Personal Identity, *Philosophical Studies*, 102(3): 259–279.

Dennett, D., 1978, Toward a Cognitive Theory of Consciousness, in *Brainstorms: Philosophical Essays on Mind and Psychology*, Cambridge, MA: MIT Press.

Dennett, D., 1981, Where Am I?, in *Brainstorms: Philosophical Essays on Mind and Psychology*, Cambridge, MA: MIT Press, pp. 310–323.

Dennett, D., 1987, Fast Thinking, in *The Intentional Stance*, Cambridge, MA: MIT Press, pp. 324–337.

Dennett, D., 1997, Consciousness in Humans and Robot Minds, in *Cognition, Computation, and Consciousness*, Ito, M., Miyashita, Y., and Rolls, E. T. (eds.), New York: Oxford University Press, pp. 17–29.

Dennett, D., 2013, *Intuition Pumps and Other Tools for Thought*, New York: W. W. Norton and Co.

Dent, E. B. and Goldberg, S. G., 1999, Challenging "Resistance to Change," *Journal of Applied Behavioral Science*, 35: 25–41.

Double, R., 1983, Searle, Programs and Functionalism, *Nature and System*, 5: 107–114.

Dretske, F. 1985, Presidential Address (Central Division Meetings of the American Philosophical Association), *Proceedings and Addresses of the American Philosophical Association*, 59(1): 23–33.

Edwards, J. E., Thomas, M. D., Rosenfeld, P., and Booth-Kewley, S., 1997, *How to Conduct Organizational Surveys. A Step-by-Step Guide*, Thousand Oaks, CA: Sage.

Eisen, S., Cherbeneau, J., and Worley, C., 2005, A Future-Responsive Perspective for Competent Practice in OD, in *Practicing Organization Development*, 2nd Edition, Rothwell, W. and Sullivan, R. (eds.), San Diego: Pfeiffer.

Emery, F. E. and Trist, E. L., 1965, The Causal Texture of Organizational Environments, *Human Relations*, 18: 21–32.

Freedman, A. and Zackrison, R., 2001, *Finding Your Way in the Consulting Jungle*, San Francisco: Jossey-Bass.

French, W. L., 1969, Organization Development: Objectives, Assumptions, and Strategies, *California Management Review*, 12: 23–24.

Fodor, J., 1987, *Psychosemantics*, Cambridge, MA: MIT Press.

Fodor, J., 1991, Yin and Yang in the Chinese Room, in *The Nature of Mind*, Rosenthal, D. (ed.), New York: Oxford University Press.

Fodor, J., 1992, *A Theory of Content and Other Essays*, Cambridge, MA: MIT Press.

Fodor, J., 2009, Where Is My Mind? *London Review of Books*, 31(3): 13–15.

For materials on change specifically related to total quality management (TQM) and the source of the materials on IBM Rochester, see the book by J. W. Spechler that reports on companies that have been successful in competing for the Malcolm Baldrige Award: *Managing Quality in America's Most Admired Companies*, San Francisco: Berrett-Kohler, 1993.

Ford, J., 2010, Helen Keller Was Never in a Chinese Room, *Minds and Machines*, 21: 57–72.

Foss, A., Lipsky, D., Orr, A., Scott, B., Seamon, T., Smendzuik-O'Brien, J., Tavis, A., Wissman, D., and Woods, C., Practicing Internal OD, in *Practicing Organizational Development*, 2nd Edition, Rothwell, W. and Sullivan, R. (eds.), San Diego: Pfeiffer, 2005.

Gardiner, H., 1987, *The Mind's New Science: A History of the Cognitive Revolution*, New York: Basic Books.

George, J. M. and Jones, G. R., 2002, *Understanding and Managing Organizational Behavior*, Upper Saddle River, NJ: Prentice Hall.

Gerber, J., 2006, *Inside and Out: Universities and Education for Sustainable Development*, Amityville, NY: Baywood Publishing, pp. 81–82.

Greiner, L. and Cummings, T., 2009, *Dynamic Strategy Making: A Real-Time Approach for the 21st Century Leader*, San Francisco: Jossey-Bass.

Greiner, L. and Poulfelt, F., 2010, *Management Consulting Today and Tomorrow*, New York: Routledge.

Hanley, R., 1997, *The Metaphysics of Star Trek*, New York: Basic Books.

Hardy, C. and Clegg, S. R., 1996, Some Dare Call It Power, in *Handbook of Organizational Studies*, Clegg, S. R., Hardy, C., and Nord, W. R. (eds.), London: Sage, pp. 622–641.

Harnad, S., 1989, Minds, Machines and Searle, *Journal of Experimental and Theoretical Artificial Intelligence*, 1: 5–25.

Harnad, S., 2002, Minds, Machines, and Searle 2: What's Right and Wrong about the Chinese Room Argument, in *Views into the Chinese Room: New Essays on Searle and Artificial Intelligence*, Preston, J. and Bishop, M. (eds.), New York: Oxford University Press, pp. 294–307.

Harrington, H. J., 1995, *Total Improvement Management*, New York: McGraw Hill.

Harrington, H. J., Conner, D. R., and Horney, N. L., 2000, *Project Change Management*, New York: McGraw-Hill.

Harrington, H. J. and Trusko, B., 2014, *Maximizing Value Propositions to Increase Project Success Rates*, Boca Raton, FL: CRC Press.

Harrington, H. J. and Voehl, F., 2004, What CEOs Need to Know about Quality, *Quality Digest*, September.

Harrington, H. J. and Voehl, F., 2015, Cultural Change Management, *Innovation Forum*, 7(1): 55, March 2015, International Association for Innovation Professionals, Houston, TX.

Harvard Business Review, 2006, available at http://www.amazon.com/Make-It-Stick -Embedding-Organizational/dp/B001GLLRVS.

Haugeland, J., 2002, Syntax, Semantics, Physics, in *Views into the Chinese Room: New Essays on Searle and Artificial Intelligence*, Preston, J. and Bishop, M. (eds.), New York: Oxford University Press, pp. 379–392.

Hauser, L., 1997, Searle's Chinese Box: Debunking the Chinese Room Argument, *Minds and Machines*, 7: 199–226.

Hayes, P., Harnad, S., Perlis, D., and Block, N., 1992, Virtual Symposium on Virtual Mind, *Minds and Machines*, 2(3): 217–238.

Heller, F., Pusic, E., Strauss, G., and Wilpert, B., 1998, *Organizational Participation. Myth and Reality*, New York: Oxford University Press.

Heller, F., Pusic, E., Strauss, G., and Wilpert, B., 2000, Organizational Participation: Myth and Reality, Reveiw by William Finlay. *Administrative Science Quarterly*, 45(3): 628–630. Sage Publications, Inc. on behalf of the Johnson Graduate School of Management, Cornell University.

Hinings, C. R. and Greenwood, R., 1988, *The Dynamics of Strategic Change*, Oxford, UK: Basil Blackwell.

Hofstadter, D., 1981, Reflections on Searle, in *The Mind's I*, Hofstadter, D.R. and Dennett, D. C. (eds.), New York: Basic Books, pp. 373–382.

Holbeche, L., 2011a, *The High-Performance Organization: Creating Dynamic Stability and Sustainable Success*, New York: Taylor & Francis/Routledge Press, pp. 37–39.

Holbeche, L., 2011b, *Understanding Change*, New York: Taylor & Francis/Routledge Press.

Hornstein, H., 2008, Using a Change Management Approach to Implement IT Programs, *Ivey Business Journal*, January/February.

Jackson, F., 1986, What Mary Didn't Know, *Journal of Philosophy*, LXXXIII: 291–295.

Jick, T. D., 2001, Vision Is 10%, Implementation the Rest, *Business Strategy Review*, 12(4): 36–38.

Jick, T. D., 2003, *Managing Change: Cases and Concepts*, 2nd Edition, New York: Irwin Publishing.

Johnson, G., Whittington, R., and Scholes, K., 2012, *Fundamentals of Strategy*, Pearson Education.

Jones, C., 2010, *Software Engineering Best Practices: Lessons from Successful Projects in the Top Companies*, New York: McGraw-Hill.

Kaarst-Brown, M., 1999, Five Symbolic Roles of the External Consultant-Integrating Change, Power, and Symbolism, *Journal of Organizational Change Management*, 12: 540–561.

Kaernbach, C., 2005, No Virtual Mind in the Chinese Room, *Journal of Consciousness Studies*, 12(11): 31–42.

Kanter, R. M., 1983, *The Change Masters*, New York: Simon and Schuster.

Kanter, R. M., 1989, *When Elephants Learn to Dance*, New York: Simon and Schuster.

Kanter, R. M., Stein, B. A., and Jick, T. D., 1992, *The Challenge of Organizational Change*, New York: The Free Press.

Kast, F. E. and Rosenzweig, J. E., 1985, *Organization and Management: A Systems and Contingency Approach*, 4th Edition, New York: McGraw-Hill.

Kirkhart, E. and Isgar, T., 1936, Quality of Work Life for Consultants: The Internal-External Relationship, *Consultation*, 5, Spring: 5–23.

Kotter, J. P., 1996, *Leading Change*, Boston: Harvard Business School Press.

Kotter, J. P., 1998, *The Leadership Factor*, New York: The Free Press.

Kotter, J. P., 2007, *Leading Change: Why Transformation Efforts Fail*, Boston: Harvard Business Review.

Kotter, J. P. and Schlesinger, L. A., 1979, Choosing Strategies for Change, *Harvard Business Review*, 57(2): 106–114.

Kotter, J. P., Schlesinger, L. A., and Sathe, V., 1979, *Organization. Text, Cases, and Readings on the Management of Organizational Design and Change*, Homewood, IL: Irwin.

Kurzweil, R., 2000, *The Age of Spiritual Machines: When Computers Exceed Human Intelligence*, New York: Penguin.

Lacey, M., 1995, Internal Consulting: Perspectives on the Process of Planned Change, *Journal of Organizational Change Management*, 8(3): 75–84.

Levy, A. and Merry, U., 1986, *Organizational Transformation. Approaches, Strategies, Theories*, New York: Praeger.

Lewin, K., 1945 and 1951, *Field Theory in Social Science: Selected Theoretical Papers* by Kurt Lewin, Ed. D. Cartwright, Boston: MIT Research Center for Group Dynamics and New York: Harper and Brothers Publishers.

Lewin, K., 1947, Frontiers in Group Dynamics: Concept, Method and Reality in Social Science; Social Equilibria and Social Change, *Human Relations*, 1: 5–41.

Lippitt, R., 1961, Dimensions of the Consultant's Job, in *The Planning of Change*, Bennis, W., Benne, K., and Chin, R. (eds.), New York: Holt, Rinchart, and Winston, pp. 156–161.

Lippitt, R., Watson, J., and Westley, B., 1958, *The Dynamics of Planned Change*, New York: Harcourt, Brace and World.

Maloney, J., 1987, The Right Stuff, *Synthese*, 70: 349–372.

Mann, D., 2014, *Creating a Lean Culture: Tools to Sustain Lean Conversions*, 3rd Edition, Boca Raton, FL: Productivity Press.

Maudlin, T., 1989, Computation and Consciousness, *Journal of Philosophy*, LXXXVI: 407–432.

Mento, A. J., Jones, R. M., and Dirmdofers, W., 2002, A Change Management Process: Grounded in Both Theory and Practice, *Journal of Change Management*, 3(1): 45–59.

Miller, D. and Friesen, P. H., 1984, *Organizations: A Quantum View*, Englewood Cliffs, NJ: Prentice Hall.

Millikan, R., 1984, *Language, Thought, and Other Biological Categories*, Cambridge, MA: MIT Press.

Miranda, E., 2011, *Time Boxing Planning: Buffered MoSCoW Rules*, Institute for Software Research, New York: Carnegie Mellon University.

Moravec, H., 1999, *Robot: Mere Machine to Transcendent Mind*, New York: Oxford University Press.

Mullins, L. J., 1999, *Management and Organisational Behaviour*, 5th Edition, London: Financial Times/Prentice Hall.

Nadler, D. and Tushman, M., 1989, Organizational Frame Bending: Principles of Managing Reorientation, *The Academy of Management Executive*, 3(3): 194–204.

National Science Foundation Blue Ribbon Panel, 2007, *Simulation-Based Engineering Science: Revolutionizing Engineering Science through Simulation*. Report of the National Science Foundation Blue Ribbon Panel on Simulation-Based Engineering Science, North Arlington, VA: NSF Press.

Neilsen, E., 1984, *Becoming an OD Practitioner*, Englewood Cliffs, NJ: Prentice Hall.

Nelson, K. and Aaron, S., 2007, *The Change Management Pocket Guide: Tools for Managing Organizational Change*, Cincinatti, Ohio, 5th Edition, Changeguides, p. 5.

Newhouse, D. R. and Chapman, I. D, 1996, Organizational Transformation: A Case Study of Two Aboriginal Organizations, *Human Relations*, 49(7): 995–1011.

Nöteberg, S., 2009, *Pomodoro Technique Illustrated*, Raleigh, NC: Pragmatic Bookshelf.

Nute, D., 2011, A Logical Hole the Chinese Room Avoids, *Minds and Machines*, 21: 431–433.

Pendlebury, J., Grouard, B., and Meston, F., 1998, *The Ten Keys to Successful Change Management*, Chichester, UK: Wiley & Sons.

Penrose, R., 2002, Consciousness, Computation, and the Chinese Room, in *Views into the Chinese Room: New Essays on Searle and Artificial Intelligence,* Preston, J. and Bishop, M. (eds.), New York: Oxford University Press, pp. 226–249.

Pettigrew, A. M., 1990, Longitudinal Field Research Methods for Studying Processes of Organizational Change, *Organization Science*, Special Issue 1(3): 267–292.

Pinker, S., 1997, *How the Mind Works*, New York: Norton.

PMI, 2014, *Pulse of the Profession® In-Depth Report: Enabling Organizational Change through Strategic Initiatives*, Newtown Square, PA: Project Management Institute. GAIA Research & Development, Ltd. *Standard Categorisation of Risks*. http://www.gaiainvent.com/services.html.

Porras, J. I. and Robertson, P. J., 1983, Organization Development: Theory, Practice, and Research, in *The Handbook of Industrial and Organizational Psychology*, Dunette, M. D. and Hough, L. M. (eds.), Palo Alto, CA: Consulting Psychologists Press, Vol. 3, pp. 719–822.

Preeti, S., 2011, Risks and Dangers of Change Management, http://www.buzzle.com/arti cles/risks-and-dangers-of-change-management.html.

Preston, J. and Bishop, M. (eds.), 2002, *Views into the Chinese Room: New Essays on Searle and Artificial Intelligence*, New York: Oxford University Press.

Program Management Institute, 2013, *The Standard for Portfolio Management*, 3rd Edition, Newton Square, PA: Program Management Institute.

Rapaport, W., 1984, Searle's Experiments with Thought, *Philosophy of Science*, 53: 271–279.

Revans, R., 2011, *The ABCs of Action Learning*, Burlington, VT: Gower Publishing.

Revising Bloom's Taxonomy, *Theory into Practice*, 41(4), Autumn 2002, pp. 212–264.

Rey, G., 1986, What's Really Going on in Searle's "Chinese Room," *Philosophical Studies*, 50: 169–185.

Richards, J. W. (ed.), 2002, *Are We Spiritual Machines: Ray Kurzweil vs. the Critics of Strong AI*, Seattle, WA: Discovery Institute.

Robbins, S. R. and Duncan, R. B., 1988, The Role of the CEO and Top Management in the Creation and Implementation of Strategic Vision, in *The Executive Effect: Concepts and Methods for Studying Top Managers*, Hambrick, D. C. (ed.), Greenwich, CT: JAI Press, pp. 205–233.

Rock, D. and Schwartz, J., 2006. The Neuroscience of Leadership. Breakthroughs in brain research explain how to make organizational transformation succeed. Issue 43, Booz & Company.

Rogers, C., 1971, *On Becoming a Person*, Boston: Houghton Mifflin.

Romanelli, E. and Tushman, M. L., 1994, Organizational Transformation as Punctuated Equilibrium: An Empirical Test, *The Academy of Management Journal*, 37(5): 1141–1166.

Rosenthal, D. (ed.), 1991, *The Nature of Mind*, Oxford, UK: Oxford University Press.

Schank, R. and Abelson, R., 1977, *Scripts, Plans, Goals, and Understanding*, Hillsdale, NJ: Lawrence Erlbaum.

Schank, R. and Childers, P., 1985, *The Cognitive Computer: On Language, Learning, and Artificial Intelligence*, New York: Addison-Wesley.

Schein, E., 1979, OD Experts Reflect on the Major Stills Needed by Consultants: With Comments from Edgar Schein, *Academy of Management OD Newsletter*, Spring: 1–4.

Schwaber, K., 2009, *Agile Project Management with Scrum*, New York: O'Reilly Media, Inc.

Schweizer, P., 2012, The Externalist Foundations of a Truly Total Turing Test, *Minds and Machines*, 22: 191–212.

Searle, J., 1980, Minds, Brains and Programs, *Behavioral and Brain Sciences*, 3: 417–457 (Preprint available online.)

Searle, J., 1989, Artificial Intelligence and the Chinese Room: An Exchange, *New York Review of Books*, 36: 2.

Searle, J., 1990a, Is the Brain's Mind a Computer Program? *Scientific American*, 262(1): 26–31.

Searle, J., 1990b, Presidential Address, *Proceedings and Addresses of the American Philosophical Association*, 64: 21–37.

Searle, J., 1998, Do We Understand Consciousness? (Interview with Walter Freeman), *Journal of Consciousness Studies*, 6: 5–6.

Searle, J., 1999, The Chinese Room, in *The MIT Encyclopedia of the Cognitive Sciences*, Wilson, R. A. and Keil, F. (eds.), Cambridge, MA: MIT Press.

Searle, J., 2002a, Twenty-one Years in the Chinese Room, in *Views into the Chinese Room: New Essays on Searle and Artificial Intelligence,* Preston, J. and Bishop, M. (eds.), New York: Oxford University Press, pp. 51–69.

Searle, J., 2002b, The Problem of Consciousness, in *Consciousness and Language,* Searle, J. R. (ed.), Cambridge, UK: Cambridge University Press, pp. 7–17.

Seashore, S. E., 1987, Surveys in Organizations, in *Handbook of Organizational Behavior,* Lorsch, J. W. (ed.), Englewood Cliffs, NY: Prentice-Hall, pp. 140–154.

Shaffer, M., 2009, A Logical Hole in the Chinese Room, *Minds and Machines,* 19(2): 229–235.

Sharvy, R., 1985, It Ain't the Meat It's the Motion, *Inquiry,* 26: 125–134.

Shepard, K. and Raia, A., 1931, The OD Training Challenge, *Training and Development Journal,* 35: 90–96.

Sherman, S., 1999, Wanted: Company Change Agents, *Fortune,* December 11: 197–198.

Shields, J., 1999, Transforming Organizations, Methods for Accelerating Culture Change Processes, *Information Knowledge Systems Management,* 1(2): 105–115.

Simon, H. and Eisenstadt, S., 2002, A Chinese Room That Understands, in *Views into the Chinese Room: New Essays on Searle and Artificial Intelligence,* Preston, J. and Bishop, M. (eds.), New York: Oxford University Press, pp. 95–108.

Sloman, A. and Croucher, M., 1980, How to Turn an Information Processor into an Understanding, *Brain and Behavioral Sciences,* 3: 447–448.

Sonnenberg, F. and Goldberg, B., 2015, It's a Great Idea, but. Questia On-line Research, retrieved from https://www.questia.com/magazine/1G1-12112236/its-a-great-idea-but.

Sprevak, M., 2007, Chinese Rooms and Program Portability, *British Journal for the Philosophy of Science,* 58(4): 755–776.

Stanfield, R. B., 2002. The Workshop Book: From Individual Creativity to Group Action, New York: New Society Publishers.

Sullivan, G. R. and Harper, M. V., 2007, *Strategic Leadership and Decision Making, Chapter 18 (Strategic Vision),* Washington, DC: National Defense University.

Sullivan, R. and Quade, K., 1995, Essential Competencies for Internal and External OD Consultants, in *Practicing Organization Development,* Rothwell, W., Sullivan, R., and McLean, G. (eds.), San Diego: Pfeiffer.

Tanaka, K., 2004, Minds, Programs, and Chinese Philosophers: A Chinese Perspective on the Chinese Room, *Sophia,* 43(1): 61–72.

Tannenbaum, B., 1993, Letter to the Editor, *Consulting Practice Communique, Academy of Management Managerial Consultation Division,* 21(3): 16–17.

Tannenbaum, B., 1995, Self-Awareness: An Essential Element Underlying Consultant Effectiveness, *Journal of Organizational Change Management,* 8(3): 85–86.

Thagard, P., 1986, The Emergence of Meaning: An Escape from Searle's Chinese Room, *Behaviorism,* 14: 139–146.

The importance of groups and teams to the issues raised here is summarized in R. A. Guzzo and G. P. Shea, Group Performance and Intergroup Relations in Organizations, in M. D. Dunnette and L. M. Hough (eds.), *Handbook of Industrial and Organizational Psychology,* 2nd Edition, Vol. 3, Palo Alto, CA: Consulting Psychologists Press, 1992.

The Organizational Excellence Five Building Blocks, Chico, CA: Paton Press, 2006 to 2009.

Tichy, N. and Ulrich, D., 1984, Revitalizing Organizations: The Leadership Role, in *Managing Organizational Transitions,* Kimberly, J. R. and Quinn, J. B. (eds.), Homewood, IL: Irwin, pp. 240–264.

Tolk, A., 2014. *Engineering Management Challenges for Applying Simulation as a Green Technology*. Conference Paper: 2010 International Annual Conference of the American Society for Engineering Management.

Trice, H. M. and Beyer, J. M., 1984, Studying Organizational Cultures through Rites and Ceremonials, *The Academy of Management Review*, 9(4): 653–669.

Turing, A., 1948, *Intelligent Machinery: A Report*, London: National Physical Laboratory.

Turing, A., 1950, Computing Machinery and Intelligence, *Mind*, 59: 433–460.

Voehl, C., Harrington, H. J., and Voehl, F., 2014, *Making the Case for Change: Using Effective Business Cases to Minimize Project and Innovation Failures*, Boca Raton, FL: CRC Press.

Voehl, F., 1994, *Deming: The Way We Know Him*, Delray Beach, FL: St. Lucie Press.

Watson, G., 1969, Resistance to Change, in *The Planning of Change*, 2nd Edition, Bennis, W. G., Benne, K. D., and Chin, R. (eds.), New York: Holt, Rinehart & Winston, pp. 488–498.

Weinberg, G., 2011, *Anticipating Change*, New York: Weinberg & Weinberg.

Weiss, T., 1990, Closing the Chinese Room, *Ratio*, 3: 165–181.

Wischnevsky, J. D., 2004, Change as the Winds Change: The Impact of Organizational Transformation on Firm Survival in a Shifting Environment, *Organizational Analysis*, 12(4): 361–377.

With regard to readiness for change, a perceptive introduction is found in M. Sashkin and K. J. Kiser, *Putting Total Quality Management to Work*, San Francisco: Berrett-Kohler, 1993.

W. L. French and C. H. Bell provide a comprehensive treatment of organizational development in their book *Organizational Development: Behavioral Science Interventions for Organizational Improvement*, 3rd Edition, Englewood Cliffs, NJ: Prentice-Hall, 1984.

Worley, C. and Feyerherm, A., 2003, Reflections on the Future of Organization Development, *Journal of Applied Behavioral Silence*, 39: 97–115.

Worley, C. and Varney, G., 1998, A Search for a Common Body of Knowledge for Master's Level Organization Development and Change Programs—An Invitation to Join the Discussion, *Academy of Management ODC Newsletter*, Winter: 1–4.

Worley, C., Hitchin, D., and Ross, W., 1996, *Integrated Strategic Change*, Reading, MA: Addison-Wesley.

Worley, C., Rothwell, W., and Sullivan, R., 2005, Competencies of OD Practitioners, in *Practicing Organization Development*, 2nd Edition, Rothwell, W. and Sullivan, R. (eds.), San Diego: Pfeiffer.

Worren, N., Ruddle, K., and Moore, K., 1999, From Organization Development to Change Management: The Emergence of a New Profession, *Journal of Applied Behavioral Science*, 35: 273–286.

Writings on organizational change are voluminous. Writings on change that fit the model we espouse—total organizational change—can also be found in: E. E. Lawler, III, *High Involvement Management*, San Francisco: Jossey-Bass, 1986.

Index

Page numbers followed by f, t, and n indicate figures, tables, and notes, respectively.